PR4381 BEA

BYRON'S WAR

Roderick Beaton re-examines Lord Byron's life and writing through the long trajectory of his relationship with Greece. Beginning with the poet's youthful travels in 1809–11, *Byron's War* traces his years of fame in London and self-imposed exile in Italy that culminated in the decision to devote himself to the cause of Greek independence. Then comes Byron's dramatic self-transformation while in Cephalonia, from Romantic rebel to 'new statesman', subordinating himself for the first time to a defined, political cause in order to begin laying the foundations during his 'hundred days' at Missolonghi for a new kind of polity in Europe – that of the nation state as we know it today. *Byron's War* draws extensively on Greek historical sources and other unpublished documents to tell an individual story that also offers a new understanding of the significance that Greece had for Byron and of Byron's contribution to the origin of the present-day Greek state.

RODERICK BEATON is Koraes Professor of Modern Greek and Byzantine History, Language and Literature in the Centre for Hellenic Studies at King's College London.

Frontispiece. Theodoros Vryzakis (1819–78), *The Reception of Lord Byron at Missolonghi*, 1861, oil on canvas, 155 × 213 cm (Athens, National Gallery–Alexandros Soutzos Museum, inv. 1298, donated by the University of Athens. Photo: Stavros Psiroukis)

BYRON'S WAR

Romantic Rebellion, Greek Revolution

RODERICK BEATON

 CAMBRIDGE
UNIVERSITY PRESS

CAMBRIDGE UNIVERSITY PRESS
Cambridge, New York, Melbourne, Madrid, Cape Town,
Singapore, São Paulo, Delhi, Mexico City

Cambridge University Press
The Edinburgh Building, Cambridge CB2 8RU, UK

Published in the United States of America by Cambridge University Press, New York

www.cambridge.org
Information on this title: www.cambridge.org/9781107033085

First published 2013

Printed and bound in the United Kingdom by the MPG Books Group

A catalogue record for this publication is available from the British Library

Library of Congress Cataloguing in Publication data
Beaton, Roderick.
Byron's War : Romantic Rebellion, Greek Revolution / Roderick Beaton.
pages   cm
Includes bibliographical references and index.
ISBN 978-1-107-03308-5 (hardback)
1. Byron, George Gordon Byron, Baron, 1788–1824 – Criticism and
interpretation.   2. Byron, George Gordon Byron, Baron, 1788–1824 –
Knowledge – Greece.   3. Greece – Civilization – Influence.
4. Greece – In literature.   I. Title.
PR4392.G65B43   2013
821'.7 – dc23   2012048501

ISBN 978-1-107-03308-5 Hardback

For what is poesy but to create
From overfeeling good or ill; and aim
At an external life beyond our fate,
And be the new Prometheus of new men,
Bestowing fire from heaven . . .

Lord Byron, *The Prophecy of Dante* (June–July 1819)

And I will war, at least in words (and – should
    My chance so happen – deeds) with all who war
With Thought; – and of Thought's foes by far most rude,
    Tyrants and Sycophants have been and are.
I know not who may conquer: if I could
    Have such a prescience, it should be no bar
To this my plain, sworn, downright detestation
Of every despotism in every nation.

It is not that I adulate the people:
    Without *me*, there are Demagogues enough
                            . . . I wish men to be free
As much from mobs as kings – from you as me.

Lord Byron, *Don Juan*, Canto ix (August 1822)

Contents

PART IV MISSOLONGHI: THE HUNDRED DAYS
(JANUARY–APRIL 1824)

The plates will be found between pages 142 and 143

Plates and maps

Images are reproduced by kind permission of the following: the National
Gallery–Alexandros Soutzos Museum, Athens; the Trustees of the National
Library of Scotland; the Benaki Museum, Athens; RMN (Musée du Louvre), Paris; Mr John R. Murray; the Gennadius Library, American School
of Classical Studies at Athens.

MAPS

Acknowledgements

The research on which this book is based was carried out thanks to the award of a Major Leverhulme Fellowship from 2009 to 2012. Work in Greece was based upon the British School at Athens, where I had the privilege of being elected Visiting Fellow from October to December 2010. I wish to record a sincere debt of gratitude to those two institutions, and to the following that also greatly assisted my research: the Bodleian Libraries, Oxford; the Centre for Hellenic Studies and Maughan Library, King's College London; General State Archives, Athens; Gennadius Library, Athens; Benaki Museum, Athens; Messolonghi Byron Research Center; National Historical Museum, Athens; National Library of Greece; National Library of Scotland; Templeman Library, University of Kent; University of London Library. Debts to individuals are numerous, and particularly to: Peter Cochran, Melvin Dalgarno, Angelos Delivorrias, Rosa Florou, Elena Frangakis-Syrett, Amalia Kakissi, Chris Kenyon-Jones, Paschalis Kitromilides, David McClay, Giorgos Mavrogordatos, Margarita Miliori, Catherine Morgan, Evangelia Panou, Argyros Protopapas, David Roessel, and Maria Schoina.

Unpublished material from the Abinger papers and from the Murray archive is reproduced by kind permission, respectively, of the Bodleian Libraries, University of Oxford, and the Trustees of the National Library of Scotland.

Names, dates, references

Greek names in the non-Greek sources for the period usually appear phonetically rendered into Italian. Thus 'Karaiskakis' becomes 'Caraiscachi'. Where these forms occur in quotations I have retained them. Elsewhere I have regularised them in a manner more readily recognisable in English today, preserving so far as possible a balance between phonology and orthography.

The calendar in use in the Ottoman empire and Greece during the nineteenth century (known as Old Style) was twelve days behind the western European (New Style). Byron went ashore at Missolonghi on 5 January 1824, but in the Greek calendar this was 24 December 1823. Conventionally, dates at the period were written in the form 'Old Style/New Style', but this double system is rarely used in the sources drawn on in this book. In the main text I have harmonised all dates to New Style, occasionally adding a reminder of the local date. In the notes, the dates of documents are cited first as they appear in the document. In the case of Old Style dates, the New Style equivalent has been added in the form '[/New Style]'. Where it has not been possible to determine which style applies, a '?' has been added.

In the notes, frequently cited primary sources are indicated by the abbreviations listed on pages 273–6, all others by author's name and short title. Full bibliographical references are listed at the end of the book.

Maps

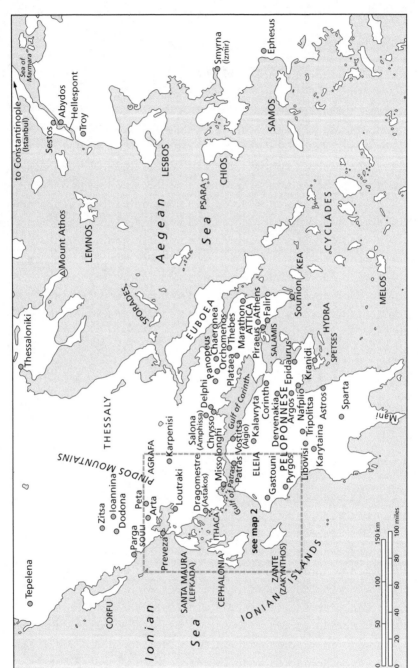

Map 1. Byron's Greece

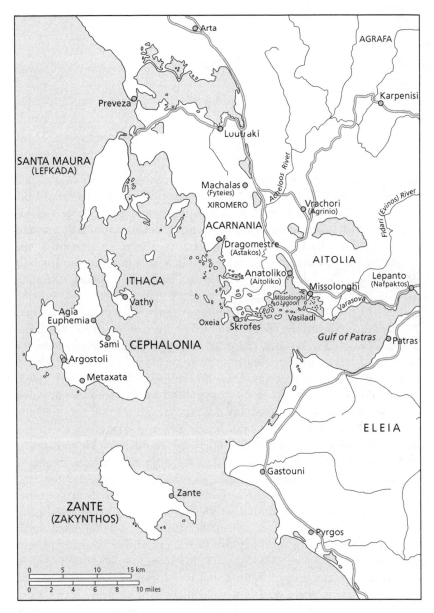

Map 2. Cephalonia, Missolonghi, and environs

Prologue

Late in the evening of Wednesday, 16 July 1823, an English coal brig named *Hercules* sailed from the port of Genoa. Aboard were a British peer of the realm, who happened also to be one of the most famous writers of his day, a Cornish adventurer, an Italian count, a Greek count, a doctor and a secretary (both Italian), half a dozen servants of several nationalities, five horses, two dogs, and a prodigious amount of money in silver coin and bills of exchange. Their destination was Greece. Revolution against Ottoman Turkish rule had broken out there two years before. Since then, horrific stories had been reaching Europe about extreme violence on both sides. None of those aboard the *Hercules* knew very much about the details of the conflict, not even who was in charge or what their policies were, except for the overriding one of liberation from tyranny. None had the least inkling of the political storm that was slowly breaking over Greece as they sailed, and would prove to be the last testing-ground for George Gordon Noel, the sixth Baron Byron, whose story this is.

Byron, by the summer of 1823, 'mad, bad, and dangerous to know', had single-handedly invented the modern cult of celebrity. He was adored and reviled throughout Europe, and as far away as America, as one of the defining spirits of the Romantic movement in poetry and the arts. He had just received the highest praise possible for a writer at the time, a letter expressing warm admiration for his work from Johann Wolfgang von Goethe, the revered poet and intellectual of the age. So, what made Byron decide at the age of thirty-five to risk everything by going to join the revolution in Greece? What impact did his coming have on the course of Greece's modern history? Why does it matter today?

The answers to these questions make a compelling story. It is a story that has never been told in full before. This may seem extraordinary when something over 200 biographies of Byron are already in existence. Since Harold Nicolson published *Byron: The Last Journey* in 1924, to mark the centenary of its subject's death, almost every conceivable aspect of Byron's

xvi

life and work has been turned over by scholars, travel writers, and celebrity hunters. The Greek 'adventure' has proved no exception, and important studies published over the last forty years have brought more modern perspectives to bear.[1] But only Stephen Minta, in three important articles so far, has begun to explore the rich resources of the Greek historical archives which provide an essential understanding of the political context in which Byron found himself in Greece in 1823 and 1824.[2]

Nicolson began his tale in the spring of 1823, on the eve of the departure of the *Hercules* from Genoa. But Byron's decision for Greece was not the result of the whims and pressures of the moment. The ground had been laid years earlier, during his 'Grand Tour' to the eastern Mediterranean from 1809 to 1811 and its aftermath. The traces of this story are there: in letters, in records of conversations, above all in the poetry – once memorably described by Byron as 'the lava of the imagination whose eruption prevents an earth-quake'.[3] Many of the moments and characters that make up this story will be familiar in themselves. But they have never before been joined up to reveal the course of Byron's long and often unexpected trajectory that would take him from the Romantic rebelliousness of his most famous poems to political action in the cause of a revolution, in Greece.

That is the first part of the story. The second tells what Byron actually did once he got there, how his high-profile involvement was understood at the time by the people he had gone to help, and the effect he had on the outcome of the Greek Revolution. Much new primary material is now available, particularly in Greek. New interpretations by Greek historians, during the last ten years or so, have largely overturned many of the stereotypes of the past – including the conspiracy theory that Byron and other philhellenes went to Greece as the baleful agents of foreign powers – and opened the way to a much more nuanced understanding of the political forces at work during the crucial years of the Revolution when Byron was there.[4] Byron himself does not yet figure as largely in this revisionist thinking as he probably deserves to. To that extent, the second part of this book offers a modest contribution to the revision of history going on in Greece today.

Seen from this perspective, the story of Byron in Greece turns out to be much more than the familiar set of anecdotes reported by those who were with him at the time. Pietro Gamba, Leicester Stanhope, William Parry, Dr Julius Millingen, and later Edward Trelawny, all published blow-by-blow accounts of Byron's last months. But none of them had much idea of the internal dynamics of the revolution they were there to serve. George Finlay, who did, and who would go on to write one of its most authoritative histories, mostly kept his private recollections to himself. Much of the material that makes up the second half of this book has never been available in English before. A good deal of it remains unpublished. Taken together with the landmarks familiar from the biographies, it adds up to a quite different understanding of the political maelstrom into which Byron found himself catapulted, and his own, tragically uncompleted, contribution to the eventual outcome of the conflict.

This is the story of Byron's remarkable achievement in inventing and reinventing himself – first in imagination as the rebellious Childe Harold and the doomed heroes of the 'oriental tales', then as the 'new Prometheus of new men', who would eventually settle on the revolution in Greece as the cause to which he would devote his final transformation – into the embryonic statesman and political leader of his last months in Cephalonia and Missolonghi. But it is not the story of one man only. Others – notably his fellow-poet Shelley – played a crucial part in bringing Byron to commit himself to Greece. The role of the Greek aristocrat from Constantinople, Alexandros Mavrokordatos, with whom Byron would forge a crucial alliance in Greece, has not been fully appreciated until now. Finally, thanks to that alliance and the effect that Byron had on the internal politics of the Greek Revolution, the story of this 'new Prometheus' forms part of the story of how Europe, including liberated Greece, became modern.

PART I

The rebel imagination
(1809–1816)

CHAPTER I

Land of lost gods . . .

A CHILDE IS BORN

Byron was only twenty-one years old when he set out on his version of the Grand Tour in the summer of 1809. The wars against France were in their second decade. Towards the end of the previous century, an improving itinerary had been becoming standard for young British aristocrats. But the overland route to Italy, and Italy itself, were out of the question. The entire continent was controlled by Napoleon. So Byron set out instead, by sea, for Portugal. With him went his friend from student days at Cambridge, John Cam Hobhouse. From Portugal, their journey took them through southern Spain and then to the British naval outpost of Malta, which they reached in September. The plan at this time was to continue by sea to Smyrna (Izmir) and on to Constantinople, capital of the Ottoman empire, seeing something of the ancient sites of Greece on the way.[1]

At Malta, Byron and Hobhouse fell under the spell of Spyridon Forresti, the long-serving British consul at Corfu who had been ousted by the French. As well as introducing Byron to a married woman who features in *Childe Harold* and some other poems, Forresti persuaded the travellers, for the next stage of their journey, to take a passage on a Royal Navy escort vessel bound for Preveza in western Greece. From there, they were to pay a courtesy visit to the semi-independent despot Ali Pasha, in his capital at Ioannina. For more than a decade, Ali had been playing off competing French and British interests in the region. Astute diplomacy, coupled with extreme violence towards his own subjects, had enabled him to consolidate his hold over much of today's northwest Greece and southern Albania. Still nominally subject to the Ottoman Sultan, Ali was already preparing the ground for his own bid for full independence ten years later.[2]

Now, while Byron and Hobhouse were in Malta, a British naval expedition was preparing to set sail to capture the Ionian Islands, off the west coast of Greece, from the French. Ali had long had these islands in his own sights. This made it important for British diplomacy to keep him onside while the Royal Navy went into action. It has been suggested that Byron was charged by Forresti with some sort of secret mission to Ali.[3] This is unlikely. The serious business was in the safe hands of His Majesty's representative at Ioannina, Colonel William Martin Leake – who was understandably put out when the dandified young travellers turned up there. But a courtesy visit from a high-ranking young Englishman, fortuitously seeming to coincide with British action in the Ionian Sea, might help to smooth any ruffled diplomatic feathers in the region. If this was the idea, it can only have been Forresti's. Afterwards, neither Byron nor Hobhouse would ever explain why they had diverted so far out of their way to visit a country that, as Byron would become fond of boasting, had until then been visited by hardly any other Englishmen.[4] And whether they knew it or not, the scheme involved a real possibility of danger. Ali Pasha, as they would discover, was a ruler whose feathers were not ruffled with impunity.

Those were the auspices under which Byron and Hobhouse had their first sight, as Hobhouse put it, of 'ancient Greece', across the Gulf of Patras. It was at nine o' clock in the morning, on Saturday, 23 September 1809. Three days later, they first set foot on Greek soil. In a field outside Patras, Byron and Hobhouse practised pistol shooting for a few hours, before being summoned back on board to continue their journey to Preveza.[5]

Of all his eastern travels, the experience that seems to have impressed Byron the most deeply was this unplanned diversion into northwest Greece and Albania. What excited him was not their first sight of ancient ruins (the Roman city of Nicopolis, outside Preveza) but the landscape. 'The scene was savage, but the scene was new', he would exclaim shortly afterwards, in *Childe Harold*.[6] Later, he would take up the theme of antiquity and its traces. But after leaving Preveza there *were* no ancient ruins.[7] It was the primitive, raw *newness* of this world, its different-ness from anything he had known before, that first caught the imagination of the twenty-one-year-old Byron.

It took them ten days to reach Ioannina. Heavy rain made the going difficult. Their first sight of Ali Pasha's capital was not encouraging: 'under a tree, hanging to a twig – an arm torn from the shoulder (this belonged to a priest executed for rebellion about five days [ago])'.[8] Efthymios Vlachavas had been quartered alive on the order of Ali and his remains distributed strategically around the town. He had been only the latest of many Orthodox Christians who had attempted to rouse a revolt against the Pasha's rule, in Thessaly the previous year. Byron can have had no illusions about the kind of man he had been sent here to meet, and to greet on behalf of His Britannic Majesty. As Hobhouse laconically recorded, 'Lord Byron and myself a little sick.'

It was perhaps some relief, after this, to discover that Ali was not at home, but was on campaign against a rival pasha several days' ride to the north, at Tepelena, in today's Albania. It flattered Byron's vanity to discover that word of his arrival had gone before him. Ali had decreed that he was to be his personal guest for as long as he stayed in his dominions. No expense was to be spared to entertain the visiting lord and his companion. Nothing was to be paid for (though gratuities could still prove expensive). This was when Byron and Hobhouse 'Tried on Albanese dresses as fine as pheasants'.[9] Back in England, Byron would later be painted by Thomas Phillips wearing his, the famous portrait whose original hangs in the British Ambassador's residence in Athens.

Rain again hampered their onward journey. Near the first stop, at the village below the monastery of Zitsa, Byron became separated from Hobhouse in a thunderstorm and turned up at three in the morning, soaked but exhilarated by his adventure. They arrived at Tepelena on the nineteenth.[10]

During the four days that they stayed there, Byron met Ali Pasha at least three times. He was moved equally by the elderly, fatherly figure who received him with dignity and kindliness, as by all that he had heard of the cruelties perpetrated by the man 'they call the Mahometan Buonaparte'. The diplomatic mission, if that is what it was, passed off well. News that the British had succeeded in capturing several of the Ionian Islands from the French had reached Tepelena just ahead of the visitors. Ali may have been reassured by the arrival of such a high-ranking Briton. Far from showing any sign of displeasure at the British move, he sent Byron on his way with gifts, a promise of protection, and a letter of introduction to his son, Veli Pasha, who ruled over the Peloponnese.

There is an amusing sequel to these manifestations of pleasure and esteem. The following summer, Byron, now without Hobhouse, travelled to the Peloponnese and presented Ali's letter to Veli Pasha, at his capital, Tripolitsa. This would be the only time that Byron ever saw the town that a decade later would play a central role in the Revolution. Veli received him even more graciously than his father had done at Tepelena – and was more blatant, too, in making a sexual advance that Byron seems to have found disturbing. But Veli, having read his father's letter of introduction, reserved the highest favours for another English lord, the young Marquis of Sligo, with whom Byron shared some of his travels during that summer and autumn.[11] The Marquis, Veli wrote to inform his father, was related to King George III, and had been sent to him on a secret mission from the British government. (The first was untrue, the second implausible.) The letter goes on to list the gifts that Veli had given to this important personage, together with their value, to a total of 11,000 piastres. As an afterthought, Veli added: 'Strané the English consul from Patras also came to pay his respects, and brought with him milord Biron.'[12] It was Sligo who was deemed to deserve all the honours, and took away the most expensive presents. Poor Byron was just a playboy, who might amuse the pasha. Whatever Byron might have hoped or believed, the Ottoman authorities in Greece harboured no illusions that he might be a person of political consequence.

Leaving Tepelena, on their way back south to Preveza, the travellers again stopped at Ioannina. Once again they dressed up as Albanians. They witnessed a performance of the Karagiozis shadow-puppet theatre and visited the Greek school run by the educational and linguistic reformer Athanasios Psalidas.[13] While they were there, on the last day of October, Byron began to write 'a long poem in the Spenserian stanza'. In time this would become *Childe Harold's Pilgrimage*.[14] Its disaffected, youthful, aristocratic hero is at once Byron and not Byron. 'Childe' was the title given to an aristocratic male heir around Spenser's time – and, like some of the poem's diction, already archaic long before the poem was written. In Ioannina, the hero was not yet called Harold, but the more transparent 'Burun'. The first canto, based on the first stage of his journey with Hobhouse, through Portugal and Spain, would be written during the travels of the next two months.

The next planned destination was Patras. The British consul there, Samuel Strané, was already an acquaintance. Strané had been visiting Malta while they were there, and had agreed to provide a *poste restante* for Byron's letters from England. The journey was an eventful one. When they got to Preveza, there were reports of raids by mountain bandits not far away. As they were still under the protection of Ali Pasha, it was decided that from Preveza they would go direct, by sea, to Patras. But their ship was wrecked and they came ashore at a wild place on the coast of Souli.[15] This episode gave Byron not only the shipwreck in the second canto of *Don Juan*, but also his lifelong admiration for the Souliots, who would come near to being his undoing, many years later at Missolonghi.

A mountain people who spoke Greek and dressed in the Albanian manner, the Souliots had for years fought with terrible ferocity against the annexation of their villages to Ali Pasha's domains. For the time being they had been subdued, but their reputation was fearsome, and their welcome to the shipwrecked travellers could not be taken for granted. Byron already knew the story, still told to every child in Greek schools, of the women of Zalongo, who when their men had all been killed by Ali's troops, danced in a line over a cliff to their deaths rather than submit.[16] But these Souliots gave shelter to the castaways, and an escort so that they could return to Preveza overland. For these kindnesses Byron would repay them fulsomely in verse, not long afterwards.[17]

Back at Preveza, neither Byron nor Hobhouse was anxious to take to the waves again. So, despite the risk from bandits, they set off with a military escort round the bay for Loutraki. It was here that bandits had struck, only a few days before. In *Childe Harold*, Byron calls the place Utraikey. There, in the evening, round the soldiers' campfire, Byron had an experience which, taken together with his recent rescue by the Souliots, had as great an effect on his future life and poetry as any other single experience of these travels. While a goat was roasted whole on a spit, the escort began to sing and dance. In *Childe Harold* Byron gives a free translation of what they sang, and in the notes added a transcription of the words in Albanian.[18] But Hobhouse in his journal quotes a refrain in Greek. From his account it is evident that the songs and stories he and Byron heard that night were of the type now known in Greek as 'kleftic' songs or 'songs of the klefts'.

Hobhouse describes the threat at Loutraki, and on their passage over the mountains the next day, as being from 'robbers'. Byron in the poem calls them 'marauders'.[19] Both are translating the Greek word *kleftis*, which means literally a thief, but at this time referred to a phenomenon widespread in the Greek mainland, and known to modern anthropologists as 'social banditry'. Often idealised as Robin Hood figures, these social bandits preyed on flocks, settled villagers, and travellers in the mountain areas, regardless of creed or ethnicity. This kind of banditry was a seasonal occupation – the raids that Byron and Hobhouse narrowly avoided came at the very end of the bandit season. In winter, the bandit would return to his village and his family, before taking to the mountains again in spring. Throughout the previous century, it had been common practice for local Turkish rulers to recruit armed bands from the villages, and pay them to keep these klefts in check. In practice, this meant that the roles of cop and robber were constantly interchanging, as the same individuals slipped in and out of the pay of the authorities. One of the NCOs of their escort boasted to Hobhouse that this had been his case. Four years ago he had been the leader of a kleftic band 200 strong. The great Ali Pasha himself, the travellers learned, had started out from less.[20]

A little over ten years later, these armed bandits would become the main fighting force of the Greek Revolution. Ever since then, the songs that celebrated their lives and violent deaths have been venerated as part of the Greek national heritage, and appear prominently in every anthology of the oral tradition.[21] Those published anthologies were not, of course, available to Byron (the earliest would be published in Paris in the year of his death). But at Loutraki on the night of 14 November 1809 he had direct experience of that oral tradition of song, and of the anecdotes that went with it.

Much has been written, since, about the 'ideology' of these social bandits, at a time before there was a national revolution to fight for. Their songs that have been preserved reveal an obsession with pride, daring, and a will to freedom, all of which consists in nothing but the absolute assertion of the individual in the face of violent and inevitable death.[22] Was it on that November night, on the shore of the Ambracian gulf, that the 'byronic hero' was born? The self-destructive urge that pits the 'giaour', Conrad the Corsair, Lara, Manfred, and other future creations of Byron's imagination against all comers in an ultimate, doomed assertion of their own individual, anti-social freedom has much in common with what is celebrated in these traditional Greek songs. Or, to put it another way, did Byron, hearing those songs and these stories that November night, instinctively recognise something in himself?

They stopped briefly at Missolonghi to take a boat through the fortified lagoon and across the gulf to Patras on the opposite shore. From there they were to travel the short distance round the coast into the gulf of Corinth, to Vostitsa (modern Aigio, pronounced 'Eyio'). Their next planned destination was the site of the ancient sanctuary of Delphi below Mount Parnassos, on the northern side of the gulf. But bad weather kept them at Vostitsa for nine days. There they enjoyed the hospitality of Andreas Londos, son, they were told, of the richest man in the Peloponnese, whose wealth was based on currants. The Londos family were 'primates', that is, Greeks who had risen to a position of local power and influence under their Ottoman rulers, in this case Veli Pasha, son of Ali. When Veli was deposed three years later, Londos *père* would lose his head and the family their property. It would take the outbreak of Revolution in 1821 to restore Andreas and his brothers to something like the prominence they enjoyed at the time when Byron met them. Today, Andreas Londos is remembered in Greece as a hero of the Revolution. A portrait of about 1830, which may be his, shows its subject in traditional costume with a long, lugubrious face (indeed, wearing a rather byronic expression) but sitting down

(Plate 2). It was Hobhouse who noted that their host was 'a very little fellow with an enormous cap', while Byron would much later describe Londos, affectionately, as having 'the face and figure of a chimpanzee'.[23]

The elder Londos seems to have been absent, but the son held court among the locals in a style that impressed the visitors. His household included a native of the Ionian Islands who spoke Italian and an Albanian doctor with whom they could also communicate, it is not clear in which language. Through these intermediaries, Byron and Hobhouse learned a great deal from Londos that was new to them. This was, as Hobhouse later explained, the first time they had encountered 'the singular spectacle of a Greek in authority', and they clearly were not expecting it.[24] This Greek had had some education too, though on his own admission only in politics. Londos had read – or at least possessed – the Greek translation of the treatise on crime and punishment by Beccaria, made in Paris by Adamantios Korais (Coray). Byron probably never read anything by Korais, but it was in this house that he heard him described as 'the most learned of the modern Greeks'. He would encounter the name of Korais again on his travels, and pay tribute to his famed erudition in the notes to *Childe Harold.*[25]

In Londos' household, after the initial reserve had been broken, there were high spirits and hard drinking late into the night. The travellers heard yet more anecdotes of the klefts ('strange stories of the superiority of the Greeks in deeds of arms – in robbing, &c.'), but also of the terrible aftermath of the rising of 1770, that had greatly reduced the Greek population – and would later provide the historical setting for Byron's poem *The Giaour.* It was in Londos' presence that the travellers first heard of Rigas Velestinlis (also called Pherraios), the writer, translator, and political thinker who had exhorted the Greeks of the Ottoman empire to rise up and proclaim a republic modelled on that of revolutionary France. Rigas had published his ideas in Vienna in 1797. Arrested by the Austrian authorities, he had been handed over to the Turks, who executed him at Belgrade. Neither Hobhouse nor Byron ever quite got this story straight. Rigas had indeed been the author of a 'famous war song', but this had nothing to do with the imitation of the 'Marseillaise' in a crude form of semi-learned Greek that Hobhouse transcribed into his diary at Vostitsa. Later, Byron would make his own translation of this doggerel, which he, too, thought was the work of Rigas.[26] But Londos 'at the mention of Riga's name, was in an ecstasy, and tumbled over ye draft board on which he was playing with the Doctor'. Hobhouse thought this 'odd in a man in so high employ under the Turks' before adding: 'we have observed the professed hatred of their masters to be universal amongst the Greeks'.[27]

Byron would not have been so eager to rationalise. What he had encountered so far in Greek lands was extremes of attitude and behaviour such as were hardly imaginable in the England he had known. Finding these coexisting in the same individual must have fascinated him all the more. This had been the case with Ali Pasha, with the former kleft turned loyal soldier at Loutraki, and now with his host at Vostitsa. Like Hobhouse, Byron would have been brought up on the ancient Greek maxim, 'nothing in excess'. Tradition, indeed, associated this teaching with the sanctuary of Apollo, that would be their next stop across the Gulf of Corinth. But the classical 'golden mean' can never have held much appeal for Byron. It must have delighted him, instead, to discover that here, in modern Greece, *everything* was in excess, even the contradictions. The tangled, tortured, above all excessive characters and plots of the later 'Turkish tales' were continuing to be forged, as Byron travelled through Ottoman Greece.

A LAME BRAT LOOKS AT THE ACROPOLIS

It was only after leaving Vostitsa that Byron for the first time came face to face with *ancient* Greece, that Hobhouse had thought he had glimpsed before they even landed. The travellers were rowed across the gulf and came ashore at the tiny harbour and customs post on the site of the modern (and ancient) port of Itea. From there, the ride through the 'forest of olive trees' towards the ancient sanctuary of Delphi, on the flank of Mount Parnassos, impressed even Hobhouse as 'very romantic'.[28] Byron interrupted the narrative of Childe Harold's adventures in Spain to write this:

> Oh, thou Parnassus! whom I now survey,
> Not in the phrenzy of a dreamer's eye,
> Not in the fabled landscape of a lay,
> But soaring snow-clad through thy native sky,
> In the wild pomp of mountain majesty![29]

What Byron saw and what he remembered from his classical schooldays had nothing to do with moral maxims against excess. He knew that Parnassos, ever since ancient times, had been sacred to the god Apollo, patron of the Muses. This was the fountainhead, the ultimate source of artistic inspiration for every poet from Homer down to his own day. None of the great English poets had ever seen Parnassos. But all had paid tribute to the *idea*. Now he, Byron, was seeing the real thing. Before him, as he and Hobhouse rode up from the landing place, rose not a legend out of a book but a mountain, at this season bright with fresh snow on the upper slopes. Hobhouse fretted that the highest peaks were out of his sight. But Byron was overwhelmed by the actuality of what he was seeing.

It probably helped that the remains of the ancient sanctuary of Delphi at that time lay under the modern village of Kastri. Almost nothing was visible except a few ancient walls and inscriptions, many of them approachable only through tunnels and cellars. At Delphi, Byron did not have to confront the ruins of the ancient past.

As they travelled southeastwards over the next ten days, he and Hobhouse turned aside to identify places that had been important in classical history. There was little to see at the battle sites of Plataea and Chaeronea. At Thebes, home of the legendary King Oedipus and an important city in classical history, as at Delphi, the modern town completely covered the ancient, so little could be seen (as is still the case at Thebes today). Little more remained at the site of ancient Orchomenos – if the travellers were even looking in the right place.[30]

It was at Athens, where they arrived on Christmas Day, 1809, that Byron found himself for the first time face to face with the ancient world in the form of monumental ruins. At Athens, more than any other place that he would visit until many years later he went to Rome, the ancient ruins still possessed the power to dominate the present-day landscape and the modern inhabitants. The experience seems at once to have impressed him and to have depressed him.

Athens at this time was a walled town of about 12,000 inhabitants, built on the northern slopes of the natural fortress of the Acropolis, and spreading a little way to the north and west. Roughly it comprised the modern districts of Plaka, Monastiraki, and Psyrri – the only old parts of the modern city, though hardly any buildings that were there in Byron's day are still standing. The Acropolis itself was a separate citadel that housed the garrison. It had its own governor, who had to be bribed with gifts of sugar and tea before he would allow foreigners access. Engravings of the period show houses, often built into the parts of the monuments that stood above ground, with gardens and even a few farmyard animals (Plate 1a). A small mosque nestled inside the great temple of Athena, the Parthenon, whose roof had been blown off in a gunpowder explosion during the Venetian siege of 1687. Below the southern walls of the Acropolis the view stretched unimpeded to the sea. Outside the town were olive groves, garden plots for vegetables, ploughed land that Hobhouse noted was full of 'a thousand pieces of marble', then bare, stony ground without cultivation. The three rivers described by ancient authors, that have since been built over, were still visible. Characteristically, Hobhouse went over the ground, identifying landmarks in the guidebook to Greece that had been written seventeen hundred years before, during the heyday of the Roman empire, by Pausanias.[31] Byron slept late, and did not accompany his friend on these expeditions.

It is often said that Byron was uninterested in the ruins of antiquity. In later life he would say so categorically, seeming to contradict much that by that time he would have written in the second and fourth cantos of *Childe Harold*. It was not lack of interest. In part, this was a matter of deep-seated principle. But there was also a more practical reason for Byron's attitude.

Within days of arriving in Athens, he had embarked on the second canto of his poem, which brings his 'childe' hero to Greece. 'Come', the poet addresses a contemporary inhabitant,

> – but molest not yon defenceless urn:
> Look on this spot – a nation's sepulchre!

In the stanzas that follow, Byron seems to be imagining the whole of Athens as the 'urn', the burial place, of the long-dead civilisation of ancient Greece: 'Abode of gods, whose shrines no longer burn'. The ruined state of the ancient temples seems to the poet to prove that no religion can offer true consolation, let alone protection, against 'Doubt and Death': 'That little urn saith more than thousand homilies.'

Before long, the poet has moved on from ancient remains to human ones:

> Remove yon skull from out the scatter'd heaps:
> Is that a temple where a God may dwell?

A pun is probably intended. But it is more than wordplay. The death's-head skull and the whitened shells of ancient marble buildings become equivalent in the poet's imagination: each, in its own way, the temporary receptacle of the 'divine spark', life. The juxtaposition is well caught visually in an engraving included in the travel book by Christopher Wordsworth, published in 1839 (Plate 1b).[32] For Byron, the ancient ruins when he saw them were too much bound up with human death for him to share in his friend's excitement at exploring them. It was perhaps for this reason, too, that he came out so strongly, and so publicly, against Lord Elgin and other collectors from the west, who vied with one another to strip the artworks from these monuments and ship them home. Lord Elgin had left Athens exactly seven years before, in January 1803. During the two years before that, Elgin and his agents had dug up, and in some cases even cut from the building, the frieze and some of the sculptures from the metopes of the Parthenon on the Acropolis – the so-called 'Elgin Marbles'.[33]

The stanzas of *Childe Harold* deploring Elgin's 'violation' of the Acropolis were written on 3 January 1810, just after the opening ones about the 'urn' and the skull.[34] What aroused Byron's visceral ire against Elgin was not what has incensed many Greeks and many archaeologists ever since: the removal of the artworks from their rightful home, or from their archaeological context, or both. When he complained that Elgin 'could violate each saddening shrine' and 'displace Athena's poor remains', he meant it literally. What Elgin had done and others were still doing was in Byron's eyes sacrilege against the dead. In those days there was no perceived distinction between today's science of archaeology (yet to be named) and the trade in looted antiquities. Byron's distaste extended equally to both, and this was why.

There was also a more practical reason. When Byron wrote those stanzas denouncing what Elgin had done to the Acropolis, he had still only seen the Parthenon from a distance. The whole passage is written from the point of view of someone looking up, while sitting on one of the broken columns of the Temple of Olympian Zeus, on the flat land by the Ilissos river, towards 'yon fane [i.e., temple] / On high'.[35] So far as we can tell, during the two months of his first stay in Athens, Byron made only a single visit to the Acropolis. That was on 29 January, by which time he and Hobhouse had been living there for over a month. Hobhouse had already spent a long and satisfying day among the ruins three weeks earlier, poking about on foot. Hobhouse's diary is methodical in recording, on every outing, whether he walked or rode. Only when he goes out on horseback does he ever add: 'with Byron'. This was not a matter of attitude, like lying in late. Byron could not walk far.

He had been born with a severe disability in one foot. The precise nature of the disability, and even which was the affected foot, have long been the subject of speculation. But its effect was to make any form of exercise involving walking or running impossible. Walking even quite short distances outdoors caused him great pain, as well as the humiliation of not being able to keep up with others. About this infirmity he was extravagantly sensitive, and would do all he could to conceal it. As a child it had caused him agonies, especially when his mother had taken him to doctors to have it 'cured'. Even worse, at moments of stress while she had been bringing him up alone, as an only child, deserted by his father, she used to bawl him out as 'a lame brat'. For this he was never able fully to forgive her, even years after her death.[36]

So, even if he had wished to, Byron could not have participated in most of the expeditions that Hobhouse made alone, or with others, to inspect ancient sites. His antipathy towards Lord Elgin and the removal of the 'Elgin Marbles' from Greece has perhaps been doubly misunderstood. The pleasures of the antiquarian (whether or not legitimate by modern standards) had to be rather differently experienced from horseback. And anything that Byron could not share in, he was inclined to resent.

Years later, he tried to explain part, at least, of his attitude:

Ask the traveller what strikes him as most poetical – the Parthenon, or the rock on which it stands? The COLUMNS of Cape Colonna [Sounion]? or the Cape itself? . . . There are a thousand rocks and capes – far more picturesque than those of the Acropolis and Cape Sunium in themselves . . . But it is the '*Art*' – the Columns – the temples . . . which give them their antique and their modern poetry – and not the spots themselves.[37]

What affected Byron was neither the ancient nor the modern in itself, neither the ruins of human achievement nor their natural surroundings, taken in isolation, but the conjunction of both. Lawrence Durrell was later to try to capture a similar idea in the phrase 'spirit of place'. Sigmund Freud, when he first stood on the Acropolis, reported a 'disturbance of memory' that years afterwards he would explain as the shock of discovering that something he could remember, as an idea, from early childhood, *actually existed*.[38] Something comparable seems to be reported by Byron when he described, a little over a year later, how

> the sense aches with gazing to behold
> The scenes our earliest dreams have dwelt upon[.][39]

If the ruins of a dead civilisation were to be seen as extensions of human remains on a larger scale, then the living traces of the past, preserved through memory and the arts, must be equivalent to the half-lost childhood dreams of mankind itself. Revisiting those primal scenes would enable a kind of visionary reconnection to a past otherwise unreachable. Greece offered a secret conduit, a back-channel, through which something that had gone for ever could possibly be recovered. Byron was ready, now, to move on.

BEYOND RUINS

In Athens, the travellers were lodged in two adjacent houses in Thekla Street, owned by two sisters, one of them the widow of a Greek who had been British consul. Byron is supposed to have flirted with all three teenage daughters of the widow Makri. To the youngest, the twelve-year-old Theresa, he addressed the poem that guaranteed her fame for the rest of her long life: 'Maid of Athens, ere we part . . .'. It has a refrain in Modern Greek. From this it can be seen that either Byron's language was faulty or he was not on close enough terms with the beloved to address her familiarly. It was not, in any case, a very romantic affair. Just before he and Hobhouse left Athens, Hobhouse drily records: 'Teresa, twelve [years] old brought here to be deflowered, but Byron would not.' Later, Byron would claim that the widow had offered to sell her youngest daughter to him for 30,000 piastres.[40] So it may have been the price, rather the girl's age, that put him off.

The *firman*, or official edict, granting permission for Byron and Hobhouse to continue their travels to the east was despatched from Constantinople on 7 February. It would have arrived not long after the middle of the month. The day after the episode with Theresa and her mother, a British naval captain offered them a passage from Piraeus to Smyrna and they hastily accepted. They arrived on 10 March, and stayed just over a month. This was their first landfall outside Europe. It was also their first experience of an Ottoman city, which in this case was also a busy commercial port. They did not like what they saw.

The time that Byron spent at Smyrna seems to have marked a low point in his travels. He and Hobhouse were put up at the house of the Consul-General, Francis Werry. Byron was often bored. The consul's wife flirted with him, undeterred by being 'fifty-six at least', in Hobhouse's perhaps uncharitable estimation. 'Werry very sulky, so Byron and myself determined to be very proud all dinner time', Hobhouse recorded about halfway through their stay.[41] Byron sounds sulky too, in a letter to his mother written the day before: 'I have written to no one but yourself and Mr. Hanson [the lawyer responsible for his financial affairs], and these are communications of duty and business rather than of Inclination.' This must have been hurtful to Mrs Byron to receive. He continued, harping on a theme that recurs throughout these letters: 'I keep no journal, but my friend Hobhouse scribbles incessantly.'[42]

The truth was that Byron, too, was scribbling incessantly in Smyrna. Curiously, although there is evidence that he showed it to Hobhouse while he was working on it, he never so much as hinted at the existence of *Childe Harold* in any of his letters until he was on his way back to England, a little over a year later.[43] On 28 March, the first draft of Canto II was finished. He would make some important additions between now and its publication, two years later almost to the day. But, for the time being, his first large-scale work was done. He would wonder, during the next leg of his travels, about continuing it with another canto.[44] But in the event it would be six years before he took up *Childe Harold* again. He had been writing intensively for five months. It would not be surprising if the effort had drained him.

From Smyrna, he made only one significant excursion with Hobhouse. This was to the ancient site of Ephesus, some fifty miles to the south. They rode through farmland that at first reminded Hobhouse of England. Further on were marshes and wooded hills. Ephesus in ancient times had been a seaport, but the sea has since receded many miles. Their first night was spent in a Turkish village. A stork had built its huge nest in a tree. At its foot was a small Muslim cemetery. On their way they stopped to rest in the shade of the trees by some more gravestones. A little further on, they found camels and goats grazing.[45]

An air of languor and gloom hangs over the expedition to Ephesus. This was the scene that would come back to Byron six years later, when he incorporated it into the poem 'The Dream', that in turn would become the basis for the painting by Thomas Eastlake, 'Byron's Dream'. What would stimulate that memory, six years on, was talk with his new friends, the Shelleys, about ghosts. There was certainly something ghostly about this expedition as he and Hobhouse experienced it. They had been told that they should expect to hear jackals howling on their journey. What they in fact heard was probably only the croaking of frogs in the marshy ground. But Byron would ever afterwards insist that he had heard, and even seen, 'the hyaena and the jackall' among the ruins of Ephesus.[46]

The temple of Diana, one of the seven wonders of the ancient world, had vanished so completely that another century would pass before its foundations could be identified. Very little of the city that has since been excavated would have been visible in 1810. But the site is so vast that much of it still remains in the form of the overgrown shapes of masonry sticking up out of the marshes, that Byron and Hobhouse would have seen. Sometimes the ruins themselves had evidently been built out of yet older ruins: Hobhouse recorded an inscription from blocks that had been incorporated into a building, upside down. Even he was infected with the mood of the place. His first impression was of 'a scene of the most perfect desolation'. Later on, wandering the ruins at twilight, both he and Byron 'found it most desolate and melancholy'.[47]

Back in the consul's house in Smyrna, sitting up late into the night, Byron was intensely nostalgic for the other side of the Aegean that he had left behind. It was at about this time that he wrote the stanzas of *Childe*

Harold in which he meditates on the possibility that Greece might ever, one day, be 'restored':

> A thousand years scarce serve to form a state;
> An hour may lay it in the dust: and when
> Can man its shatter'd splendour renovate,
> Recall its virtues back, and vanquish Time and Fate?[48]

It was the baleful operations of time and fate that had been most in evidence at Ephesus and on the way there.

In the same section of the poem he wrote wistfully of Greece as a 'Land of lost gods and godlike men!' In Athens the temples at least still stood, even if plundered and decayed. But at Ephesus Byron seems to have felt the presence only of death. Even more depressing than ruins was the absence of ruins, where one of the ancient world's greatest buildings should have been. This sense would become intensified at the travellers' next stop after Smyrna, Troy.

With *Childe Harold* for the time being finished, and neither Byron nor his host in any better humour, it was time to leave Smyrna. The *Salsette*, a thirty-six-gun frigate of the Royal Navy, would shortly be on its way through the Dardanelles to bring home the ambassador from Constantinople, at the end of his tour of duty. Byron and Hobhouse were glad to embark.

The *Salsette* was obliged to wait, at anchor off the Dardanelles, for a *firman* to arrive from Constantinople granting permission to pass the forts that guarded the entrance to the straits. Hobhouse reread the opening of Homer's *Iliad* and was prepared to concede that the beach off which they were anchored, 'flat, broad and shelving', could well have been the place where the Greek ships had been drawn up, during the ten-year siege of Troy. Where the city itself had been was more difficult to determine. It was not until the excavations of Heinrich Schliemann in the 1870s that the site known at the time as Hissarlik was identified beyond reasonable doubt. Until then, opinion had been fairly evenly divided whether there had ever been such a city, or whether the epics of Homer and other ancient myths had been pure invention. Hobhouse approached the question with scholarly enthusiasm and a dose of scepticism.[49] What mattered to Byron was the intense reality of a place in which the present could be experienced, lying superimposed on the past. As before at Ephesus, it troubled him in the Troad that the visible signs of such a famous past were so few.

With Hobhouse and several of the ship's officers, Byron rode for miles over the scrubby, low-lying landscape. The only antiquities that were clearly identifiable were burial mounds. Tradition had attributed these, ever since Roman times, to illustrious Greeks who had fallen during the siege of the city. To his mother two days later, Byron wrote bleakly, 'all the remains of Troy are the tombs of her destroyers'.[50] Years later, his comic creation Beppo would be 'cast away / About where Troy stood once, and nothing stands'. This scene of absence would be recreated again in *Don Juan*.[51] The next day the whole party set out on horseback in a different direction, overland to the Hellespont, the narrow strait that divides the Asian shore from the Gallipoli peninsula in Europe. Here, Byron and one of the ship's officers tried to swim the channel, but were driven back by the cold and the strong adverse current.[52]

Over the next two weeks, while the *Salsette* was still held at anchor waiting for the *firman* to arrive, Hobhouse records several trips ashore, but on foot, which means that Byron was not with him. Byron might possibly have gone exploring on horseback elsewhere, but there is no indication that he did. He seems to have spent the entire time cooped up on board. Perhaps he was imitating the behaviour of Achilles, the hero of the *Iliad*, who had famously sulked in his tent, a few hundred yards away, while the battle raged across the plain. Or perhaps he was practising swimming from the ship. Byron, more than most people, hated being thwarted. He would not have given up hope of swimming across the Hellespont, if another opportunity were to present itself. Aboard the *Salsette*, inactivity caused tempers to flare. Captain Bathurst bawled out Byron for 'getting up late'. Ordinarily, he would have been quick to take offence, and his response to insult could be extreme (in Malta he had challenged an officer to a duel). But aboard a British ship of war the captain's word was law. Byron appeared at breakfast the next morning – for the first time since joining the ship at Smyrna.[53]

Then on Thursday, 3 May, Byron got the chance he had been hoping for. The *Salsette* had permission to proceed. But for several days the wind had been blowing strongly from the northeast, making the passage of the straits impossible for a ship whose only means of propulsion was sail. While they lay at anchor off the European shore, Byron and his companion from his last attempt, Lieutenant Ekenhead of the Marines, swam from one shore to the other, the lieutenant in one hour and five minutes, Byron in one hour and ten.[54] It was one of the greatest exploits of Byron's life. He would boast of it repeatedly in prose, in verse, and in conversation as long as he lived.

It is worth pausing to wonder why this particular feat mattered so much to him. It was not just that he had overcome the natural hazards of intense cold, a treacherous current, and his own disability. The exploit also had a literary dimension. The ancient Roman poet Ovid had told the story of the love of Leander, of Abydos in Asia, for a girl called Hero, who lived in Sestos on the European side. Leander used to swim across the Hellespont each night, until he lost his way in a storm and drowned. The story had been retold in English verse by Christopher Marlowe, and a few years later Byron himself would invoke its setting in one of his 'Turkish tales', *The Bride of Abydos.*[55] In re-enacting Leander's exploit, Byron temporarily *became* the hero of an ancient legend, a character in a treasured story. A moment from the remote past was made real, and lived, again. It was the very opposite of the *absence* that had so oppressed him at Ephesus and now, most recently, in the Troad.[56]

A few days afterwards, while the elation of the event was still on him, Byron wrote a light-hearted poem about it. In these lines, he says something more about the motive that had prompted him to risk his life in these dangerous conditions. Leander had swum 'for Love', but 'I for Glory'.[57] Homer's heroes had accepted that they would die young, in order to live for ever in the 'fame of men'. Much the same ethos held true for the contemporary Greek klefts, as Byron probably by this time knew. It was an idea to which he would return, many years later.

LIBERATION

Byron's impressions from the two months that he and Hobhouse spent in the Ottoman capital, Constantinople (today's Istanbul), were of a rather different sort. They left no trace upon the early editions of *Childe Harold*. But, in the seventh edition, in 1814, he would add seven stanzas that celebrate the brightness, colour, and movement of a city that had once been the capital of the Greek-speaking eastern Roman empire. He knew that Greeks such as Londos dreamed of restoring Constantinople as a Greek and Orthodox capital city once more (this, minus the Orthodoxy, had been the political vision of Londos' hero, Rigas, before him). But Byron had also seen the Ottoman state in all its pomp and splendour, as well as its squalor and occasional horrific cruelty. He had been present at an audience with Sultan Mahmud II in the Topkapi palace. As he saw it from the perspective of 1814, the great city might conceivably change masters:

> But ne'er will freedom seek this fated soil,
> But slave succeed to slave through years of endless toil.[58]

It was decided at this time that Hobhouse would go back to England with the *Salsette* and the returning ambassador. Byron thought he would stop off in Greece and stay there on his own, perhaps for another year. As he acknowledged about himself while in Constantinople: 'I am quicksilver, and say nothing positively.'[59] He also began to draw wider conclusions from his travels. These he summed up for the benefit of a friend back in England, namely: 'that all climates and nations are equally interesting to me; that mankind are every where despicable in different absurdities; that the farther I proceed from your country the less I regret leaving it . . . I would be a citizen of the world'.[60]

The *Salsette* left Constantinople on 13 July. Four days later, at the harbour of the small island of Kea, not far from Athens, Byron said goodbye to Hobhouse. The parting was 'non sine lacrymis' (not without tears), as the latter recorded, quoting the Roman poet Horace. Byron's comment was more brutal: 'got rid of Hobhouse . . . [T]hough I like him, and always shall, . . . he will never be any thing but the "*Sow's Ear*" . . . I feel happier, I feel free.' The same night, Byron was back in Athens – a place, he quickly decided, despite the searing heat, 'which I think I prefer upon the whole to any I have seen'.[61]

For the first time in his travels, Byron was on his own. His only link to England was William Fletcher, the faithful valet who would remain with him until his death at Missolonghi fourteen years later. But even Fletcher was under notice that he would be sent back to England ahead of his master. It was now, and in all probability not before, that Byron sought liberation in a form that would remain a taboo subject until the 1960s.

Ever since setting out, the already promiscuous Byron had been alert to the possibility of discovering new forms of sexual experience on his travels in the East. While waiting to sail from Falmouth, in June 1809, he had been excited, in anticipation, by the presence of so many young sailors, and may have gone swimming in the harbour with some of them.[62] From his Cambridge friends William Bankes and Charles Skinner Matthews, he certainly knew about homosexual practices. In student circles such as theirs it was well known – and the fact was much discussed – that sex between adult males and adolescent boys had enjoyed particular esteem in the ancient world, especially in classical Athens. Neither Byron nor Hobhouse seems to have been much surprised by the discovery that the latter records in his diary during their first month in the modern country, and that would even find its way into the notes to *Childe Harold*: 'paederasty is practised underhandly by the Greeks, but openly carried on by the Turks'.[63]

Probably, up to the time when he left England, Byron had had no homo-sexual experience. The story that he had 'corrupted' his pageboy, Robert Rushton, has been dismissed as just that. For the choirboy John Edleston, whom he had befriended at Cambridge, his feelings were surely sexual. But the poems he wrote addressed to Edleston (or 'Thyrza') surround their object with a romantic aura of untouchable purity. In real life Byron recog-nised a strong need to keep his distance from Edleston. It was not only that homosexual behaviour in England was illegal, and could even carry the death penalty. For all his later courting of scandal, in many ways Byron the late-arrived aristocrat could be socially conservative. Though his most recent biographers have tended to suppose he was as promiscuous with men as with women, it is quite possible that Byron never had sex with a man in England.[64]

In Greece, where others did, Byron did too.

In the Londos household at Vostitsa, his eye had been caught by a young man whom he must have befriended quite openly, because when he met up with him again he could describe him to Hobhouse as 'my dearly-beloved Eustathius' and 'the dear soul'. Returning six months later without Hobhouse, when he left Vostitsa he took young Efstathios Georgiou with him. But, despite the youth's apparently ardent devotion, the idyll was a dismal failure. Byron wrote an exasperated account of these adventures to Hobhouse, in which it does not appear that he is being anything less than frank. There is no reason to suppose that anything happened that could not have been witnessed by Fletcher, who must have been present throughout. Homoeroticism was in the air. But, the way Byron tells it, there were too many elements of farce for anything more serious to have happened.[65]

Opportunity came his way in Athens. By this time he had moved out of the Makris household to the Capuchin Convent round the corner, in today's Plateia Lysikratous. All that stands from Byron's day is the 'lantern of Demosthenes', the monument built in the fourth century BCE that was at the time incorporated into the convent walls and functioned as a kind of monastic cell. Here he found he could happily relive his student days, with none of the annoyances or demands of Cambridge. Apart from the Father Abbot and himself, the other occupants of the convent were six young students with whom, Byron reported, 'We have nothing but riot from Noon till night.' One of the students was Nicolo Giraud, whose sister was married to Lusieri, the Neapolitan painter who was still being employed by Lord Elgin to bring the last of the sculptures from the Parthenon frieze out of the country. (Despite this association, Byron was on excellent terms with Lusieri.) Nicolo was about fifteen. His parents were French but he had been born in Athens, spoke Italian like a native and Greek fluently. Soon he was helping Byron to practise both languages. In return, Byron took Nicolo swimming at Piraeus. He affected to be shocked that the boy bathed naked, as he himself did not.

On 23 August, Byron wrote to Hobhouse of the progress he was making. Heavy hints indicate that this was to be understood as more than linguistic. Using a cryptic abbreviation from Latin that had originated with Matthews' homosexual circle at Cambridge, Byron declared, 'I must arrive at the pl & opt C, and then I will write to [Matthews]'. *Coitum plenum et optabilem* ('full intercourse as much as I could wish') is the narrator's reward in a scurrilous episode of the novel *Satyrica*, by the Roman author Petronius, written in the first century CE. The point of the code was that in Petronius' story the intercourse had been between an adult male and an adolescent boy. Byron had no need to resort to code to report his *female* conquests to his friends, including Hobhouse.[66] Although he *could* have been referring only to the new prospect of sex with Giraud, having previously 'arrived at' the desired point with others, it is more likely that a line was about to be crossed for the first time. Matthews (himself inexperienced) had promised Byron at the time when he left England: 'of the pl&optC, should I be so happy as to obtain one, or of the progress towards it, you shall be fully informed'. Byron hoped soon to be able to return the compliment, via Hobhouse.[67]

It worked. The first 'pl & opt C' took place at the monastery below Mount Penteli that Byron and Hobhouse had visited together. Thereafter, Nicolo Giraud became his constant companion for the remainder of his time in Greece. Fletcher, now seriously an inconvenience, was despatched to England in November, and young Giraud was promoted to be his 'Dragoman [interpreter] and Major Domo'.[68]

On his first (and longest) trip with Nicolo outside Athens, to the ancient site of Olympia in the Peloponnese, Byron caught a fever and became seriously ill at the house of Strané, the consul in Patras. Probably it was malaria, caught from the mosquitoes of the Alpheios riverbed whose silt at that time almost completely covered the site of the ancient Olympic Games. Nicolo nursed him with such devotion that he too fell ill, and it was Byron's turn to perform the same offices for his nurse. While he still recovering, he wrote a high-spirited account for Hobhouse of all that he had suffered, for which he blamed the local doctors as much as the disease. But in a sober exchange of opinions with a clergyman friend, after he had returned to England, he would confide that he had thought he would die in Patras.[69] By 4 October, recovering with Nicolo from the fever and only six weeks after he had reported his early progress, Byron boasted that he had 'obtained above two hundred pl & opt Cs' and was 'almost tired of them'. If that was anywhere near true, it might have been another reason for his near-death experience in Patras and the extreme fatigue that followed, after he returned to Athens.

There seems to have been something joyous and extravagant about the affair. When Byron came to make a will, back in England, the principal bequest, outside his family, went 'To Nicolo Giraud, subject of France, but born in Greece' – to the tune of 7,000 pounds. As late as 1815, Nicolo would write in a mixture of English and Greek, 'Oh my dear master I cannot express the pain my heart endures from not seeing you for so long. Oh that I might become a bird and fly, to come and see you even for an hour[.]'[70]

During his second winter in Athens, in the disorganised but collegiate atmosphere of the Capuchin Convent in Plaka, Byron became a student again. He was keeping company with antiquarians and artists from several countries of Europe. These foreigners were harsh in their judgements of the people among whom they lived. The accounts of the country that he had read, by western travellers, tended to be disparaging too. None of the friends he made at this time was Greek. But, perhaps through Nicolo, who had never lived anywhere else, Byron was roused to try to imagine how all this must seem from a *Greek* point of view. As he put it in a short essay on the present-day Greeks dated 'Franciscan Convent, Athens, January 23, 1811', 'instead of considering what they have been, and speculating on what they may be, let us look at them as they are'.[71]

To pursue these enquiries, he had to have a tutor – a native of the country, and someone of more advanced education than young Nicolo. His choice was probably severely limited. Athens was not, at that time, among the several centres of Greek learning in the Ottoman empire. Ioannis Marmarotouris is regularly described by editors and biographers as 'a leader among the Greek patriots'. All that Byron himself tells us is that he was 'a Greek of Athens'.[72] Marmarotouris is not otherwise known to Greek history or Greek literature. He had collaborated in a translation into modern Greek of the influential work of historical fiction, *The Travels of Anacharsis the Younger in Greece*, that had first appeared in French in 1788, and hoped – against all probability – that his pupil could help him have it published in London. A printed prospectus for this work, with a list of subscribers, that Byron brought home with him, is dated 1799, so Marmarotouris' hopes cannot have been very high when he gave it to Byron twelve years later.[73] Otherwise, Marmarotouris appears in print only as the translator into Greek of an edifying treatise in Italian, written 'by a merchant' for the benefit of those wishing to go into business, and published in Trieste in 1800.[74]

Throughout the first months of 1811, at the Capuchin Convent, Byron seems to have worked diligently with Marmarotouris. It was during this time that he assembled all the miscellaneous material on modern Greece that he would later publish in the 'Notes' to *Childe Harold*. Only some of this material is included in the standard modern editions.[75] It was no doubt with his tutor's help that he produced a series of translations of popular poems from the 'Romaic' (or Modern Greek). One of these was the Greek version of the 'Marseillaise' that he had first encountered with Hobhouse in Londos' household at Vostitsa. Another is a love song about a beautiful girl called Haidee. From Candia (the modern Heraklion, capital of Crete), his friend John Galt sent him the manuscript of a narrative poem, *The Shepherdess*, that had been written in the Cretan dialect around the year 1600. Byron refers disparagingly to this in his letters at the time, perhaps reflecting his tutor's opinion. He would not have been able to read it without assistance from Marmarotouris. But it must have left its mark, because almost ten years later he would combine the story of the *Shepherdess* with the name in the love song to produce the Haidee episode in *Don Juan*.[76]

Marmarotouris' first language was probably Albanian, as was the case with very many inhabitants of the region until the twentieth century.[77] Judging from the short poem that he wrote as a present for Byron on his twenty-third birthday, the tutor was confused between the ancient and modern forms of Greek, a terrible speller, and a worse versifier:

> Scion ever-blooming of Renownèd Britain
> He blossomed like a phoenix over Greece
> In Strength, wisdom exceeding all others
> As those of Bengal exceed among Pearls;
> Now let us bless this glorious day
> That makes to rise anew this star.[78]

Following an old Greek tradition, the first letter of each line spells (more or less) Byron's name: VERONN, and just in case the recipient of this gift failed to notice it, the acrostic is spelt out again in letters down the side.

Probably, Marmarotouris scored more highly on politics than on language or poetry. When Byron wrote on 23 January 1811, 'To talk, as the Greeks themselves do, of their rising again to their pristine superiority, would be ridiculous', he was probably responding to something Marmarotouris had said in that day's lesson – or perhaps had been dinning into him, day after day. In this and other notes written at the time, Byron tries hard to do justice to the Greek point of view, as he had glimpsed it at Vostitsa in the Londos household and was now learning it more thoroughly from his tutor.

A year ago, while he had been writing the second canto of *Childe Harold*, he had lamented Greece's 'lost Liberty' and all but urged the subject Greeks to 'strike the blow' that would set them free.[79] Now he was not so sure: 'The Greeks will never be independent; they will never be sovereigns as heretofore, and God forbid they ever should! but they may be subjects without being slaves. Our colonies are not independent, but they are free and industrious, and such may Greece be hereafter.'[80]

He was familiar with the claim that was increasingly at this time being made by educated and partly educated Greeks (like Marmarotouris): that the Greeks of today were the lineal descendants of the Hellenes of old. Among European visitors it was fashionable to scoff at this. Fauvel, for instance, the French consul and rival to Elgin in the plunder of antiquities, was reported by Byron as refusing to believe that a people who were now so debased could possibly be descended from the originators of the world's greatest civilisation. Perhaps exasperated by both sides, Byron wrote:

As to the question of their descent, what can it import whether the Mainotes are the lineal Laconians or not? or the present Athenians as indigenous as the bees of Hymettus, or as the grasshoppers, to which they once likened themselves? What Englishman cares if he be of a Danish, Saxon, Norman, or Trojan blood? or who, except a Welchman, is afflicted with a desire of being descended from Caractacus?[81]

Byron may not yet have read the first volumes of the *History of Greece* by William Mitford, that would accompany him on his final voyage to Greece, many years later. But he had already found a position on this vexed topic that appealed to him, not least because he liked to provoke, and this one could be guaranteed to provoke *everyone*. 'A Mr Roque' (the French uncle of Theresa, the 'maid of Athens'), Hobhouse had reported the previous winter, 'said that Athenians today were the same *canaille* [rascals] as those in the times of Miltiades and the other heroes whom they maltreated'.

In the 'Notes' to *Childe Harold*, Byron tactfully rephrased this to make it sound more complimentary to the Greeks than it was. Later, when he found the same opinion expressed in Mitford's *History*, he would adopt it as his own. The ancients, whom so many in his time revered, had been no better than the moderns.[82]

Byron abandoned his researches without finding the answer to these questions. 'My own mind is not very well made up as to ye. Greeks', he would write to Hobhouse while *Childe Harold* was in press, 'but I have no patience with the absurd extremes into which their panegyrists & detractors have equally run'.[83] Even at the time he died, in and for Greece, it is not clear that Byron had really made his mind up. But long before that it would have become a different question.

A LOVER'S DUST

What made it a different question was not anything that happened to him in Greece, but a series of events just after his return to England.

Byron in the spring of 1811 had reached an impasse. From his lawyer, John Hanson, he had learned that financially he faced ruin at home. The problems he had inherited with his title were beyond the lawyer's powers to resolve. His own debts, run up at Cambridge and in London, had made things much worse. Hanson urged him to sell his inherited home, Newstead Abbey. This Byron refused even to consider – in all the languages he knew, including both ancient and modern Greek.[84] There was nothing else for it. He had no idea what he would do, once he got there, that would change matters. But on 22 April 1811, he set out to return to England.

Byron returned from his Grand Tour not so much a 'citizen of the world', as he liked to think of himself, as in today's terms a *relativist*.[85] It was this that marked out his way of thinking from that of so many of his contemporaries and makes him in some ways seem so modern today. Byron's increasing scepticism about absolute values anticipates late-twentieth-century and twenty-first-century attitudes at many points. On the Greeks, as indeed on his own self, he was capable of simultaneously observing from different points of view, without judging between them. He enjoyed provoking his friends by comparing English society with what he had found in Turkey – not always favourably to the former.[86] He could not accept the received consolations of religion. As he wrote to a friend in holy orders, shortly after he came back from Greece, 'I will have nothing to do with your immortality; we are miserable enough in this life, without the absurdity of speculating upon another.' Well aware of the instability of his own will and moods, he saw no refuge, either, in the supposed integrity of the individual personality: 'what nonsense it is to talk of Soul', he wrote to the same correspondent, 'when a cloud makes it *melancholy*, & wine – *mad*'.[87] These ways of thinking are so familiar today, after more than a century of psychoanalysis, Modernism, and Postmodernism, that it is hard to grasp how disturbing they would have been in the first decades of the nineteenth century, not least to a character as volatile as Byron, still in his early twenties.

With these ideas and this temperament, Byron had nowhere to turn when first his mother and then three young male friends all died within a few months of his return to England. He had been on his way home to Newstead when news reached him that his mother was ill. By the time he arrived, she was dead. Just days later, he learned that Charles Matthews, he of the 'pl & opt Cs', had drowned in the River Cam. Another friend from student days, John Wingfield, had died a few months previously, while serving in the Peninsular War. This news, too, reached Byron at the same time. 'Some curse hangs over me and mine', he wrote on 7 August, when the experience was still raw.[88] But what seems to have crystallised his feelings was none of these, but another death, that of John Edleston, whom he had known as a choirboy at Cambridge and had cherished ever since as an ideal of homoerotic desire.

Edleston had died in May, but it was not until October that the news caught up with Byron. 'I heard of a death the other day that shocked me more than any of the preceding of one whom I once loved more than I ever loved a living thing', he wrote on 10 October.[89] The phrase 'whom I *once* loved' is telling. Whatever his feelings for the young man had been at Cambridge, they were already in the past. Evidently, Byron had made no attempt to contact Edleston since reaching England in mid-July. Unlike the other recent deaths, this was of someone younger even than himself. With the loss of Edleston (really, of the *idea* of Edleston), it was youth itself, and his own youthful desires, whose passing Byron found himself forced to face.

Everything that he had written while under the immediate impressions of his first sight of the ruins of ancient Athens came back to him now, with redoubled force. Sitting on a column-drum fallen from the Temple of Olympian Zeus below the Acropolis, he had made the imaginative connection between 'a nation's sepulchre' and a human skull, picked out from a burial urn. Revising the poem a year later, either in Athens or on the journey home, he had added the lines that memorably encapsulate this idea:

> Cold is the heart, fair Greece! that looks on thee,
> Nor feels as lovers o'er the dust they lov'd[.][90]

But, even then, there had been something impersonal about it. Not any more. The physical appearance of death was nothing new to Byron: at Newstead he had no fewer than four human skulls in his study (allegedly they were even on occasion pressed into service as drinking cups). In the same spirit he had contemplated the ruins of Athens. But the actual death of someone who had been close to him was something quite different.

During the weeks that followed the news about Edleston, Byron wrote several short poems in the young man's memory, one of them in Latin. He also inserted three new stanzas into his long poem about Greece and its ruins, which by this time was in proof:

> Thou too art gone, thou lov'd and lovely one!
> Whom youth and youth's affection bound to me;
> Who did for me what none beside have done,
> Nor shrank from one albeit unworthy thee.[91]

So far as is known, Edleston never performed any particular 'services' for Byron at Cambridge. Even while he lamented that youthful idol of unfulfilled desire, the poet was thinking also of Nicolo Giraud, who had nursed him back to life in Patras. With Nicolo left behind in Malta, and Edleston dead, Byron was mourning something in himself: the possibility of a fulfilment that he would never (probably) experience in England.

It has often been said that these personal losses, and particularly that of his own 'youth and youth's affection' in Edleston, give human depth and immediacy to a poem that is otherwise about exotic places and the traces of antiquity.[92] But the equation works the other way, too. From this time on, Byron's memories of Greek antiquities, of the Greek landscape, of places 'hallowed' by a past even whose ruins have vanished, will become the gigantic emblem of human mortality. From now on, the question he had argued over with Marmarotouris and his cosmopolitan friends in Athens – the question of a 'revival' of ancient Greece in the modern world – will be not just a question of politics in a remote country. It will be a question of the most urgent, pressing, terrible relevance. Could *anything*, ever, as he had written in *Childe Harold* while he was in Athens, 'Restore what Time hath laboured to deface'?[93]

It was entirely characteristic of Byron (hypersensitive, quick to take offence) to take these experiences of the common condition of humanity as a personal affront. With the addition to *Childe Harold* of those three stanzas in October 1811, and the sudden success of the poem when it was published the following March, the precocious 'childe' of the Grand Tour begins to be transformed into something else. It was time for the 'byronic hero' to step forward, and Byron himself to launch his own far-reaching brand of the great artistic movement of the day, Romanticism.[94]

Byron's 'war', in the beginning, was against mortality.

CHAPTER 2

. . . and modern monsters

PUBLIC FAME, 'PRIVATE WOES'

The field of battle had yet to be determined. Even before his Grand Tour, Byron had been preparing himself to make his mark on British politics in the House of Lords. As he recovered from the shocks of the summer and autumn of 1811, and while *Childe Harold's Pilgrimage* was being printed by John Murray, he returned to the political offensive. He made his maiden speech to the House on 27 February 1812. A second followed in April. Both speeches addressed liberal causes. The first opposed legislation to introduce capital punishment for the kind of industrial protest that had recently broken out in his home county of Nottinghamshire. The second proposed extending civil rights to Roman Catholics, who were still excluded from full participation in public life in Great Britain.[1]

Both these speeches were passionate, eloquent, and wholly sincere. Because Byron's liberal position seems self-evident, even unremarkable, today, it takes an effort of imagination to realise that in 1812 both of these were lost causes. Byron will not have imagined for a moment that he would persuade their lordships. He had no idea, at this time, of the practical art of politics. It was enough for him to make an impression. Midway between the dates of his two speeches, on 10 March, Murray published the first two cantos of *Childe Harold*. Overnight Byron was a celebrity. Probably not coincidentally, his political career in the House of Lords was all but over.

But not his political ambitions. A year and a half into his literary fame, in November 1813, he would confide to the pages of a short-lived journal: 'To be the first man – not the Dictator – not the Sylla, but the Washington or the Aristides – the leader in talent and truth – is next to Divinity.' And as for literature, the very next day: 'Who would write, who had anything better to do?'[2] Byron might have put the formalities of the British House of Lords behind him, but not necessarily the stage of world history. There was always a potentially 'political' Byron, right from the beginning. But in the years that immediately followed the success of *Childe Harold*, this was not the path that he chose to follow. Only a few months after these remarks, and while fully immersed in writing the 'Turkish tales', he seems to shrug off political engagement altogether – again in the privacy of his journal: 'by the blessing of indifference, I have simplified my politics into an utter detestation of all existing governments'. The prevalence of *any* system, he thought, would be sufficient to drive him into support for its opposite. And he concluded: 'The fact is, riches are power, and poverty is slavery all over the earth, and one sort of establishment is no better, nor worse, for a *people* than another . . . [A]s to *opinions*, I don't think politics *worth* an *opinion*.'[3]

The years of the 'Turkish tales' were also Byron's 'years of fame', the celebrity years, when he was lionised by London society. This was when Lady Caroline Lamb, one of many married women with whom he had affairs, notoriously described him as 'mad, bad, and dangerous to know' – though here the pot was surely calling the kettle black. The great love of his life at this time seems to have been his half-sister Augusta Leigh. The threat of exposure, either for incest or for nameless crimes committed on his eastern travels, presumably related to his homosexual affair with Giraud, was a real and constant presence, no less in Byron's life than in the fictions he created during these years. Forbidden love is a more-or-less veiled theme in every one of the five tales, and continues into the later *Parisina* and *Manfred*, where the exotic setting has been replaced by more-familiar, western backdrops.

Partly to protect a fraying reputation, at the end of 1814, Byron decided to marry. His choice fell on Annabella Milbanke, whose high principles and intelligence he would afterwards mock bitterly when he disparaged her as 'the princess of parallelograms' and his 'moral Clytemnestra'. The marriage was a disaster. It lasted only just over a year. After the birth of a daughter, Ada, in 1815, threatened by bankruptcy and renewed scandal, Byron obtained a formal separation from Annabella. In April 1816, he determined to leave England for good. He never saw his daughter again, though he continued to think of her, not least while he was dying at Missolonghi.

During these years from 1812 to 1816, Greece was eclipsed but not forgotten. Nostalgia for the warmer climate and the freedoms experienced on his travels is a frequent theme in Byron's letters for about a year after his return. Thereafter, it reappears sporadically, but with diminishing frequency and ardour. He seems never altogether to have given up the idea of returning to Greece.[4] On the other hand, after 1813, he never sounds quite serious about it either. Late in 1814, while he was waiting for Annabella's reply to his proposal of marriage, he plotted an escape to the east in case she should refuse him. Even during the time of his marriage, he toyed with revisiting Greece – with or without his wife.[5]

Meanwhile, the 'Turkish tales' poured one after another from his pen: *The Giaour* and *The Bride of Abydos* in 1813, *The Corsair* and *Lara* the year after, *The Siege of Corinth* in 1816. Byron himself would tend to denigrate these fictions as crowd-pleasers, but their boldness of conception has been reclaimed by criticism since the mid-twentieth century.[6] All five draw deeply on his experiences in the east. Variously described as 'Turkish', 'Eastern', or 'Oriental', what these tales are *not* is conspicuously *Greek*. True, all but *Lara* are set in Ottoman lands that Byron would have thought of, through their historical associations, as Greek. Landscape and local customs are lovingly portrayed, and often bulked out with notes and anecdotes to remind the reader that all this is based on first-hand observation. But none features a Greek as a main character. Greece, ancient and modern, as Byron had experienced it and thought about it on his travels, in these poems as in his letters seems to tug him strongly only at the beginning, in 1812 and 1813. Thereafter, as the tales progress, the subject drops out of sight. The Byron of the oriental tales is not yet looking for a cause that could be called political. Instead, during these years, he devoted himself to honing his distinctive version of the Romantic rebel, the figure of the solitary, 'byronic' hero that would soon become fatally entwined with his own reputation.

It is well known that the heroes of these tales have a long pedigree. It goes back to the first murderer, Cain, in the Book of Genesis, to myths of cosmic disobedience by Satan in the Jewish and Christian traditions and by the titan Prometheus in the Greco-Roman, to the legend of Faust, recently refashioned by Goethe, and to the rebellious heroes of the dramas of Schiller, that Byron knew at second hand.[7] Another avatar, closer to the geographical setting and to their creator's own experiences on his travels, is surely the Greek kleft, or his equivalent at sea, the privateer – a role actually assumed, for a time, by both the 'giaour' and Selim in *Bride*, and entirely consistent with the career and actions of Conrad the Corsair in the Aegean (Plates 2 and 3).[8] The 'excess' that had so excited Byron on his first acquaintance with the Greek landscape and the tales and songs he heard about these klefts marks every one of these fictional heroes too.[9] Other ingredients of the mix derive more directly from Byron's own obsessions and experiences: the secret guilt that is hinted at but never revealed; the hero as victim of past wrongs, usually not specified either; forbidden love (with clear echoes of his incest with Augusta in *Bride*, and pederastic relationship with Giraud in *Lara*);[10] the willed refusal of any form or possibility of redemption.

There is something determinedly self-destructive about all these heroes – another trait that ever since the 'tales' were first published has appealed to those seeking the secrets of Byron's own life. The metaphor of the scorpion, supposedly turning its venom on itself, duly appears in *The Giaour*, even though tempered by Byron's sceptical note.[11] And it is not only their lives that they destroy. These heroes have forfeited any claim on posterity either. The 'giaour' leaves no memorial other than his story, which is protected by the secrecy of the confessional. Selim's rebellion claims 'no land beyond my sabre's length'. When he is killed, his body is washed out to sea and never found, any more than Conrad is, alive or dead, at the end of *The Corsair*. *Lara*, too, ends with all three main characters 'gone, / Alike without their monumental stone'.[12] The Greek klefts, like the Homeric heroes before them, had at least been compensated for an early death by having their deeds commemorated for generations afterwards. But even this is denied the protagonists of the 'tales'. As one modern study puts it, 'The heroes of the *Tales* live in an existential and moral cul-de-sac.'[13]

They do have one other quality, though, that may have a bearing on Byron's own subsequent trajectory. Lara is described, by the dispassionate narrator, as 'Lord of himself', a phrase that Byron had first tried out in a fragment of 1812, the time of the gestation of the tales.[14] The heroes of these tales have the power to invent or transform themselves. The 'giaour', actually, we are meant to suppose, a Venetian nobleman, at one point becomes an Albanian leader of a band of klefts when he ambushes and kills his enemy Hassan (Plate 3), at another a hermit living among Catholic monks. Selim, in *Bride*, first appears as the rather dandified son of the pasha, who dotes on his sister. Then in a dramatic reversal – the setting is at night, in a cave 'hewn / By nature, but enlarged by art' – he reveals himself to Zuleika in pirate clothes and tells her a story that entirely reinvents his past, and even his relationship to her.[15] Lara seems visibly to create his own public persona in the first part of the poem, but nothing in it prepares us or anybody else for the violent transformation of the second, as he takes up arms against his fellow nobles.[16] The Turkish champion Alp was once Lanciotto, in Venice, and in love with the lovely Francesca. Along with his political allegiance, he has changed his name, his religion, his costume, we must suppose even his language. Identity is not stable in these poems, but *willed* by the protagonists – or the controlling hand of their creator.

Throughout the 'Turkish tales', the political is very firmly subordinated to the personal. A fragment from 1812, usually understood today as
the abandoned starting-point for the tales, suggests that Byron may have
begun with an idea of balancing what he called the 'private woes' of an
individual character with the idealised historical struggles of the Greeks
in modern times, as he had heard about them on his travels.[17] But, as the
tales developed, the balance came down decisively in favour of the 'private'.
The rebel hero is *not* a revolutionary, even when he seems to behave like
one.[18] Most revealing of all is Lara, who cynically adopts the cause of the
oppressed populace to take up arms against his own class, in what is actually
only a private quarrel:

> By mingling with his own the cause of all,
> E'en if he failed, he still delayed his fall . . .
> What cared he for the freedom of the crowd?
> He raised the humble but to bend the proud.[19]

The conflict implied in these 'tales', between the private and the public
spheres, between rebel and revolutionary, between the claims of poetry and
the claims of political action, would play itself out across the rest of Byron's
life and work.

In only one of the 'Turkish tales' does Byron break new ground in his
thinking about Greece, past and future. This is in *The Giaour*, the earliest
to be written. The question that had preoccupied Childe Harold and the
Byron of the 'Notes' to that poem is asked again at the beginning. Passing
by an ancient Athenian's grave, the poet-narrator demands to know, 'When
shall such hero live again?'

This is in Byron's earliest version.[20] When he began to prepare the poem
for press, he introduced an entirely new and disturbing idea about what
it might mean to 'live again'. He added a self-contained passage in which
an unnamed Muslim, perhaps the mother of the murdered Hassan, lays a
curse on the 'giaour' who has killed him (Plate 3):

> But first, on earth as Vampire sent,
> Thy corse shall from its tomb be rent;
> Then ghastly haunt thy native place,
> And suck the blood of all thy race,
> There from thy daughter, sister, wife,
> At midnight drain the stream of life;
> Yet loathe the banquet which perforce
> Must feed thy livid living corse[.][21]

On his travels, Byron had been deeply impressed by the superstition, prevalent in eastern Europe and particularly in Greece, about the living dead, or vampire. In his notes to this passage, he cites a literary source, *The Curse of Kehama* by Robert Southey. But Southey had never been to the east. Byron had, and drew his readers' attention to the fact: 'I recollect a whole family being terrified by the scream of a child, which they imagined must proceed from such a visitation. The Greeks never mention the word ["vampire"] without horror . . . The stories told in Hungary and Greece of these foul feeders are singular, and some of them most *incredibly* attested.'[22]

It had been Hobhouse who first came into contact with these stories, while he and Byron had been in Athens, at the end of 1809. Hobhouse had come back one day from exploring below the Acropolis and would have reported to Byron, as he wrote in his diary, that he had 'passed by the Turkish burying ground where the headstones are composed of pieces of ancient small pillars, and where is the carved turban of a Mussulman who is buried at Constantinople and at Smyrna likewise, and is said often to appear amongst the living'.[23]

The classic account, at the time, of the modern Greek superstition had been published a century earlier by the French traveller Joseph Pitton de Tournefort. Byron's note to *The Giaour* reproduces this passage, in translation, from Southey's notes to *his* poem, where he had no doubt looked it up.[24] But the volumes of Tournefort's travels had accompanied Byron and Hobhouse around the Levant. One of these was certainly with them on that sinister visit to Ephesus, when they rested, not once but twice, in Turkish graveyards.[25] Thanks to Hobhouse, Byron too would have been familiar with Tournefort's account of the vampire superstition at the time when they toured the spooky remains of Ephesus.

Having introduced this macabre theme into his poem, Byron was not yet done with it. In his next revision, included in the first edition, he considerably expanded the end of the story. Confessing the visions that continue to haunt him, six years after the events, in the monastery where he has found refuge, the dying 'giaour' refuses the blessing of religion:

> I would not, if I might, be blest,
> I want no paradise – but rest.

The curse has struck home. Life for him has become a living death. He already anticipates his future condition as 'That lifeless thing the living fear' – invoking the physicality of the recently dead corpse. He cannot accept the loss of his beloved, believes that he still sees her even though he knows she is dead. 'I knew 'twas false', he cries out in the frenzy of his vision, 'she could not die!'[26] He still speaks of Leila and Hassan in the present tense. He refuses to let go of the dead. It is Leila's corpse that he clasps in his vision, and prays in his last reported words never again to be parted from.[27] *The Giaour* ends not with the redemption dear to Romantic poets, but with the prolongation, in death, of the appearance of life, which is the essence of the vampire – ''twas a hideous tale!' indeed, as the hero himself exclaims.[28]

It was not until June 1813, after the first edition of *The Giaour* had been published and there was immediate demand for a second, that Byron went back to the beginning and added almost a hundred new lines, most of the prologue in which the poet in his own person meditates on the fate of Greece:

> 'Tis Greece – but living Greece no more!
> So coldly sweet, so deadly fair,
> We start – for soul is wanting there.
> Hers is the loveliness in death,
> That parts not quite with parting breath;
> But beauty with that fearful bloom,
> That hue which haunts it to the tomb –

That Byron was still thinking about vampire stories when he wrote these lines is evident from their similarity to one of his notes to the passage he had already written: 'The freshness of the face, and the wetness of the lip with blood, are the never-failing signs of a Vampire.'[29]

The prologue continues:

> Spark of that flame – perchance of heavenly birth –
> Which gleams – but warms no more its cherish'd earth!

A few lines on, the Greeks of today are urged: 'Snatch from the ashes of your sires / The embers of their former fires.'[30] What, Byron was implicitly wondering now, would it *mean*, if that heavenly spark were somehow to be rekindled? In *Childe Harold*, the ruins of Greece had reminded the poet of human remains, but quite lifeless ones: the bones in a burial urn, the skull, 'a lover's dust'. Here, there is something newly sinister about a corpse that is 'coldly sweet' and 'deadly fair'. Looking back with hindsight, and perhaps remembering moments like his first sight of Parnassos, or his swim across the Hellespont, Byron imagines the entire ancient world of Greece as still having the deceptive appearance of life.

Commentators on the finished poem have noted a parallel between the narrator's devotion to the idea of Greece and the hero's to his idealised beloved. Both, it is sometimes suggested, are vindicated, if not quite saved, by a form of Romantic transcendence.[31] But the idea behind *The Giaour* is much darker. Recalling the heroes who fought for freedom in ancient Greece, the poet celebrates the 'graves of those that cannot die!' No more could Leila die, in the obsessive fantasy of the 'giaour'.[32] The equivalence is a deadly one. Supposing that the dangerously fresh, 'fair' corpse of ancient Greece *could* be brought back to life, as enthusiasts like Londos and Marmarotouris had seemed to want, would not the result be a kind of living death, a monster like the vampire of modern Greek superstition? Would not a modern champion, were he to take up the cause of a Greek 'revival' in the political world of the second decade of the nineteenth century, end up like the obsessed 'giaour', whose inability to let go of the dead drags him down to insanity and an early death?

Here would be no victory in the fight against mortality, but only a horror story. These reflections might well explain why Byron lost interest in the political cause of Greece, during his 'years of fame'. He had progressed no further when, three years after *The Giaour* was published, in the course of his flight from England in 1816, he met the Shelleys, and the greatest of all modern horror stories was born in his house.

CREATURES OF PROMETHEUS

It was the year without a summer. Violent eruptions on the other side of the world are now believed to have been the cause of the freak weather that affected all of Europe, that summer of 1816. Byron's party travelled in a grand coach drawn by four horses, that he had had built in imitation of Napoleon's. With him went his faithful retainers from earlier years, Fletcher and Rushton, and a new recruit, the young and impressionable half-Italian doctor, John Polidori. Since landing from Dover at Ostend in April, Byron had written approximately half of a new canto of *Childe Harold's Pilgrimage*. This continues the adventures of a now grown-up 'childe' with the immediate impressions of its author's travels as he embarked on his new, self-imposed exile.

They arrived at Geneva on 25 May 1816, and put up at the Hotel d'Angleterre in Sécheron, on the lakeside not far from the city. It was there, on the doorstep of the hotel, two days later, that Byron for the first time met Percy Bysshe Shelley. With Shelley was Mary Wollstonecraft Godwin (not yet the second Mrs Shelley), their infant son William, and Mary's step-sister Claire Clairmont, who then went by the name Clara Godwin. Claire is often wrongly described as Mary's half-sister. In fact, she was not a blood relation at all, but the daughter of William Godwin's second wife by a previous relationship. Claire had been brought up in Godwin's household along with Mary, Mary's half-sister Fanny, and Claire's half-brother William. Confusion was understandable.

It was Claire who had brought this meeting about. Byron had met Clara Godwin before. Probably he was not best pleased to find her here, in Geneva. He had had a brief affair with her while he had been preparing to leave London. She was now blatantly pursuing him, under the pretext of introducing him to her stepsister and her stepsister's poet-lover.

Shelley was not quite twenty-four. He stood at least a head taller than Byron. He had probably not yet developed the stoop to his long sinuous body that later would remind Byron of a snake. His broad, open face and curly brown hair exuded an air of youthfulness. Shelley's appearance in those days, as remembered by a friend, was 'wild, intellectual, unearthly; like a spirit that has just descended from the sky; like a demon risen at that moment out of the ground'.[33] In his lifetime, Shelley was better known for his heterodox opinions than for his poetry. It had been his enthusiasm for the political radicalism of William Godwin, the author of *Political Justice*, that had brought him into contact with Godwin's daughter, Mary (causing him to abandon his first wife, Harriet, and their two small children). Shelley professed to be an atheist. A pamphlet entitled *The Necessity of Atheism* had been the cause of his being sent down from Oxford. Free love, though Shelley never quite called it that, was another of his principles whose notoriety had preceded him. Polidori's initial idea of Shelley would have been Byron's too, at that first meeting: 'separated from his wife; keeps the two daughters of Godwin, who practise his theories'.[34]

Much has been written about the web of personal and literary entanglements that began that day and would leave none of the five unscathed, and about the fraught and elusive poetic dialogue between Byron and Shelley that it set in train.[35] Within a fortnight of that first meeting, the two parties had rented houses some ten minutes' walk from one another on the lakeside, near the village of Cologny on the opposite shore from Geneva. Byron's was the spacious Villa Diodati, that had been built on four floors in the first half of the seventeenth century, with a view over the lake. Shelley, with the two women, the infant William, and their servants, found more modest accommodation in the hamlet of Montalègre.[36] Day after day, thunder, lightning, rain, and unseasonal cold kept the whole party cooped up together in the Villa Diodati, often sitting up very late into the night. The evanescent conversations of those days and nights left traces in the letters and reminiscences of those who were there, and have been seized on by biographers ever since. But one subject that was present throughout, and would prove to have a lasting effect on the future lives and work of Byron, Shelley, and Mary has barely surfaced in all the subsequent retellings. That subject is Greece.

Shelley already had his own passionate idea of Greece. It could hardly have been more different from Byron's. Shelley saw in ancient Greece nothing less than the proof of the perfectibility of the human race. Shelley knew Greece only from books, and through the ancient language, which he loved and knew far better than Byron did. The possibility of Greece as contemporary and actual had probably never occurred to Shelley before he met Byron. In turn, for Byron, Shelley's enthusiastic Hellenism rekindled memories, and set him thinking again about his own never-resolved dilemma about 'ye. Greeks'. The two poets had much to learn from one other, that summer.

On one of their first boating expeditions together on the lake, Byron regaled the company with 'a strange, wild howl' that 'he declared, was an exact imitation of the savage Albanian mode'.[37] This made such an impression that, ever afterwards, the private nickname for Byron in the Shelley household would be 'Albè' (short for 'Albaneser').[38] When Claire gave birth to Byron's daughter the following winter, their first name for her would be 'Alba'. Then, on the night of 13 June, they all watched a spectacular thunderstorm. The thunder and lightning seemed to emanate from all over the lake, from the peaks of the Jura on one side and the Alps on the other, all at once. Byron would have made to his friends the comparison that he later put into a note to the third canto of *Childe Harold*: 'I have seen among the Acroceraunian mountains of Chimari several more terrible, but none more beautiful.'[39] He was remembering, and would have recalled for his friends, his journey with Hobhouse, from Ioannina to Tepelena.

Three days later, when the talk turned to the supernatural and at Byron's instigation they each agreed to write a ghost story, he at once launched into a tale based on his adventures in the east. In a few pages, drafted on Monday 17 June, Byron recaptured for his friends the atmosphere of sinister desolation that he remembered from his expedition with Hobhouse from Smyrna to Ephesus. The narrator of Byron's unfinished story is a young man travelling with an older companion, named Augustus Darvell. On their way to visit the ruins of Ephesus, Darvell is mysteriously taken ill. They stop, as Hobhouse and Byron had done, in a deserted Turkish graveyard. There, amid strange portents, Darvell dies in the narrator's arms – but not before he has extracted from him a bizarre promise. This is as far as Byron progressed with his tale.[40]

During the next few days and evenings, there was further scary talk at the Villa Diodati. Draft stories were read and their plots discussed. This is how Polidori knew how Byron's story was supposed to end: with the narrator 'finding [Darvell] alive, upon his return, and making love to his sister'.[41] Evidently, Byron had told the others what he knew of the contemporary Greek superstition about vampires. With this information, Polidori had enough to go on, after Byron had announced he was giving up the story, to complete it in his own way. Polidori moved the setting to a better-known destination on Byron's travels, namely Athens, turned the chief character into a recognisable caricature of Byron himself, and gave the completed story a title that shows he had been listening attentively. He called it *The Vampyre*.

At least one other member of the party had been listening too. The story that Mary began during those same days has long since eclipsed every other consequence of that late-night pact at the Villa Diodati. *Frankenstein* is not, of course, a vampire story. The 'Creature' that Victor Frankenstein creates is the product of his own human ingenuity. But the raw material Frankenstein uses for the purpose ensures that the unfortunate 'Creature' (Mary never calls him a 'monster') has all the appearance, as well as the destructive capability, of the living dead of Greek superstition. Frankenstein's method is to reassemble human body-parts taken from 'vaults and charnel houses', and then to reanimate the 'lifeless thing' that results, by infusing it with 'a spark of being'.[42] At an early stage of his experiments, he even contemplates raising the dead as an alternative: 'if I could bestow animation upon lifeless matter I might in process of time (although I now found it impossible) renew life where death had apparently devoted the body to corruption', he muses.[43] Modern criticism often emphasises that the 'Creature' is imagined in the novel as a kind of *alter ego*, or doppelgänger, of Frankenstein himself, his own 'dark side'. In the words of the hero (whose creator had obviously absorbed Byron's tales from Greece): 'I considered the being whom I had cast in among mankind... nearly in the light of my vampire, my own spirit let loose from the grave and forced to destroy all who were dear to me.'[44]

One of the most unexpected subtleties of the novel is the *innocence* of the Creature. 'Every where I see bliss from which I alone am irrecoverably excluded', he cries, at the beginning of his confrontation with his creator on the Mer de Glace, above Chamonix. 'I was benevolent and good: misery made me a fiend.' Then, at the climax of that scene, the Creature renews his accusation: 'I am malicious because I am miserable. Am I not shunned and hated by all mankind?'[45] This aspect of the novel has invited comparison with Rousseau's ideal of the 'natural man', with the forces unleashed by the French Revolution, or with the condition of the negro slaves that Mary would have seen in chain gangs at Bristol – not to mention Mary's own self-image as the precocious intellectual 'creation' of her father, William Godwin.[46] To this list (in principle, open-ended) could be added Byron's account of the modern Greeks, that he had published in the 'Notes' to the second canto of *Childe Harold*: 'they suffer all the moral and physical ills that can afflict humanity... They are so unused to kindness, that when they occasionally meet with it they look upon it with suspicion, as a dog often beaten snaps at your fingers if you attempt to caress him.'[47]

These are not the only ways in which Byron's reminiscences of Greece left their mark on Mary's novel. *Frankenstein*, now considered a 'modern myth', is connected to an ancient one through its subtitle: *The Modern Prometheus*. The original Prometheus was not only the fire-bringer, punished by the king of the gods, Zeus, for daring to bestow the gift of fire on mortals (and for that reason counted among the inspirers of the 'byronic hero'). According to a less-well-known version of the myth, Prometheus had also been the creator of mankind, fashioning the first humans out of clay. It is in this sense that Frankenstein can claim to be his modern equivalent. Since the 1960s, scholars have supposed that Mary's source for this version of the myth was Dryden's translation of the *Metamorphoses* of Ovid. No doubt she did look up what Ovid had written, in the first century CE, once she was back in England. But Byron knew the story too.[48]

It is in Pausanias' guidebook to Greece, written in the second century, that had travelled all round Greece with Byron and Hobhouse, mostly consulted by the latter. According to Pausanias, the very spot where Prometheus had created the first humans could still be seen in his day. The place is called Panopeus.[49] There is no reason to suppose that Byron and Hobhouse actually went there. But, both in Pausanias' text and on the ground, Panopeus is right next to Chaeronea, the site of an ancient battle that they did visit. This and other battlefields of antiquity are invoked in the new canto of *Childe Harold*, part of Byron's tirade against what he saw as the hollow victory of Wellington over Napoleon at Waterloo.[50] While he was working on this part of his canto, he more than once wrote to Hobhouse in England, urging him to bring with him his copy of Pausanias when he came out to visit – and Hobhouse must have complied, because the book would later be found among Byron's effects at Missolonghi.[51]

There was certainly talk of Prometheus at the Villa Diodati, and of what the ancient myth might mean, today, to those who were present. Shelley's apocalyptic celebration of universal liberation, *Prometheus Unbound*, was still some way off in the future. But the two poets reread together the original Prometheus drama by Aeschylus – or rather, according to Byron's later account, Shelley translated it for him, since he himself was a lazy classical scholar and since leaving school had 'never open[ed] a Greek book'. Byron wrote his own ode, 'Prometheus', in July or early in August.[52] In this poem, Prometheus is no longer the benefactor of mankind, but rather 'a symbol and sign', a reminder to man that he too is 'in part divine' and so capable of making his own bitter victory out of defiance.[53]

Then, in the autumn, Byron would begin his drama *Manfred*, which in many ways is his own counterpart to *Frankenstein*, and draws on the same geographical setting as the novel and some of the same ideas. In Byron's play, the hero avows 'The mind, the spirit, the Promethean spark, / The lightning of my being'.[54] Manfred, no less than Victor Frankenstein, has engaged in dark arts in his doomed quest to 'seek the things beyond mortality'.[55] Not long after finishing the play, Byron explained: 'The Prometheus – if not exactly in my plan – has always been so much in my head – that I can easily conceive its influence over all or any thing that I have written.'[56] In the context of that summer of 1816, this has less to do with the ancient drama that Shelley translated for him at the Villa Diodati than with the composite myth of Prometheus as the creator who uses fire to bring his creatures to life. This is what Frankenstein does in Mary Shelley's novel – and, although the company of the Villa Diodati may not have known it, had earlier been imagined by Beethoven in his ballet score *The Creatures of Prometheus* and by Jean-Simon Berthélemy in his painting of 1802 *The Creation of Man*, with its evident allusion to Michelangelo's famous depiction of the creation scene from Genesis (Plate 4).[57]

The figure of Prometheus would appear yet again, more subtly this time, in the next and final canto of *Childe Harold*, written the following summer in Italy.[58] And, as we shall see in the next chapter, once Byron had read *Frankenstein* in its published form, he would return to the idea and add yet another resonance to the growing 'modern myth' that had been born that summer in Switzerland.

LOVE CARNAL AND DIVINE

The ghost stories had been first thought of on the night of Sunday, 16 June. By the following Saturday the weather had cleared sufficiently that the two poets decided to hire a boat and embark on a week-long tour of the lake together. Polidori was not invited. Neither were the ladies.

The poets had had enough of ghosts and darkness. With them in the boat, along with the hired crew, they took the novel of romantic love by Jean-Jacques Rousseau, *Julie or the New Heloise*. The unrequited but unquenchable love between its hero, St Preux, and Julie had been acted out at the far end of the lake from Geneva and Cologny, at Clarens. Byron had read the book before and urged it enthusiastically upon his companion. Shelley, a reluctant reader of novels, now came to it for the first time. But Shelley had long been an admirer of Rousseau's political ideas, and was easily captivated.[59] To reach the scene of the famous love story they had first to make their way along the southern shore of the lake, which at the time was part of the Kingdom of Savoy.

By comparison with Switzerland, where they were living, they found the Savoyards disturbingly backward. Their first stop, on the evening of Saturday, 22 June, was at the small village of Nernier.[60] The inn where they deposited their baggage was 'gloomy and dirty', the children they watched playing by the lakeside 'deformed and diseased'. One child stood out, as Shelley remembered the scene a little over a fortnight later: a 'little boy' who 'had such exquisite grace in his mien and motions, as I never before saw equalled in a child. His countenance was beautiful for the expression with which it overflowed.' Byron gave the boy a coin. For Shelley, this scene by the peaceful lakeside was all innocence. Not so, perhaps, for Byron. Back at the inn, the pair found that their rooms had been made up during their absence. Shelley recorded: 'They reminded my companion of Greece: it was five years, he said, since he had slept in such beds. The influence of the recollections excited by this circumstance on our conversation gradually faded, and I retired to rest with no unpleasant sensations.'[61]

What can have struck Shelley as so 'unpleasant' about his friend's reminiscences that its impression had first to 'fade' before he could sleep easily that night? How much might Byron have confided, during that first evening when the two poets were alone in one another's company at the inn at Nernier, to the strikingly good-looking younger man? The beds Byron was reminded of were surely the ones he had shared with Nicolo Giraud, beginning at the Penteli monastery. He must have hinted at something, at least, of the sexual liberation he had found in Greece. Shelley's radical opinions on sex and religion, as Byron would have realised by now, were tempered by an extreme fastidiousness. This would explain the lingering effect of the conversation that Shelley could not entirely elide from his account of it, written a fortnight later – and perhaps also for the unexpected harshness of this judgement, that closely followed: 'Lord Byron is an extremely interesting person, and as such is it not to be regretted that he is a slave to the vilest and most vulgar prejudices, and as mad as the winds[?]'[62] Later, there would come other grounds for Shelley's often wildly oscillating judgements of Byron's character. But, in mid-July 1816, less than two months into their friendship and with the lake tour recently behind them, the likeliest spur to this one must have been what Byron told Shelley about those beds in Greece, recalled for him so vividly by the inn at Nernier.

This conversation, brief and probably mutually embarrassing, was to have a sequel that would leave its mark on the life and work of both poets. Shelley, either that same evening or in the boat during the days that followed, now had all the prompting he needed to embark on a favourite hobby horse of his own. Byron in his letters of the time never mentions his companion on these travels, let alone what they talked about. But another new acquaintance reported of Shelley, when he met him not long after this, that 'His principle [*sic*] discourse was . . . of Plato.'[63]

Ever since his last year at Eton, Shelley had known Plato's philosophical dialogue on sex and love, written at the beginning of the fourth century BCE, the *Symposium*.[64] The following summer, he would go back to the Greek text, and in 1818 would translate it, at the same time crafting a thoughtful introductory essay. In this essay Shelley would engage directly with an aspect of ancient Greek society, and more particularly of Plato's ideas in the *Symposium*, that would not be acknowledged in print in English until much later in the century. As Shelley expressed it in 1818, in ancient Greece, 'beautiful persons of the male sex became the object of that sort of feelings, which are only cultivated at present as towards females'. To explain this to Byron now was all that Shelley needed in order to elevate the two poets' discourse to a level more congenial to his own sensibility. Most probably Shelley kept to himself his sense of revulsion from what, a few lines later in the essay, he would term 'the ridiculous and disgusting conceptions which the vulgar have formed on the subject' – apparently referring to anal intercourse between men.[65] This sudden outburst, which breaks into an otherwise elevated context, is rather reminiscent of Shelley's words on Byron.

Byron in 1816 had not read Plato. Indeed, he probably never did, and later would rely for his information on Shelley. In his down-to-earth way, Byron seems to have thought that Plato's ideas were humbug.[66] But, that summer, he was ready to seize on what Shelley told him about the idea of 'intellectual beauty'. This phrase was Shelley's own translation of Plato's Greek, *To Kalon*, which literally means 'the beautiful'. *To Kalon*, according to the ancient philosopher, is the ultimate object of all love, whether carnal or divine. It was this idea that Shelley would address in his poem 'Hymn to Intellectual Beauty', and would also intrude upon Byron's latest canto of *Childe Harold*.

The poets reached Clarens on the Tuesday. It may have been during their twenty-four-hour stay there, or more likely during the days that followed, while their progress was held up by yet more stormy weather, that Byron penned the six stanzas that were almost the last to be added to the canto. The first of them begins: 'Clarens! sweet Clarens, birth-place of deep Love!'[67] These stanzas, in which Shelley's influence has often been noted, are Byron's own 'hymn to intellectual beauty'. Ostensibly written in praise of Rousseau and the heterosexual tussle between love and virtue that blights the lives of Julie and St Preux, these stanzas address a male god, the Eros of the Greeks, who is also presented as the supreme force that drives both animate and inanimate Nature.[68] 'All things are here of *him*', the poet declares:

> the gush of springs,
> And fall of lofty fountains, and the bend
> Of stirring branches, and the bud which brings
> The swiftest thought of beauty, here extend,
> Mingling, and made by Love, unto one mighty end.[69]

Byron was ever shy of the kind of philosophical abstraction or gener- alisation in which Shelley delighted. It is often suggested that 'Shelleyan' moments such as these sit awkwardly in their context, or go against the grain of Byron's own poetic instincts.[70] In this case it is worth remem- bering that Canto III of *Childe Harold* was already finished. These stanzas were written as one of several afterthoughts, or codas. The separateness of this one was then quite deliberately disguised by inserting it to follow the description of the thunderstorm over the lake that Byron had witnessed on 13 June, and before the original ending of the canto. It may have been because he recognised something too personal concerning Shelley, in these stanzas, that after the two poets had returned to Cologny, Byron neglected to give them to Mary to include in the fair copy of the poem that he had asked her to make.[71]

When these stanzas are read in their *biographical* context, rather than the literary one that Byron created for them after the fact, it becomes clear that the 'deep Love' addressed in them reaches far more deeply into the poet's experience and aspiration even than his genuine admiration for Rousseau and the beauties of Clarens. In these stanzas Byron was grasping at an understanding of love sufficient to encompass his own transgressive adventures in Greece, as well as all that his new friend had just been telling him about a transcendent 'intellectual beauty' to which all human love aspires. Shelley, surely, was the catalyst for this poetic outburst of feeling.

It is also possible, in some way that may never have been fully acknowledged by Byron, and of which Shelley would have remained always blissfully unaware, that the handsome younger poet had himself stirred something of those deepest feelings in Byron.

The lake tour ended on the last day of June. The two poets would in future get to know one another better, and to misunderstand one another worse, than they had during those eight days together on the Lake of Geneva. But they would never again be as close. On Thursday, 2 August, Byron summoned Shelley and Claire to the Villa Diodati. 'I do not [go] for Lord B. did not seem to wish it', wrote Mary in her journal.[72] Claire was pregnant. Byron was reluctant to acknowledge the child as his. It was probably Shelley who persuaded him, but, when he did, it was with conditions that would impose a formidable burden on the Shelley household for the rest of Shelley's life, and would mark the beginning of Claire's undying enmity for Byron. With such practical and embarrassing matters to be haggled over, much of the zest will have gone out of the conversations at the Villa Diodati. At about the same time, Shelley received another summons, this time from his father. For financial reasons, he and Mary and Claire would have to return to England. The summer was ending early.

Shelley, Mary, and Claire left Montalègre on their journey to England on 29 August. A month later Byron wrote to his friend and banker, Douglas Kinnaird: 'Pray continue to like Shelley – he is a very good – very clever – but a very singular man – he was a great comfort to me here by his intelligence & good nature.'[73] Commentators have noticed ever since that Byron always estimated Shelley more as a man than as a poet. It was Shelley's conversation that held Byron's attention. Byron would often concede that he could easily be influenced, but this was never truer than in the case of Shelley, for whom eventually he would come to entertain feelings close to awe.[74]

Meanwhile, beginning in the immediate aftermath of that summer, Shelley would have no compunction about capitalising on the ascendancy he felt he had gained, though probably without ever divining its cause. It was time, he risked urging in his very first letter, for Byron put behind him the mere popular success he had achieved so far, and devote his talents, instead, to an 'Epic Poem' suitable for the age.[75] Less than two months later, Shelley would allude with easy familiarity to his own radical opinions on politics back home. Clearly this subject, too, had been part of those elusive conversations in Switzerland: 'I earnestly hope that, without such an utter overthrow as should leave us the prey of anarchy, and give us illiterate demagogues for masters, a most radical reform of the institutions of England may result from the approaching contest.'[76]

The summer of 1816 would prove a turning point. Byron's inchoate 'war' against the entire human condition was for the first time, since he had abandoned the House of Lords, touched by the possibility of engagement with a defined cause. By the end of 1816, there can have seemed little likelihood of that ever happening. Byron the rebel had still no great inclination to turn himself into a revolutionary, still less to make common cause with others in the hope of changing the world around him. But, although he probably did not realise it, a start had been made.

The idea had come to him at the Villa Diodati, sitting up late on the night when the pact to write ghost stories had been conceived, after the others had gone to bed:

> I do believe,
> Though I have found them not, that there may be
> Words which are things . . . [77]

It was an idea he had first tried out, back in 1813, in the same journal in which he had imagined for himself a future career as a political leader.[78] Byron could often be disparaging about his own craft. But here he moves towards faith in the poet as a maker: his words have power in the world. It is a cruder, but more immediate and tangible, expression of the claim that would later be made by Shelley, that 'poets are the unacknowledged legislators of the world'.[79] The stanza ends with a similarly guarded affirmation about his fellow human beings:

> That two, or one, are almost what they seem, –
> That goodness is no name, and happiness no dream.[80]

These were the new thoughts that had been aroused in the author of the 'oriental tales' by the congenial company of that evening at the Villa Diodati. It was a beginning.

PART II

The road to revolution
(1816–1823)

CHAPTER 3

Reluctant radical

'SOMETHING NOBLER THAN TO LIVE AND DIE'

Byron left Switzerland a month after Shelley, Mary, and Claire had departed
for England. Once again in the company of Hobhouse, who had now
arrived from England, he turned his Napoleonic coach in the opposite
direction and headed south across the Alps. From his first sight of Italy,
first in Milan, then in Venice, Byron threw himself into Italian intellectual
society. His poems were translated, and the translators got into trouble with
the Austrian censors. Here, the rulers were not just hated conservatives,
as they were in England. They were servants of a foreign monarch, the
Habsburg emperor. Byron's experience of political oppression in Milan
and Venice was nothing like the dramatic, exotic condition of 'slavery' he
had witnessed in Ottoman lands. Its victims were people like himself, of
a class and education that did not exist beyond the bounds of Christian
Europe. These experiences came early on, in the autumn of 1816, and were
never forgotten.[1]

For the next three years, Byron chose to make his home in Venice. There
he wrote a fourth (and as it turned out final) canto of *Childe Harold*,
based on the journey he made, in the spring of 1817, by way of Ferrara
and Florence, to Rome. In Venice, he found a new poetic voice, one that
perfectly captured both his love of the dissolute lifestyle he experienced
there and his sardonic distance from it. This emerges in his first comic
poem, *Beppo*, based on a real anecdote from Venetian life. *Beppo* was
written in the autumn of 1817 and published the following March. For the
first time, in this poem, Byron adopts the Italian verse form, *ottava rima*,
and also shows his delight in a range of minor and major Italian poetry
of the previous centuries.[2] By the summer of 1818, he had embarked on a
more ambitious poetic venture, using the same verse form and the same
sardonic narrative voice. This was to become the first canto of his epic
poem *Don Juan*.

51

Greece, it seemed, had been left far behind. To a visiting American, who tracked him down to his idyllic country retreat on the mainland of the Veneto: 'His residence in Italy, he said, had given him great pleasure; and spoke of the comparatively small value of his travels in Greece, which, he said, contained not the sixth part of its attractions.'[3] What set Byron thinking again about Greece, and his youthful adventures there, was the arrival of Shelley, at three in the afternoon of Sunday, 23 August, 1818, at the Palazzo Mocenigo on the Grand Canal, where he was now living.[4] In all, Shelley would spend a little over twenty days in Venice, spread over the next two months, to the end of October.

Shelley was now married to Mary, after the suicide of his first wife, Harriet, at the end of 1816. The couple had set out from England in the spring, with Claire and little 'Alba', who was now to be delivered to Byron and baptised Allegra. While they were in Venice, the younger of the Shelleys' two children died – Clara Everina, aged one year and twenty-two days. Against this unhappy private background, the two poets would go riding in the late afternoons on the Lido, the long, narrow island that protects the Venetian lagoon from the sea, and was then uninhabited. As the sun was setting they would be rowed back in Byron's gondola to the Palazzo Mocenigo. There they would talk long into the night.[5] Shelley's masterly conversational poem 'Julian and Maddalo' includes a distillation of these meetings and the intense debates he held with Byron over those two months.

Byron read to Shelley the first canto of *Don Juan*. It was not quite, perhaps, what the younger poet had had in mind, when he had first presumed to direct his new friend's energies towards the epic of the age. Shelley was generous enough, though, to recognise in the new poem 'a thing in the style of Beppo, but infinitely better'.[6] On the other hand, the fourth canto of *Childe Harold*, that had been published in England since the Shelleys had left, and which Byron also now read to him, Shelley disliked intensely.[7] He will not have said so to Byron's face, but he hated its tone of personal defiance, that had troubled him in *Manfred* too. In this latest canto, Byron seemed to be proposing a cyclical, perhaps a fatalistic, view of history. 'For Time hath not rebuilt them', one of Byron's stanzas begins, referring at once to the ruins of Roman Italy and of ancient Greece, 'but uprear'd / Barbaric dwellings on their shattered site'. Further on, the poet tries to draw a 'moral of all human tales; / 'Tis but the same rehearsal of the past[.]'[8] This Shelley saw as defeatism. He refused absolutely to endorse it. The heart of Shelley's quarrel with Byron, as he expressed it in 'Julian and Maddalo', came down to this:

We are assured
Much may be conquered, much may be endured,
Of what degrades and crushes us. We know
That we have power over ourselves to do
And suffer – what, we know not till we try;
But something nobler than to live and die[.][9]

Shelley's poem even includes a hint, in its prose preface, as to what that 'something nobler' might be, in his friend's case. Count Maddalo, the lightly fictionalised version of Byron, is not only 'a person of the most consummate genius'. He is 'capable, if he would direct his energies to such an end, of becoming the redeemer of his degraded country'.[10] For the purposes of the poem, Byron's determination to go native in Italy (which Shelley deplored) has been turned into a fact: Maddalo is an Italian, of an ancient Venetian family. So while they rode together along the edge of the Adriatic on the Lido Shelley must have been urging Byron to take a hand, directly, in the political revival of Italy. Of the two poets, it was always Shelley who had the makings of the true revolutionary.[11] There is no indication that Byron was at all receptive to the idea at the time. Still, a seed had been sown.

As well as talking politics, the poets revived their older discussions about Greece. It was now that Shelley did his best to persuade his friend to read Plato, though probably without success.[12] When Byron next took up his epic poem *Don Juan* in the aftermath of Shelley's visit, he decided to bring his young hero from his native Spain to Greece. In this way, Byron brings his 'unplann'd' epic into contact with the fountain-head of the epic genre, Homer's *Odyssey*.[13]

The idea of linking up his own epic with the world of Homer's heroes may have been prompted, or encouraged, by his recent conversations with Shelley. But Homer's world, for Byron, meant primarily his own, the one that he had experienced on his travels in Greece. The material that makes up most of the next three cantos of *Don Juan* derives very largely from his memories of those travels. This was when he remembered the folksong about a beautiful girl called Haidee, and amalgamated with it what he remembered of the manuscript poem from Crete, *The Shepherdess*, that Marmarotouris would have helped him construe at the convent in Athens. In the spontaneous passion that unites the shipwrecked hero with the beautiful Greek girl, far from social constraints, rules, pieties, or even loyalty to past love, Byron relives his own sense of sexual liberation that had come to him in Greece in 1810 and 1811. At the same time, he finds a way to acknowledge his friend Shelley's admiration for the classic beauty

of ancient sculpture, and so, briefly, to unite his own and Shelley's very
different ideals of Greece:

> And thus they form a group that's quite antique,
> Half naked, loving, natural, and Greek.[14]

Canto II of *Don Juan* was written during December 1818 and January
1819. Its later stages indicate that the idyll and its tragic end, that take
up most of the following two cantos, had already begun to take shape in
Byron's mind. But nine months would elapse before he returned to the
poem, to produce the most famous of all the lines that he ever wrote on
the subject of Greece, its past, and its future. What happened during these
months had nothing to do with Greece. But it would shape the course of
the remainder of his life.

Byron fell in love. And in the process he found a political cause to
which – just possibly – he thought he might be able to commit himself.

WORDS AND THINGS

Her name was Teresa (Plate 5a). She was twenty-one years old and had
recently become the third wife of a much older man, Count Alessandro
Guiccioli. Byron met her after the theatre, at a late-night *conversazione*,
a party for the intellectual and aristocratic elite of Venice, on either the
second or the third of April 1819. Teresa's father, Count Ruggero Gamba,
despite his aristocratic title and lineage, was a committed republican. Both
her own and her husband's families came from Ravenna, the provincial
city near the Adriatic coast in Romagna, a part of Italy that belonged at
the time to the Papal States. Freedom for Italy from rule by the Pope, the
hated Austrians, or their dynastic allies in different parts of the country,
was an article of faith for all the Gambas.[15]

After that first meeting, Byron and Teresa spent ten days together in
Venice, meeting in gondolas and at a 'little house' that he used as a place
of assignation. Byron claimed to have had hundreds of affairs of this sort,
in two and a half years in Venice. That this one was going to be different
emerged only after Teresa's husband intervened to take her back to Ravenna.
There she became seriously ill after a miscarriage. Byron, for all the bravado
of his letters in which he makes light of his feelings, followed her to her
home town. To a normally hard-headed correspondent he confessed: 'I do
not know what I *should* do – if She died – but I ought to blow my brains
out – and I hope that I should.'[16]

Teresa recovered. Soon, when his horses had arrived from Venice, Byron would go out riding with her in the huge pine forest that separates Ravenna, once a thriving seaport, from the sea. In mid-June, she asked him to write a poem for her, on a favourite subject. He had already published a poem about one great Italian poet, Torquato Tasso. Here in Ravenna lay buried the greatest of them all, Dante Alighieri: 'his tomb is within fifty yards of my "locanda", the effigy & tombstone well preserved', wrote Byron to Hobhouse.[17] Would he write a poem for her, on Dante? He agreed at once. The four short cantos that make up *The Prophecy of Dante* were begun on 18 June 1819, and finished within a month. The poem's publication, in April 1821, would fortuitously coincide with breaking news, in western Europe, of revolution in Greece.[18]

The Prophecy of Dante is the most overtly political poem that Byron ever wrote on an Italian theme. Writing to his publisher, John Murray, he explained that its subject was 'a view of Italy in the ages down to the present'.[19] Its strongly polemical tone suggests that what Dante will ultimately prophesy will be nothing less than the awakening of national consciousness and the imminent political liberation of Italy. The poem was never finished according to this plan. By the spring of the following year Byron had become sufficiently involved in the politics of Italian liberation to realise that he would need real gifts of prophecy to guess what might happen next. So he decided to publish the four cantos as they stood, leaving the 'prophecy' suspended rather vaguely in the period of the Renaissance.

Like the earlier heroes of the 'Turkish tales', Dante in the second canto turns to politics as a way of relieving a personal sense of injury:

> And hast thou still to bleed,
> Italia? Ah! to me such things foreshown
> With dim sepulchral light bid me forget
> In thy irreparable wrongs my own[.][20]

Canto IV of the *Prophecy* makes it clear that the cause in which the medieval Dante has learned to subsume his private wrongs is the very modern one of the Italian nation: 'Who toils for nations may be poor indeed / But free'.[21] Canto II had ended with a rousing call to the Italians of the future to avoid 'Division' that 'sows the seeds of woe' and instead 'with *one* deed – Unite!'[22] In very similar terms, but in prose and with a practical object, Byron would in future address the leaders of the Greek Revolution. For now, he can have understood little of the political process in Italy. But he did know that Dante, in the early fourteenth century, had prefigured the idea of Italian unity, and that certain passages of the *Divine Comedy* had been taken to heart by Italians of Teresa's generation and her father's as prophetic of a united Italy.[23] Although he seems not yet to have realised the significance of his discovery, Byron had stumbled into one of the most potent ideologies that would come to dominate the next two centuries in Europe: nationalism.[24]

The final canto shows Byron, through the persona of Dante, straining for a new role in life:

> For what is poesy but to create
> From overfeeling good or ill; and aim
> At an external life beyond our fate,
> And be the new Prometheus of new men,
> Bestowing fire from heaven . . .[25]

By this time, and probably quite recently, Byron had read *Frankenstein*, with its subtitle *The Modern Prometheus*. Evidently, Mary's novel impressed him.[26] In these lines, Prometheus is, again, at once the fire-bringer and the giver of life. Byron's 'new' version of the mythical hero will create, through poetry, a new generation of human beings. Boldly disregarding all the cautionary force that most readers have detected in Mary's tale, the poet of *The Prophecy of Dante* takes upon himself the mantle of Victor Frankenstein, albeit in a different cause: to become a 'modern Prometheus' and create new life – that is, a new generation of minds attuned to a new way of political thinking, that today we call nationalism (Plate 4).

The Prophecy of Dante does not yet suggest exchanging the role of poet for that of the man of action. It is as a poet that Dante speaks. The inconclusive call to the Italian people to a war for political liberation does not yet go beyond words. But, in a telling reminiscence of what he had written in *Childe Harold*, at one of the happiest moments at the Villa Diodati three years before, Byron makes Dante invoke 'days of Old, / When words were things that came to pass'.[27] The difficult passage from words to things was once again on his mind. However tentatively, he was again beginning to contemplate the possibility of political action. There was a long way still to be travelled. But the idea was there. *Words* might yet become *things*. The poet might yet be empowered to go beyond the confines of his art and become the 'new Prometheus of new men'.

October 1819 saw Byron, with Teresa, back in the vicinity of Venice. The setting for a short-lived idyll, before her husband was due to return and reclaim her, was a house on the mainland not far from the Venetian lagoon: the Palladian Villa Foscarini on the river Brenta at La Mira, on the road to Padua.[28] This became the background to the idyll that Byron now began to write for his hero Don Juan, whom he had left being tended, after his shipwreck, by Haidee in her island cave, back in January. It was within that idyll, in turn, that Byron chose to embed his passionate lyrical stanzas on 'the isles of Greece', that have been read, ever since they were first published in 1821, as a call to the modern Greeks to take up arms against their oppressors. The truth is more complex.

While he was at La Mira with Teresa, Byron wrote approximately 100 stanzas for the third canto of *Don Juan*.[9] In these stanzas the idyllic situation of the lovers is prolonged, but little described. Juan and Haidée (her name has acquired an acute accent since the previous canto) have forgotten all about her father, the piratical chieftain now named as Lambro. But the reader knows that a vengeful Lambro is on his way home. The lovers are doomed – in much the same way and for the same reason that Byron's current idyll with Teresa at La Mira was doomed.

It is while the blow is about to fall, and Lambro is waiting in the wings, that Byron stops the action to describe the entertainment that the couple have been enjoying during her father's absence. At the end of a long list of exotic diversions comes a song. Here Byron inserts the sixteen stanzas, in a different metre, that begin, 'The isles of Greece . . . '. Best known are the lines:

> The mountains look on Marathon –
> And Marathon looks on the sea;
> And musing there an hour alone,
> I dream'd that Greece might still be free[.][30]

Modern editors and commentators do not take seriously the evidence of Thomas Medwin, who reported two separate conversations with Byron, not long after these cantos had been published, in 1821, in which he claimed that 'The Isles of Greece' had been written years before, at the same time as the second canto of *Childe Harold*.[31] Byron may have been deliberately 'mystifying' Medwin. But even if the stanzas were entirely new in 1819, Byron was looking back to the days when he had indeed ridden round the bay of Marathon, and to the younger, more impressionable self of that time. What may have triggered this unexpected throwback was news from Greece that will have reached Venice some months before, but may have thrust itself literally under his nose while he was writing, in the form of an article in the October issue of the *Edinburgh Review*.[32]

A delayed and unintended consequence of the arrangements concluded at the Congress of Vienna in 1814 and 1815, that had given Great Britain control of the Ionian Islands, was that the mainland town of Parga had to

be ceded to Ali Pasha. In April 1819, some 800 Souliot families chose to
dig up the bones of their ancestors from beneath their houses and decamp
en masse to Corfu rather than submit to their arch-enemy, Ali. Byron had
never forgotten those warriors who had rescued him and Hobhouse when
they had been shipwrecked not far from Parga in 1809. Among the patriotic
verses he inserted into the entertainment for Juan and Haidée at this point,
are these:

> On Suli's rock, and Parga's shore,
> Exists the remnant of a line
> Such as Doric mothers bore;
> . . .
>
> Trust not for freedom to the Franks [i.e., western Europeans] –
> They have a king who buys and sells . . . [33]

Not the least shocking aspect of the cession of Parga, to liberal sensibil-
ities at the time, was that the British government in Corfu had accepted
a substantial sum of money from Ali in return for ceding the territory.
In reality, this was paid as compensation for the displaced townspeople.[34]
But this was not how matters were presented in the *Edinburgh Review* –
hence Byron's jibe that the king of an unnamed England 'buys and sells'.
In these stanzas, as once before in *Childe Harold*, the Greeks are urged, if
they want freedom enough, to trust no outside help but to stand up for
themselves.

But apart from this glancing topical allusion to an event that will have
excited Byron's sympathy for the losers, everything else about 'The Isles
of Greece' is ambivalent.[35] For all their tone of revolutionary fervour, it is
not even clear whether the stanzas as a whole are an exhortation to action
or to fatalism. 'Fill high the bowl with Samian wine!' the hearers are three
times urged, before the peroration: 'Dash down yon cup of Samian wine!'[36]
Are the hearers being urged to throw down the cup, untasted, in an act of
defiance, or only to drain it dry and accept their inglorious lot?

When they are quoted out of context, it is easy to assume the stanzas
of 'The Isles of Greece' are spoken by Byron, even if he *is* striking a
byronic pose. In fact, the whole inserted poem is part of a performance.
The lines are to be imagined as sung by the poet who has been brought
on to entertain Haidée and her foreign lover. What we are told about this
poet is not calculated to inspire confidence. He is a 'sad trimmer', a word
which can mean either the assistant of a lowly tradesman, or a turncoat in
politics.[37] This trimmer, we are told, is a consummate performer who can
satisfy an audience of any nation with what it likes to hear. Where he comes

from, what his own nationality is, we are not told. The verses themselves
are contradictory. At one point he speaks of Greece as 'my country', then
later addresses the Greeks as 'you'.[38] It is impossible to pin down where this
voice is coming from. Even the words we have just been reading turn out
to be no more than hypothetical:

> Thus sung, or would, or could, or should have sung,
>   The modern Greek, in tolerable verse[.][39]

Poets in general, we are next told, in a critique as old as Plato, are 'liars'.[40]
But then, as happens so often in *Don Juan*, the voice of the author takes
over. He continues, and the tone changes again:

> But words are things, and a small drop of ink,
>   Falling like dew, upon a thought, produces
> That which makes thousands, perhaps millions think[.][41]

The thought is familiar from *The Prophecy of Dante*, and before that
from the addition to the third canto of *Childe Harold*, made on the night
of the ghost stories at the Villa Diodati. Here, it leads into a meditation
that lasts for several stanzas and develops in a different direction from the
expected one. It turns out that Byron is thinking not about words as the
motive for action, but rather more subtly, that history is all in the telling.
Even the most heroic or inspired action is given meaning only through
being memorably told. If it had not been for the poet of the *Iliad* and
the *Odyssey*, the fame of Achilles, Odysseus, and all the other heroes of
the Trojan War would have disappeared along with the traces of the city
they had fought over, that Byron had searched for in vain, in the Troad.
As he now understood it, a person's glory owes more to what he calls 'the
historian's style' than to any intrinsic quality of the individual or actual
deed he has done. He was once again recalling Homer's 'fame of men',
the idea of posthumous glory that had motivated the legendary heroes of
Homer and the modern-day Greek klefts – though not the heroes of the
intervening 'Turkish tales'.

THE '*POETRY* OF POLITICS'

The idyll at La Mira ended at the end of October, with the expected return
of Teresa's husband. Now back at the Palazzo Mocenigo on the Grand
Canal, sitting up late at night, while the domestic drama was played out by
day, Byron brought the idyll of Juan and Haidée to its violent conclusion.[42]
Juan is sold into slavery. Haidée dies of grief, taking her unborn foetus with

her. Real life was superficially, at least, more civilised, certainly subtler and more surprising. On Christmas Eve, 1819, having already closed up the Palazzo Mocenigo, and with the agreement of both Teresa's father and her husband, Byron moved to Ravenna, there to make his home, for the next two years, bizarrely enough in the house of the man he was cuckolding.

There was no question, in Catholic Italy, of divorce for Teresa. But strings were pulled and the next best thing achieved. In July 1820, she was granted a legal separation from her husband. It came with a condition: either she must live with her father, Ruggero Gamba, or retire to a convent.[43] Byron could never live openly with Teresa, as man and wife. But the papal dispensation had an unintended consequence. From this time on, until his departure for Greece, Byron too would live, if not quite under the paternal roof, then in ever closer proximity to the whole Gamba family. Liked by all the Gambas, he would soon find himself made warmly welcome by these aristocratic republicans.

Within days of the dispensation allowing the separation, in July 1820, Teresa's brother Pietro returned to Ravenna from studying at Rome. He was two years younger than his sister, so only twenty when Byron first met him. Before long, Byron, too, would be calling him Pierino, as he was known affectionately to his family. Accounts emphasise his physical resemblance to Teresa, his impetuosity, bordering on naivety, and above all his enthusiasm for revolutionary politics. Pierino's devotion to Byron from that time on would be unshakeable – until he too died an early death from fever in the cause of the Greek Revolution. There could well have been an unstated homoerotic element to this relationship on Byron's side.[44]

In the circles in which Byron now moved, talk of revolution had been going on since March, when news had reached Italy of a liberal putsch in Spain. King Ferdinand VII had been forced to restore a liberal constitution. For the time being – indeed until the spring of 1823 – it looked as if the Spanish liberals were going to win the day. Now, in July, with Pierino from Rome came breaking news of another revolution, this time closer to home. In Naples, on 5 July, the restored Bourbon king had also been compelled to accept a constitution and to call a parliament in October. Young Pietro Gamba was wild with excitement. The rebels who had triumphed in Naples all belonged to the secret society of which he and his father Ruggero were also members, the Carbonari.[45]

Whether Byron actually ever became a member of the Carbonari is uncertain. Their initiation rituals were based on those of Freemasonry, a movement that had been growing in Europe since the last decades of the previous century. Clandestine meetings in the forest, the storing of arms, and an aura of conspiracy all clearly appealed to Byron. For a time, his admiration for Ruggero and a half-amused, half-romantic attachment to Pierino seem almost to have trumped his feelings for Teresa. Added to this, he found that, in those circles, people looked up to the English milord – or so, at least, the Austrian authorities believed.[46]

It was all very exciting. Here, at last, was the possibility of taking an active role, as once he had dreamed of doing. But as the hour for action (possibly) approached, Byron found himself violently torn. On the one side, he had seen enough of the effects of autocratic rule, since he had first come to Italy four years ago, to know that he hated it. His thoughts about England, too, had been turning increasingly belligerent, ever since he heard that unarmed demonstrators had been shot and killed by the militia outside Manchester, the previous August (the event known as the 'Peterloo Massacre').[47] On the other hand, at the very time when he found himself more and more drawn into the conspiracy of the Carbonari in Ravenna, the idea of radical *social* reform threw him on to the defensive. Byron, to the end, would remain fiercely loyal to his class.[48] To take up arms against the aristocracy would be to make war against his own self.

He tried to explain this to Hobhouse, who at the time, and to his alarm, was standing for parliament as a Radical Whig. There was a distinction to be drawn, he insisted, one that went back to the French Revolution. With moderate reformers, such as Mirabeau and Lafayette, Byron could sympathise. But Robespierre and Marat had been no better than 'ruffians'. 'I do not think the man who would overthrow all laws – should have the benefit of any', he insisted. And he went on: 'I protest, not against *reform* – but my most thorough contempt and abhorrence – of all that I have seen, heard, or heard of the persons calling themselves *reformers, radicals*, and such other names.'[49] The trouble was, these were the very names, with only the difference of language, that were being used by his new friends the Gambas and their like-minded compatriots in Romagna.

No wonder Byron found it so hard, during 1820, in Ravenna, to throw in his lot wholeheartedly with the cause of Italian liberation. Unable to resolve the conflict for himself, he turned it, instead, into a drama in verse. A month after the revolution in Spain, and within days of Hobhouse's election to the House of Commons, in April he embarked on the tragedy *Marino Faliero*.[50] The subject is taken from an episode in Venetian history that seems to have attracted his attention on his very first days in the city: the revolution against the established political order that the head of state himself had led, in the year 1355, thereby forfeiting both his life and his posthumous reputation.

Marino Faliero, the way Byron tells it in his play, is the story of a nobleman who joins a revolution against his own social class. Like his own version of Dante, and the enigmatic Lara before him, Byron's Doge resorts to political action as the means to pursue a private grudge by wrapping it up in a public cause.[51] Faliero struggles to make this a respectable position. The way he is described by others in the play is transparently a projection of how Byron saw himself in 1820. First and foremost, 'a child of greatness', it comes across as a secondary consideration that 'his mind is liberal'.[52]

The drama of Faliero's inner conflict comes to a head near the mid-point of the play. Contemptuously, and gratuitously, the Doge insults his plebeian accomplices, even while he promises to be ruthless in destroying the class to which he belongs. In language that recalls the doomed Manfred, and Lara before him, he cannot even decide whether he is acting of his own free will or not:

> And thou dost well to answer that it was
> 'My own free will and act', and yet you err,
> For I *will* do this! . . .
> And yet I act no more on my free will,
> Nor on my own feelings – both compel me back;
> But there is *hell* within me and around,
> And like the demon who believes and trembles
> Must I abhor and do.[53]

These lines bear witness to the intensity of the inner pressures that were tearing Byron, too, apart that spring and summer, while he wondered whether, or how far, to throw in his lot with his new friends, the Gambas, and their political hopes for Italy.[54]

There *was* a solution. He had glimpsed it the year before, when he had written *The Prophecy of Dante*. He had toyed with it teasingly, inconclusively, in the episode of *Don Juan* that includes 'The Isles of Greece'. But of this solution there is no sign in the play. What is missing from *Marino Faliero*, that was present in these poems of 1819, is the new idea of the *nation*. To have found room for this idea in a play set in fourteenth-century Venice would have been anachronistic. And Byron was proud of his historical accuracy. But the omission must have a deeper cause. It has been said that *Marino Faliero* looks deliberately backwards. The political resonances of the play have more to do with the England Byron had left behind than with Italy in 1820.[55] In Italy, the new struggle was for *national* liberation, as it could not be in England. In fighting for a nation, which in principle ought to include *all* social classes, including his own, Byron would be able to honour his commitment to 'reform' and 'liberation', without tying himself into the self-destructive, and ultimately absurd, bind that in his play costs Faliero his head and does nothing to change the political constitution of Venice. But, in the summer of 1820, Byron could not yet see this.

There was another reason, too, for holding back from full commitment in 1820. If he was sceptical about his own motives, he was still more so about the Carbonari themselves. Were they even serious? What chance of success did they have? Politically and strategically, they were weak. This was apparent to Byron from the beginning. One of his very first references to taking an active role comes in a letter to Murray from April 1820:

I shall if permitted by the natives remain to see what will come of it – and perhaps to take a turn with them . . . in case of business – for I shall think it by far the most interesting spectacle and moment in existence . . . I . . . feel more for them as a nation than for any other people in existence – but they want Union – and they want principle – and I doubt their success.[56]

Repeatedly through the letters of that year, Byron's favourite word to refer to the hostilities that he believes are imminent is 'row'.[57] There is a schoolboyish air to this bravado. When he jokes grimly about the risks, it is hard to tell whether he is talking about a glorious battlefield or the threat of ambush by a *bravo* in the pay of Teresa's jealous husband.[58] This was not so much politics as a personal vendetta projected on to a grand stage – the scenario, indeed, of so many of Byron's poems and plays.

The anticlimax came early in the new year, 1821.

The year in Ravenna began with a succession of snow, thaw, mist, and mud that clogged the forest paths. During its first two months, Byron once again embarked on a journal. The long deferred 'row' was finally imminent. Austrian troops were expected to begin crossing the river Po, on their way to crush the constitutionalist rebels in Naples. The local Carbonari were preparing to resist them.

While tension mounted in the streets outside, Byron began to occupy himself with writing another tragedy. This time, he quarried the theme from the *History of Greece* by William Mitford, that he had been rereading. Sardanapalus, whose name gives the play its title, according to a Greek story had been the last king of the Assyrians, who abandoned his regal duties to a life of selfish, sensual pleasure. Only when it is too late does he rouse himself to lead his followers in a heroic rearguard action against rebels determined to depose him. Finally, rather than submit, he has himself immolated on a funeral pyre which is a true bonfire of the vanities.

Like the previous play, this one too projects dilemmas of Byron's own at the time when he was writing it. The debauched Sardanapalus, deaf to the duties of his office, is Byron of the Venice years. In the portrayal of his two women characters, Byron embeds coded allusions to his estranged wife, to Teresa, and to his half-sister Augusta.[59] The historical backcloth may be changed, but the dilemma of *Sardanapalus* is once again between the personal and the political. In imagining himself as the Assyrian king, awakened at the last moment to his true nature and his true role in life, Byron goes further than he ever had, until now, in disavowing his own past career as a poet. But he still does so *in a poem*. Writing these plays was not political action. It was an alternative to political action.

On 9 February, Pierino brought news that the Austrian army was expected at the Po in six days' time. That would be the signal for a general uprising, to prevent the troops from crossing. But the day came and nothing happened. Byron noted in his diary only: 'Last night finished the first act of Sardanapalus. To-night, or tomorrow, I ought to answer letters.' By next day, he knew that the 'Barbarians', as he called the Austrians, were already across the river. Perhaps they had been forewarned of the plan. Even then, while the fate of the whole movement hung in the balance, and he was still affirming his commitment to it, the language of his journal betrays him: 'It is no great matter, supposing that Italy could be liberated, who or what is sacrificed. It is a grand object – the very *poetry* of politics. Only think – a free Italy!!! Why, there has been nothing like it since the days of Augustus.'[60]

The exclamation marks, the bravado, the carefree assumption that the ancient past could be brought back to life (this from the author of *Childe Harold* and *The Giaour*), all tell the same tale. All along, this has been not real politics, but only the '*poetry* of politics'. Byron the poet remains a poet. The cause of Italian liberation will not transform him into a man of action. His dramatic hero Sardanapalus, when the moment came, might show true courage, playing at being a king, but it could only ever be a futile gesture. *Words* are not, after all, not yet, ready to become *things*.

The complete collapse of the Carbonaro movement in northern Italy came six days later, on 24 February. For a few days longer, Byron kept up his journal, and the last of his hopes. The final defeat of Neapolitan forces came on 7 March, and on the twenty-third, a month after the collapse in the north, Naples was back under the rule of Ferdinand, its Bourbon king, with the Austrian army to enforce it.[61] It was all over. Ruefully, Byron summed up his feelings for the benefit of his friend, the Irish poet Tom Moore, quoting an unnamed Teresa: 'As a very pretty woman said to me a few nights ago, with the tears in her eyes, as she sat at the harpsichord, "Alas! the Italians must now return to making operas." I fear *that* and maccaroni are their forte, and "motley their only wear."'[62]

From that time on, Byron's loss of interest in the cause of Italian liberation was sudden, total, and permanent.

CAUGHT WRONG-FOOTED

If Byron had really been looking for a political cause to embrace that winter and spring, he need not have looked very far beyond the shores of Italy. The day before the final defeat of the liberals in Naples, on 6 March, the standard of revolt against Ottoman rule was raised above the river Pruth, in what is today Romania. The Greek Revolution had begun. A month later, much of what is now Greece was up in arms. All over Europe, during the next few months, liberal opinion rallied to the side of the Greeks, while governments everywhere condemned the uprising. Soon, volunteers were descending from all parts of the continent (though not, yet, from Great Britain).[63] Byron might well have felt a twinge of responsibility, as he read of these expeditions. True, he had never in his own person given explicit public support to the idea of a Greek revolution. But popular awareness of the present-day condition of Greece owed a good deal to his own literary fame. The latest cantos of *Don Juan* were in press – they would be published on 8 August. The lines inserted into the story of Juan and Haidée, 'The Isles of Greece', would be there for all to read, topical now in a way that Byron could never have imagined during his idyll with Teresa by the Brenta. How many of the new wave of volunteers would be setting out with copies of *Childe Harold* or *The Giaour* tucked into their rucksacks? What was he to say when even Pierino, Teresa's brother, threatened to become one of them, and earnestly exhorted him to go with him?[64]

By the middle of April, news from Greece was in all the European newspapers. And throughout April and May, Byron was scouring the papers in all the languages he could read – not to find out what was happening in the country that had once meant so much to him, but for reports of the unauthorised stage production of *Marino Faliero* in London.[65] It is not until 20 May that he so much as mentions the Greek Revolution, for the first time, in a surviving letter. Tucked in among other items is this, written to Hobhouse on that day: 'Our Greek acquaintances are making a fight for it – which must be a dilemma for the Allies – who can neither take their part (as liberals) nor help longing for a leg or a wing & bit of the heart – of Turkey.' *Realpolitik* meets the language of the nursery dinner table. Two weeks later, he would add, apparently as an afterthought, in a letter to Moore: 'The Greeks! what think you? They are my old acquaintances – but what to think I know not. Let us hope howsomever.'[66]

Byron's throwaway style can be deceptive. When he is laconic it does not necessarily mean that he is indifferent. Events in Greece had caught him unprepared, coming so soon after his disillusion with the political cause of Italy. He writes no less than the truth when he confesses that he does not know what to think about them. For the last five years, he had made his home in Italy. He had embedded himself deeply into Italian society, history, and culture. Nothing, if he could help it, would move him from the comfortable routine he had established with the Gambas in Ravenna. Too bad if there was not, after all, going to be a 'row' with the Austrians, in which he could have made common cause with his Italian friends. But he had never been happy with the idea of throwing in his lot with a bunch of 'ruffians' like Hobhouse's radical friends in England – and he knew perfectly well that not all of the Carbonari were as well-born or as cultivated as the Gambas. During the opening stages of the Greek Revolution, Byron became more defensive than ever. He said nothing in public, and in private so little that the rare, half-amused, half-grudging asides in his letters only make the surrounding silence the more clamorous. In the spring and summer of 1821, faced with the news from Greece, Byron could neither think nor act. He had gone to ground.

Instead, once again, he wrote a play. Again, he set it in his beloved Venice. He began *The Two Foscari* on 12 June (a week after the second mention of Greece in a letter), and finished it in a month. Jacopo Foscari, son of the Doge, is on trial for unspecified crimes against the state.[67] His father places his civic duty above all ties of sentiment and family, acquiescing even in the judicial use of torture and the eventual sentence of banishment on his son, which together are enough to cause the young man's death. This time, the dramatic conflict that had divided Doge Faliero against himself is played out between two different characters, the older Foscari and his son. But, as the title and the family relationship together imply, these two separate individuals are inseparably and fatally bound together. Both love Venice with a deep passion. Each, by the end, has died for the city he loves. In the case of old Francesco Foscari, the Doge, this means the civic constitution of the state. For him the independent, self-governing Venetian state is, as it was for Byron, the best achievable form of human organisation in an imperfect world. For young Jacopo, whose eulogy on the beauties of his native city provides the play with one of its few lyrical passages, Venice is the site of *personal* happiness, fulfilment, freedom – something that it *also* was for Byron.[68] *The Two Foscari*, more even than *Marino Faliero* or *Sardanapalus*, pits the private sphere against the public, individual happiness against civic duty and the good of the community.[69]

In dramatising this conflict, Byron has exaggerated a detail that was already in his sources, and which seems never to have been noticed.[70] Young Jacopo has already served time (whether as a tour of duty or as punishment is not made clear) in Venice's overseas possessions in Greece. He recalls with horror

> The hot gales of the horrid Cyclades,
> Which howl'd about my Candiote dungeon, and
> Made my heart sick.[71]

To be sent back to the colonial outpost of Candia, as Crete was known at the time, will be a fate literally worse than death:

> In that accursed isle of slaves, and captives,
> And unbelievers, like a stranded wreck
> My very soul seem'd mouldering in my bosom,
> And piecemeal I shall perish, if remanded.[72]

Jacopo's principled, lyrical, but also at times rather petulant refusal of his civic duty takes fire, in lines like these, from Byron's own inner conflict during the early summer of 1821.

This was Byron as he began to digest the news that kept arriving from Greece: disillusioned by his foray into political action with the Carbonari, and refusing as stubbornly as his dramatic projection, Jacopo Foscari, to uproot himself from the Italian world he had made his own, still less to acknowledge any political 'duty' to stand up for the Revolution that had broken out in the country to which he owed so much.

With the outbreak of revolution in Greece, the author of *Childe Harold* and the 'oriental tales' found himself in a bind from which there was no easy escape. It was not until Byron was visited for a second time by Shelley, this time in Ravenna in August 1821, that his thinking would begin to change. By that time the Shelleys would have come far closer to the politics of events in Greece than Byron himself was yet ready to do. How that came about, and what effect it had, will be the subjects of the next chapter.

CHAPTER 4

'Prophet of a noble contest'

ITALIAN PLATONICS, GREEK PASSIONS

While the year 1820 was drawing towards its close, and all Italy waited to see if the summer's revolution in Naples would lead to the 'row' with Austria that Byron anticipated, a chance acquaintance brought to the Shelleys' home in Pisa the most intellectually gifted among the future political leaders of the Greek Revolution.[1]

Born in 1791, Alexandros Mavrokordatos was a year and a half older than Shelley, three years, almost to the day, younger than Byron. The impression he made on the Shelleys at that first meeting seems never to have been recorded. This is how he struck another young Englishman, who encountered him three years later at Missolonghi:

The ensemble of his head was excessively fine, being very large in proportion to his body; and its bulk was not a little increased by his bushy jet black hair and prodigious whiskers. His thick eye-brows and huge mustachios gave a wild, romantic, expression to his features, which could not but produce a striking effect on a stranger. The expression of his physiognomy was that of a clever, penetrating, ambitious man. His large Asiatic eyes, full of fire and wit, were tempered by an expression of goodness. His looks had not, perhaps, sufficient dignity; for they had a kind of indecision, and timid flutter, which prevented him from looking any one stedfastly [*sic*] in the face. His stature was much below the usual size and his carriage altogether . . . unmartial[.][2]

The author of that portrait, Julius Millingen, has been unjustly treated by posterity, partly because he was one of the doctors who bled Byron to death, and partly because after the Revolution was over he made his home in Constantinople and for almost forty years served as court physician to a succession of Sultans until his death in 1878.[3] But Millingen could be an acute observer, and we will meet him again. What must have astonished the Shelleys most of all about their 'turbaned friend', as Shelley soon took to calling him, was his dress. Mavrokordatos had not yet adopted the thick

68

spectacles that he would use to counteract his myopia, or the western frock coat that later, in Greece, would mark him out as westernised. In Pisa he still wore the robes and turban of the Ottoman court that he had fled two years before (Plate 6a).[4]

Mavrokordatos owed the courtesy title 'prince' to his uncle, Ioannis Karatzas (Caragià). The family belonged to the Orthodox Christian, Greek-speaking elite of Constantinople known as 'Phanariots', after the Phanar district of the city where the Ecumenical Patriarchate of the Orthodox Church has its seat. The Phanariots were among the most highly educated subjects of the Sultan. During the preceding centuries, many of them had risen to positions of trust and influence within the empire. Since the early eighteenth century, the principalities of Wallachia and Moldavia, that make up two-thirds of today's Romania, had been fiefdoms handed out by the Sultan to these Greek families to rule. From 1812 to 1818, Mavrokordatos' uncle had been *hospodar*, or prince, of Wallachia, ruling from his semi-feudal court at Bucharest. The young Mavrokordatos had gained political experience working in his uncle's administration, where over six years he had risen to the rank of *megas postelnikos*, or secretary to the government.

Then, in 1818, Karatzas had fallen foul of the Ottoman authorities. He and his immediate family had to flee Bucharest for their lives. They took refuge in the west, first in Geneva, then in Pisa. There had been for some time a sizeable Greek community in the nearby seaport of Livorno (known to the English as 'Leghorn'). Pisa had already been chosen as the place of his exile by another high-profile fugitive from Bucharest, the Orthodox Metropolitan (bishop) Ignatios of Hungary and Wallachia, who still retained the title of his former see, although now officially living in retirement. Ignatios was already proving something of a magnet for young Greeks eager to study abroad. Greek students had begun enrolling in ever greater numbers at the university of Pisa, and the Tuscan authorities were keeping a watchful eye on their activities. Ignatios and the Orthodox community he led were at this time suspected (quite rightly) of close and possibly subversive links with Russia.[5] Later, the bishop would become an influential, if always somewhat inscrutable, figure behind the scenes of the Greek Revolution (Plate 6b). For several years, Mavrokordatos would continue to look up to Ignatios as a political, rather than a spiritual, mentor.

At the time when he met the Shelleys, Mavrokordatos had recently turned his political mind to the great conundrum of nineteenth-century geopolitics that would soon become known as the 'Eastern Question'. How long would the Ottoman empire last? How could the balance of the European powers be maintained during its dissolution and after? These questions Mavrokordatos addressed in a treatise that he wrote in French in 1820, but which remained unpublished during his lifetime. Like Ignatios, Mavrokordatos thought that a new war between Russia and Turkey was likely, if not inevitable. Victory this time would most likely go to Russia. But the Greek population of the empire was a force to be reckoned with, in its own right. Either by their own efforts or with outside help the Greeks would be capable of establishing an 'empire' of their own, favourably disposed towards the western powers, and strong enough to guarantee the future 'political balance of Europe'.[6] It was the beginning of a far-reaching vision to which Mavrokordatos would later endeavour to convert the British Foreign Secretary. Later still, it would become Byron's too.

As well as possessing a rare grasp of politics, Mavrokordatos had a prodigious command of languages. At the time the Shelleys met him he was proficient in seven. To those he was about to add English, thanks mainly to Mary. Mavrokordatos' intellect and the romantic glamour of his appearance and background appealed to each of the Shelleys in different ways and to differing degrees.

According to Thomas Medwin, Shelley's biographer, who was staying with them at the time, Shelley and Mavrokordatos read *Paradise Lost* and Aeschylus' *Agamemnon* together, both in the original. Shelley prided himself on his classical scholarship and soon began to be riled by the claims of an educated native-speaker of the modern language. Like most English classical scholars, Shelley refused to pronounce the ancient language in the modern way. Mavrokordatos, in common with most Greeks to this day, insisted on the pronunciation that came naturally to him. Mavrokordatos tried to interest Shelley in the commentaries by Adamantios Korais on the first four books of the *Iliad*, that were just then being published in Paris, in Modern Greek. Although Medwin muddles the details, he was surely correct in saying that 'Shelley's knowledge of the language as at present spoken, was very superficial'. For the rest, we know only that Shelley and Mavrokordatos would sometimes play chess together – badly.[7]

Shelley's irritation with Mavrokordatos was occasioned by more than arguments about pronunciation or textual criticism. To Claire, in May 1821, he would confide, 'The Greek Prince comes sometimes, & I reproach my own savage disposition that so agreable [*sic*] accomplished and aimiable [*sic*] a person is not more agreable to me.'[8] The truth was that the prince was visiting a good deal more frequently than that suggests. But it was not Shelley that he came to see. Mary's journal records meetings on no fewer than twelve days during that month, and sometimes two or three meetings on the same day. Between April and June 1821, Mavrokordatos wrote eighteen letters to Mary, in French, that she preserved. Only half of these letters have ever been published, very imperfectly, in a private publication that is now very rare.[9] In a lightly joking tone which he probably borrowed from Mary, in a letter of 31 May, Mavrokordatos would add to his punctiliously observed 'complimens à Mr Shelley': 'I have not had the honour of meeting him for quite some years.'[10] No wonder, then, that when a ship arrived at Livorno to convey their new friend to play his part in revolutionary Greece, Shelley's feelings, as he expressed them confidentially to Claire, were that 'He is a great loss to Mary, and *therefore* to me – but not otherwise.'[11]

At some point, probably in January, it was agreed that Mavrokordatos would teach Mary Greek – that is, the ancient language in which her husband was already proficient. In exchange she would teach him English.[12] By the middle of March, Mary had taken to indicating what were probably private meetings, by the Greek initials of his name, in lower case. Sometimes these appear on the same day when she also records a meeting with 'Prince M.' or some other variant of his name, which she was never very certain how to spell. Before news of the outbreak of the Greek Revolution arrived at the beginning of April to change the rhythm and the nature of their friendship, Mary and Mavrokordatos were enjoying one another's company, and often meeting alone. This is not to say that the relationship was overtly sexual. Nothing in his letters to her suggests that, and on her side it would not have been in character. But Mary's relationship with Mavrokordatos went hand in hand with Shelley's infatuation for the underage daughter of the governor of Pisa, Teresa Viviani. This was the episode, later consigned wearily by Mary to 'Shelley's Italian platonics', that gave rise to the poem 'Epipsychidion'.[13] The poem is Shelley's poetic declaration of love for 'Emilia', as his fantasy had renamed the sixteen-year-old convent girl whom he and Mary had both befriended.

Written during January and February 1821, 'Epipsychidion' ends with a fantasy of fulfilment in which 'Emilia' is transported to Greece, to an idyllic shore in the island group, the Sporades.[14] The landscape Shelley evokes is one of an earthly paradise, inhabited by only a few 'pastoral people' who 'Draw the last spirit of the age of gold'.[15] There is no sign, here, of Shelley's revered ancient Greeks. No ruined temples obtrude upon the lovers' solitude. In his own way, Shelley has re-imagined Haidee's island and the beginning of her idyll with Don Juan, from Canto II of Byron's epic (he had not yet read the continuation of the story in the next two cantos). If Byron had met Shelley half-way in bringing his epic hero into the classical world that Shelley so admired, the younger poet was now returning the compliment, in decamping with his beloved Emilia to a Greece that is recognisably *Byron's* from that canto. Shelley had always idealised Greece, but only in relation to the remote past. Now, while Mavrokordatos became an ever more frequent visitor to their house, for both the Shelleys the idea of Greece was becoming grounded in the present and beginning to open towards the future.

This was how matters stood with the Shelleys when news reached Pisa that the Greek Revolution had begun. Their response could not have been more different from Byron's.

ECHOES OF REVOLUTION

It was the first of April. But this was no April Fool. The day was Sunday, the first day of fine weather after a week of rain and gales, brought by the *libeccio* blowing in from the sea. The Shelleys at the time were living in the centre of town, on the Lung'Arno. It was there that Mavrokordatos called, as Mary's diary recorded: 'with news about Greece – he is as gay as a caged eagle just free'.[16] He was back the next day with the text, in Greek, of the declaration of his country's independence. Mary, certainly, and probably also Shelley, would have needed his help to translate it. No sooner had Mavrokordatos left again, than Mary wrote to him, considerately offering to suspend her Greek lessons. He agreed at once. (This is the first of his letters that Mary preserved.) In the event, the lessons would continue sporadically, and their meetings would become more frequent than ever. In a postscript to the same letter, Mavrokordatos added, 'I am preparing a small task for Mr Shelley. He has promised me to have it inserted in an English publication, and I am counting on him to fulfil his promise.'[17]

Two days later, on 5 April, the Shelleys dispatched their translation of the declaration of independence, together with two short letters summarising the news from Greece. One of these went to the *Examiner*, the radical journal edited by their friend Leigh Hunt, the other to one of the most widely circulating British newspapers of the day, the *Morning Chronicle*. The declaration of independence had already appeared in the British press, but the Shelleys' letters were duly published. These letters have been assumed by modern scholars to be the Shelleys' own work. But this is to overlook the guiding role of their 'turbaned friend' – and also the fact that most of the 'news' reported in these letters had either not yet happened by the day they were posted from Pisa, or was not yet known in Italy. Already on that April day, the Shelleys had become willing agents of what today would be called a propaganda campaign, whose author was Mavrokordatos.

In all probability the text published in the *Examiner* represents a faithful translation of the 'task' that Mavrokordatos had prepared for Shelley. His original text, which has not survived, would have been in French, the language in which he wrote to Mary. Mary, or Shelley, or both, will have done little more than put this into English:

An express from Wallachia informs us that the Prince [Alexander] YPSILANTI, a Greek General in the Russian service, who has been aid-de-camp to the Emperor ALEXANDER, has entered Wallachia, declaring the liberty of Greece, with a force of 10,000 Greeks, collected from those serving under the Russians, and has now already advanced to Bucharest, his army increasing every hour ... His proclamation, which I enclose, has been the signal for a simultaneous insurrection throughout Greece. The Servians, the Epirotes, and the Sulliotes have revolted ... The Turks are completely driven from the Morea[.][18]

Ypsilantis had crossed from Russia into Ottoman territory, in what is today Romania, on 6 March. The more general insurrection in the Peloponnese (or Morea) had in fact only just begun, on 2 April. News of its success would not reach Pisa for another two weeks.[19] Ypsilantis' troops were not yet at Bucharest. The other revolts announced were still no more than wishful thinking. When Mavrokordatos wrote to unnamed Greek friends in Paris on 2 April, he did not include these inflated claims that he had passed to the Shelleys.[20] That this is Mavrokordatos speaking, and not a Shelley, is further proved by a sentence that begins, 'The war of the Cross against the Crescent, for which our fathers bled ... '. Mary repeats this, with the rest, in a private letter to her friend Maria Gisborne of the same day. But this is simply a more informal version of what she would have received from Mavrokordatos.[21]

The version of this communiqué that reached the *Morning Chronicle*, and was published on 23 April, has been touched up with the addition of opinions that are recognisably Shelley's.[22] Shorn of the tell-tale reference to religion, it subtly qualifies the announcement that Ypsilantis' action has already provoked sympathetic revolts throughout Greece: 'or rather it has been the signal before determined on of that measure'.[23] Shelley knew, in other words, that this was what was *supposed* to happen. Thanks to Shelley's connivance, Mavrokordatos was later jubilant that the *Morning Chronicle* had been the first newspaper to announce the uprising in the Peloponnese – in effect, before it had happened. But he was annoyed, too, that Shelley by a careless, or perhaps a face-saving, opening sentence had all but given away the source of his information. To Mary, Mavrokordatos would complain, 'This declaration has caused me some pain, for you know that I am already sufficiently watched by the enemies of our cause.'[24]

Medwin, who had left Pisa at the end of February, was no doubt correct in remembering:

There was at that time little prospect of a Greek revolution, though the subject frequently formed part of our conversation. It was a favourite speculation of Shelley's, and with a prophetic spirit he anticipated the emancipation of that oppressed race; and Mavrocordato . . . half resolved to believe, almost against reason, that an insurrection in Greece was possible; but had no idea it was so near at hand.[25]

Mavrokordatos knew more than Medwin realised. At some point between Medwin's departure and the beginning of April, it seems that he had taken the Shelleys part way, at least, into his confidence.

The *Philiki Etairia* (Friendly Society, or Society of Friends) was a clandestine organisation, very similar in its rituals, codes, and secrecy to the Italian Carbonari, and like them based ultimately on Freemasonry. Often supposed to have been founded in the Ukrainian city of Odessa in 1814, the Society effectively began its operations between two and three years later.[26] Its nucleus was made up of expatriate Greek traders and businessmen with interests and connections in Russia, a country long seen by many Greeks as their future liberator and protector, because of their shared Orthodox religion. The chief political objective of the conspirators was to win over highly placed Greeks in the ruling elite of the Russian empire, in the hope that in this way Russia could be induced to support a revolution in Greece, if necessary by making war against Turkey. To this end they had tried, and failed, to recruit the Corfiot nobleman Ioannis Kapodistrias (Capodistria), who at the time had risen to become foreign minister to Tsar Alexander. Instead, they had only recently persuaded another high-ranking officer in the Russian imperial service to lead them. This was the Alexander Ypsilantis named in the communiqué that the Shelleys had transmitted to England.

By early in 1821, the conspirators had come up with a plan for action: a universal uprising of the Greeks on the symbolically chosen feast of the Annunciation, 25 March (6 April in the western calendar). A meeting of leading 'Friends' in the Peloponnese at Vostitsa (where Byron's former host, Andreas Londos, was now primate), debated whether this might not be too soon. Letters, of seemingly anxious content, were despatched on 10 February to Ypsilantis in Russia and Metropolitan Ignatios in Pisa. The conspirators agreed to stay their hand until they should receive replies.[27] It is not known for certain how Ignatios responded. According to Mavrokordatos, later, both he and the bishop had tried to persuade the conspirators to abandon their plans, believing that 'in a few years' the nation would have progressed to the point where liberty could be won without bloodshed.[28]

The messengers from the Vostitsa meeting would have reached Pisa by the end of February. Mavrokordatos, living in the same house as Ignatios, would certainly have been in the bishop's confidence. Throughout March, Mavrokordatos will have known that revolution was imminent, even if he was actually exerting himself, along with Ignatios, to postpone it. So the news he brought to the Shelleys that April day was not entirely unexpected. As Shelley confided to Claire the next day, 'Prince Mavrocordato has made us expect this event for some weeks past.'[29]

Ten days earlier, he had written to his friend Thomas Love Peacock in England to commission a gem with the head of Alexander the Great and two seals with the words engraved, in Greek, from Sophocles' play *Oedipus at Colonus*, 'I am the prophet of a glorious contest.'[30] These must have been intended as presents from both the Shelleys to Mavrokordatos, who shared his name with the conqueror of old, and in this way was to become emblematically the new Alexander the Great. Mary had just finished reading Sophocles' play, with his help.[31] Evidently, in the minds of all three, the resonant Greek phrase had become a touchstone for discussion of imminent revolution in Greece. When Mavrokordatos wrote to break the news to his Greek friends in Paris, on the same day that he brought Ypsilantis' proclamation to the Shelleys, he would quote the same phrase from the play as an epigraph or heading.[32] And Shelley would quote it again, also in the original Greek, as the epigraph of his verse drama, *Hellas*, that he would write later in the year and dedicate to Mavrokordatos.

Mavrokordatos may have had reservations about the timing of the revolution beforehand. But, once hostilities had broken out, his enthusiasm was wholehearted from the beginning. There was never any doubt in his mind that he would be departing for Greece at the earliest opportunity.[33] For the remainder of his time in Pisa, Mavrokordatos would loyally maintain his promise to keep Mary abreast of every development that was reported to him from Greece, both in person and by letter. Although he wrote only to her, it is clear that he expected the news he reported from Greece to be shared with Shelley, and perhaps also with others.[34]

The first news was not good. On Saturday, 7 April, when reports of the outbreak were less than a week old, Mavrokordatos wrote to Mary:

I am in despair. The Russians, the Austrians, perhaps even England, are making common cause against the unhappy Greeks, offering them their mediation, and threatening them should they not accept. You can well imagine that at such a moment I am not master of myself. The only thing I beg of you is to speak of this to no one, unless to Mr Shelley. I may come to see you this evening to seek your consolation.[35]

It was worse than that. News of Ypsilantis' action had reached the assembled sovereigns of Europe and their diplomatic retinues at a summit in the Austrian town of Laibach (today's Ljubljana, the capital of Slovenia). The occasion was one of a series of such high-level meetings which served to consolidate the conservative policies that had been ushered in by the Congress of Vienna at the end of the Napoleonic wars. In the company of other heads of state, not only had the tsar refused to the insurgent Greeks the support on which the *Philiki Etairia* had been counting, he had publicly dismissed Ypsilantis from his service and disowned his actions, even going so far as to make common cause with the Turks to ensure the defeat of the rebels.[36] From that moment, the revolution in the Danubian principalities was doomed. And there was as yet no news that the conspirators had been any more successful with the second prong to their plan than the first, in raising sympathetic revolts in Greece itself.

Soon this would change. In the Peloponnese, where Turkish-speaking Muslims were few outside the towns, the revolt spread quickly during the first half of April. Within weeks, much of the country was in the hands of the insurgents, while the Turks took refuge in the fortresses and fortified towns. Mary's journal for 24 April records, 'αμ [Mavrokordatos] calls in the evening with good news from Greece – The Morea free.'[37] This time it was true. Soon there would be confirmed news from further afield. In northwest Greece, there was a revolt of the Souliots, the warlike mountaineers whose spirit had so impressed Byron. The islands of Hydra, Spetses, and Psara had joined in, contributing a combined fleet of merchantmen and privateers to begin enforcing a naval blockade in the Aegean.

All this Mavrokordatos reported throughout April and May. While news was slow to arrive from Wallachia, he continued to express anxiety that Ypsilantis had not yet crossed the Danube, on his way south to relieve his countrymen in Greece. He confessed to Mary that no one seemed to know what the Prince's plans were.[38] Even while the fate of Ypsilantis' venture hung in the balance, Mavrokordatos seems to have been remarkably candid in what he told Mary about its prospects:

I believe that I have told you more than once that the Greeks' efforts are not for Wallachia and Moldavia, which are two provinces quite foreign to Greece, and I foresaw that immediately upon the departure of Ypsillanti [sic] these two countries would have either to pass under the power of Russia, or else come to an accommodation with the Porte [the Ottoman government].[39]

Meantime, disturbing news was arriving from Constantinople. From the outset, the Greeks had been braced for savage reprisals by the Ottoman authorities.[40] On 21 May, Mavrokordatos wrote to Mary that he feared the Patriarch of the Orthodox Church had been put to death, as well as several of the higher clergy and 'a Prince Mavrocordato (who must be either my cousin, or my uncle)'.[41] Three days later he was able to confirm the execution of the Patriarch. Gregory V had been hanged from the gate of his own palace on Orthodox Easter Sunday, 21 April, along with three archbishops. The fate of Mavrokordatos' relative remained unknown. In time it would be confirmed. A Mavrokordatos is included in the list of high-ranking citizens beheaded on 16 April.[42]

If Mavrokordatos had initially hoped to leave for Greece in a matter of days, he was to be disappointed. On 27 May, in a passage marked 'Secret', he announced to Mary that a ship had been sent for him from Greece, but would not be departing immediately. At the same time, he was unable to resist scoring a point against her husband: 'If Mr Shelley was full of pride at being able to have at his disposal a barque and two cannons, you may imagine how proud must I be now to have at mine a brigantine with eighteen.'[43] He also asked her to burn this letter after reading it. Whether this element of melodrama was aimed at Shelley or at the Tuscan authorities is not clear.[44]

By now the Shelleys had moved some five miles outside Pisa, to the spa resort of Bagni di San Giuliano. Prince Karatzas was a frequent visitor to the baths. This made it easy for Mavrokordatos to send letters by a family servant, or to call on the Shelleys while accompanying his uncle.[45] With the tempo of preparations speeding up during June, there were fewer meetings. To compensate for this, on Wednesday, 13 June, Mavrokordatos wrote to Mary promising to 'come to see you on Friday at 7 and stay until five, perhaps a little later'. Mary's journal duly reports that the visit took place, though not its duration.[46] A week later, having met her unexpectedly in Pisa, he wrote to her immediately afterwards to announce that his departure from Livorno had been fixed for the following Monday. He would make every effort to see her on Sunday. At the same time he passed on a report, admittedly unconfirmed, that Ypsilantis had won a great victory over the

Turks. The reality, though Mavrokordatos could not have known of this before he left Italy, was that Ypsilantis' forces had been routed at the battle of Dragashan on 19 June.[47]

From Sunday to Monday, when Mavrokordatos was expected, Shelley absented himself from Bagni di San Giuliano, perhaps tactfully.[48] But there was no sign of Mavrokordatos. On Monday, the day she expected that he would sail, Mary wrote to him in what must have been considerable distress, to judge from her covering note to Maria Gisborne: 'Would you have the kindness to get the enclosed delivered immediately to its address? Pardon me for troubling you with this, and pray let it be sent without *any delay* – You will hear of the Prince at M. Constantin Argyropoli, a merchant at Leghorn. If he has sailed, then let the letter be sent *back to me*[.]'[49]

This probably crossed with Mavrokordatos' letter to her. Events had kept him in Pisa. He would be leaving in all probability today. 'If I cannot come [to visit you] I count greatly on your indulgence. I have no doubt at all of the interest that you take in our cause, and in me in particular, and I thank you with all my heart.'[50] This is more formal than most of what he had written to her over the last few months. It does not sound as though he was in fact planning to visit, and Mary's journal does not record that he did. After promising, at the end of the same letter, that he would write to her 'as often as possible', Mavrokordatos sailed from Livorno aboard a Hydriot ship flying the Russian flag on Tuesday, 26 June, bound for Marseille. There he would pick up military supplies, a printing press, his future right-hand man Georgios Praidis, and a score of French and Piedmontese volunteers, before sailing for Missolonghi in Greece.[51]

Mavrokordatos never wrote to Mary again, except once, almost twenty years later, when he was serving as his country's ambassador in London. Politely declining her invitation, he did promise to visit on another occasion and to introduce her to Madame Mavrocordato.[52] But if their friendship during these seven months in 1820 and 1821 left little detectable mark on the private life of either, the same cannot be said of Mavrokordatos' future political career in Greece. Between the outbreak of the Revolution and, at the latest, 1823, both Mavrokordatos and his political mentor Ignatios had withdrawn their principal foreign allegiance from Russia and turned, with careful qualifications, to Britain instead. During the exact same period, Mavrokordatos, the former privileged minister of an enlightened despot in Wallachia, would re-emerge into the political limelight as a constitutional nationalist with liberal leanings. It has been suggested that these developments may owe much to the influence of the Shelleys during those months at Pisa.[53]

Finally, whatever Shelley's feelings may have been at the personal level, a consequence of his wife's closeness to Mavrokordatos was that during the first three months of the Greek Revolution he, too, had had the benefit of extensive and privileged information about the progress of events there, updated on an almost daily basis. This information Shelley would soon have the opportunity to share with Byron.

REUNION IN RAVENNA

When Byron rather peremptorily summoned Shelley to visit him in Ravenna, at the end of July, the reason had nothing to do with Greece. Two more urgent matters pressed upon him.

The first was Allegra, his illegitimate daughter by Claire. To the extent that Byron had kept in touch with Shelley at all after their time together in Venice, it had been to complain whenever Claire pestered him about Allegra. The girl was now four years of age, and at the beginning of March Byron had sent her away to be educated in a convent. It fell to Shelley and Mary to pass on this news to Claire. She wrote at once to Byron, and begged him, instead, to have the child educated in England. Shelley wrote to him too. Shelley had been appalled by the way Teresa Viviani, the 'Emilia' of his poem 'Epipsychidion', had been kept a virtual prisoner in a Catholic institution while others arranged a loveless marriage for her. In a little more than ten years time, this must surely be Allegra's future, too.

From that exchange, the idea of a meeting between the two men took root – 'alone', as Byron stipulated. But the months went by at Bagni di San Giuliano without any word from Ravenna. Then, suddenly, at the end of July, Byron was in such a hurry for Shelley to visit him that he even offered to pay the expenses for his journey – something which later, if not then, Shelley might have found insulting. Impatiently, not to say imperiously, Byron followed this up a few days later with the briefest of curt notes: 'D[ea]r S. – I wrote to you last week.'[54] Byron need not have worried. By the time this reached Pisa, on 8 August, Shelley was already in Ravenna.

There was a reason for this urgency. On 10 July, Pietro Gamba, Teresa's brother, had been arrested. Soon after, both Pierino and Ruggero, Teresa's father, had been given notice to leave the Papal States within twenty-four hours. It was part of a round-up of all those who had been implicated in the revolutionary movement that had ended so ignominiously in February.[55] This meant that Teresa had to leave Ravenna too. Under the terms of her separation from her husband, if she was not living with her male relatives, it would be *her* turn to be shut up in a convent. What Byron saw as good for his four-year-old daughter would not do for his mistress. To escape this fate, Teresa, at Byron's insistence, left Ravenna on 25 July. No sooner had she gone, than she began to badger him by letter, writing 'sheer lunacies', as he complained to her brother.[56] The way he explained it to Shelley, Byron had no appetite to return to his old Venetian habits (of which he knew his friend disapproved). There was nothing for it, then, but for Byron to leave Ravenna himself and, soon, to rejoin Teresa and her family.[57] But where was he to go? The Gambas were proposing Switzerland. If he were to leave Italy, what should he do about Allegra? Within a week of Teresa's departure, Byron had despatched his hasty summons to Shelley. To Pierino he explained that the visitor was 'a relative of Allegra's', whom he was expecting so as 'to decide about the child's future'.[58]

This was the immediate spur to the meeting. But Byron had made decisions on Allegra's behalf before, without thinking to consult Shelley. There was another reason why Byron urgently needed a meeting with Shelley that summer. In April, the Poet Laureate, Robert Southey, had published an adulatory poem in memory of King George III, who had died the previous year. It was called *A Vision of Judgement*. In his preface to this poem, Southey had seen fit to attack certain unnamed poets

of diseased hearts and depraved imaginations, who, forming a system of opinions to suit their own unhappy course of conduct, have rebelled against the holiest ordinances of human society, and hating that revealed religion which, with all their efforts and bravadoes, they are unable entirely to disbelieve, labour to make others as miserable as themselves, by infecting them with a moral virus that eats into the soul!

To this detested 'school' of contemporary poetry Southey gave the name 'Satanic', because of the writers' 'Satanic spirit of pride and audacious impiety'.[59]

Byron was used to attacks of this sort, though he would never grow a thick skin. This one was different, for two reasons. The first was that he was being attacked not as an individual but as one of a 'school'. Perhaps his friend Tom Moore was implicated too. But the real thrust of the Poet Laureate's attack was directed against Shelley. Like it or not, Byron was being lumped together with a self-proclaimed atheist, the author of *Queen Mab* and of its still more stridently political 'Notes'. Whether or not Southey had been the origin of the rumours that linked Byron's name with Shelley's in a so-called 'league of incest', as Byron believed, he certainly knew the story and now seemed to allude to it publicly.[60] The attack concluded: 'This evil is political as well as moral, for indeed moral and political evils are inseparably connected.' Rumour, personal slurs, political radicalism, and religious heterodoxy were forced together, just as unavoidably as Byron's name as a poet was joined implicitly with that of Shelley in the 'Satanic school'.

Byron read this tirade, almost certainly, on 7 May.[61] He must have realised at once that he was going to have to make his mind up, finally, about Shelley, and take a public position. At the personal level, he knew the allegation of incest to be untrue, at least in the literal sense, since Mary and Claire were not blood relations.[62] But he was not at all sure about the nature of Shelley's relations with Claire, a suspicion that has been shared by modern biographers. Byron was capable of being as much shocked by Shelley's private life as Shelley was by Byron's. When the future of Allegra was at stake, and stung to cruelty by Claire's persistence, he could even blame the deaths of the Shelleys' own children on the irregular lifestyle of a household that included Claire as well as Mary.[63] On the other hand, when Claire or Allegra were not involved, Byron's judgement of Shelley was usually generous. That June, he wrote to a friend, without any sign of irony: '*Shelley* is *truth* itself – and *honour* itself – notwithstanding his out-of-the-way notions about religion.'[64]

To this new dilemma Byron responded in the same way as he had done to others over the course of the past eighteen months. He set about dramatising it in verse. If the British public had been informed that he and Shelley were conspiring together to form a 'Satanic school' of poetry, then he, Byron would come up with something to fit the bill. On 16 July, exactly a week after he had finished *The Two Foscari*, and a fortnight before he summoned Shelley to join him, he began to write a new drama that could truly, and literally, be called 'satanic', since the Devil is one its main characters. He called it *Cain*. It was finished three weeks after Shelley's departure.[65]

Cain is one of the most Shelleyan of all Byron's works.[66] The knowledge that God forbids to the faithful is granted to Cain by Lucifer. This turns out to be the knowledge, not of Good and Evil, as in Genesis, but of life and death. It is Byron's old theme of mortality. Lucifer in this play at times talks very like Shelley:

> Nothing can
> Quench the mind, if the mind will be itself
> And centre of surrounding things – 'tis made
> To sway.[67]

This was the affirmative belief that Shelley's Julian had tried without success to instil in Count Maddalo. Cain is convinced, and falls.

It looks as though Byron had made up his mind, by the second half of July 1821, to make common cause and be publicly damned along with Shelley. But even once he had embarked on writing *Cain*, and at the point when the departure of Teresa from Ravenna gave a practical edge to his thinking, he may still have wavered. Then came news of yet another attack published in the British press. Once again Byron's name was linked with Shelley's. According to an article in the *Literary Gazette*, the 'Notes' to *Queen Mab*, recently re-published in a widely circulated pirated edition, had been the work not of Shelley, but of Byron.[68]

It may have been that article, rather than the question of Allegra's future, that decided him. Or it may have been both together. Before he could go on with the drama, before he could answer Southey in public, before he could decide what to do about Allegra and whether or not to join Teresa and the Gambas in Switzerland or somewhere else, Byron had first to have it out with Shelley. Hence the peremptory summons to Ravenna at the end of July.

Shelley arrived at the Palazzo Guiccioli in Ravenna at ten o'clock in the evening on Monday 6 August. The two men sat up talking until five the next morning. Byron had prepared a test for Shelley, and lost no time in springing it on him. In Venice, the British consul, Richard Hoppner, and his Swiss-born wife had acted for a time as unofficial guardians of Allegra. The couple had grown fond of the girl, and had also got to know the Shelleys and Claire when they had visited in 1818. A year ago, Hoppner had written to Byron to pass on a series of allegations he had heard from the Shelleys' former maidservant, Elise. At the time, Byron had been content to allow this letter to reinforce his prejudices against allowing Allegra ever to return to Claire and the influence of the Shelleys. Now, a great deal more was at stake. In defiance of its writer's explicit request, Byron gave Shelley Hoppner's letter to read, and then watched for his reaction.

According to Elise, who had been with the Shelleys at the time, Claire had had a child by Shelley when she and the Shelleys had been in Naples at the end of 1818. Byron may still have been hoping to wring from Shelley an admission that *he*, rather than Byron, was the father of Allegra, even though he had long ago seemed to accept the reasons why this could not be so.[69] It was not this that shocked Shelley to the core. Elise had told the Hoppners that Shelley was habitually cruel to Mary and beat her, that he had attempted to force an abortion on Claire, and then that he had abandoned Claire's child after it was born. Shelley may or may not have confessed to Byron the truth that lay behind these smears. A child *had* been born in Naples. Shelley had falsely registered the birth, giving himself and Mary as the parents. His 'Neapolitan charge', a girl, had died eighteen months later.[70] If he did, he may also have revealed a secret that has eluded all modern biographers, namely the true parentage of Elena Adelaide Shelley. Mary, when at Shelley's request she wrote to Mrs Hoppner, passionately denying the allegations, made no reference to this fact.[71] It is possible that Shelley did not, either.

However frank he may have been with Byron about these matters, Shelley's horrified outrage at the charge of cruelty comes through with ringing candour in the account of the evening he wrote at once for Mary. Byron, observing this face to face, cannot have been less than impressed. Shelley had passed the test, and more.

A number of consequences followed. Shelley was surprised and delighted to find Byron easily persuaded to change his plans and choose Tuscany as the place of his exile with the Gambas. Bemused by this success, Shelley suddenly found himself charged with writing to Teresa, whom he had never met, to persuade her of the advantages of this new plan. He was also expected to find a house for Byron, his entourage, his horses, and his menagerie in Pisa, as soon as he went back. The only casualty of these arrangements was little Allegra. Shelley did at least take the trouble to visit her in the convent, something that Byron never did. But, despite Shelley's attempt to persuade Byron to bring her with him to Pisa, Allegra remained where she was.

The drama *Cain* went forward. Byron's own *Vision of Judgment*, his brilliant comic parody of Southey's poem, would soon be completed. Within a couple of weeks of Shelley's departure from Ravenna, Byron would add an appendix to *The Two Foscari*, that he had recently sent to Murray to be published. In this appendix, he explicitly hit back at the preface to *A Vision of Judgement*, but also implicitly rose to the challenge contained in Southey's diatribe against a 'Satanic school'. Without naming Shelley either, Byron took the opportunity to dispose of the other allegation he had recently received, that concerned the two poets. Not only was he, Byron, *not* the author of the 'Notes' to *Queen Mab*: 'No one knows better than their real author, that his opinions and mine differ materially upon the metaphysical portion of that work; though in common with all who are not blinded by baseness and bigotry, I highly admire the poetry of that and his other publications.'[72]

This was the first time that Byron praised Shelley's poetry in public. And if he was at pains to keep his distance from his friend's opinions on matters metaphysical, he went on to ally himself with the radical politics of the 'Notes' to *Queen Mab*. Overcoming the misgivings that he had dramatised in his two Venetian plays, Byron now declared his conviction 'that a revolution is inevitable' in England, even as he disclaimed any personal benefit, as an aristocrat, that he could expect from it. The reluctant Radical was edging closer to the position of his radical friend and fellow-poet. In this passage he even uses the plural: 'Mr Southey accuses us . . .'.[73] Against the grain of his own nature, Byron was beginning to make common cause with others – even in a 'Satanic' school of poetry.

In the same spirit, by the time Shelley left Ravenna, Byron had agreed to join with him and his politically radical friend Leigh Hunt in a new project, that would be at once literary and political. This was to be a periodical called *The Liberal*. The initial outlay would be provided by Byron. *The Liberal* would be published in England, but controlled jointly by the three of them from Pisa. After the failure of the Carbonari, here was another way for Byron to attempt to convert 'words' into 'things' and to contribute directly to political life in England. Again, the willingness to cooperate in a higher interest – however hedged about – is new.

In tribute to the persuasive powers that had brought these things about, it was now that Byron devised a new nickname for Shelley: 'the Snake' or 'serpent'. The nickname was derived, as Byron explained it, from 'the Serpent who tempted Eve', according to a mildly humorous allusion to the story in Goethe's *Faust*. Shelley was tall and thin, particularly when set beside a short, and at this time rather portly, Byron, and so reminded him of one of the serpent's 'Nephews – walking about on the tip of his tail'.[74] Byron himself termed this a 'buffoonery'. But it was more than that. After all, the story of the tempter in Paradise, and its fantastical sequel in his own drama *Cain*, had been preoccupying him all through the time of Shelley's visit. But Shelley either missed this, or misunderstood it. Byron would never know the crippling effect that he was to have on the final year of Shelley's life. But Shelley would have been even more surprised, could he have had any inkling of the true power the devilish 'Snake' would come to exercise over Byron's last years, beginning with those ten days in Ravenna.

'WE ARE ALL GREEKS'

By the time of Shelley's visit to Byron in Ravenna, the Greek Revolution was five months old. Byron – the celebrity who had made his name with poetry written 'in Greece or of Greece' – had still made no public statement on what was happening there.[75] He had finished *The Two Foscari* on 9 July, still implicitly jibbing as furiously as Jacopo against the prospect of returning to the 'hot gales of the horrid Cyclades' or acknowledging the political and moral 'duty' that the new situation in Greece might possibly impose on him.

It was Shelley who began to winkle him out.

It turned out that Byron at Ravenna did have access to news from Greece, even if his own letters make no mention of the fact. We have Shelley to thank for the information that 'We have good rumours of the Greeks here.'[76] Byron seems to have tried to dampen his friend's zeal by lending him the novel by Thomas Hope, *Anastasius, or Memoirs of a Greek*, that had been published two years before. Byron loved this scurrilous, picaresque story of a modern Greek trickster and chameleon, who will try anything to stay alive. He assured Shelley that the thoroughly debased picture it gives of 'modern Greek manners' was true to life.[77]

But Shelley had an answer to this. Thanks to what Mavrokordatos had told him in Pisa, Shelley had newer information about the Greeks than had been available to the author of *Anastasius*:

the flower of their youth returning to their country from the universities of Italy, Germany, and France, have communicated to their fellow-citizens the latest results of that social perfection of which their ancestors were the original source . . . The munificence and energy of many of the Greek princes and merchants, directed to the renovation of their country with a spirit and a wisdom which has few examples, is above all praise.[78]

Not, perhaps, Shelley's exact words to Byron at Ravenna. But this is how he would write up his rebuttal of *Anastasius* some two months later, back in Pisa, in the Preface to *Hellas*.

Byron's immediate response to Shelley's enthusiasm seems to have been grudging at best. On the day of his guest's departure from Ravenna he was tetchily fuming about the financial consequences for himself, should the revolution in Greece spark a war between Russia and Turkey. 'There "*will* be a Turkish war" –', he wrote to his banker, Douglas Kinnaird, 'and yet you tell me not to be disturbed "about the funds"?' And to his publisher: 'I am in great discomfort about the probable war – and with my damned trustees not getting me out of the funds.'[79]

But 'the Snake' had proved persuasive yet again. In early September, three weeks after Shelley had left him, Byron wrote to Murray to announce his imminent departure for Pisa. The letter is full of grumbles – about the careless printing of the new cantos of *Don Juan*, and about the revolution that had failed to happen in Italy last winter. But if Byron has washed his hands of the Italian cause once and for all, this letter introduces a new tone. And this may well reflect something of the tenor of his conversations with Shelley. The Italians, he wrote: 'will rise again some day – for these fools of the Government are blundering – they actually seem to know *nothing*; for they have arrested & banished many of their *own* party – & let others escape – who are not their friends. – What thinkst thou of Greece?'[80]

This is only the third recorded mention by Byron of the Greek Revolution. This one is prompted by a more positive reflection on the failure of the Carbonari. History might still, in the long run, turn out to be on their side – as indeed would prove to be the case, forty years later. Nothing would induce Byron to throw in his lot with that particular cause again, after having been let down so badly, as he saw it, last winter. And so his thoughts turn to Greece.

This was the time when he was putting the finishing touches to the drama *Cain*, with its bleak but resolute conclusion. A few days later, he was still thinking of Greece: 'At present I am going into Tuscany – and if the Greek business is not settled soon – shall perhaps go up that way . . . But my going will depend upon more certain information than is yet to be obtained – things are so disguised there.'[81] This comes in one of Byron's rare letters addressed to his estranged wife. This one, probably, was never sent. These occasions bring out his most solemn side. Transposed into a more jocular tone, more suitable to a very different recipient, the poet Tom Moore, the idea appears again, all within the space of a few days. It is from this second letter that we learn of the role of Pierino, who had probably been the first to urge Byron to think of going to Greece, and who eventually would accompany him there:

It is awful work, this love, and prevents all a man's projects of good or glory. I wanted to go to Greece lately (as every thing seems up here) with her [Teresa's] brother, who is a very fine, brave fellow (I have seen him put to the proof), and wild about liberty. But the tears of a woman who has left her husband for a man, and the weakness of one's own heart, are paramount to these projects, and I can hardly indulge them.[82]

These words were written just over a month after Shelley's departure from Ravenna. During that visit, or in its immediate aftermath, an idea had taken root. But, as often happened with Byron, the impulse did not last long. Already, by the time of his letter to Moore, he had put it behind him, not to be mentioned again for many months to come.[83] As September progressed, Byron began to apply himself to the more immediate plans he had laid with Shelley and the Gambas, although he still kept putting them off.

Shelley, on the other hand, returned to Pisa fired up with the project for his most ambitious composition since *Prometheus Unbound*. Soon, it would take shape as the 'lyrical drama' *Hellas*. In this play, Shelley updates Aeschylus' *The Persians*, written to celebrate the Greek victory over the Persian invaders in the battle of Salamis in 480 BCE, so as to comment upon the present conflict in Greece. But with one very significant difference. Aeschylus' drama had been written and performed eight years after the event. Victory for the Greeks, and their future freedom from Persian rule, were assured before Aeschylus began writing. This was not the case in the Peloponnese in the autumn of 1821, however 'glorious' the contest as reported in Pisa. Shelley *could* have written a propaganda play, simply endorsing what Mavrokordatos had told him and Mary earlier in the year: that in the present struggles of the Morea the ancients were being reborn and history was about to repeat itself. But this was not Shelley's way. As the chorus of Greek captive women expresses it, half-way through:

> Greece and her foundations are
> Built below the tide of war,
> Based on the crystàlline sea
> Of thought and its eternity[.][84]

Greece – that is, ancient Greece – is not history, but an *idea*, the product of thought. By the end of the play, 'thought' has triumphed over 'mutability', Shelley's term for the unstable, unpredictable flux of history.[85] In the drama, the Greeks of 1821 are not victorious. Their revolution is crushed by the Ottomans. It is in quite a different sense that the political claim of Mavrokordatos and the Greeks the Shelleys knew at Pisa is endorsed towards the end, again in the words of the chorus: 'Greece, which was dead, is arisen!'[86] The ultimate triumph of Greece, as Shelley conceives it, will be in the mind. It will come about regardless of the vagaries of real history, and will touch everybody. This is what Shelley means by his famous statement in the Preface, that 'We are all Greeks.'[87] We are all equally the inheritors of an idea that is not bounded by history but exists for all time, and may be endlessly renewed. Greece is no longer fixed in a remote and unredeemable past. Greece, as an idea, has become an aspiration to be realised in the future.

When Byron read *Hellas* the following April, Mary reported that he 'seem[ed] pleased with it'.[88] Whether or not the poem chimed with the conversations that Byron remembered having with Shelley in Ravenna, it offered him, and anyone else who read it, a way of thinking about the Greek Revolution that excused him from having to think about any *particular* Greeks, ancient or modern. It also solved Byron's old problem in thinking about a Greek revival: would not a reborn Greece be as unnatural and as deadly as the vampire of contemporary Greek superstition, or as Victor Frankenstein's ingeniously animated 'Creature'? No, according to Shelley, because Greece is eternal and so can never die.

Byron may not have read the poem very closely. If he did, he would no doubt have been sceptical. Shelley's idea of Greece had never been his. But one thing was clear. In the words of the poem's epigraph, that Shelley left in the original Greek but incorporated, translated, into the Preface: the Greek Revolution was a 'glorious contest', and he, Shelley, was its prophet.

Hellas was finished by the end of October. Dutifully, perhaps, on 1 November 1821, Shelley inscribed the dedication to 'His Excellency Prince Alexander Mavrocordato' in token of his 'admiration, sympathy, and friend-ship'. On the same day, Byron arrived in Pisa.

CHAPTER 5

Death by water, transfiguration by fire

The group of British expatriates that within a few months would gain notoriety as the 'Pisa circle' was now almost fully formed.[1] Thomas Medwin,
Shelley's cousin, who had shared a house with him and Mary the winter
before, returned from Rome shortly after Byron's arrival. Medwin's friend
from the Indian Army, Edward Williams, with his common-law wife Jane,
had been near neighbours and good friends of the Shelleys for most of the
past year. Williams had been drawn to Pisa by his admiration for Shelley
as a poet. He himself had ambitions as a dramatist. The latest house moves
had brought both couples back into the centre of Pisa. The Shelleys were
now renting the top floor of Tre Palazzi di Chiesa on the Lung'Arno. The
Williamses lived in the flat below them. Almost opposite, across the river,
was the Casa Lanfranchi. This building of the fifteenth century had been
judged suitably grand for Byron and his large household. All the arrangements at the Tuscan end had been made by Shelley. Teresa, obedient to
the terms of her separation from her husband, lodged with her father and
brother, a few streets away.

The Irishman John Taaffe had been introduced to the Shelleys at about
the same time as Mavrokordatos. In some ways the odd man out in the
group, being a staunch Catholic and conservative in his politics, Taaffe had
become a regular visitor before Byron's arrival, and was quickly accepted
by Byron too.[2] Last to arrive, in mid-January, was Edward John Trelawny.
'Incurable romancer' or, to those who knew him later in Greece, 'Lord
Byron's jackal', Trelawny was a Cornishman of wild and exotic appearance
who had once served in the Royal Navy as a midshipman.[3] He was often
supposed to have been the original on which Byron had based the character
of Conrad, the Corsair. The reality was the other way round. Ever since
he had begun reading Byron's poems in the 1810s, Trelawny had created
for himself a personality and a past based on Byron's fictional creations. At

his first appearance in Pisa, Trelawny made a strong impression on the rest of the group, and particularly on Mary.[4] Only Byron seems to have seen through the facade to detect, or at least to suspect, the fantasist beneath. That would not prevent him from coming to rely on Trelawny, at moments when a 'jackal' was called for.

Finally, there was a missing member, an invisible planet whose distant orbit exerted a gravitational pull on those of the 'circle' proper. This was Leigh Hunt, former editor of the *Examiner*, poet and fearless columnist who had earned the friendship of Shelley and the respect of Byron when he had spent two years in Surrey Gaol after libelling the Prince Regent.[5] Hunt was the key to the two poets' plans, hatched in Ravenna, to establish a new radical journal that they would edit together from Pisa. *The Liberal* was the only practical or tangible rationale for the circle to exist at all. From the beginning, Byron had had the ground floor of the Casa Lanfranchi fitted out to accommodate Hunt, his wife Marianne, and their six small children. A leitmotiv throughout the six or so months that the 'Pisa circle' lasted is news, and more often the lack of it, of the Hunts' ever-expected arrival from England.

While the 'Pisa circle' was still coming together, the Shelleys, Williams, and perhaps also Medwin were full of excitement as news continued to come in from Greece. Now that Mavrokordatos had left Pisa, they kept in touch with the Greek community through Georgios Argyropoulos, whose wife Ralou was the daughter of Karatzas, the former *hospodar*, and Mavrokordatos' cousin.[6] It was Argyropoulos who called at the Tre Palazzi di Chiesa on 11 November, a Sunday, with news of what in hindsight would become one of the most significant events in the whole course of the Greek Revolution.[7] On 5 October 1821, the large fortified town of Tripolitsa (today's Tripoli), in the centre of the Peloponnese, had fallen to the Greeks after a prolonged siege. It was a victory of immense strategic importance. It also marked the first widely reported occasion on which the Greeks proved themselves no less capable than their enemies of treachery and indiscriminate slaughter. Despite a guarantee of safe conduct given to the Muslim inhabitants of the town, at least 8,000, including women and children, were massacred. In a gratuitous excess of violence against all who were not Orthodox Christians, the victors turned with equal ferocity on the small Jewish community.[8]

Once the scale of the savagery at Tripolitsa became known in Europe, it undoubtedly did the Greek cause much harm. On the other hand, in the eyes of most Greeks, at the time and for long afterwards, the Muslim population of Tripolitsa had merely paid a small part of the debt of violence perpetrated against Greek Christians during hundreds of years of slavery. Mary, at least, seems to have had no difficulty in accepting the Greek view. Writing to Maria Gisborne in England a few weeks later, she would brush aside anticipated criticism: 'Some cruelties have ensued – But the oppressor must in the end buy tyranny with blood – such is the law of necessity.'[9] Shelley, too, was still enthusiastic in December, writing to Claire: 'The news of the Greeks continues to be more & more glorious – It may be said that the Peloponnesus is entirely free, & Mavrocordato has been acting a distinguished part[.]' He and Mary were even considering moving to Greece to settle there permanently, once the revolution was over.[10] At the end of November, Mary had gone back to learning Greek, though with Mavrokordatos gone she now had no one to teach her. Until the end of the year, Greek fever still ran high in the Shelley household.[11]

The same cannot be said of Byron. No sooner had Shelley heard the news from Tripolitsa, than he arranged to accompany Argyropoulos to the Casa Lanfranchi to introduce him to Byron.[12] Byron's response has not been recorded, but the evidence suggests that he reacted quite differently from Shelley. He never mentions the capture of Tripolitsa in a surviving letter. If he ever returned the call or met Argyropoulos again, there is no record of it. During all the time that the 'Pisa circle' lasted, there is no indication that Byron took any interest in the Greek exiles living nearby, corresponded with them, or met any of them. For almost a year, in Pisa, Byron lived within a few hundred yards of Metropolitan Ignatios. Later, the bishop would lend his moral authority to Byron's expedition to Greece (though not without caveats). But it seems the two never met.

Something of what Byron felt about the violence at Tripolitsa may perhaps have been carried over into Canto VIII of *Don Juan*, written the following July. The subject is the horrors of the siege and sack of a Turkish town in an earlier war. The cause of liberty is not forgotten. But it is not uppermost in the poet's mind, in a canto that reads overwhelmingly as a denunciation of the senseless destruction of war.[13] A fictional episode from that canto, in which Juan saves the life of a young Turkish girl among the victims, would later be played out in real life when Byron imitated Juan's action, at Missolonghi.[14] Magnanimity towards the losers, and a horror of the kind of indiscriminate cruelty that had been in evidence in the sack of Tripolitsa, would distinguish Byron's behaviour and attitudes later, when he arrived in Greece. Now, at the end of 1821, it probably mattered more to Byron that he had actually been to Tripolitsa. He had been treated with respect (if a trifle louchely) by Veli Pasha. It made sense for him to sympathise with the losers.

After reports of the massacre at Tripolitsa had become current, by the end of the year, only the Shelleys still made sporadic efforts to keep in touch with news from Greece. No member of the 'Pisa circle' ever mentions the first Provisional Constitution of free Greece, drawn up near the site of the ancient sanctuary of Epidaurus in January 1822. Dismissed by some as a paper exercise, at the time and ever since, this document nonetheless laid the foundations for the kind of democratic nation state that most western supporters, including Byron and the Shelleys, wished to see in Greece. Among the chief architects of this constitution, as Byron would come to appreciate later, had been Mavrokordatos, who was also voted President of the Executive for the first year of its operation. But although the Shelleys had continued to follow Mavrokordatos' career with evident approbation until the end of 1821, these later developments, that should have interested them both, seem to have made no impression, either on them or on anyone else in their circle.[15]

Only one event reported from Greece during the first half of 1822 seems to have made any impact at all on Byron and his new friends, and that was muted. The event was the death of Ali Pasha. Since Byron had met him at Tepelena in 1809, the pasha had gone on consolidating his position in northwest Greece and Albania. In 1820, in his old age, Ali had overreached himself, coming out against the Ottoman government in open rebellion. This action probably had the unintended consequence of hastening the outbreak of the Greek Revolution. Inveterate enemy of the Greeks that he was, Ali inadvertently gave great assistance to their cause, as his rebellion tied down Turkish forces elsewhere in the region. Finally, on 24 January 1822, the Sultan's armies entered Ioannina, Ali was executed, and his head sent to be displayed in Constantinople. By 13 March, news of these events had reached Pisa. Recollection of his meetings with Ali moved Byron to retell an anecdote from his travels in Greece that had more to do with his own poem *The Giaour* than with the pasha. His laconic epitaph on the 'Mahometan Buonaparte', flattened by Williams' plain style, but in essence probably conveyed faithfully, was merely: 'a brave man but an infamous tyrant'.[16]

As spring began to turn to summer, the 'Pisa circle' cannot have been unaware of one of the most widely reported atrocities of the entire Greek Revolution. Between mid-April and the end of June, the prosperous island of Chios had been razed on the order of the Sultan, in a calculated act of reprisal. Contemporary estimates put the number of Greek dead at 25,000, with 45,000 taken into slavery.[17] These acts provoked the outrage even of Lord Castlereagh, the British Foreign Secretary detested by both Byron and

Shelley as the arch-enemy of liberal causes everywhere. An official protest to the Ottoman government followed. Byron may never have known this, or have chosen to believe it if he did, but it was actually Castlereagh, as a direct result of these events, and not his successor Canning, who first among the representatives of the Great Powers of the day went some way towards recognising the rights of the Greeks as belligerents.[18] It might not have been much, when weighed against the horrors that had been perpetrated in Chios, but it was the first step towards an international policy on Greece that Byron would later do his utmost to promote.

Byron's refusal to talk about events in Greece during these months in Pisa is of a piece with his policy – or lack of one – that he had begun at Ravenna before Shelley's visit. Even when the Revolution was a year old, and beyond, Byron was still not ready to take up a public position on a subject so strongly associated with his own reputation as a poet. Still less, among this new circle of friends, was he prepared to reveal his short-lived thoughts from last autumn, of going 'up that way' himself. Instead, when he resumed work on *Don Juan*, at some point between January and April 1822, from then until the end of July he laid his hero's adventures among the Turks.[19]

In any case, the members of the 'Pisa circle', and Byron and Shelley in particular, had matters of their own to preoccupy them during the first half of 1822. The growing tensions between Byron and Shelley, and the underlying as well as more obvious causes of these, need to be understood if one is to make any real sense of what Byron did next.

FALLEN ANGELS

A month after Byron's arrival, Mary marvelled that 'Pisa . . . has become a little nest of singing birds'. On the surface, at least, all went well for several months more. In January, Shelley reported that he and Byron were 'constant companions'.[20] A routine had quickly become established. Most afternoons the men rode out of Pisa by the Porta alle Piagge to practise pistol shooting at targets in the grounds of a nearby farmhouse. Once a week, in the evening, Byron hosted dinners for the men at the Casa Lanfranchi. Mary, finding herself relegated to the company of Jane and Teresa, missed the intellectual stimulus she had always been used to. For Shelley, too, the new social Byron that emerged on these communal occasions must have come as a shock. Averse as he was, equally, to alcohol and gossip, Shelley soon found evenings at the Lanfranchi a strain: 'my nerves are generally shaken to pieces by sitting up, contemplating the rest making themselves vats of claret &c. till 3 o'Clock in the morning', he wrote towards the end of January.[21]

With the arrival of Trelawny, who had a friend in the boatbuilding business, it suddenly became possible for Shelley to realise a lifelong dream, to own a seagoing boat of his own. Byron, acting on impulse, had to have a bigger and a better one. There was much excited talk of how they would spend the summer, all together, sailing up and down the Tuscan coast. Already, in the first half of February, Shelley and Williams were scouting for a summer base where the whole group could be together, by the sea.[22] As late as 5 March, Mary could still write of these summer plans, paraphrasing Wordsworth for the benefit of Marianne Hunt, 'we are a colony "which moves altogether or not at all"'. Mary had a reason for encouraging the Hunts to delay no longer in joining them. Two days later, writing to Maria Gisborne, she was more frank: 'We shall have boats & go somewhere on the sea coast where I dare say we shall spend our time agreably [*sic*] enough for I like the Williams' exceedingly – though there my list begins & ends.'[23]

Something had happened to change the dynamics of the 'nest of singing birds'. Already, Shelley was confiding to Hunt that 'Particular circumstances, – or rather I should say, particular dispositions in Lord B's character render the close & exclusive intimacy with him in which I find myself, intolerable to me.'[24] Three weeks later, Shelley had made up his mind. The plan for the summer was off. He wrote to Claire, 'I shall certainly take our house *far* from Lord Byron's, although it may be impossible suddenly to put an end to his detested intimacy.'[25]

Part of the problem was, again, Allegra. Claire, who was now living in Florence, had been approached by Elise Foggi, the Shelleys' former maid who had been responsible for the allegation that had reached Byron the year before, that Claire had given birth to Shelley's child in Naples. Claire panicked, and decided she must leave Italy at once. She wrote to Byron, announcing this intention, and begged him to let her visit Allegra in the convent at Bagnacavallo before she went. At the same time, she also wrote to the Shelleys. Shelley at once fetched Claire back to Pisa. Over four days staying with them Claire agreed not to leave the country. During this time, Mary learnt something that shocked her very much, to judge from the tone of her journal entry for 25 February.[26] There was no obvious reason for Byron to refuse Claire's request. In her letter she made no claims on him. In the past he had promised her access to Allegra, and once, in Venice, had even granted it. But Shelley may have been rattled too, and at once rushed off to Byron to intercede for Claire. It was the worst possible thing he could have done.

Byron turned on Shelley, as only he was capable of doing. There was at least one face-to-face quarrel, probably in the last days of February. Its echoes can be heard in Shelley's letter to Hunt on 2 March. They can be heard again in a joint letter he and Mary wrote to Claire three weeks later, and yet again in the words of an acquaintance who had heard Shelley speak of what had happened. Shelley had seen 'a gleam of malicious satisfaction' pass over Byron's face. '"I saw his look," Mr Shelley said; "I understood its meaning; I despised him, and I came away."'[27] The informant seems not to have understood what it was that Shelley feared in that moment. Byron must have said something to remind him that he knew of the allegations about Shelley and Claire, and the child born in Naples. Shelley had seen, at those weekly dinners at the Lanfranchi, how carelessly and how cruelly Byron could dissect the affairs of absent friends and acquaintances. The very scandal that Claire was preparing to flee Italy to avoid was liable to break any day, right here in Pisa, thanks to Byron's propensity to malicious indiscretion. Shelley never had any proof that Byron did this, and probably in fact he did not. But he *might*, at any time when Shelley was absent, have entertained the company with a version of the story that Elise Foggi had brought to the Hoppners in Venice. If that were to happen, Shelley confided to Claire, he might have no choice but to challenge Byron to a duel.[28] Only this fear explains Claire's complaint to Mary, that 'you wished to keep me as much out of L.B.'s mind as possible, that he might not mention me to the people by whom he is surrounded'.[29]

On Shelley's side, by the end of March, the friendship with Byron was over. He continued to admire him as a poet, and he was determined to fulfil his obligations to Leigh Hunt over *The Liberal.* But 'intimacy' with Byron was a thing of the past.

Byron, having vented his feelings, was not going to back down over Claire and Allegra. But he knew he had been in the wrong to round so violently on Shelley. Within days of when the quarrel must have happened, he was defending Shelley from the latest attack by Southey, in a letter to Moore: 'As to poor Shelley, who is another bugbear to you and the world, he is, to my knowledge, the *least* selfish and the mildest of men – a man who has made more sacrifices of his fortune and feelings for others than any I ever heard of.' Mary surely read Byron correctly, when she wrote to Maria Gisborne on 7 March, 'For the present S[helley] is entangled with Lord B[yron] who is in a terrible fright lest he should desert him.'[30] With their differences over Claire and Allegra threatening to turn friends and collaborators into enemies, the advantage was not all on Byron's side. He knew he needed Shelley, at least as much as Shelley needed him. The 'Pisa circle' continued to meet as regularly as before.[31] But the time was not far off when it would be Byron's turn to be on the defensive.

All this was only part of the story, the part on the surface. These spats and tantrums were no more than the outward symptoms of a tension between the poets whose origins lay far deeper, in the character and the imaginative life of each of them. Shelley's growing loss of self-esteem, as it might be termed today, would culminate in talk with Trelawny about suicide, and the cry of despair at the human condition that is his last long, uncompleted poem, *The Triumph of Life*. Byron's presence, his wealth, and his status all had this effect on Shelley, though there might well have been other causes too. The evidence has been sifted by Charles E. Robinson, who concludes that Shelley was distressed by his own feelings of envy towards Byron. At the same time, he felt trapped in a vicious circle: 'without fame, he could not earn money; without money, he was too depressed to write; unable to write, he could never attain fame'.[32]

At some time between November and 22 January, perhaps as an immediate response to reading *Cain*, which he admired above anything that Byron had written, Shelley adapted some discarded lines from *Hellas* to make a sonnet addressed to Byron. Its conclusion reveals Shelley at his most abject, in this bitter twist to an image drawn from Schiller's 'Ode to Joy':

> the worm beneath the sod
> May lift itself in homage of the God.[33]

The 'worm' here is kin to the serpent, 'shut out from Paradise', according to another poem of the same time, a love poem addressed to Williams' wife Jane.[34] Worm, serpent, or 'Snake': in Shelley's imagination, he felt himself excluded, demeaned, inferior. It had been meant in play, but for a poet who had also likened himself to a 'tender plant', a metaphor like that was not harmless fun.

Nor was it for Byron. If Shelley was now the 'Snake' – the nephew of the serpent in the Garden of Eden – the Devil had always been Byron's own part. Behind all the 'byronic' heroes of his poems and dramas lies Milton's depiction of Satan, the defiant rebel angel in *Paradise Lost*. According to Lady Byron, during the short time that he had lived with her, Byron's 'imagination [had] dwelt so much upon the idea that he was *a fallen angel* that I thought it amounted nearly to derangement'. Echoing the same idea (and quite probably something Byron himself had said in conversation), Shelley could describe Byron, in a letter written in January, as 'this spirit of an angel in the mortal paradise of a decaying body'.[35]

Byron as the fallen angel, Shelley as 'the Snake'. Southey's libel against the 'Satanic school' of poetry had really struck home. And, as luck would have it, it was on the evening of 4 February that Southey's second onslaught reached the Casa Lanfranchi. Medwin gives a vivid account of the scene, and Byron's immediate rage.[36] The next day Byron drafted a long rebuttal, addressed to the editor of the *Courier*, which had carried Southey's attack, but it seems he never sent it. To everyone in Pisa he ranted that he was going to 'call out' Southey. A letter addressed to the Poet Laureate, amounting to a challenge to a duel, was actually sent, care of Byron's banker, Douglas Kinnaird. But Byron's instructions were perhaps intentionally ambiguous, and Kinnaird ignored them. The challenge never reached Southey.[37]

It was in this fervid atmosphere that Shelley attempted to intervene, at the end of that month, as the voice of Byron's conscience in the matter of Allegra. The fury of Byron's reaction, his otherwise quite gratuitous intransigence, and Shelley's lurid fears of having to fight a duel over it, now begin to make sense. While Shelley was debasing himself in his imagination as the 'worm' before his God, Byron saw in Shelley a rival for a role he had long ago reserved for himself. In the person of Shelley, Byron was confronted with what he might himself have been, if he had not been Byron.

During January, at the Casa Lanfranchi, they talked about doubles. The idea of the doppelgänger, the sinister other, or dark side of the self, was not new to this company. It had cropped up during the ghostly conversations in Switzerland, five and a half years before. Now, a translation of Goethe's *Faust* had been sent from England. It arrived on 12 January and at once they began eagerly to discuss it. In the introduction to the translation, they read this: 'the easiest clue to the moral part of this didactic action is, to consider Faust and Mephistopheles as *one person*, represented symbolically, only in a two-fold shape'.[38] Shelley, who had been learning Spanish, thought he had found the source for this idea in a play by the seventeenth-century Spanish poet Calderón. He entertained the company with an account of its story.

Not long after this, towards the end of January 1822, Byron embarked on what is surely his strangest work, the unfinished play *The Deformed Transformed*. In Medwin's hearing, he described it as 'a *Faustish* kind of drama'. Before he sent it to be published, he would add a note acknowledging the debt to Goethe.[39] In this play Byron gave an entirely new twist to the theme of the doppelgänger. *The Deformed Transformed* has an urbane wit and a lightness of tone, that derive in part from Goethe and in part from the Byron of *Don Juan*. But just like his previous plays, it dramatises personal and immediate anxieties of Byron's own, in this case to do with the 'Pisa circle' out of which it grew.

The play's hero, Arnold, is a hunchback, deformed so hideously that his crude and simple-minded peasant mother rejects him. On the point of killing himself from despair, he is prevented by the miraculous apparition of the 'Stranger' – the Devil in light disguise. The Stranger offers to exchange Arnold's crippled body for that of a mighty hero of his choosing. Arnold accepts the deal. There follows a brief beauty contest, in which the Stranger conjures up the images of victorious generals from antiquity, and the philosopher Socrates (ugly, but with a mind to compensate). Arnold opts for the body of Achilles. Reincarnated in his new body, he is now ready to distinguish himself as a hero in war, and sets out for the field. With him goes his shadow – his old deformed body, now occupied by the Stranger. This image of his former self Arnold will never shake off. It is the price of the deal. The pair then head for Rome. The year is 1527, and Arnold performs valiantly during the siege and sack of the city, while the devil who accompanies him has all the best lines. Having saved the beautiful Olimpia from the mayhem, Arnold is disconcerted to find his advances to her rebuffed, despite his gorgeous body and chivalrous action in saving her. At this point the text breaks off.

In this bizarre concoction, Byron outdoes Goethe, Calderón, the Shelleys, and himself in earlier works, in *doubling* the doppelgänger. One pair is formed by Arnold the hunchback and the suave Stranger/Devil. Arnold's deformity is Byron's own, exaggerated to extremes. So, too, is his sense of physical inferiority. Byron had never forgotten being scolded by his own mother as a 'lame brat', just as Arnold is by his, in the play's opening scene. That is one side of the coin. The other is the Stranger, who can fix everything by the magic of an incantation. The Devil's wit and way with words are Byron's too.

But Arnold's transformation and reincarnation in the body of Achilles involves a *second* doubling. It is not a two-way exchange of identities that the Stranger offers. While the Stranger/Devil adopts Arnold's old identity, Arnold himself acquires an entirely new one, a *third* identity that he picks, as it were, off the shelf. Achilles is described:

> The god-like son of the Sea-goddess,
> The unshorn boy of Peleus, with his locks
> As beautiful and clear as the amber waves
> Of rich Pactolus rolled o'er sands of gold,
> Softened by intervening chrystal, and

Rippled like flowing waters by the wind . . .
      Look upon him as
Greece looked her last upon her best, the instant
Ere Paris' arrow flew.[40]

This is an Achilles imagined at the very moment before his early death, a moment made timeless by the devil's magic power – or the poet's imagination. Byron may not yet have read *Hellas* when he wrote these lines, but he surely had its author in mind. The ideal specimen of manhood that he conjures up from ancient Greek mythology for his *alter ego* Arnold to adopt is made of the very same stuff as Shelley's Greece, that was 'Based on the crystàlline sea / Of thought and its eternity'. From this point on, *The Deformed Transformed* becomes Byron's fantasy of exchanging his own identity (the composite made up of Arnold and the Stranger/Devil), not quite for that of Shelley, but, rather, for the embodiment of the Shelleyan *ideal*.

By comparison with Byron's idea of his own deformity, physical and perhaps also moral, Shelley was tall and physically whole. He still had his absurdly youthful good looks, while Byron was becoming appalled by the signs of premature ageing in himself. Shelley's beliefs had something unearthly about them that Byron often deplored. But – a rare thing for him – he never ridiculed them either. 'Shelley believes in immortality', he wrote to Moore, with something like awe, just after their quarrel at the end of February.[41] Byron the sceptic, the railer, the scoffer, 'lame brat' or cloven-hoofed fallen angel, could never match up to an imaginary ideal like Shelley's Greece in *Hellas*, or Achilles as he is described in *The Deformed Transformed*. On this reading, Shelley and his unearthly ideals tormented Byron as the 'other' that he himself could never be. After all, almost from their first meeting, nearly six years before, Shelley had been nagging Byron to transform himself from what he was into something that better matched Shelley's idealistic conception, be it the great poet of the age or the saviour of Italy.[42]

In the play's working-out, Byron probably intended to get his own back. The beautiful Olimpia would have fallen for the scoffing devil in Arnold's old, hideous body. Arnold would have been beside himself with jealous rage. Even in the written parts, there is something vacuous about Arnold's role inside his gorgeous carapace. He has little to say for himself. But if this was to be Byron's imaginative victory over Shelley, it would still have been a pyrrhic one. What may have been intended as the final consummation is summarised in an account that derives from Medwin's recollection of another Pisa conversation. Here the hero's name is given as Alfonso. He challenges his rival

and demands *satisfaction*. They fight; his rival scarcely defends himself; at the first thrust he receives the sword of Alfonso in his bosom; and falling, exclaims, 'Are you satisfied!'
The mask and mantle of the unknown drop off, and Alfonso discovers his own image – the spectre of himself – he dies with horror![43]

For Arnold to kill the devil inside his own discarded body will be to kill himself.

The fury that Byron turned on Shelley, in real life at the end of February 1822, was the fury that he had imagined for Arnold rounding on his devilish double. They were both of them rebel angels. Each was in awe of the other to such an extent that both nurtured fantasies of self-destructive violence, as the only way to end a coexistence that was at once intolerable and as inescapable as Arnold's with the Stranger and the body of Achilles.

If *The Deformed Transformed* was indeed planned to end with Arnold killing his other self, this might also explain why, after Shelley's death, Byron had not the heart to finish it. What Shelley himself thought of the parts of the play that he read is lost in the conflicting recollections of Medwin and Trelawny.[44] Mary, when she copied Byron's manuscript in Genoa that autumn, while coming to terms with her bereavement, would enjoy the play enormously – perhaps because she recognised its backhanded tribute to her husband.[45]

THE END OF THE 'PISA CIRCLE'

An incident on 24 March had the temporary effect of healing over these divisions. It was a Sunday. Byron and his party were riding back to town from their regular pistol shooting practice. As they approached the Porta alle Piagge they were overtaken by a horseman in a hurry. Taaffe briefly lost control of his mount. Byron decided that he and his party had been deliberately insulted, and overreacted as only he could. There was an affray at the gate, when the guard had to intervene. Shelley was knocked to the ground and briefly lost consciousness. A visiting English friend of Byron's had his face slashed open with a sabre. One of Byron's servants was badly wounded. Byron forced a way through the soldiers and set off to notify the police. Returning to the scene, on his way he encountered the offender again, and challenged him on the spot. To his chagrin, the man turned out to be a mere sergeant of dragoons. It came down to class. Sergeant

Masi was unworthy to fight a duel with a peer of England. It was left to Byron's coachman (probably without his master's knowledge) to ambush the sergeant shortly afterwards and stick a pitchfork into his side.

For several days, it looked as though the sergeant would die of his wound. Local sympathy now turned against the English party. Masi recovered. But for a fortnight the members of the 'Pisa circle' were all treated by the Tuscan authorities like the suspects in a classic detective story. With the exception of the inglorious Taaffe – now nicknamed 'Falstaaffe' – the group presented a united front under pressure and the threat of danger. This was the more striking as the Shelleys and the Williamses between them had three very small children in their care. Depositions were taken. Byron enlisted the aid of the British consul at Florence, Edward Dawkins. Gradually, tensions eased. Two of Byron's servants and one of Count Gamba's remained in prison pending charges. Otherwise, on the surface at least, by the middle of April the affair had blown over.[46]

It had all been avoidable. Byron's extreme sensitivity to insult had magnified a trivial annoyance into the 'Masi affair' that still takes up several pages in most biographies of the protagonists. Its most serious repercussions were yet to come. Afterwards, Byron laid all the blame on Taaffe, a poor horseman and inconsistent in his version of what had happened. So incensed was all the 'circle' with the Irishman's conduct that Byron had to restrain Trelawny from 'breaking his bones', or so he would later claim.[47] But the truth is that Byron was spoiling for a fight, that Sunday afternoon. He had already threatened the poet laureate, Southey. In the previous month, Shelley had feared he might be goaded into fighting a duel with him over Claire and Allegra. Now, Sergeant Masi turned out to be beneath his notice. Byron seemed to have no luck in picking his antagonists.

A fortnight after the affray, on 9 April, Byron signed a six-month lease on the Villa Dupuy at Montenero, in the hills outside Livorno.[48] The following day, Shelley was confident that his own party, which would now include Claire, would be leaving for the Gulf of Spezia, 'the moment the weather permits'.[49] With the relaxation of tension, the two parties – Byron's and Shelley's – were again making plans to spend the summer apart.

Then, on the evening of Monday 22 April, a courier arrived at the Casa Lanfranchi from Ravenna. Allegra had died two days ago, in the convent at Bagnacavallo.[50] Byron's first thought was for the Shelleys. 'Lord Byron did not have the courage to give Shelley the melancholy tidings himself', Teresa remembered, almost half a century later. She was sent in his stead. Calling at the Tre Palazzi di Chiesa on the twenty-third, Teresa must narrowly have missed meeting Claire, who had just left. 'Evil news', Mary noted in her journal.[51]

Shelley seems to have been ready to go across to the Casa Lanfranchi at once. Byron intervened to pre-empt him:

There is nothing to prevent your coming to-morrow; but, perhaps, to-day, and yester-evening, it was better not to have met. I do not know that I have any thing to reproach in my conduct, and certainly nothing in my feelings and intentions toward the dead. But it is a moment when we are apt to think that, if this or that had been done, such event might have been prevented, – though every day and hour shows us that they are the most natural and inevitable.[52]

Whatever his own personal feelings may have been about the loss of his natural daughter, Byron's extreme constraint here, perhaps even masking alarm, has everything to do with his relationship with Shelley. Byron had already put himself badly in the wrong with Shelley, after refusing so intemperately to allow Allegra's mother to visit her. Now the wrong could never be put right. Worse, all Claire's fears, everything that Shelley had been urging on Byron, ever since the girl had been consigned to the convent, had been proved absolutely correct. This is the letter of a proud man who can no longer hide from himself that he has been in the wrong, but still cannot bring himself to admit the plain fact that shines through his words. We can be sure that Byron was not moved to this by consideration for Claire, the bereaved mother. It is Shelley's reaction that Byron dreads.

Shelley and Mary now determined to leave Pisa at the earliest opportunity, and spirit Claire away from Byron's vicinity before they broke the news to her.[53] Byron was no doubt relieved by their precipitate departure, whether or not he knew that Claire was with them. When Shelley wrote to him thereafter, it was without rancour, but without apology, either, for conveying the grieving mother's last requests. Shelley wrote to Byron four times before they next met. Only one letter from Byron survives, though he did write at least one other.

Shelley is at pains to salvage the outward form of the old friendship, referring to the boats that are imminently expected, and the still-awaited Hunts. He almost, but not quite, invites Byron to visit.[54] Byron is less forgiving. He reverts to an old habit in forwarding to Shelley a letter of violent recrimination received from Claire, that Shelley had been unable to intercept. He is tetchy about the Masi affair, and bitter about the critics who had once praised what he terms the 'exaggerated nonsense' of his own earlier works, but now rubbish his more recent plays. In this mood of angry self-pity, Byron quite forgets that Shelley, too, has written plays. He never so much as mentions *Hellas*.[55]

At almost exactly the same time, Shelley was writing to another correspondent: 'I do not write – I have lived too long near Lord Byron & the sun has extingushed [*sic*] the glowworm; for I cannot hope with St. John, that *"the light came into the world, & the world knew it not"*.' By the end of May, Shelley was convinced there was no risk that Byron would visit. Between Byron and himself, he confided to Claire, 'I suspect there is a great gulph fixed, which by the nature of things must daily become wider.'[56]

There was something eerie about the Casa Magni, on the coast near Lerici on the Gulf of Spezia. This was now home to the Shelleys, the Williamses, their children, and their respective servants. Built right on the edge of the sea, with the woods rising steeply behind and no other house within miles, it was a lonely spot. Often, even when there was no wind, a heavy swell would break along the beach and under the arches of the lower floor, disturbing the sleep of those in the rooms above.[57] There was a local community of peasants or fishermen, whose extreme poverty, coarse dialect, and noisy festivities on the shore disgusted Mary and seem not to have been noticed at all by anyone else. Mary loathed the place. Shelley loved it.[58] Once his boat arrived from Genoa, he and Williams spent all their time sailing and overhauling her. Particularly at sea, he seems to have been elated and serenely happy. But these moods would swing wildly and unpredictably to bitter despair and thoughts of suicide. Mary's state of mind cannot have been helped by being three months pregnant at the time when they moved there. On 16 June she suffered a miscarriage, and would have died from loss of blood had it not been for Shelley's decisive intervention. This left her very weak for some time afterwards.

During June, there seems to have been no direct contact between Shelley and Byron. Trelawny sailed Byron's schooner down from Genoa, and made a stop at the Casa Magni on the way. He carried news of the Shelleys to Byron in Pisa. From there, he reported to Shelley by letter that Byron had finished two more cantos of *Don Juan* before the end of the month.[59]

After the departure of the Shelleys and the Williamses, Byron had stayed on in Pisa until the third week of May.[60] The Villa Dupuy at Montenero was in the hills immediately above Livorno. From there he intended to sail his newly acquired schooner, with Trelawny as captain of its small crew. It is not clear how seriously Byron ever took the plans for a summer exploring the coast from the sea, that had been excitedly plotted by Shelley and Williams, with the encouragement of Trelawny, back in January and February. His new acquisition, when Trelawny sailed it into the harbour of

Livorno on 18 June, was large enough to attract the attention of the Tuscan authorities, the more so as the vessel carried cannon and was named *Bolivar*, after the hero of the revolutionary wars in South America.[61] It was now that the aftermath of the Masi affair began to have unpleasant consequences for Byron. Restrictions were placed upon his use of the *Bolivar*. He at once gave up the idea of ever sailing in her.

Life at Montenero was not easy. The Tuscan authorities were watching the Gambas as well as Byron, as Pierino had also been involved peripherally in the affray with the dragoon. As June went on, the heat worsened. There was a shortage of water in the house. It began to look as if the residence permits for Ruggero and Pietro would not be renewed. In that case, Teresa would have to leave Tuscany too. By 26 June, Byron was so annoyed at what he saw as harassment of himself and his friends by the government, that he was threatening to quit the country as soon as the last legal formalities resulting from the Masi affair were dealt with.[62]

The flashpoint came at the end of June. In towns and villages, processions of priests were praying for rain.[63] On the afternoon of 28 June, one of Byron's servants ran amok. Pierino was slightly injured in the affray, the second to involve Byron's household in only a few months. The police were called. By the time they arrived, it seems that Byron's authority had been sufficient to restore order. But the damage had been done. As luck would have it, that was the afternoon when Leigh Hunt, having finally reached Livorno, came out to Montenero to look for Byron. Hunt arrived in the middle of what he later described as a scene out of the classic gothic horror novel, *The Mysteries of Udolpho*. It was the worst possible start to the collaboration on *The Liberal*.[64]

The following day an order went out from the *Buongoverno* in Florence to the local judicial authorities in Pisa and Livorno. In view of their conduct in the affair of Sergeant Masi, Counts Ruggero and Pietro Gamba were to have their residence permits revoked and be told to leave the Duchy, pending a formal order of exile.[65]

This was the situation into which Shelley and Williams sailed in Shelley's boat, named the *Don Juan* after Byron's epic poem, intending to meet Hunt and help him and his family install themselves in the Casa Lanfranchi in Pisa. They arrived in the harbour of Livorno late in the evening of Monday 1 July and spent the night on board. Hunt had in the meantime returned from his harrowing visit to Montenero, and was greeted by Shelley with rapturous enthusiasm on the quayside next morning.[66] Byron was in town too. The Gambas, father and son, had received a summons that morning to attend a tribunal, at which the order from the *Buongoverno* was handed down to them, with the additional stipulation that they had only four days in which to leave Tuscan soil.[67] Byron had accompanied them from Montenero and must have been raging by the time Shelley, Hunt, and Williams caught up with him outside Henry Dunn's general store in the port. They were in time to witness him deliver a mortal snub to Captain Roberts, who had built his boat.[68]

Over the next few days, Williams kicked his heels in Livorno while Shelley, assisted by Byron and Teresa, helped the Hunts settle into their new home in Pisa.[69] From there Shelley reported to Mary: 'Lord Byron is at this moment on the point of leaving Tuscany . . . His first idea was to sail to America, which was changed to Switzerland, then to Genoa, & at last to Lucca. – Everybody is in despair & every thing in confusion.' Byron too, in a letter written the same day, gives the same list of possible destinations, although in a different order. To Medwin, a couple of months later, he would declare that he had actually been on the point of embarking for America, 'the only country which is a sanctuary of liberty'.[70] By 'liberty', all Byron meant was a place where he could live in peace and quiet with Teresa. The last thing in his mind, more than a year into the Greek Revolution, was Greece.

Even before the Hunts' arrival, Shelley had already thought the prospects for *The Liberal* were bleak. Now they looked bleaker still. Shelley had not revised his opinion of Byron, and determined to see little of him from now on. Byron, he wrote, is 'so mentally capricious that the least impulse drives him from his anchorage'. What Shelley's plans were for himself at this time is hard to determine.[71] But, during the five days that he spent with Hunt and Byron in Pisa, he exerted himself to the utmost to secure what he could for the joint project, with or without his own future participation.

By the time Shelley left Pisa to return to Williams and the *Don Juan* at Livorno, on Sunday, 7 July, he had extracted from Byron a number of promises. This way, the new journal had at least a fighting chance. Byron would ensure that the stricken Hunt family had the means to subsist in Italy. Probably also as a result of Shelley's persuasion, Byron was prevailed upon not to leave Tuscany immediately with the Gambas. In slightly more emollient mood, he was now urging Dawkins in Florence to intercede with the authorities in neighbouring Lucca to allow them to remain there.[72] In the meantime, in defiance of both the order from the government and the terms of her legal separation from her husband, Teresa remained at the Casa Lanfranchi.

After Shelley left Pisa, Byron seems to have had no inclination to return to the Villa Dupuy at Montenero. A new rhythm was beginning to be established, albeit uneasily, on the Lung'Arno. Byron embarked at once on a new canto of *Don Juan*. Earlier, he had promised Teresa that he would give up the poem, then secretly started work on it again in the spring. Very possibly it was thanks to Shelley's persuasive powers that Teresa now relented and gave her blessing to its continuation. By the end of the first week of the new regime, Byron was still serious enough about the joint project with Hunt and Shelley to write to his poet friend Tom Moore to solicit contributions for *The Liberal* – though he confessed at the same time that Hunt 'seems sanguine about the matter, but (entre nous) I am not'. Whatever the state of their relations at the time when Shelley left for Livorno – and such evidence as exists suggests that they were at least cordial – this new and more serious Byron was surely the consequence of Shelley's presence. The 'Snake' had proved persuasive yet again.[73]

The heat wave had finally broken on Monday 8 July, with thunder, violent rain, and wind. Reports reaching Pisa from the coast prompted Hunt to send a note to Shelley at the Casa Magni, probably on Wednesday: 'pray write to tell us how you got home'.[74] It was Trelawny, according to his own account, who first raised the alarm. This would have been on Thursday, 11 July. Trelawny had seen Shelley, Williams, and their boy sailor, Charles Vivian, off on board the *Don Juan* shortly before the storm broke. Since then, he had been trying to get news of them from the ships' crews as they came into port. Trelawny says that he confided his fears to Hunt first, then went upstairs to Byron. 'When I told him, his lip quivered, and his voice faltered as he questioned me.'[75]

It was after midnight on Friday night, and Teresa was standing on the first-floor balcony of the Casa Lanfranchi watching an eclipse of the moon, when she heard a carriage in the street below. Mary and Jane, seriously alarmed after the arrival of Hunt's letter, had come straight from Lerici to find out what he knew. Hunt had gone to bed, but Byron was still up, as usual. Teresa met the women on the stairs. Mary looked like a ghost, from worry and the effects of her recent miscarriage. 'Sapete alcuna cosa di Shelley?' – Do you know anything of Shelley? she managed to ask. The visitors stayed only long enough to discover that nothing was known. In the small hours of the morning, they left again for Livorno, in search of Trelawny or Roberts, the boatbuilder who had also been in the harbour when the *Don Juan* put to sea. By Sunday, 14 July, Byron had received an answer to his own separate enquiry to Roberts. 'Your opinion has taken from me the slender hope to which I still clung', he wrote in reply, and authorised the use of the *Bolivar*, implicitly to search for the bodies.[76]

By the time they were washed ashore, they had been more than a week in the sea. As soon as he heard that they had been found, Byron rode out to the coast on two successive days 'for the purpose of ascertaining the circumstances – and identifications of the bodies'. But the local quarantine authorities had got in first. The remains of Shelley and Williams had already been buried in quicklime where they were found.[77]

What happened aboard the *Don Juan* on the afternoon of Monday, 8 July has been the subject of speculation that continues to this day. Byron will have wondered, as others did at the time and biographers have ever since, *was* it an accident? Was the *Don Juan* seaworthy? Was Williams a competent sailor? – almost certainly not. Was any other boat involved? – again, almost certainly not, despite a number of claims. Was Shelley's death in some sense suicide? – if so, what was Williams doing, and did neither of them think of young Charles Vivian, who drowned with them and is hardly ever remembered?[78] We will never know. But Byron's biographer, Leslie Marchand, surely understates the case when he says, 'The death of Shelley made a greater impact on Byron than he expected.'[79]

'AND I WILL WAR . . .'

The sequel must surely be one of the most bizarre episodes in English literary history. On 15 August, the festival of the Dormition of the Virgin and one of the most celebrated days in the Catholic year, a handful of bemused onlookers, some in boats, others apparently smart ladies in carriages, were drawn to a spot on the beach near the mouth of the river Serchio, close to the border that in those days divided Tuscany from Lucca. The day was windless, there was no shade on the beach, the sand was scorching to the touch. There, under the watchful eyes of a small detachment of dragoons and officials from the Health Department, and under the direction of four foreign gentlemen, soldiers in workmen's overalls began digging at the sand, not far above the tideline. When they had found what they were looking for, using hooks mounted on long poles, the soldiers removed a bulky object and several smaller pieces from the sand and manoeuvred them into a cage-like contraption made of iron bars and sheet metal. Two cartloads of wood now appeared. When a quantity of wood had been heaped up below and around the cage, it was set alight. The fire was then fed continually for several hours, during which time a nearby coastguard shelter went up in flames too. While the flames were at their height, three of the foreign gentlemen stripped off their clothes and swam out to the schooner that was riding at anchor, a mile or two offshore. When they came back, the soldiers were instructed to carry the red-hot cage, supported on long poles, down to the water to douse it. What it contained was then scooped into a casket, conveyed to a carriage that was waiting behind the beach, and driven off with two of the gentlemen to Pisa. The other two foreigners stayed that night at a nearby inn.

The following day the same procedure was repeated some miles further north, nearer to Viareggio, in the territory of Lucca. Here, because the site was close to a town, the crowd of onlookers was larger. Some effort was required to keep them at a distance.[80] In this way, the bodies, first of Williams, then of Shelley, both badly decomposed, five weeks after death, were exhumed and cremated, the one to be reburied in England, the other in the Protestant cemetery in Rome.

What the devout peasants, soldiers, and well-dressed ladies thought of what they witnessed has not been directly recorded. But Trelawny, who masterminded the entire process and ensured its lasting fame through a series of vivid narratives, here and there allows a trace of the local reactions to peep through. On his way to carry out these obsequies, Trelawny presented his credentials to the provincial governor, who at first 'hesitated at complying with so unprecedented an order'.[81] Trelawny had to persuade him 'as to its being the custom of our Country, and permitted by our creed &c'. This was stretching the truth for England in 1822. One of his earliest accounts dismisses the unfortunate official as 'a very weak and superstitious man'. The common soldiers, stoical enough when called upon to exhume the badly decomposed corpses, once the burning began 'appeared superstitiously fearful [and] had withdrawn themselves as far as possible'.[82] Elsewhere, although he tends as a rule to play this down, Trelawny takes a certain quiet pride in the shocking 'novelty' of the manner chosen to dispose of the bodies of his friends.[83] Not untypical of the general local response to these events will have been the distaste of Teresa. She did her best to dissuade Byron from taking part in an action that was not only contrary to the religion of the country but also, as she correctly predicted, would leave a permanent mark on his health.[84]

The explanation usually given for the gruesome rituals on the beach, at the time and ever since, is that they were required by local quarantine regulations. Mary and Jane were anxious to have their husbands' bodies moved for proper burial. At first, it seemed that the authorities were prepared to allow this. But, at the very end of July, almost two weeks after the bodies had been washed ashore, the Health Department intervened. Permission was refused. It was at this point, as Medwin reports, that over the next few days, 'A consultation took place between Byron, Hunt and Trelawny' – to decide what to do.[85] The intermediary in these negotiations was once again Dawkins, the British consul who had done his best to smooth over the consequences of the Masi affair. Dawkins' next application to the authorities contained a significant new phrase: he asked to be allowed to move either a body 'or else its ashes'. Quarantine regulations, it turned out only now, in response to this renewed appeal, did allow for this possibility, in cases where the terrain made the usual practice of burial in quicklime impossible.[86] Cremation was *not* normal practice, as most biographers of the participants have supposed. But it *was* within the regulations.[87] A loophole had been found, one that would satisfy both the widows and the health authorities.

But whose idea was it? Trelawny had been energetic in the search for the bodies, and tireless in his efforts to secure official permission for their removal and reburial.[88] Once permission had been granted, Trelawny's practical skills and expertise would be essential to the success of his commission. He had been in India and half-remembered 'the practice of the Hindus in using a funeral pyre'.[89] He organised every detail and oversaw its execution. Trelawny was a natural Romantic. During those weeks he saw a succession of roles for himself. He acted out each of them with tact, ingenuity, and courage. Afterwards, he would relive the whole experience in powerful prose. In all his accounts of the cremations, Trelawny takes credit where it is due, perhaps here and there a little more. But he never claims to have been the originator.[90] Hunt, by his own accounts as much as by Trelawny's, went along passively with the whole thing. Of Medwin's triumvirate, Hunt had been closest to Shelley for longest. The shock of his friend's sudden death seems to have left Hunt helpless. And Hunt was a newcomer, still struggling to grasp the essentials of life in a country he barely knew. Mary seems not to have been a party to the discussions. All she said at the time was that she did 'not dislike' the solution found.[91]

That leaves Byron. The idea must have been Byron's. It is consistent with what he had written in the aftermath of his Grand Tour, within days of the death of his mother and several of his friends: 'I cannot strip the features of those I have known of the fleshly covering even in Idea without a hideous Sensation.' 'Surely', he had concluded then, 'the Romans did well when they burned the Dead.'[92]

From the earliest accounts, it is clear that the intention to mimic an ancient rite was there from the beginning. 'I then procured incense, honey, wine, salt, and sugar to burn with the body', writes Trelawny, not long after the event.[93] Byron had determined that his fellow poet and rival 'fallen angel' would leave the world surrounded by the obsequies for a Homeric hero. The requirements of contemporary quarantine laws had been met, but in a manner probably not seen on that shore since antiquity. In this way, Shelley, who had so idealised the ancient Greeks, thanks to Byron and his friends finally became one.

For Byron, this was not mere antiquarianism. Whether or not he planned this consciously, it cannot have escaped him, while the plans for the cremations were going forward, that life was imitating his own art. Near the end of the play *Sardanapalus*, the hero had given instructions for his own immolation:

> Now order here
> Faggots, pine-nuts, and wither'd leaves, and such
> Things as catch fire and blaze with one sole spark;
> Bring cedar, too, and precious drugs, and spices,
> And mighty planks, to nourish a tall pile;
> Bring frankincense and myrrh, too, for it is
> For a great sacrifice I build the pyre[.][94]

All these things Trelawny faithfully accomplished to honour Williams and Shelley. But there is more. Sardanapalus' immolation was perhaps intended to remind the play's readers of the legendary phoenix, renewed by fire. To this idea Byron had very recently returned, in the first part of *The Deformed Transformed*. As part of the deal with the Stranger, once Arnold has been reincarnated in the body of Achilles, his old deformed body is left behind like a corpse on the ground. The Stranger then performs an incantation over it, invoking fire to revive it so that the devil-stranger himself can enter it:

> Fire! assist me to renew
> Life in what lies in my view
> Stiff and cold!
> His resurrection rests with me and you!
> One little, marshy spark of flame –
> And he again shall seem the same;
> But I his spirit's place shall hold![95]

Behind these passages and the real-life rituals on the beach lies the myth of Prometheus – at once benefactor of mankind through the gift of fire and creator of life. For Byron, too, the bizarre obsequies would become a rite of passage.

There is only one surviving letter in which Byron gives any account of the cremations. It was written eleven days afterwards. In it, he approaches the subject in a curious way:

The other day at Viareggio, I thought proper to swim off to my schooner (the Bolivar) in the offing, and thence to shore again – about three miles, or better, in all. As it was at mid-day, under a broiling sun, the consequence has been a feverish attack, and my whole skin's coming off, after going through the process of one large continuous blister, raised by the sun and sea together. I have suffered much pain; not being able to lie on my back, or even side; for my shoulders and arms were equally St. Bartholomewed. But it is over, – and I have got a new skin, and am as glossy as a snake in its new suit.

We have been burning the bodies of Shelley and Williams . . .⁹⁶

A very brief account of the cremations follows. Before he even mentions the most important event, Byron has described his *own* experience of burning: the blistering and removal of his skin, the pain that followed, which he compares to being flayed alive (the fate of St Bartholomew). While Shelley's body is being consumed on the pyre, Byron submits his own to an extreme ordeal in the same two elements that had brought about the final transformation of Shelley: water and fire. What emerges from the experience is a new outer man, 'as glossy as a *snake* in its new suit'. Among the 'Pisa circle', 'the Snake' had always been Shelley. Byron, at the end of August, with the cremations and his own experience of being 'St. Bartholomewed' behind him, felt himself ready to take on the mantle of the man he had been playfully casting as his own doppelgänger in *The Deformed Transformed*. He may even have said something of this to Trelawny, who concluded his eulogy of Shelley, intended for publication in *The Liberal* a few months later, with the words, later deleted, 'The "Pilgrim of Eternity" [Byron] has declared his intention of doing that justice to his [Shelley's] character & genius, which his long intimacy and great talent can so nobly execute.'⁹⁷

Trelawny thought Byron had in mind a poem, an equivalent, perhaps, to Shelley's epitaph for Keats, 'Adonais'. But Byron was contemplating something else entirely.

Byron's usual response to a crisis was to write more furiously than ever. Already, since the death of Allegra, he had been working on the resumed *Don Juan* at a terrific pace. During July, beginning in the aftermath of Shelley's death, he wrote the whole of Canto VIII. At the start of the week leading up to the cremations, as he reported to Moore, he was 'hovering on the brink of another (the ninth)'.⁹⁸

In its original form Canto IX began with an extended passage that has been recognised as Byron's undeclared epitaph on Shelley.[99] 'Death laughs', the passage begins, and the words are repeated with the effect of a refrain or an incantation through three stanzas. This macabre meditation on the physical signs of death as a cruel mockery of life must surely have been written in the immediate aftermath of the exhumation of the corpses of Williams and Shelley on the fifteenth and sixteenth. The hideous condition of his friends' bodies, from the action of the sea and the lime in which they had been buried, comes through clearly in the lines that insist on death *smiling* (the emphasis is Byron's):

> He strips from man that mantle (far more dear
> Than even the tailor's) his incarnate skin,
> White, black, or copper – the dead bones will grin.[100]

Byron is still smarting from his own ordeal by sunburn. As he writes these lines his own flesh is peeling from him. In verse, he identifies himself with the condition of the corpse, just as he would do again in prose, a few days later, in the letter to Moore already quoted.

The upshot of this meditation is a profound melancholy. Then the mood changes abruptly. The snake has sloughed off its old, burnt skin. This is the new Byron that suddenly bursts out:

> And I will war, at least in words (and – should
> My chance so happen – deeds) with all who war
> With Thought[.]

He goes on to announce his 'downright detestation / Of every despotism in every nation', and then to articulate the newfound political principle that he had several times glimpsed, but never until now been able to come to terms with, since at least his Carbonaro days:

> It is not that I adulate the people;
> Without *me*, there are Demagogues enough . . .
> I wish men to be free
> As much from mobs as kings – from you as me.[101]

Byron's tribute to Shelley, finally, will be not a poem, but a war. His will be a tribute not of words but ('should . . . chance so happen') of deeds.

By the time he wrote his one and only account of what had taken place at Viareggio, Byron was already turning over in his mind ways and means. The same letter to Moore ends: 'I had, and still have, thought of South America, but am fluctuating between it and Greece . . . where I shall probably take a part of some sort.' Like Arnold reincarnated in the body of Achilles, Byron is once again thinking of covering himself with 'glory'. It is the first time he has mentioned the revolution in Greece since leaving Ravenna for Pisa almost a year before.

Against the enemies of 'Thought'. *For* a new kind of freedom, that will somehow be more than just a change of masters. This, from now on, will become the essence of Byron's war.

CHAPTER 6

The deformed transformed

A PLAN IN EMBRYO

There was nothing now to keep Byron in Pisa. By the beginning of September 1822, he was making plans to move his whole establishment to Genoa. This included, as well as the eight Hunts: the menagerie, several horses, the Napoleonic coach, and three geese, bought to be consumed at Michaelmas but destined in the event to last longer in Genoa than did Byron himself. Mary Shelley had elected to stay on in Italy for a time and was there already. So was Pierino, who had found a mansion huge enough that Byron could live in one part of it and Teresa and her relatives in another, thus satisfying the strict terms laid down by the Pope.[1]

Byron was impatient to be gone. But, as often happened, he dragged his feet. During his last weeks at Pisa, he confided to friends a little more of the scheme that he had touched on at the end of his letter to Moore, in which he had described the cremations of his friends. To Medwin, he called it 'a plan I have in embryo. I have formed a strong wish to join the Greeks.' And, according to Trelawny, it was now, and not before, that 'his thoughts veered round to his early love, the Isles of Greece, and the revolution in that country – for before that time he never dreamt of donning the warrior's plume, though the peace-loving Shelley had suggested and I urged it'.[2] Trelawny's is the only direct evidence we have that Shelley, while he was alive, had actually urged this course upon Byron. It was only now, with Shelley dead and posthumously made into an ancient Hellene, that Byron was – perhaps – beginning to take the idea seriously.

He was certainly beginning to talk that way. Hunt, who ought to have been in his confidence but it seems was not, would wonder afterwards if his patron 'had already made arrangements for going' to Greece, at the time he left Pisa for Genoa. And at least one person who should not have been, the Cavaliere Luigi Torelli, who was reporting on Byron's activities to the Tuscan authorities, was in a position to report: 'Mylord has expressed his intention of not remaining in Genoa but of going on to Athens in order to make himself adored by the Greeks.'[3] Trelawny, who knew him better, was not convinced. Recognising what he thought was another short-lived whim, he says that at the time he 'took little heed'.

Then, on 15 September, Hobhouse arrived in Pisa. Accompanying his sisters on the Grand Tour of Italy, Hobhouse was bound to remind Byron of all that they had experienced together in Greece, on their own version of the Tour. For the next six days, Hobhouse spent a large part of each day with Byron. To judge from both men's accounts, and from Teresa's, there was something bitter-sweet about this meeting, after a gap of four years.[4] Too much had changed, for both of them.

Hobhouse's visit has been credited with inspiring Byron's decision to depart for Greece ten months later.[5] If anything, it probably had the opposite effect. Hobhouse was no visionary like Shelley. Now a Member of Parliament for the Radical Whigs, he took a serious, politician's interest in Greek affairs, and may have hoped that Byron would too. But if the two men did talk about Greece, no trace of their conversation remains, either in Hobhouse's diary or in Byron's letters. What Hobhouse does record is a reunion with a patriotic young Greek lawyer from Zante, Niccolò Carvelà (Karvelas), who had recently come to live in Pisa. He and Byron had met Carvelà, with his brother Francesco, in Switzerland and at Milan, six years before.[6] But it was on Hobhouse, not on Byron, that Carvelà called, with news of Greek affairs. There is nothing in Hobhouse's account to suggest that Byron was present during their conversation, and no mention of Carvelà or Greece in Byron's surviving letters from this time.[7] Later, when Byron urgently needed information about Greek events, Carvelà would be one of the first to whom he would turn. But that was still several months in the future. At Pisa it seems likely that he still held himself aloof, as he had done earlier from Shelley's Greek friends.

That Byron did have some larger scheme in mind, while he was preparing to leave Pisa for Genoa, is evident not from anything he said about Greece, but from what he wrote to his friend and banker, Douglas Kinnaird, on quite a different subject. That subject was money. Since the death of Lady Noel, the mother of his estranged wife, in January 1822, Byron had been corresponding furiously on the subject of the considerable fortune that would now be his. The letters to Kinnaird become extremely frequent at this time. There are eleven of them written during September up to the eve of his departure from Pisa on the twenty-seventh. All of them are to some extent about money.

This is a new preoccupation for Byron. Friends noted it at the time. Biographers have done their best to explain it ever since. It is not, perhaps, so surprising, if we remember that at the time when Byron had been living with his wife the bailiffs had been camping in their house – a circumstance he chose to recall in other letters written during this same month.[8] Byron has often been accused of avarice during the last two years of his life. With a varying mixture of apology and bravado he would acknowledge as much in himself. But, right from the beginning, there was more to it than that. As he explained it to Kinnaird: 'In short – Doug. – the longer I live – the more I perceive that Money (honestly come by) is the Philosopher's Stone ... [M]y avarice – or cupidity – is *not* selfish ... I want to get a sum together to go amongst the Greeks or [South] Americans – and do some good.'[9]

Within weeks of arriving in Genoa, Byron would begin the twelfth canto of *Don Juan* with an astonishing paean addressed to the *political* power of money. His ideas here are ahead of their time for the early nineteenth century. The 'true lords of Europe', the poet declares, are not kings, princes, or generals, but bankers:

> Every loan
> Is not a merely speculative hit,
>   But seats a nation or upsets a throne.
>
> . . .
>
>   Cash rules the grove, and fells it too besides;
> Without cash, camps were thin, and courts were none[.][10]

The idea was still forming. But this, when the time came, would emerge as the cornerstone of Byron's policy for Greece. '*Cash*' would become the foundation upon which a newly liberated nation would have to be built. These are the words not of the miser, but of what today we would call an economist. Or, as Byron would more jokily put it, using the terms available to him at the time, 'my best Canto ... / Will turn upon "Political Economy"'.[11]

Whether he knew it or not, as he set out from Pisa on 27 September, the embryo was growing.

AGES OF MAN

For the journey to Genoa, Trelawny's services had once again been requisitioned to take command of the *Bolivar*. Byron himself had no thought of travelling that way, even though it would have made for a much easier journey. Medwin reported that, since the loss of Shelley and Williams, Byron 'has not made one voyage in his yacht . . . and has taken a disgust to sailing'.[12] He arranged for the Hunts to travel by sea. He himself, with the rest of his retinue, set out with the Napoleonic coach, picking up Ruggero Gamba at Lucca as they passed through. The two parties met up half way, at Lerici on the Bay of Spezia.

This was the nearest town to the Casa Magni, Shelley's last home and the place to which he and Williams had been returning when they were drowned. 'This place fills me with gloomy and desponding thoughts', wrote Trelawny to Claire as soon as he arrived there aboard the *Bolivar*. The others must have felt the same. Next day, after Byron's party arrived, they all went aboard with Trelawny to be shown Shelley's house. Neither Byron nor Hunt had ever been there, while Shelley was alive.[13] This was probably the only voyage Byron ever made in the *Bolivar*. He became ill on board. It is not even certain that they reached their destination. When they returned to Lerici, he was overtaken by what Trelawny described as 'Spasms' and Byron, more graphically, as 'a violent rheumatic and bilious attack – constipation', and later as 'a fever and a portentious [*sic*] Constipation and inflammation'. He was then laid up for four days at the only inn in Lerici, a sorry place from the sound of it. When it was over, he would joke about the indignities to which he had been subjected by an inept local doctor, until he took matters into his own hands and cured himself.[14] But he never afterwards referred to the expedition to the Casa Magni.

To all appearances, Byron was fully restored when the party set out on the next leg of the journey, by sea as far as Sestri. He still would not go with Trelawny in the *Bolivar*, but chartered another boat instead. As they sailed up the coast, Teresa would recall, half a century later: 'a cloud of grief passed over his eyes as he gazed at Villa Magni'.[15]

Through the winter that followed, and into the spring, Byron's health never quite got over this episode. During the same period, he also lost a great deal of weight. From his letters, it is difficult to make out whether this was caused by his condition or was the result of deliberate dieting. In Genoa, an English doctor attended him 'every other day', and attributed his patient's 'melancholy' to lack of physical activity.[16] This will not have helped. But, in his own mind, the problem went back even further than the episode at Lerici. 'I never quite recovered that stupid long swim in the broiling Sun and saline Sea of August', he wrote to Hobhouse in mid-December. The same tale will be repeated, for different recipients, with minor variations until April of the next year.[17] Although Byron never mentions the fact, this had been the swim (in fact two swims, on two successive days) while the bodies of Shelley and Williams were being cremated on the shore.

Physical decline, that winter, was beginning to oppress him. Health was part of it. Another was ageing. For some years now, he had been aware of the signs in himself. In the autumn it seems he acted on a threat he had made light-heartedly in *Don Juan*, to have a wig made.[18] In January, he would pass the traditional midpoint of a man's life, thirty-five – the year 'in the middle of the way' in which Dante's *Divine Comedy* is set. Unlike other birthdays after his thirtieth, this one passed unremarked by Byron on the day. Instead, he brooded on this watershed all winter.

He had been in Genoa only a fortnight, when he began his new canto of *Don Juan*, Canto XII (the one that goes on to extol the power of money and bankers):

> Of all the barbarous Middle Ages, that
> > Which is the most barbarous is the middle age
> Of man;
> . . .
> Too old for youth, – too young, at thirty-five,
> > To herd with boys, or hoard with good threescore, –
> I wonder people should be left alive[.][19]

The premature death of Shelley, who had always seemed to him the embodiment of youth, and what he saw as the protracted death of his own youth, as health and vigour left him during that winter in Genoa, brought Byron face to face with his old enemy, mortality. What, when a life is over – or all but over – had it all been *for*?

The Casa Saluzzo (today called Mongiardino), on the edge of the village of Albaro, high on the hills above Genoa, would be Byron's last home in Italy. Just outside the gates, the spacious Villa Negrotto housed the Hunt family and, separately, the grieving Mary Shelley. In this way, the remnants of Shelley's 'Pisa circle' regrouped for a last, half-hearted stand – and the blighted project for *The Liberal*, despite everything, managed to produce four not inconsiderable issues.

If life with Teresa and the Gambas was harmonious within the walls of the Casa Saluzzo, the same cannot be said for Byron's other relationships during this winter. He went out of his way to help Mary, paying her to copy his manuscripts and offering the services of his lawyer to help deal with Shelley's estate and family in England, but only succeeded in offending her in her fragile state.[20] With the Hunts, things were far worse. Marianne Hunt could not bring herself to acknowledge the existence of

Teresa, let alone to be civil to her. The Hunts' six children, aged between one and thirteen, were allowed to run wild. Byron warned Mary, 'They are dirtier and more mischievous than Yahoos; what they can't destroy with their filth they will with their fingers.'[21] Even before they all left Pisa, Hunt had become sufficiently attuned to Italian ways to recognise the double edge to Byron's generosity in accommodating him and his family in the ground-floor apartments of the Casa Lanfranchi. In Italian households, the ground floor was traditionally used, if not for animals, then for servants or paid retainers, while the owners lived upstairs, on the *piano nobile*. Although the arrangement at Genoa was less demeaning, and involved a good deal less proximity, Hunt had taken umbrage. As the association continued, the list of Hunt's grievances against his patron lengthened.[22]

By the end of February, Byron had made up his mind to extricate himself from *The Liberal*. At the time, only the first two issues had appeared. Such was the outcry against the new periodical, not least among his own friends, it was easy for Byron to persuade himself that his 'connection with the work will tend to any thing but its success'.[23] Even then, he would continue to support the Hunts financially, and to give Mary what assistance she would accept, for as long as he remained in Genoa.

Another quarrel that had been simmering for more than a year had also come to a head. A little over a month after arriving in Genoa, Byron sacked John Murray as his publisher. For years, Murray had been not just a publisher but a valued confidant. It would not be quite the end of the friendship, or at least of their correspondence. Byron would continue to write to Murray and sometimes even to confide. But the winter in Genoa saw the end of what had been perhaps the most stable collaborative relationship of his life.[24] From now on, his publisher would be the political Radical, John Hunt, brother of Leigh. Both socially and politically, Byron the poet was finding himself pushed more and more into the radical position that had been Shelley's, but never quite his own.

The weather was cold and stormy, the Genoese hillside exposed to the elements. Byron became reclusive. Visitors were turned away from the Casa Saluzzo. All that winter, he remained out of sorts: irritable, listless, angry. In December, taking a break from *Don Juan*, he tried to work off his dissatisfactions by writing political satire. From Genoa, he had been closely following reports of the latest of the congresses at which the conservative Great Powers of Europe periodically came together to uphold their alliance and deliberate the foreign policy issues of the day. This one had begun at Verona on 20 October and continued into December. On the agenda were the continuing revolution against the monarchy in Spain, recent anti-Austrian movements in Italy, and the Greek Revolution.

During the first half of December, while in Verona the Congress was slowly winding up, Byron weighed in with 'a poem of about seven hundred and fifty lines . . . being all on politics &c. &c. &c. and a review of the day in general . . . a little . . . stilted and somewhat too full of "epithets of war" and classical & historical allusions'.[25] The résumé is Byron's, written just after he sent the poem to Mary at the Villa Negrotto to have a fair copy made. *The Age of Bronze* has had its supporters in modern times – not least the late leader of the British Labour Party, Michael Foot.[26] But Byron's assessment is close to the mark. The poem trumpets its author's long-held and rather broad-brush views on the failure of Napoleon, on the evils of the post-Napoleonic regimes, and on liberal revolution. There is nothing, here, of the subtler, tormenting doubts that had animated the play *Marino Faliero* two years before. Nothing, either, of the insight that Byron had put into the mouth of Dante, in his poem of 1819, that the cause of 'nations' might be different. One liberal revolution, in this poem, sounds much like another:

> On Andes' and on Athos' peaks unfurled,
> The self-same standard streams o'er either world[.][27]

For someone who had been thinking, a few months before, of going to take part in one of these conflicts, Byron in this poem shows surprisingly little interest in detail. There is certainly no sense that Greece means any more to its author than any of a dozen liberal causes, drawn from ancient and medieval history as well as modern, and rather indiscriminately lumped together.[28]

The Age of Bronze shows Byron ready to pick a fight. But he has no more found his target in the poem than he had in letters in which he wondered about going to South America, Greece – or even Australia.[29] Only days after he completed the poem, in January 1823, he was writing once again to Kinnaird about his financial affairs: 'I wish to have these things settled as I think of going to Greece [or] perhaps to America.' But there is no other mention of these plans the whole winter long. If Byron was serious, he had yet to do his homework, and the poem shows it. By far the most important political insight of *The Age of Bronze*, that *is* new, is carried over from his correspondence of the autumn and winter on the subject of money. In the poem, he amplifies at length the insight he had first begun to develop in Canto XII of *Don Juan*, about the controlling power of finance in the affairs of states.[30]

The Age of Bronze is presented as satire. Its title implies that the present age is a degraded successor to the ages of gold and silver before it. According to the ancient Greek poet Hesiod, later echoed in Latin by Ovid, the men of the age of bronze had destroyed themselves by warfare. The pessimism implied by this choice of title all but outweighs any sense that the revolutions championed in the poem can possibly bring any real good into the world. The whole age is doomed to self-destruction.

Early in the new year, and before he went back to work on *Don Juan*, Byron turned his imagination loose by transporting his reader to another of Hesiod's five ages:

> To lands where, save their conscience, none accuse;
> Where all partake the earth without dispute,
> And bread itself is gathered as a fruit;
> Where none contest the fields, the woods, the streams: –
> The Goldless Age, where Gold disturbs no dreams . . .[31]

The scene is set among the islands of the South Pacific, imagined by Byron as an amalgamation of Hesiod's idyllic age of gold with the primitive condition of mankind as envisaged by Rousseau half a century before. Hesiod's age of gold was not *literally* that, but a time of universal harmony and happiness – hence Byron's play on words. Such an age must surely have been 'gold*less*', redeemed from the corrupting love of wealth. *The Island*, written in January and February 1823, is the last poem of any length that Byron completed.

In this poem Byron creates the idyllic counterpart to his satire on the present 'Age of Bronze'. Like most literary golden ages, this one is under threat in its natural state, and is all but unattainable to the modern European. The natives of Otaheite (Tahiti) and the surrounding islands live in a state of nature and perfect harmony, like Hesiod's men of the first age, and like Rousseau's 'noble savage'. This is a 'field o'er which promiscuous plenty poured'. An 'equal land without a lord', it is the perfect antithesis of the Europe represented at the Congress of Verona. Into this earthly paradise Byron inserts the fugitive mutineers from HMS *Bounty*, and thereby creates the poem's narrative.[32]

The well-known story of the mutiny and its consequences is treated very freely by Byron. Having despatched the hated Captain Bligh in his open boat, the mutineers make their home on an island that Byron calls Toobonai. There they are made welcome by the natives, especially the women. Of the real-life mutineers, Byron retains only the leader, Fletcher Christian. By suppressing his first name, and calling him only 'Christian',

Byron quietly and provocatively reminds his readers of the Christian allegory by John Bunyan, *The Pilgrim's Progress*. Needless to say, in the hands
of the 'pilgrim of eternity', any element of allegory in this poem is not of
the expected sort. Christian is one of the poem's two heroes. The other is
a younger man, the inexperienced, idealistic, and tender-hearted Torquil.

The action of the poem is triggered by the appearance of the Royal Navy
off Toobonai, in pursuit of the mutineers. An unequal fight ensues, in
which the natives make common cause with the pursued and are routed.
All take to their canoes, with the Navy after them. Torquil is saved by
the native girl he loves, Neuha, who leads him to a submarine cave where
they can make love to their hearts' content in a setting of perfect natural
solitude. Meanwhile, the remaining mutineers are hunted down. Christian
refuses to surrender and finally throws himself over a cliff to a gory death.
By the end of the poem, the alien ships have gone, the mutineers are dead
or captured – all except Torquil, who returns with Neuha to be accepted
by her people and to live happily ever after in their island paradise.

The South Pacific setting in this poem is not quite as exotic as it sounds. It
has been described as 'B[yron]'s Greece in Polynesian trappings'.[33] Neuha's
cave, improbably provisioned ahead of time for love-making and banquet-
ing, is Haidee's cave from Canto ii of *Don Juan*. Indeed, Neuha resembles
Haidee very closely, not least in that she takes all the initiatives. There is
a further echo of the same episode in *Don Juan*: the war song sung by the
islanders recalls the song sung to entertain Juan and Haidée, 'The Isles of
Greece', particularly in its refrain.[34]

But it had been Shelley, not Byron in *Don Juan*, who had first imagined
an idealised Greek landscape as a primitive earthly paradise or age of
gold, and made that the setting for the fulfilment of an idealised love. In
'Epipsychidion', Shelley had written:

> It is an isle under Ionian skies,
> Beautiful as a wreck of Paradise,
> And, for the harbours are not safe and good,
> This land would have remained a solitude
> But for some pastoral people native there,
> Who from the Elysian, clear, and golden air
> Draw the last spirit of the age of gold,
> Simple and spirited; innocent and bold.[35]

This is the landscape to which Byron has added only a sprinkling of exotic
touches drawn from his reading of travels in the South Pacific, to create
the imaginary world of *The Island*.

It has been argued, on good evidence, that Byron had also been reading or rereading some of Shelley's poems, and that *The Island* is, in part, his 'elegy' for Shelley.[36] On this reading, young Torquil is an imaginative projection of Shelley, as Byron now thought of him. But, if this is so, where is Byron himself in the poem? One answer is that Torquil is not *only* Shelley. The young mutineer's Scottish childhood and his skill at swimming have been transposed from Byron's own life – as one of his notes to the poem effectively points out.[37] So it is not precisely Shelley who is vindicated and given the rare privilege, in a poem by Byron, of finding happiness at the poem's end. Torquil is an idealised version of Shelley plus Byron – of what might have been, if Shelley had learned to swim and if he, Byron, had not also been the poem's other hero, Christian.

Christian has been well described as 'the last of the Byronic heroes'. We see him first, quite late in the poem:

> But Christian, of an higher order, stood
> Like an extinct volcano in his mood;
> Silent, and sad, and savage[.][38]

This is after the first battle, when his first thought is for young Torquil, the undeserving victim of what Christian now calls 'my madness'. It is not often that a hero of Byron's regrets the actions that have brought him to an extreme situation. But Christian does, and this is the reason.

By the time of the second battle, Torquil has been spirited away by Neuha. Christian gives no ground. Like every 'byronic hero' before him, he will die as he has lived. The surviving mutineers are down to just three. The narrator compares them to the 300 Greeks who stood against the Persian armies at Thermopylae, but then immediately corrects himself:

> But, ah! how different! 'tis the *cause* makes all,
> Degrades or hallows courage in its fall.
> O'er them no fame, eternal and intense,
> Blazed through the clouds of death and beckoned hence;
> No grateful country, smiling through her tears,
> Begun the praises of a thousand years;
> No nation's eyes would on their tomb be bent[.][39]

The last stand of the mutineers will *not* bear comparison to the 300 at Thermopylae. Theirs was a selfish act and will be remembered as such. No matter how heroically Christian fights and dies, he will never deserve 'the praises of a thousand years'. The '*cause*' (the italics are Byron's) determines everything. Christian fights for 'no nation' and therefore deserves no posthumous gratitude. The narrative voice is unforgiving: 'Their life was shame, their epitaph was guilt.'[40] If *The Island* is Byron's elegy for Shelley plus the best of himself (imagined as Torquil), it is also his damning epitaph on the worst of himself, imagined as Christian. At the moment of his death:

> The rest was nothing – save a life mis-spent,
> And soul – but who shall answer where it went?[41]

Ill throughout that winter, thinking himself aged before his time, and still shaken by the premature death of Shelley, Byron was thinking about his own posthumous fame. He needed, now, as never before, what the doomed trajectories of so many 'byronic' heroes, and now of the *Bounty* mutineers, had never had: a cause. Not just any cause, but one that would earn the plaudits of a 'grateful country' and draw a '*nation*'s eyes'.

THE CALL COMES

'Attended a committee summoned by Joseph Hume [M.P.] to examine into the chance of doing something for the Greeks.'[42] So wrote Hobhouse, in his diary, on 1 March 1823. The meeting had been held the evening before, at the Crown and Anchor Tavern in the Strand. In this seemingly rather breathless way, the London Greek Committee came into existence. Such groups had existed on the continent for some time, but organised support for Greece in England was something new. It began with a secretary and twenty-five members, most of them Members of Parliament belonging, like Hobhouse, to the Radical wing of the Whigs. Within a month, that number would have doubled. The final list runs to just over eighty.[43] According to a declaration drafted that first evening, they were 'friends of Greek Independence', their purpose to advance 'by all the means in their power the most important and most interesting cause'.[44] As that wording suggests, the Committee had at this time only the vaguest notion of what it was about. Far more influential than the MPs in directing the activities of the group, were two individuals who had only very recently begun to take an interest in Greece.

John Bowring, the Committee's secretary, was four years younger than Byron. Already he had made a name for himself all over Europe as a supporter of liberal causes. Ahead of him still lay a distinguished and varied career. During the past year, Bowring had corresponded occasionally with the Provisional Government in Greece, but until the end of 1822 his chief interests had lain in revolutionary Spain.[45] It was on the initiative of the ubiquitously connected Metropolitan Ignatios in Pisa that Bowring had been approached, that autumn in Madrid, by a Greek businessman from Ioannina, of about his own age. This was Andreas Louriotis (Luriotti), who had been working in his uncle's business at Livorno at the time when the Shelleys had been living in Pisa, and had since followed Mavrokordatos to Greece. Louriotis was now on a mission from the Provisional Government to seek financial support from the liberal revolutionaries of Spain.[46]

Bowring must have been impressed by his new Greek acquaintance. Before long he had introduced Louriotis to his friend Edward Blaquiere. Blaquiere, on his own admission, at this time knew nothing of Greece. A former lieutenant in the Royal Navy during the Napoleonic Wars, he had just published a 600-page book glorifying the revolution in Spain.[47] Towards the end of the year, with the Congress of Verona in session, and the outlook for the Spanish liberals darkening, the newly formed trio began to gravitate towards England. Louriotis was easily persuaded that London might present better prospects for raising support for his government than were on offer in Madrid. Bowring on his way home was arrested by the French police and found to be carrying confidential papers detailing plans by France to invade and restore the ousted Spanish monarchy. A minor diplomatic incident ensued and he was lucky to be quickly released.[48] Blaquiere and Louriotis travelled together, avoiding anything so compromising en route, and reached London probably about the end of January.

Blaquiere now set himself to assist his new Greek friend with all the zeal of the recent convert. It was almost certainly at Blaquiere's instigation that the veteran philosopher and constitutionalist Jeremy Bentham, who was susceptible to his flattery, was prevailed upon to comment in detail on the Provisional Constitution of free Greece, that had been drawn up the previous year. Bentham set to work on 9 February. When the newly formed London Greek Committee met for the first time on the twenty-eighth, at the Crown and Anchor, Bentham was one of the few attending who was not a Member of Parliament. Out of that meeting came the decision to send Blaquiere to Greece immediately. He would accompany Louriotis on his way home to report to his government.[49]

Everything about Blaquiere's mission was (perhaps purposefully) obscure: its precise purpose, the capacity in which the emissary was supposed to act, and even the role of the Committee in sending him at all.[50] How much this was due to muddle, and how much to well-maintained secrecy, is hard to tell. In general, the Committee's activities tended more towards the former. But it must have been by prior arrangement that Blaquiere's reports directed to Bowring's home in London were addressed to a 'Mr Henry Murdoch' – no doubt to avoid the watchful eyes of mail interceptors on the continent, to whom Bowring's name was known.[51]

However it had been arranged, Blaquiere's responsibilities were numerous and overlapping. For Bentham, who covered his expenses, he was to deliver to the Provisional Government of Greece the great man's *Observations* on their constitution, together with instructions on their publication in Greek.[52] He also carried letters from Bowring and Thomas Gordon (the only Committee member who had first-hand knowledge of the conflict).[53] But Blaquiere was not only a confidential courier. His mission was at the same time a fact-finding one. Bowring even tried to persuade the British government to recruit his agent for its own purposes – presumably without success.[54]

Finally, there was one more task for Blaquiere and Louriotis, as they prepared to leave London. A committee needs members. Names were discussed, at that first meeting. Hobhouse ventured to hope that his friend Lord Byron might lend his 'kind and cordial support in this good cause' and allow his name to be added to the list.[55] This was as much as the Committee or any of its members would ever ask of Byron.

So it was agreed. For the emissaries to call in at Genoa would not take them far out of their way. When Blaquiere and Louriotis set out from London, on 4 March, they were preceded by Hobhouse's warning to Byron to expect them.

Byron received this warning on the nineteenth, and so was well prepared by the time Blaquiere and Louriotis turned up on 5 April. But what Hobhouse had told him was so brief as to be almost in code. It takes the form of a postscript written across the top of the first page of a letter, positioned so that it is the first thing anyone unfolding the paper will read: 'Blaquier [*sic*] is going thro' Genoa on a sort of mission to Greece – he will call on you.' Nothing in the rest of the letter explains these words, or why Byron should have replied, equally tersely, by return: 'I shall be glad to see Blaquiere.'[56]

The explanation is that Hobhouse had *already* written, and this letter does not survive. Pietro Gamba would remember the earlier letter arriving, and roughly when ('towards the end of February').[57] In fact, since Hobhouse had been expecting a reply before he wrote to Byron again on 2 March, and the normal time taken for letters to travel between Genoa and London was two weeks, the missing letter will have been written close to the beginning of February and received around or shortly after the middle of the month. All we can infer about its contents is that it will have mentioned Greece, explained who Blaquiere was, and said something about the latest developments in Spain, where Blaquiere had just come from. This would explain why Byron wrote to Kinnaird on 1 March: 'If my health gets better and there is a war – it is not off the cards that I may go to Spain – in which case I must make all "sinews of War" (monies that is to say) go as far as they can – for if I *do* go – it will be to do what I can in the good cause.'[58] Hobhouse's missing letter had set Byron thinking once more about going to fight in a war – but not necessarily in Greece.

At the time this letter was written, the London Greek Committee had not yet come into existence. Blaquiere may have begun talking of going to Greece himself. But no one in London had any thought of Byron doing so. Before long, when he discovered the full extent of what his friend was planning, Hobhouse would be horrified, and would do his best to dissuade him.[59] This first letter, though, whatever it contained, was enough to start Byron off along an entirely new train of thought. Its traces can be found in the new canto of *Don Juan* that he began on 23 February and in several letters written over the next few weeks. Canto XIV starts off with one of the longest and most personal digressions of the whole famously digressive poem. The ostensible theme is the meaning of life and the purpose of action. This leads into a vivid passage about the impulse towards self-destruction. The suicide, the narrator suggests, acts impetuously 'Less from disgust of life than dread of death'. If ever you have been afraid, looking down from the top of a precipice, that you may suddenly have an uncontrollable urge to throw yourself over, the reason is:

> The lurking bias, be it truth or error,
>   To the *unknown*; a secret prepossession,
> To plunge with all your fears . . .[60]

Thoughts like these could have been prompted by the sudden prospect of taking part in violent action, whether in Spain or Greece.

The long digression that follows becomes an anatomy of the melancholy that Byron had been experiencing during the winter at Genoa. His own word for it is '*Ennui*'. But now it has begun to affect him even as a poet:

> In youth I wrote, because my mind was full,
> And now because I feel it growing dull.[61]

This is a new admission for Byron. He had often enough, before, been sceptical about the worth of poetry. Suddenly he had been forced to confront the worth of his own. During the weeks that followed the writing of these lines, beginning the very next day after he started the canto, he would elaborate upon these thoughts in a series of letters:

Every publication of mine has latterly failed; I am not discouraged by this, because writing and composition are habits of my mind, with which Success and Publication are objects of remoter reference . . . I have had enough both of praise and abuse to deprive them of their novelty, but I continue to compose for the same reason that I ride, or read, or bathe, or travel – it is a habit.[62]

Then at the end of March, just over a month after beginning his new canto, Byron's mood turned. Suddenly, he was sociable again. Within the space of a few days, no fewer than three separate sets of callers were received with courtesy, even with enthusiasm, at the Casa Saluzzo. No doubt, by this time, he was expecting one of them to be Blaquiere. Instead, April Fool's Day brought to Albaro the Irish peer Lord Blessington, travelling with his second wife who had been born a commoner, and the young French dandy who completed an ambiguous *ménage à trois*, Count D'Orsay.[63] In his new mood of outgoing anticipation, Byron at once struck up a vivacious friendship with this trio that would last for the next two months.

With Lord Blessington, Byron joked about everything, including his fast-forming plans for Greece. With Lady Blessington he flirted, and allowed himself to be drawn out in conversations that he probably knew she was writing down and would eventually publish. He was especially charmed by the French count, whose witty observations on English aristocratic manners he thought matched his own in the cantos he was just then writing of *Don Juan*. He probably competed, in a playful way, with Lord Blessington for the attention of the handsome and accomplished D'Orsay. The count returned the compliment by drawing a series of sketches in which Byron appears stooped, balding at the front, rather gaunt – in short very much as he describes himself in his letters of the winter (Plate 5b).[64]

This was the scene upon which Blaquiere and Louriotis entered on Saturday, 5 April, having reached Genoa the previous night. At ten in the morning Blaquiere despatched a note to the Casa Saluzzo, explaining that he was on his way to Greece: 'I could not pass through Genoa without taking the liberty of communicating with your Lordship and offering you my best services in a country which your powerful pen has rendered doubly dear to the friends of freedom and humanity.'[65] Blaquiere makes it look as if the visit is unpremeditated, and respectfully requests, along with his companion, 'to be permitted to pay our respects in person'.

Byron was ready for them. He had been waiting for this moment for the last three weeks. He agreed at once. His brief note, addressed to a complete stranger, is unexpectedly defensive. It is as though the writer feels the need to counter an imagined reproach:

I cannot express to you how much I feel interested in the cause – and nothing but some Italian connections which I had formed in Italy – connections also in some degree referring to the political state of this country – prevented me from long ago – returning to do what little I could as an individual – in that land which is an honour even only to have visited.[66]

What Byron said to his visitors that April afternoon, none of those who heard it recorded. According to his own report to Hobhouse: 'Of course I entered very sincerely into the object of their journey – and have even offered to go up to the Levant in July – if the Greek Provisional Government think that I could be of any use.'[67] But at once he had qualms. These he would not have spelt out to his visitors, but did to his old friend, the companion of his youthful travels. He was uncertain of his health, he explained to Hobhouse. His financial affairs in England were still unresolved. Then there was Teresa. She had appeared in this role in his letters before, whenever he had toyed with the idea of Greece. Teresa was still an obstacle to his going. The letter tails off in an excited ramble. Even if he were not actually to go in person, Blaquiere has suggested there is much that he might do, without leaving Genoa. He is anxious 'in no way to interfere with Blaquiere'. Can Hobhouse help him think of supplies he could buy for the Greeks? He ends by placing himself at the disposal of the Committee, and then worries immediately because he has heard that 'Strangers are not very welcome to the Greeks – from jealousy.' There is something of the excited schoolboy about this letter. It is as though he cannot quite believe his own resolution.

In a very specific way this is a new Byron. At the beginning of the letter, he subordinates his own intentions to what the Greek Government might find useful. At the end, he writes in very similar terms of the Committee. 'Use' and 'useful' will become very frequent terms, from this time on, in Byron's correspondence on the subject of Greece. This submission to a temporal authority higher than himself marks a complete break from the conduct of all the 'byronic heroes', from Childe Harold to Christian, to say nothing of his own up till now. From now on, the *legitimacy* of the cause he is engaged in will matter more and more to Byron.

It was a perfect misunderstanding. The London Greek Committee was anxious to secure Byron's name for the cause. Most of its members knew nothing about the revolution they had pledged to support. Information and advice from anyone who did, even if it was ten years out of date, would be most welcome. 'I venture to hope that your Lordship will favor us with any suggestions which may advance our common objects. Your knowledge both of places and individuals would be very valuable if any part of it were transferred to us', wrote Bowring to Byron on 14 March.[68] That was all. But these letters were delayed in the post and would not reach Genoa until long after Blaquiere and Louriotis had departed. So they formed no part in shaping Byron's thinking.

For Byron, providentially, the call had come. Now, when he most had need of one, he had a cause to live for – if need be, to die for. Within weeks, the cause of Greece would have become 'the Cause', with the capital letter.[69] But the call to which Byron responded that spring had not come from London, from the newly formed Committee, or its emissaries.

The formation of the London Greek Committee, the vague indications he had had from Hobhouse, and now the arrival of a deputation with an imagined invitation, all had a catalytic effect. Without them, the latent decision might never have been put into effect – just as the sufferer from vertigo is at no risk of jumping if there is no precipice in front of him. But none of these things was the reason for Byron's unexpected offer to go to Greece. This was a call to which he had first begun to respond, tentatively, in the autumn of 1821 after Shelley's visit to him in Ravenna. It was the 'plan in embryo' that he had confided to Medwin, Trelawny, and others, in the weeks after Shelley's cremation. Each time, until now, the determination to 'take a part of some sort' had been outweighed by 'the tears of a woman . . . and the weakness of one's own heart'.[70] Now, for the first time the balance had shifted.

The call had come. But the call Byron heard was in his own imagination.

NO GOING BACK

Even now, he hesitated. With one foot over the edge of the precipice, for two whole months he teetered. He knew, really, that he was committed. If his offer were to be taken up by the Committee and the Greek provisional government, he could not honourably go back on it. The alacrity with which both Blaquiere and Louriotis responded made this a foregone conclusion. In London, Hobhouse relayed the news to Bowring. When Bowring wrote to Byron at the end of April, welcoming him as a full member of the Committee, Byron felt honour-bound to repeat formally what he had already said and written to Blaquiere, Hobhouse, and others: 'My first wish is to go up into the Levant in person.' When Bowring leaked parts of this letter to the press, on 2 June, Byron was too far over the precipice to draw back.[71] But still, until the middle of June, he went on subjecting himself – and his correspondents – to an exquisite agony of indecisiveness.

Blaquiere had promised to write. When no letter had arrived, after just over a week, Byron's excitement turned to petulance: 'I have heard no more from Blaquiere – who was to have written to me at length – so I suppose that he has either exceeded his powers – or repented him – for some reason or other.'[72] Then three days later he did hear from Blaquiere:

I saw the Bishop Ignatius at Pisa. He has begged me to express his gratitude for your generous intentions, and says he is sure G[reece] will be *grateful*. As to my companion [Louriotis], nothing can exceed his exultation – you would smile if I named the part he has cut out for your Lordship – It would be a novel though unnatural sight to behold the author of Childe Harold molding the energies of G[reece] in the 19th century as a minister.[73]

This is all that lies behind the supposition, repeated in many biographies, that 'some of the Greek exiles in Italy had . . . approached Byron with the offer of the crown of Greece'.[74] But it was enough to set off Byron and the Earl of Blessington weaving a tipsy fantasy that has since become part of the Byron legend. 'What think you', wrote Blessington, as the preamble to an invitation to dine the next day, 'of *Emperor of the Greeks*. You are too lean for a Greek Emperor and would not like to be a little one like *Cousin of Austria*.'[75]

What would have flattered Byron far more, in Blaquiere's letter, were the repeated terms, 'gratitude' and '*grateful*'. It was this that Christian, in *The Island*, could never deserve. Whether he knew it or not, Blaquiere had struck exactly the right note. And there was a sombre aspect, too. The letter ends with a brief account of visiting Shelley's grave in Rome. For Blaquiere to have mentioned this, it seems likely that Byron had spoken of Shelley at their meeting. Perhaps he had even told Blaquiere what he would later tell the Scottish Presbyterian medical officer in Cephalonia, Dr James Kennedy: that Shelley, had he lived, would have gone with him to Greece.[76] This may be the reason why Byron determined, right at the beginning, that if he did go to Greece, it would be in July. The planned date for his departure (if he went) was always going to be close to the anniversary of Shelley's death.[77]

As he tried out the idea of Greece in correspondence and conversation, Byron was not above introducing a strain of playful morbidity. Since 'there is some risk of not returning', he writes to Kinnaird, 'my *latest* works would bear some value merely as *such*'. By 'latest' he means 'last'.[78] To Lord Blessington, he started out robustly: 'I assure you my notions on that score are limited to getting away with a whole skin', only to shift into the same lugubrious tone: 'or sleeping quietly with a broken one in some of my old Glens where I used to dream in my former excursions; – I should prefer a grey Greek stone over me to Westminster Abbey – – but I doubt that I shall have the luck to die so happily'.[79] If Byron was dreaming of glory during those months of decision-making in Genoa, he was also thinking of death.

He still had no real idea of what he might do, once in Greece. At first he thought of it as a civilising mission – to teach both sides how to treat their prisoners better, perhaps even to protect lives.[80] Soon, he was building on the embryo plan that had been in the background since Pisa. He would put to good use the capital he had been hoarding for the best part of a year.[81] Throughout May, he was still equivocating. 'However I *will* go . . . an' it be possible – or do all I can in the cause, go or not', he wrote to Hobhouse on the nineteenth. But then, Byron knew something about himself too: 'What the Hon Dug. [Kinnaird] and his committee may decide I do not know – and still less what I may decide (for I am not famous for decision) for myself.'[82] The Blessingtons left Genoa at the beginning of June, before Byron's mind was fully made up. But Lady Blessington had already been struck by the lack of enthusiasm with which he talked of his plans.[83] In conversation, to her and others, he confessed something that he never put into a letter. As the time for an irrevocable decision approached, he was wishing he had never got himself into this 'scrape'.[84] But even while he vacillated, he was daily cutting off a little more of his retreat.

He would not yet have known about the leaking of his letter in London, when on 7 June a second letter arrived from Blaquiere. If any single factor decided Byron, surely it was this. Blaquiere, writing from Zante in the Ionian Islands, was about to cross into Greece. He would write again when he reached the seat of government, in Tripolitsa. In the meantime, Blaquiere was determined to hold Byron to the offer that he was now, in some moods at least, regretting:

From all that I have heard here, it would be criminal in me leave this [i.e., Zante], without urging your Lordship to come up as soon as possible: – your presence will operate as a Talisman – and the field is too glorious, – too closely associated with all that you hold dear, to be any longer abandoned.[85]

To Kinnaird the next day, Byron wrote: 'if the next communication from the *Greek* seat of Government – at all resembles the present – I shall proceed to join the cause forthwith'. Two days after that he had begun rather desperately trying to find someone to take care of Teresa during his absence, prefacing his request: 'My latest news from Greece gives me reason to suppose that I shall be required to go up there – and probably soon.'

Suddenly, on the fifteenth, he turned practical. He wrote to Trelawny, who was then in Florence (this is the whole of the letter):

My dear T. – You must have heard that I am going to Greece. Why do you not come to me? I want your aid, and am exceedingly anxious to see you. Pray come, for I am at last determined to go to Greece; it is the only place I was ever contented in. I am serious, and did not write before, as I might have given you a journey for nothing; they all say I can be of use in Greece. I do not know how, nor do they; but at all events let us go.[86]

After that, there really *was* no going back.

The preparations that went on during June and the first half of July have been much written about, at the time and ever since. Most famous is the story of the scarlet and gold uniforms for himself, Pierino, and Trelawny, and the helmets to go with them. These were built to Byron's own design, inspired by the description of Hector's armour in the *Iliad*. Whether Byron ever wore his helmet is uncertain. But all these accessories did travel with him to Missolonghi. After his death, one of the helmets would find its way, via Boston, Massachusetts, to the Historical Museum in Athens, where it can be seen today.[87] A few months later, Mary Shelley, who had been living in the Casa Negrotto with the Hunts at the time, wrote to Leigh from London, 'the existence of these helmets by the bye is well known here'. No doubt Mary had smiled to herself as she reassured an anxious enquirer about Byron's intentions: 'Helmets so fine were never made to hack.'[88] Only a few weeks had gone by since Lady Blessington had been complaining in her diary that the most famous poet of the age dressed in dingy old clothes far too large for him. The transformation was too extreme to avoid comment. But in truth Byron probably set no more store by his new carapace than he had by the old. In this display there is surely a wry memory of the hunchback Arnold, in *The Deformed Transformed*, suddenly emerging with the body and armour of the slayer of Hector, Achilles.

Another task was to find out what was actually happening in Greece. To Bowring on 12 May Byron had written that he was in touch with Greek exiles in Italy. But it says much for his lack of interest up to now that he had no Greek contacts to draw upon when he needed them. He wrote to Carvelà in Pisa, relying on Hobhouse's acquaintance rather than his own. The result was in any case disappointing. He mobilised the local representative of the banking firm he had used in Tuscany, Charles Barry, to take soundings on his behalf among the Greek community in Livorno. The result would again be inconclusive, but in this way Byron would gain a valued friend and supporter, the recipient of many of his last letters from Greece.[89]

As a result of these enquiries, the community that Byron had shunned, or at least ignored, during the ten months when he had been living in Pisa the previous year, soon knew all about his plans. The Casa Saluzzo was becoming a magnet for a new kind of visitor. Two German volunteers, returning destitute and disillusioned from Greece, were directed there. Byron sent them on their way with money and new shoes.[90] A colonel from Hesse, on his way from Greece with vague schemes to help the cause, asked for and received an introduction to the London Greek Committee.[91] A relative of Mavrokordatos, Count Constantin Skilitzy, travelling in the opposite direction, turned up with a letter of introduction and asked for a passage to Greece.[92]

Then there were preparations of a more practical sort. Blaquiere had advised against bringing 'the pleasure boat'. Byron now loathed the *Bolivar* in any case. He sold it to Lord Blessington who subsequently, to his rage, was slow to pay for it: 'he shan't treat me like a tradesman *that* I promise him', he would rant. Byron's aversion to paying tradesmen is one of the least forgivable of his faults, and probably one of the few that he never regarded as one in himself. It was only a couple of months since he had expressly forbidden Kinnaird to settle the coach-builder's bill, now six years overdue, for his Napoleonic coach.[93] With the *Bolivar* disposed of, Byron had now to find a way to convey himself, his companions, horses, and supplies (though not the coach) to Greece.

By 18 June, Barry had found him a ship. On the last day of the month Byron signed a contract to charter the *Hercules*, a two-masted brig of a type built to carry coal for the English coastal trade.[94] Perhaps the name appealed to the owner of the helmets. The travelling party was coming together. Soon Trelawny arrived in response to Byron's summons, and at once set about the modifications necessary to the brig so that it could transport horses. Pierino, of course, would be going. A young Italian doctor, Francesco Bruno, was recruited on the recommendation of Dr Alexander, who had been treating Byron in Genoa. A place was found for Count Skilitzy. The complement would be made up by Byron's secretary, Lega Zambelli, several servants including the ex-gondolier Tita Falcieri and the faithful Fletcher, Trelawny's black American servant Benjamin Lewis, and Byron's two dogs. Money was taken aboard: 10,000 Spanish dollars in silver coins, and bills of exchange for a further 40,000.

Right up to the day of departure, Byron was more troubled than he cared to admit about 'the absurd womankind', as he had taken to referring to Teresa, quoting a character in a novel by Walter Scott.[95] He delayed even telling her of his plans for Greece. When he could dissemble no longer, he sent Pierino to break the news. There were scenes. Teresa then begged to be allowed to go with him to Greece. His response was a kind of backhanded chivalry, crueller than kind, but perhaps not intentionally so: 'of course the idea is ridiculous – as every thing must there be sacrificed to seeing *her* out of harm's way'.[96] But his firmness cost him pain. The 'obstacles' to his going, he confessed to Lord Blessington, 'have hampered and put me out of Spirits – and still keep me in a vexatious state of uncertainty'.[97] For a time it really did look as though Teresa would have to go into a convent. Byron wrote to at least two lady acquaintances, hopelessly wondering if they could help find an alternative home for her.[98] As the day of departure approached, Teresa would sit up at night writing sentimental letters to him, then tear them up. Half a century later, she would recall his promise to her: he would soon be back, 'and then nothing will be able to part us again'.[99]

Other partings, though less emotionally charged, were no more happy. The Hunts were to move to Florence. Byron had made financial provision for them, but it was accepted with a poor grace. By a terse agreement, he did not meet Hunt to say goodbye.[100] Because of a misunderstanding over money, for which Hunt was probably to blame, Byron behaved high-handedly towards Mary at the last. There was then a mix-up (perhaps) over timing, which meant there were no farewells with Shelley's widow either. When she knew he had gone, she sent a short note after him, instead. But he had asked her to keep Teresa company at the time when the *Hercules* was due to sail, and this she did.[101]

It was a wretched end to a relationship that seems to have been like no other, on either side. One biographer has supposed that Mary was 'one of the very few women who ever wished to be on terms of frank and intimate friendship with [Byron], but no more'.[102] On his side, Byron had on occasion been roused to fury by the slander that he had had an affair with Mary, as well as with Claire. Another biographer wonders if this was because he was 'annoyed at not getting the credit for having resisted trying'.[103] Mary herself was most probably thinking of Byron when she wrote in her diary, a few months after his death, 'I was never a coquette – those who might have become my lovers became my friends & I grew rich – till death the reaper . . . '[104] For all the frictions of those final months at Albaro, Mary's first reaction, when she heard that he was dead, would be to think back to those 'evening visits to Diodati' in 1816. But then she would continue (without mentioning the much longer period when Byron and the Shelleys had again been together in Pisa): 'Can I forget his attentions & consolations to me during my deepest misery? – Never.'[105] This can only refer to the time after Shelley's death, at Genoa, that ended when Byron left for Greece, and Mary set out to return to England.

The departure, when it came, was a sadly drawn-out affair. After several delays, the expedition was due to sail on the twelfth, but there was no wind. The next day, Byron and his party were all aboard. But the *Hercules* lay becalmed in the harbour of Genoa until dawn on the fifteenth. Then twelve hours after putting to sea, a sudden storm forced the ship back to port. The following morning, the whole party went ashore. With Pierino, Byron made a brief melancholy return to the Casa Saluzzo. Perhaps it was as well that Teresa and Ruggero Gamba had already left. 'Where', Byron wondered aloud, 'shall we be in a year?' To Barry he even confessed that 'he would not go on the Greek expedition even then but that "*Hobhouse and the others would laugh at him*"'. The party spent a miserable day on shore, most of them the worse for seasickness and lack of sleep. By evening, everyone was back on board, and the *Hercules* sailed from Genoa for a second time, late on Wednesday, 16 July.[106]

WHY DID HE DO IT?

Byron's letters from these months are fervid with excitement. They convey vividly the crabwise, vacillating, but from the beginning also somehow inevitable movement towards commitment. But they give nothing away about his deeper motivation. *Why* is he putting himself through all this?

Many reasons have been suggested, both at the time and ever since, some of them originating with Byron himself. He was bored with his life in Genoa. Prematurely ageing, he was obsessed with physical decline and saw a way out in courting a violent death. It was a presentiment: he had always known he would die in Greece. He craved action. He craved glory. He loved liberty (so he told Lady Blessington, and who would doubt it?). He wanted to revisit the forbidden sexual adventures of his youth (perhaps even to regain the youthfulness of that time). He had always wanted to emulate his hero, Napoleon, and now was his chance. Trelawny even thought he did it 'to be revenged on Nature' for his deformity.[107]

On one thing, those who knew him were in no doubt. He was not doing it for the Greeks. Already, before he left Genoa, Byron could 'calmly talk of the worthlessness of the people he proposes to make those sacrifices for'.[108] This attitude troubled Lady Blessington, as it would trouble others to whom he said the same, and worse, in Greece when he got there. Plenty of philhellenes talked like this on their way home, none on their way out. But Byron had already been to Greece. Unlike so many philhellenes, he knew better than to expect to find himself transported into the company of the ancient heroes familiar from his schoolbooks.

Even more surprising was his attitude towards those ancient heroes themselves, those 'glorious beings whom the imagination almost refuses to figure to itself as belonging to our kind', as Shelley had imagined them in the Preface to *Hellas*. Despite all that he had written on the subject in the second canto of *Childe Harold*, Byron told Lady Blessington in Genoa that 'antiquities had no interest for him; nay, he carried this so far, that he disbelieved the possibility of their exciting interest in any one'. This view, too, he would repeat to several others in the months that followed.[109]

It was now that Byron began to adopt the attitude towards ancient Greece that he had found in William Mitford's *History*. The five volumes of this work travelled with him aboard the *Hercules*.[110] Far from idealising classical Greek civilisation, Mitford had drawn the attention of his readers to the 'piratical, thieving and murdering kind of petty war, to which the [ancient] Greeks at all times and in all parts were strongly addicted'.[111] It was passages like this that Byron had in mind when he told Trelawny, during the voyage, 'The Greeks are returned to barbarism; Mitford says the people never were anything better.' Mitford was his authority. But the opinion was one he had heard in Athens, on his first visit with Hobhouse.[112]

If it was not for the Greeks, what *was* it for? 'Perhaps', Lady Blessington wondered, 'Byron wishes to show that his going to Greece is more an affair of *principle* than *feeling*.' To an English lawyer a few months later, in Ithaca, he would confess 'that his undertaking had more the character of a speculative adventure, in favour of what he conceived to be a glorious principle, than any admiration or enthusiasm for the individual cause'.[113] That rings true, so far as it goes. But Byron was not the man to be guided solely by an abstract principle, no matter how 'glorious'. Feeling surely did come into it. The truth is, he may well not have known, himself, why he did it. Some of the explanations he gave, afterwards, sound almost as though he is trying to explain himself to himself.[114]

Byron's decision to go to Greece was at once the culmination and the negation of his entire career as a poet. The negation: because from the moment he left Genoa, his writing career was over. Even if he was still imagining future projects before he left, the reality was that he would write only a handful of lines thereafter.[115] The barely begun seventeenth canto of *Don Juan* travelled with him, and would be found among his effects at Missolonghi. But he never touched it again. The play, *The Deformed*

Transformed, he had sent to England to be published as it was, unfinished. 'I doubt if I shall go on with it', he had written to John Hunt, now his publisher, on 21 May.[116] He never did. He had no need to. The transformation was happening to him in life, and this was part of it. The last poetry Byron wrote in Italy is a short fragment begun a month before he sailed, and at once abandoned. It begins:

> The Dead have been awakened – shall I sleep?[117]

But it was also a culmination. The momentum that was now carrying Byron to Greece had been building up ever since the 'Frankenstein' summer with the Shelleys, in 1816. In the persona of her fictional narrator, Mary had written, then: 'Those events which materially influence our future destinies often derive their origin from a trivial occurrence' – a sentence that would be dropped before the novel saw print.[118] It could hardly have been truer of the real-life story that included the writing of *Frankenstein*. At every turn, the trivial and the accidental could have turned that momentum into any one of many possible channels. It was never a foregone conclusion that Byron would go to Greece. Often, during those years, it looked as if the chosen channel would be a quite different one. But accidental and trivial occurrences also combined, in the end, to make Greece the chosen destination. The momentum had to go somewhere.

There were several strands to this. There was Byron's war against mortality, that he had declared while completing the second canto of *Childe Harold*. There had been his early ambition, later eclipsed by the success of the 'Turkish tales', to distinguish himself in the world of action or politics. Then there had been the solipsistic rebellion of the 'byronic' heroes of those tales, that had spilled over into his own life and public reputation. Later still, there had been the tentative, never wholehearted, attempts to yoke those rebel instincts to a common, political cause. Byron had only very recently, in the aftermath of Shelley's death, begun to articulate a more nuanced position that could be called political: against tyranny and 'all who war / With Thought'. Hovering in the background, but never consistently espoused, was the new cause of nations, that still-emerging political concept of a different sort of collective freedom. To bring that about would require a 'new Prometheus of new men', as he had written in *The Prophecy of Dante*, back in 1819. Where Victor Frankenstein, the 'modern Prometheus' of Mary's fiction, had failed, he, Byron, would restore life to an entire nation.

Byron can never literally have believed the rhetoric of the Greek revival, that in the actions of the modern Greeks 'The Dead have been awakened.'

But Greece, unlike North or South America, or even Spain, did lend itself to that rhetoric. It was not the revival of *Greece* that moved him, so much as the idea that went back to his meditation below the Acropolis of Athens, in the first days of 1810, of *reviving* something – anything – that had gone. Somewhere at the back of all this, perhaps, lay the Christian idea of salvation through sacrifice, of life's ultimate victory over death – with the difference that Byron's victory would have to be won in the real, visible world, not in the hereafter.

Above all, there was Shelley. Often understated, frequently conflicted, the relationship between the two poets had brought out something in Byron that few others did, unless perhaps his youthful idealising of male beauty in the Cambridge choirboy John Edleston or the sexual liberation he had experienced with Giraud in Athens. Shelley's presence and the life-affirming brilliance of his conversation had brought Byron to believe, even if only for a moment, 'That goodness is no name, and happiness no dream'. At Clarens, on Lake Geneva, he had been infected by the younger man's platonic vision of universal love. Over the years, the persuasive 'Snake' had become his conscience, inverting the biblical role of the evil tempter. If Byron was the 'satanic' fallen angel, Shelley's was the voice of the good that he had denied in himself and in his many fictional creations. While Shelley lived, even *his* persuasive powers had had their limits. It was Shelley's death that catapulted Byron into commitment of a kind he might never otherwise have made. Byron's war, as it entered its final phase, was to be above all a tribute to everything that Shelley had come to represent in his imagination.

Byron's departure for Greece, that July evening in 1823, was the very essence of Romantic poetry translated into politics. No longer the '*poetry of politics*' from his Italian days – that had been no more than game-playing – this would be the politics inherent in the Romantic poetry that had been his life up to now, that was also the legacy of Shelley and many others: Romanticism in action, 'words' turned at last into 'things'.

PART III

Greece: ''Tis the cause makes all'
(July–December 1823)

Plate 1a. 'View of the Parthenon', showing the Acropolis as Byron and Hobhouse would have seen it in 1810, lithograph published in Edward Dodwell, *Views in Greece* (London, 1821) (National Library of Scotland)

Plate 1b. Athens 'lives in the inspiration of the poet', perhaps illustrating CHP II 82–92, lithograph published in Christopher Wordsworth, *Greece Pictorial, Descriptive and Historical* (London, 1839) (National Library of Scotland)

Plate 2. *Portrait of a Greek Wearing a Fustanela*, Louis Dupre, *c*.1830, oil on canvas, thought to depict Andreas Londos (Athens: Benaki Museum, Collection of Paintings, Drawings, and Prints)

Plate 3. *The Defeat of the Pasha*, Antoine Charles H. Vernet, 1827, oil on canvas, based on Byron's poem *The Giaour* (Athens: Benaki Museum, Collection of Paintings, Drawings, and Prints)

Plate 4. *Prometheus Creating Man in the Presence of Athena*, Jean-Simon Berthélemy, 1802, detail, repainted 1826 (Louvre)

Plate 5a. Teresa Guiccioli, by E. C. Wood, lithograph published in *The Byron Gallery*, London, 1838 (National Library of Scotland)

Plate 5b. Byron in Genoa, May 1823, at the time when he was making up his mind to take part in the Greek Revolution, sketch by Alfred d'Orsay (John Murray)

Plate 6a. Alexandros Mavrokordatos in Geneva, 1819, lithograph published in *Taschenbuch für Freunde der Geschichte des griechischen Volkes älterer und neuerer Zeit* (Heidelberg, 1824) (Athens: Gennadius Library)

Plate 6b. Metropolitan Ignatios of Hungary and Wallachia, Pisa, 1816, lithograph by Lassinus Carolus (Athens: Gennadius Library, Scrapbook no. 026,v. 4, p. 9)

Plate 7a. Alexandros Mavrokordatos, pencil sketch by Karl Krazeisen, dated 21 May 1827 (Athens: National Gallery–Alexandros Soutzos Museum, Department of Prints and Drawings, published in the catalogue: Karl Krazeisen, *Οι αυθεντικές μορφές των ηρώων του '21* [*Authentic Likenesses of the Heroes of 1821*], curated by Marilena Z. Cassimatis, 2005–6)

Plate 7b. Theodoros Kolokotronis, pencil sketch by Karl Krazeisen, dated 14 May 1827 (Athens: National Gallery–Alexandros Soutzos Museum, Department of Prints and Drawings, published in the catalogue: Karl Krazeisen, *Οι αυθεντικές μορφές των ηρώων του '21* [*Authentic Likenesses of the Heroes of 1821*], curated by Marilena Z. Cassimatis, 2005–6)

Plate 8a. Georgios Sisinis, lithograph published in Karl Krazeisen, *Bildnisse ausgezeichneter Griechen und Philhellenen*, Munich, 1828–31 (Athens: Gennadius Library)

Plate 8b. Georgios Karaiskakis, by an unknown artist, oil on canvas (Athens: Benaki Museum, Collection of Paintings, Drawings, and Prints)

CHAPTER 7

Preparations for battle

Byron's plan after leaving Genoa was to make for Zante (Zakynthos) in the Ionian Islands. The British authorities who ruled these islands under the terms of a Protectorate established in 1815 were known to be hostile to the revolution in neighbouring Greece. Under the rule of 'King Tom' Maitland, Lord High Commissioner in the capital, Corfu, official British policy of neutrality in the conflict was strictly enforced. Despite this, the islands were a natural jumping-off point for British and other European philhellenes intent on finding a route into revolutionary Greece. Blaquiere had gone this way. Byron was counting on Blaquiere to contact him in Zante and take charge of the final stage of his journey to the seat of the Greek Provisional Government.

But it turned out that he was not quite ready to leave Italian waters. Charles Barry's efforts on his behalf, to extract information from the Greek community of Pisa and Livorno, had begun to produce results after all. These were not quite the results that Byron had been hoping for, and they came while he was in the final stages of preparing for his departure. A florid epistle from Metropolitan Ignatios, Mavrokordatos' mentor and the spiritual leader of the Greek community in Tuscany, written on 3 July, reached Byron four days later. The bishop praised his mission to Greece but withheld all hint of the kind of up-to-date factual information that Byron was seeking. Ignatios did give one piece of advice: to place his trust, among the leaders of the armed bands in Greece, in the Souliot chieftain, Markos Botsaris, who was leading resistance to a Turkish counter-attack in the hinterland above Missolonghi.[1] Enclosed were six more letters of introduction for Byron, addressed in Greek to Botsaris, Mavrokordatos, and the unnamed leaders of Mainland Greece, Psara, Hydra, and Aitolia. Botsaris would be killed in battle before Byron got there. But Byron seems to have made no use of the other letters either – since they are today among his papers in the John Murray archive in the National Library of Scotland.[2]

Byron was determined to be cautious in his dealings with Ignatios. To add to his general mistrust of ecclesiastical authorities in any shape or form, he had recently been warned by Bowring: 'Ignatius (the Bishop) may perhaps be considered too closely connected with Russia.' This was a view shared by most British philhellenes as well as by the Foreign Office.[3] In reality, Ignatios and his political allies in Greece had despaired of help arriving from Russia and were increasingly turning their attention to seeking support from Great Britain. The shrewd bishop had already begun to calculate the advantages to Greece of a British alliance.[4] Ignatios could turn on the purple prose when he needed to. But writing to Mavrokordatos in Greece, in a very different style, he showed that he had the measure of his man:

The nobleman Lord Byron is on his way to see the state of affairs in Greece and to lend a helping hand. He has means. He is a member of the committee established in London in favour of the Greeks; he has important friends and can bring benefit, provided he is pleased and our compatriots can win him over with their good offices towards him.[5]

This letter, unknown to Byron, would travel with him aboard the *Hercules*. A month later, Ignatios would write again, more urgently this time, to Mavrokordatos: 'Do what you can to please him, not so much because he can provide money and material help, but most of all, because if he is displeased, he will do such damage as you cannot imagine.'[6]

The distrust was mutual. Byron, once he had decided to call at Livorno, declined a meeting with the Metropolitan, though he did receive his secretary, Dimitrios Mostras, aboard the *Hercules*.[7]

As he was about to leave Genoa, more advice began to arrive. Barry's enquiries had belatedly recruited two new supporters of Byron's mission, the merchants Giorgio and C. (probably Constantine) Mavrogordato. They would have been only very distantly related, if at all, to Mavrokordatos. The latter reinforced the recommendation of Botsaris among the military leaders, and was probably the first to suggest to Byron that once in Greece, he should make his headquarters at Missolonghi. It was from this source, too, that Byron first learned that the government in Greece had resolved to send deputies to England to negotiate a loan, a move with which he would soon become closely associated.[8] But it was not advice that Byron was looking for. He needed hard information. He had gleaned precious little by the time he left Genoa. The stop in Livorno only exasperated him still further. 'I find the Greeks here somewhat divided amongst themselves', he would write to Bowring while at anchor, on 24 July. 'What they most seem to want or desire is – Money – Money – Money.'[9] Byron would soon grow used to both these circumstances.

In the event, the decision to call at Livorno had a number of consequences, from the bizarre to the far-reaching. Before leaving Genoa, Byron had agreed to pick up two new passengers, in addition to Count Skilitzy who was already aboard. Georgios Vitalis claimed to have fought in Napoleon's infantry and was now in the seafaring business. His brother had just arrived from Greece bringing despatches for Ignatios.[10] When the *Hercules* sailed into the harbour of Livorno, the Vitalis ship fired off a thirteen-gun salute – a gesture that may not have been appreciated by the Tuscan port authorities, who had taken such exception to the cannon aboard the *Bolivar* the year before. On the voyage, the unfortunate Vitalis would become first the object of suspicion, and then the butt of rather crude pranks at the hands of Byron and Trelawny. He seems to have been a harmless enough character – but his apparent attempt to smuggle into the Ionian Islands a badly decomposed roast pig, wrapped in an expensive cloak, would earn him the contempt and scorn of his fellow-passengers.[11]

The second passenger was James Hamilton Browne. Born in Edinburgh in the same year as Shelley, Browne had recently been living outside Pisa, by coincidence in one of the many houses where the Shelleys had once lived, with a Greek mistress from whom he seemed now to have parted. Before that he had served the British administration of the Ionian Islands but had left or been dismissed over his pro-Greek sympathies.[12] Some years later, Browne would publish a lively account of his brief visit to Greece with Byron and Trelawny, but never seems to have explained his motive in going there. In his rather straight-faced way he had a good eye for detail. This is Browne's recollection of Byron's appearance, when he first set eyes on him on the deck of the *Hercules*:

The contour of his countenance was noble and striking; the forehead, particularly so, was nearly white as alabaster. His delicately formed features were cast rather in an effeminate mould, but their soft expression was in some degree relieved by the mustaches of a light chestnut, and small tuft 'à la houssard', which he at that time sported. His eyes were rather prominent and full, of a dark blue, having that melting character which I have frequently observed in females . . . The texture of his skin was so fine and transparent, that the blue veins, rising like small threads around his temples, were clearly discernible . . . Lord Byron was habited in a round nankeen embroidered jacket, white Marseilles vest, buttoned a very little way up; he wore extremely fine linen, and his shirt-collar was thrown over in such a way as almost to uncover his neck; very long wide nankeen trowsers, fastened below, short buff laced boots . . . with a chip Tuscan straw hat, completed his personal equipment.[13]

It was Browne, not long after they had left Livorno, who persuaded Byron to change his destination in the Ionian Islands from Zante to Cephalonia.[14] Each island under the British administration was ruled by a Resident, with powers delegated from the Lord High Commissioner. The Resident in Cephalonia, Colonel Charles James Napier, was not only known personally to Browne, but also, within the limits prescribed by his duties, a serious philhellene. Had it not been for Browne's inside information and advice, Byron's trajectory from this point on might have been very different. Had he persevered with the original plan for Zante, he would certainly not have been encouraged to linger there, as he was by Napier in Cephalonia.

A final consequence of the stop at Livorno was that Byron took delivery of a package forwarded from Genoa. It contained a glowing personal tribute from no less a person than Johann Wolfgang von Goethe. This was the ultimate accolade, setting the final seal on Byron's international reputation as a poet – just at the moment when he was turning his back on it. In a hasty and effusive response, Byron announced his new resolve for Greece, and promised to visit the great man at his home in Weimar, 'if ever I come back'.[15]

Byron's mood at Livorno and on the voyage that followed is hard to gauge. According to Gamba, he 'enjoyed excellent health, and was always in good spirits', allegedly throughout. Trelawny echoes this, adding anecdotal evidence that seems to bear it out. But Trelawny also notes that in the course of the voyage Byron had 'improved amazingly' – suggesting that things had not been so rosy at the start. In his later, but not his earlier, published recollections, Trelawny adds a conversation that he claims took place not long after leaving Livorno, in which Byron seems to presage his own death and expresses a wish to be buried in Greece. Browne also described Byron's 'hilarity and enjoyment' but was puzzled and disturbed by what sound, in today's terms, like abrupt mood swings: 'A cloud would instantaneously come over him, as if arising from some painful and appalling recollection; the tears would bedew his eyes, when he would arise and quit the company, averting his face, in order to conceal his emotion.'[16]

The stop at Livorno was part of Byron's programme. But even before leaving Genoa he seems to have been in two minds about it. As the delays mounted, he warned his two intended passengers that the *Hercules* might not even anchor in the port. They must be ready to be brought aboard by boat, on receiving Byron's signal.[17] In the event, the ship remained off

Livorno for some seventy-two hours. Trelawny and the others were glad to stretch their legs ashore. Byron landed only once, to pay a courtesy call on Barry's business partner and to buy additional supplies from Henry Dunn's store on the harbour front.[18] Even this experience will have been painful. The last time Byron had been here, almost exactly a year ago, on emerging from the shop he had run into Shelley, Williams, and Leigh Hunt. It had been the day the Gambas had learnt of their final exile from Tuscany. Byron had been in a towering temper. A week later, Shelley and Williams had drowned, sailing out of this same harbour. This new voyage, undertaken almost on the anniversary, was in part, at some level, Byron's homage to Shelley. The interlude at Livorno was a form of leave-taking. Whether or not he would ever return from Greece, Byron surely sensed the profound change that was taking place in himself.

This is not at all to say, with Harold Nicolson, that on leaving Livorno Byron 'knew that the only positive action of which he was still capable was death'.[19] The conflict that awaited Byron in Greece was far from being the 'glorious contest' that Shelley, translating the two-and-a-half-thousand-year-old words of Sophocles, had prophesied. Byron's war would have, in reality, very little to do with battles between Greek and Turk, or between freedom and tyranny. To *that* struggle, there was nothing that Byron, for all his wits and his wealth, could possibly have contributed. There was a different struggle beginning in Greece, that summer of 1823. This was the political struggle, among the leaders of the Greeks themselves, to determine what kind of freedom they were in the process of winning from their former masters. It was a conflict between rival liberators, between bitterly contested assumptions of what it meant to be free. This was a struggle that was only now emerging into the open, as Byron sailed for Greece. On its outcome would depend the fate of the Revolution and the future shape of what we know, today, as 'Modern Greece'.

Byron would not learn this until much later. But while the *Hercules* was sailing down the coast of Italy, events were taking place in Greece that would set the stage for the new struggle in which he would become a key player.

Much more remained for Byron to do, in Greece, than to die.

MODERNISERS AND WARLORDS

From the point of view of the insurgents, the war against the Ottoman empire had gone better, by the summer of 1823, than anyone might have dared to hope. All of the southern Greek mainland and many of the islands of the Aegean (including at this time even Crete) were in Greek hands, although many vital fortifications were still held by Turkish garrisons. At sea the balance of power remained uncertain, with partial blockades in force both by the Ottoman navy, which continued to supply its outposts in the Peloponnese, and by ad hoc Greek fleets based upon the island communities of Hydra and Spetses (Spezzia) off the northeast coast of the Peloponnese, and Psara (Ipsara) in the eastern Aegean. During the previous year, 1822, the Turks had hit back in force, with separate land expeditions launched through eastern and western Greece. The eastern force had been annihilated by a daring guerrilla action in the pass of Dervenakia, between Corinth and Nafplio. In the west, it was the Greeks and their philhellene supporters (mainly, at this time, from Germany and France) who were annihilated at the battle of Peta. The survivors had fallen back upon the main town in the region, Missolonghi, facing the Gulf of Patras. Against all expectation, Missolonghi had held out against a siege that lasted until Christmas Day, when the attackers had finally been driven back.

The year 1823 had begun with a lull in hostilities. A renewed attempt by the Sultan to regain his lost territories was imminently expected, and inexplicably delayed. As Byron sailed, the campaign in the west, in the mountains to the north of Missolonghi, was hotting up once more. Soon there would once again be a very real threat to the town. But the prime movers in these actions were the local pashas of northwestern Greece, the successors to Ali Pasha, who were more loyal subjects of the Sultan than Ali had been, but far less powerful. The concerted Ottoman counter-thrust would not come until 1825. When it did come, the consequences would be devastating for the Greeks – but that is another story.

In the meantime, the Greeks had the opportunity to recognise and to confront their internal divisions. The two years of relative inactivity on the external front, and the two civil wars that were fought in the Peloponnese during that time, have long been treated with embarrassment by Greek historians and censure in the influential foreign accounts. 'The two civil wars are black spots in the history of the Greek Revolution', wrote Finlay in 1861.[20] But recently historians in Greece have been taking a fresh look at these events. While the military history of the Revolution has been written many times, the political, social, and economic dimensions of the conflict have only of late begun to be examined. From these changed perspectives, the internal conflict, into which Byron unwittingly sailed, is now coming to be understood as a 'necessary, unavoidable, a *defining* stage' of the Revolution, in that sense comparable to the period of the Terror in France.

Far from being a shameful diversion from the main business of winning independence, the two civil wars of 1824 are today coming to be recognised as the crucible in which the future political shape of independent Greece would be forged. These wars were closely fought, and the outcome was by no means a foregone conclusion.[21]

Essentially, the conflict was between those who wished to create a modern, centralised state on the one side, and local warlords on the other. The first group were political rather than military leaders, educated either in the Ottoman system, or in the west, or both, and inspired by ideas derived from the western Enlightenment. The second were the military chieftains, the klefts and local leaders that at the time and since have always captured the popular imagination in Greece: simple and direct in their manners and speech, often without much education, but with a strong local power-base and a political understanding based on traditional practices and family-centred networks. During the time that Byron was in Greece, the chief protagonist of the modernisers was Alexandros Mavrokordatos, of the warlords Theodoros Kolokotronis, also known as the 'Old Man of the Morea' (Plate 7b). Somewhere in the middle stood Andreas Londos, Byron's host at Vostitsa in 1809 and 1810. Together with another local primate, Andreas Zaimis of Kalavryta, Londos would ally himself with Mavrokordatos and the modernisers in the first civil war, with the warlords of the Peloponnese in the second.

The divisions that these men represented were far more than personal, although individual loyalties and antipathies were so strong as to obscure, very often, the more fundamental fault lines that lay beneath. Mavrokordatos and Londos we have already met. Theodoros Kolokotronis was a whole generation older than Mavrokordatos and Byron. He had been born in 1770, in the tiny hamlet of Libovisi, high in the mountains above Tripolitsa in the centre of the Peloponnese. As a young man, he had been the embodiment of the rough independence of the kleft, honing his military skills sometimes as brigand, sometimes in the service of the local pashas, as was common at the time. Like other klefts, too, when things became too hot on the mainland, he crossed over to the Ionian Islands. During the Napoleonic wars, in Zante, Kolokotronis had served, in succession, the occupying forces of Russia, France, and Great Britain, before returning to the Peloponnese just before the outbreak of the Revolution in 1821.

Gordon, who had fought alongside him, and would later become the first historian of the Revolution, describes a character and appearance that ought to have appealed to Byron:

It would be impossible for a painter or a novelist to trace a more romantic delineation of a robber chieftain . . . tall and athletic, with a profusion of black hair and expressive features, alternately lighted up with boisterous gaiety, or darkened by bursts of passion: among his soldiers, he seemed born to command[.][22]

But Gordon, writing just after the Revolution was over, had harsh words too for a man whose 'sordid avarice, and mean ambition . . . [had] severely scourged his country'. Finlay, who also knew him, noted with his customary wariness: 'His manners had a degree of roughness well suited to conceal his natural cunning; and he had adopted an appearance of boisterous frankness as a veil for his watchful duplicity.'[23] What no one ever denied about Kolokotronis, love him or hate him, was his genius as a guerrilla commander in the field.

Forthright in speech and absolutely ruthless in action, Kolokotronis left a memoir, dictated in later life because he had never learned to read. For the same reason, contemporary documents in his name are few. But those that exist testify to these qualities. A letter to Ignatios and other political figures, after the Turkish garrison had surrendered the fortresses above Nafplio in December 1822, demands money for repairs to the ruined town: 'You're to send it to me without fail, if you don't, I'll be at war with You, war without mercy, war without end, and I'll leave it to be carried on by my descendants.'[24] A proclamation to a group of villages in the district of Corinth warns, if they should continue to resist his demands (probably for money): 'So long as there is a Kolokotronis family living in the world . . . eternally shall revenge be sought in rivers of men's blood.' This, the text continues, is its author's 'patriotic duty'.[25] Terms like 'fatherland' (*patrida*) and 'patriotic' were used at the time in quite different senses by warlords such as Kolokotronis and by political modernisers like Mavrokordatos and Ignatios.[26]

In the Greek popular imagination, and in Greek schoolbooks to this day, if the Revolution has a single, outstanding hero, it is Kolokotronis. The giant equestrian statue outside the Old Parliament building in Athens, that today houses the Historical Museum where Byron's helmet is on display, is typical. No such monuments commemorate Mavrokordatos, the politician.[27]

These divisions had come out into the open during April 1823. The delayed Second National Assembly had the task of reviewing the Provisional Constitution that had been drawn up the previous year, and deciding the membership of the two national bodies that between them were responsible for overseeing the functions of government. It met at a place on the

Gulf of Nafplio, opposite the town, known at the time as St John's Huts (Aiyannitika Kalyvia). For the purposes of a national assembly, a long-disused ancient name was resurrected. Just as its predecessor, held at the village of Piada, had appropriated the name of an ancient site in the vicinity, guaranteeing that the 'Assembly of Epidaurus' would resonate throughout Europe, so the huts on the shore became 'Astros'. By this name the village, and the assembly that took place there in 1823, have been known ever since.

By all accounts, the deliberations at Astros were bad-tempered from the start. The sticking-point proved to be what to do with the huge tracts of land expropriated from wealthy Turkish landowners. Inside the Assembly it was proposed that the lands should become the property of the state and be sold to raise revenue. Outside, according to one eyewitness, the armed 'captains' wrote out the proposition on scraps of card, hung them from the olive trees, and pretended to use them for target practice, to the consternation of those assembled within.[28] The warlords would not agree to the concentration of land, and of the revenue it might provide, in the hands of an abstract state. By temperament and upbringing, they could not identify with such a thing. Under the old Ottoman system, the state was by definition alien: their forefathers had never had a stake in it, although most had learned to exploit it for the benefits of their own families and dependants.

For the modernisers, the failure to gain control of the only asset the fledgling state possessed was a severe setback. By the time the Astros assembly broke up, any chance there had been of resolving the land issue had been lost.[29] The least contentious way to find money sufficient for the basic needs of the state was to seek loans from abroad – even if this meant offering as collateral an asset that the Provisional Government did not in fact possess. As Mavrokordatos was honest enough to concede, while skating over the reasons for it, in his very first letter to Byron, written on 14 July, 'It is true that we already possess immense riches since 4/5ths of lands belong to the nation; but the present state of things does not allow us to profit from them.'[30]

These were not the only grounds for contention. The centralisers, backed by the first contingents of philhellenes from abroad, had consistently pressed for the creation of a national army. This was seen by the war-lords and their supporters as a threat to their very existence, as well as to the traditional tactics that had worked so well in the Revolution until now. Kolokotronis' violent and often unorthodox manner of warfare had been vindicated again and again in action, most recently at Dervenakia. Mavrokordatos, by contrast, had made the mistake of taking command of a relatively conventional military force at Peta – and seeing it wiped out. Mavrokordatos' reputation, to this day, has never recovered from what most historians have condemned as a serious error of judgement in assuming direct command. At the time, opinions were more evenly divided. Napier, a military man to the core, thought that Mavrokordatos had more than made up for the disaster at Peta by his brilliant and successful defence of Missolonghi. Others, too, not naturally disposed to think well of him, thought Mavrokordatos' conduct at Missolonghi had strengthened his following at the time of the Astros Assembly.[31] On balance, though, the tide of opinion in the Peloponnese had turned against the idea of a regular, European-style army. The irregular tactics of the warlords were in the ascendant.

Above all, there was the issue of foreign involvement. In the eyes of warlords such as Kolokotronis, those educated Greeks from abroad, who had dominated the first Provisional Government after Epidaurus, were themselves foreigners. The most conspicuous of these in the Peloponnese during the first half of 1823 was Mavrokordatos, who had now abandoned the oriental robes that had so impressed the Shelleys and went about, provocatively, in a European frock coat (Plate 7a). Even some real foreigners found this off-putting.[32] Kolokotronis would complain bitterly to Byron's emissaries, Browne and Trelawny, when they reached Tripolitsa in September:

the natives of Constantinople perceiving themselves without influence and not in possession of the confidence of the people, who looked upon them as foreigners, from their possessing no property in Peloponesus [*sic*], lost no relations in the war and never resided amongst them, commenced then a series of chicanery and intrigue in order to obtain power by creating divisions. Mavrocordato . . . began to correspond with foreign courts and foreigners without informing the Govt of the nature of many of his communications, this naturally excited jealousy and suspicion[.][33]

Kolokotronis expressed the fears of many newly liberated Greeks in the Peloponnese that these 'foreigners' – Greeks with the benefits of education and privilege gained abroad – would go over the heads of the fighters on the ground to hand over the country to outside interests, in the process destroying the warlords' power-base. Even the mission to seek a loan in London would come to seem a betrayal in Kolokotronis' eyes, for the slightly circular reason that he gave to Browne at that same September meeting:

because Great Britain might thereby obtain an undue preponderance in Greece, which country he wished to be entirely unfettered, and that it might tend to aid the intrigues of Mavrocordato and the Phanariots, who . . . would contrive to appropriate to themselves the lion's share of it.[34]

It is a fear that has haunted Greek society and political life ever since – and events have often shown that it was not unfounded. Indeed, distrust of foreign interests, and still more of those fellow-Greeks who might be supposed to have sold out to them, has probably done more than any other single factor to stunt the growth and self-confidence of the Greek state, from Byron's time, through the long schism of the twentieth century, to the debt crisis that broke upon the country in 2010.

Against this background, it was only natural that Kolokotronis and his supporters should have feared the worst when Blaquiere turned up in Tripolitsa with Louriotis, an old associate of Mavrokordatos from Italy. This was in early May, soon after the end of the Astros assembly and within days of the new Provisional Government being formed. It will hardly have helped that the newcomers brought with them from London and duly handed over Jeremy Bentham's 'Observations' on the Epidaurus constitution, along with instructions for their translation into Greek.[35]

Mavrokordatos, on the other hand, saw an opportunity that could not be missed. Now was the chance to put into practice the geopolitical vision he had articulated while living in the house of Metropolitan Ignatios in Pisa, before he had met the Shelleys – and also to update it to fit the changed circumstances. Mavrokordatos had understood from the beginning that the key to the Revolution's success would lie in what today would be termed its internationalisation. So long as the conflict remained a relatively local affair, the most that could be hoped for was the kind of uneasy de facto autonomy that had already been won by Greece's northern neighbours, the Serbs, through revolts in 1804 and 1815. This was exactly the kind of arrangement that would best have suited men like Kolokotronis – in effect an extension of the relative autonomy the klefts had always claimed for themselves among their mountains. Rule would be autocratic, family-based, and unimpeded by the checks and balances that the European Enlightenment of the eighteenth century had laboured to devise for the regulation of a modern civic society. But Serbia was still nominally a part of the Ottoman empire, as indeed it would remain until 1878. Ignatios and Mavrokordatos, like the Ypsilantis brothers and most foreign philhellenes, aspired to something both more and different. In their eyes, success would not be won unless or until Greece could become a fully functioning, independent state. To achieve that, it would not be enough to chase the Muslim Turks out of the Peloponnese, or any number of islands, and replace their rule with that of a local Greek chief. Greece would have to win recognition and support from the Great Powers of Europe. And this at a time when these powers were universally hostile to anything that might threaten the old order restored throughout the continent by the Congress of Vienna at the end of the Napoleonic Wars. This was the task that faced Mavrokordatos in the months after Astros.

Blaquiere clearly talked up the prospects for the London Greek Committee and may well have given the impression that its parliamentary members (actually belonging to the Opposition) were closer to the British government than they were.[36] Mavrokordatos would have been encouraged, too, by the letters that Blaquiere brought from London. When Blaquiere wrote to Byron from Tripolitsa, soon after his arrival, he was expecting that 'the government will most probably remain here for some months', and implied that he himself would wait for Byron to join him there.[37] But then, only a month later, Blaquiere could not wait to leave. 'Circumstances have arisen which render it necessary for the interests of Greece, that I should absent myself a short time from the seat of government before your arrival', he wrote to Byron on 10 June, and ended his letter: 'I am however well assured that the object of my intended journey will be a sufficient excuse in the eyes of your Lordship.'[38]

What these circumstances were Blaquiere never directly revealed. He left Tripolitsa 'precipitately', according to Mavrokordatos, a few days afterwards.[39] Perhaps he had been intimidated by Kolokotronis or his supporters. But the main reason, sufficient even to override the promises he had made to Byron, was that Blaquiere had been entrusted by Mavrokordatos with a new mission. This was to carry personal letters to the British Foreign Secretary, George Canning, to several members of the administration of the Ionian Islands, and to a number of other influential individuals in England.[40]

Blaquiere was only one part of Mavrokordatos' plan. Within days of his emissary's departure from Tripolitsa, perhaps on the very day, Mavrokordatos used his position as Secretary of the Executive to force through a resolution appointing deputies to travel to London, to raise a loan for the Greek Provisional Government. This was a policy on which almost all at this point were agreed. Even Kolokotronis seems not to have objected.

What Kolokotronis and the Executive did not know was that two of the three deputies for London, Louriotis and Ioannis Orlandos, were also receiving secret instructions from Mavrokordatos. Far more was at stake, even, than the much-needed cash that a loan would bring. Great Britain, Mavrokordatos now advised Louriotis and Orlandos confidentially, was beginning to change its policy with regard to Greece. Under Canning, who had succeeded Castlereagh as Foreign Secretary the previous September, for the first time the rights of the Greeks as belligerents had been recognised by a foreign power. The new policy still fell a long way short of support for the Greek cause. But it did mark the first chink in the united front the allied powers had presented to condemn the uprising, ever since 1821. If the British government, even at its most conservative, thought it worth competing against Russia for influence in the region, this was an opening that Mavrokordatos now urged his emissaries to exploit. The secret part of their instructions was to sound out the British government about nothing less than a diplomatic alliance with the new Greek state.[41]

A week later, confidentially to Louriotis alone, and writing in French, which few of his opponents in Tripolitsa would have been able to read, Mavrokordatos urged the need to play on British fears of Russian designs:

Exert yourself to exploit their hostile sentiments toward Russia, while bringing home to them the impossibility of the continued existence of the Turkish dynasty in Europe, and the need to replace that spectre with a power young and dynamic, jealous of its independence and capable of supporting itself through alliances, as powerful as they are well chosen, against an invasion from the North.[42]

It was the dream that Mavrokordatos had nurtured in Pisa, long before he and Ignatios had come to consider Britain as the principal one among these potential allies. The intervention by the London Greek Committee, variously manifested through Blaquiere, Louriotis, and the news that Byron might soon be on his way, gave Mavrokordatos his chance. He was not without supporters among the members of the post-Astros Provisional Government. But he had taken an enormous risk, from a considerably weakened political position.

Within weeks of Blaquiere's departure from Tripolitsa, and during the very days while Byron was at Livorno and beginning his voyage to Greece, the simmering confrontation at the heart of the Greek Provisional Government came to a head.

The separation of the functions of government, according to well-meaning principles adopted from the western Enlightenment, and following the practice of the American Constitution, by now threatened to pit the Legislative Body against the Executive. The new Executive, with Kolokotronis as its Vice-President and the primate of Mani, Petrobey Mavromichalis, as its President, was dominated by the warlords. Mavrokordatos, as its Secretary, found himself increasingly isolated. When the Executive Body moved out of Tripolitsa on 2 July, he contrived to stay behind – to 'intrigue', as

Kolokotronis would soon indignantly claim.[43] For its part, the Legislative Body now wanted Mavrokordatos to leave his post with the Executive and assume the authority of *its* President. This was too much for Kolokotronis, who hurried back to Tripolitsa to prevent it.

Mavrokordatos was elected on Tuesday, 22 July (the tenth according to the Greek calendar at the time). The Bishop of Arta, one of three delegates sent by the Legislature to inform Kolokotronis of its deliberations, made the mistake of slapping his thigh as he sang the praises of the new President. Kolokotronis drew out his yataghan and started waving it. The horrified bishop protested that the whole Legislative Body would have no choice but to leave the Peloponnese if threats like that continued. This very soon happened. But worse was to come, first.[44]

Mavrokordatos was already in trouble with the Executive for failing to follow it on campaign towards Corinth. Relations with Kolokotronis had now reached breaking point. Kolokotronis had plans to force his own candidate upon the Legislature. As things now stood, for Mavrokordatos to accept the post risked an open breach between the two bodies. At first he hesitated. Then he refused the office. A second summons from the Legislature followed the next day, both in writing and via an emissary. The emissary found him at Kolokotronis' house, where the signs of coercion would have been unmistakable. Once again Mavrokordatos said no. The Legislative Body now resorted to emotional blackmail: 'Twice you have been called to serve as president of this Body, and now for a third time. Unless you come at once, the Nation cries out against you.'[45]

The next day, 24 July (this was the day that Byron sailed from Livorno), Mavrokordatos addressed the Legislature with a dignified but rather convoluted speech on the necessity of avoiding divisions within the government. That day and the two days following, the Proceedings record that he presided. But his tenure was to be short-lived. On the twenty-fifth, an abrupt note from Kolokotronis, little softened by the diplomatic language of an official scribe, sacked Mavrokordatos as Secretary of the Executive and called on him to give an account of himself. Obediently, and at some length, Mavrokordatos did so, invoking the higher cause of 'our national independence' as his justification.[46]

Kolokotronis would have none of it. There were no more diplomatic exchanges. On the twenty-sixth, he summoned Mavrokordatos. What he said has been repeated, with variations of wording, many times since. Closest to the event is the account that Kolokotronis himself gave to Byron's agents, when they arrived in Tripolitsa two months afterwards:

if he found him again intriguing he would mount him on a donkey and have him whipped out of the Morea. (These were his expressions) and that he only refrained then from putting his threat in execution, in consequence of the remonstrances of some friends, who represented the bad effects likely to be the cause from it.

According to long-established custom and tradition under the Ottomans, it would have been the ultimate public humiliation.[47]

In the face of these threats, Mavrokordatos resigned and the Legislature hastily decamped from Tripolitsa.[48] For a whole year after this, the Legislative Body would continue to regard Mavrokordatos as its president and would make no attempt to replace him. After the debacle, Mavrokordatos himself stayed behind in Tripolitsa for two weeks, perhaps a virtual prisoner. But Kolokotronis soon left, to extort revenues and adjudicate local disputes in the remoter parts of the Peloponnese.[49] Mavrokordatos seized his opportunity, and was smuggled out of the town with the help of the Peloponnesian primates, Londos and Zaimis.[50]

By this time, the badly scared legislators had found a temporary home at the quarters already taken up by the peripatetic Executive, in the Faneromeni Monastery on the island of Kolouri, near Athens.[51] As the seat of government, the island was immediately re-baptised in official documents with its ancient name, that would be familiar to western Europeans: Salamis. For Mavrokordatos to follow the Legislature to Salamis would have been to risk putting himself back into the power of Kolokotronis' supporters. Instead, he found refuge, from the middle of August, among the wealthy Albanian-speaking merchants and shipowners of the island of Hydra. The way was open for Greece to have two governments, in different parts of the country, in a state of undeclared war against each other.

IN LIMBO

Byron had no intention, beforehand, of stopping in the Ionian Islands for much longer than he had stopped at Livorno.[52] Everybody aboard the *Hercules* knew that their destination was free Greece. But when the brig dropped anchor in the long inlet of the sea that shelters Argostoli, the principal town of Cephalonia, on Sunday, 3 August, the news that greeted those aboard, according to Trelawny writing at the time, was 'rather appalling'. The Morea, they now learned, was under blockade, its waters patrolled by a Turkish fleet of 'between eighty and ninety ships of war'. A huge Turkish army was reported to be heading down the eastern side of the Greek peninsula 'in three divisions'.[53] The reality turned out to be less dramatic. The land force would prove much smaller than feared and its operations would reach no further south than Thessaly and Euboea. The strength of the enemy fleet, that had arrived off Patras six weeks before, was only half what Byron's informants told him on that first day.[54] But its existence had not been known in Italy. It was still a serious setback. While the blockade lasted, there would be little chance of entering a recognised Greek port, such as a vessel the size of the *Hercules* would require. In any case, Captain Scott was not willing to risk his ship in the attempt.

What upset Byron more even than this was the report that Blaquiere, far from waiting for him at Tripolitsa, as his last letter had seemed to promise, was already on his way to England. Byron probably never learned the true reason for Blaquiere's abrupt departure. At the time, and for some while afterwards, he took Blaquiere's behaviour as a personal betrayal.[55] That same night, writing 'on the binnacle of a ship by the light of a lanthorn and a Squall blowing', he dashed off a furious note to Blaquiere. 'Here am I – but where are *you*?' Beneath the anger, a glimpse of real despair peeps through: 'what ought I to do?' Suddenly, on arriving in Greek waters, Byron found himself rudderless. Thus far, he had relied entirely on Blaquiere to draw him onward to the next stage of his expedition, and on Bowring and the Committee in London to push from behind. He had left Livorno with the slightly resentful realisation: 'As the Committee has not favoured me with any specific instructions . . . I of course have to suppose that I am left to my own discretion.'[56] That first night at anchor off Argostoli, Byron understood for the first time what that might mean, and was appalled by it.

Next morning, he awoke to find the *Hercules* surrounded by small boats and a crowd of kilted Souliot tribesmen swarming over the deck, to the consternation of Captain Scott and his crew. Ever since their compatriots had saved him and Hobhouse after their shipwreck in 1809, Byron had had a weakness for these colourful warriors. For a moment it must have looked as though the Provisional Government had after all sent a guard of honour to welcome him to their country – and to transport him momentarily back to the sights and sounds of his youth. Parley with their leaders on the deck – the chieftains Fotomaras, Tzavellas, and Drakos – quickly revealed the truth. These men knew nothing of any government in Greece. They had found refuge here with their families from the fighting on the main-land. When Byron discovered that the British authorities had prudently confiscated their weapons as a condition for this sanctuary, he professed outrage, and immediately took forty of the men into his service. If the

Provisional Government in Greece had neglected to send him the guard of honour he had at first imagined them to be, Byron would create his own.

And what of the Provisional Government? As the days passed, and Byron's party kept to the ship to minimise embarrassment to the British authorities on shore, there was no sign of any reception committee or even a message from the mainland. Blaquiere was supposed to have prepared the ground for his coming. Even if Blaquiere himself had defected, why had no one been sent from Tripolitsa to receive him – or at least to bring a message? The last letter Byron had received from Blaquiere before leaving Italy had promised that Louriotis would be writing. 'Mavrocordato is also desirous of thanking you, and will most probably do too.'[57] Where were these letters? As a matter of fact, Mavrokordatos *had* written to him, on 14 July, at the same time as he had been briefing Louriotis and Orlandos for their mission to London. Thinking Byron was still in Genoa, Mavrokordatos hoped that his emissaries might be able to deliver his letter on their way. But the letter had still travelled no further than Hydra and would not reach Byron for another six weeks. Byron was not to know this, but within days of his arrival in Cephalonia, there would be nobody left in Tripolitsa who would have had either the wish or the authority to invite the noble foreigner into their midst.[58]

The day after the invasion by the Souliots, Byron received another visitor aboard the *Hercules*. This was Colonel Napier, the Resident, who had only that morning returned to the island from a meeting with the Turkish naval authorities from Patras.[59] With Napier, Byron at once struck up a friendship based on mutual respect. A veteran of Wellington's Peninsular campaigns during the Napoleonic wars, and the future conqueror of the Indian province of Sind, Napier sympathised strongly with the Greek cause and held very decided views about how it should be prosecuted. He was also an energetic, if not necessarily a very popular, governor in Cephalonia. Napier is still remembered there for the ambitious programme of public works that he pursued, conscripting the islanders for forced labour. Roads, lighthouses, and bridges built or planned by Napier can still be seen today. Back in April, Napier had risked the displeasure of the government he served, when he volunteered a memorandum of advice to the Provisional Government of Greece on the conduct of the war.

Envisioning a military advance through Thessaly to take Salonica and even Constantinople, Napier had given short shrift to the kind of constitutional debates that at the time had been preoccupying the Greek leaders gathered at Astros:

The Greek Government should have nothing to do with constitutions for a country which does not belong to them[,] which Greece does not, while a single Turkish soldier bears arms in Europe. Prince Mavrocordato should be made dictator; his success gives him a full title to that high honour, and for the present the men, the arms, the money of Greece, ought to be at his command.[60]

Napier shared these ideas with Byron, probably from the beginning. To one who had once dreamed of being 'the first man – not the Dictator – not the Sylla, but the Washington or the Aristides – the leader in talent and truth', Napier's bluntness must have been exhilarating. On the politics of the Revolution, once he was in a position to formulate ideas of his own, Byron would take a very different line. But on military matters he would ever afterwards defer to Napier. Soon, he would be confidentially recommending his new friend to the London Greek Committee as a possible commander-in-chief for Greece.[61]

Here, at last, and just when he was most needed, was someone of whom Byron could ask, as he had rhetorically demanded of Blaquiere, what was he to do now? Napier was the only person in the island with the authority to invite Byron's party to come ashore and to prolong their stay. In the circumstances, Byron could only agree. Until he knew who was expecting him in Greece, and where, he could go no further in any case. But he refused Napier's offer of hospitality at the Residency. No doubt he was jealous of his independence. And despite the suspicions of Trelawny and others, he will still have believed that his stay would be a short one. So Byron and his party kept to their cramped quarters aboard the *Hercules*. But he was soon regularly accepting invitations to dine with Napier. He had his horses put ashore, and took to riding out with Lieutenant-Colonel Duffie of the Eighth Regiment. A different kind of acquaintance began to be cemented with the Scottish Presbyterian medical officer, James Kennedy, who would keep a meticulous record of his *Conversations on Religion, with Lord Byron and Others*, the first of which took place on Sunday, 10 August.[62] As surprising to Byron as the lack of warmth shown by the Greeks he was on his way to serve, was the enthusiastic welcome extended by these representatives of his own nation, that he thought had long ago disowned him for good, in this provincial garrison town.

But these were distractions. During his first week in Cephalonia, and most likely acting on advice from Napier, Byron did everything he possibly could to establish contact with the Greek authorities on the mainland. He despatched a messenger to Corfu with his note for Blaquiere, and instructions to bring him back if by any chance he was still there. Blaquiere's intelligence from Tripolitsa would be vital, if only it could be obtained. Another messenger carried a letter through the blockade to Markos Botsaris, the Souliot chieftain recommended by his informants in Livorno. At the same time, Byron made the acquaintance of a local nobleman who promised to contact the Provisional Government in Greece on his behalf.

This was Count Demetrio Delladecima. Described as 'a gentleman of some literary acquirements', Delladecima would impress the young Julius Millingen with his 'shrewdness, sound judgment, and deep acquaintance with the Greek character'. Byron gave him the nickname '*Ultima Analise*', apparently a catchphrase of his.[63] Many of the landed families of these islands were descended from the Italian nobility that had settled there during seven centuries of rule by Venice, intermarried, and adopted the near-universal Greek Orthodox form of Christianity. It was still the custom for the men of this class to receive their education in Italy. As a result, they were more used to writing in Italian than in their mother tongue. This made it easy for Byron to converse with Delladecima.

By the end of Byron's first week in Cephalonia, Delladecima had agreed to convey his urgent message to the Provisional Government. Since he was on good terms with Mavrokordatos, and believing him still to be Secretary to the Executive Body, Delladecima wrote to the person he knew, in Italian, and giving the address, simply, as 'Peloponneso'. As well as conveying Byron's questions, the Count gave a factual account of his arrival, entourage, and demeanour so far. That Byron was to be taken seriously, he wrote, was evident from his offer to put up 1,000 dollars per month to maintain a corps of Souliots at the disposal of the Government. Delladecima added that in his own opinion this force would be of greatest use in Western Greece, where it would back Botsaris' campaign in the mountains. To this, Byron had agreed.

Next come Byron's questions, which are to be answered by the government. They reveal the immediacy, as well as the urgency, of Byron's dilemma when he had been only one week in the Ionian Islands:

1. At what place in Greece would it most advisable for him to disembark?
2. When should he arrive at the place fixed upon?
3. What route should he take after disembarking, to make contact with the Government, communicate, and present the letters that he is carrying?
4. The wishes of the Government in regard to his project for the Souliots.
5. Where should the forty Souliots that he now retains be disembarked, whom his Lordship would wish to keep by him so long as this is acceptable to the Government?[64]

Spurred, no doubt, by Byron's insistence face to face, Delladecima added a postscript: 'His Noble Lordship hopes to have an answer through me within twenty days.' In the event, it would take four times that long, and much else would have happened in the meantime. For now, with all three letters on their way, there was nothing Byron could do but wait.

On 11 August, a week after their arrival, he declared a holiday. He and his companions from the *Hercules* would recreate the Homeric quest of his younger days, when with Hobhouse he had searched for the site of ancient Troy. Just across the channel lay Ithaca, the island kingdom that had been Ulysses' destination in the *Odyssey*. They would fill the days of waiting by exploring.

CHAPTER 8

Wavering

OLD MORTALITY

The six days that Byron and his companions spent on the island of Ithaca were an idyllic interlude – nearly. The sun was hot and the skies cloudless. There were opportunities to swim and ride and talk about old times. Byron's moods and his conversation during these days are exceptionally well recorded. No fewer than four members of the party were taking notes, and would later write up their recollections.[1]

On the antiquities they were shown, while crossing Cephalonia, and in Ithaca itself, Byron was nowadays more blunt in his opinions than he had allowed Harold to be, in the days when he had been a 'childe'. 'I detest antiquarian twaddle', Trelawny recorded him as saying while they were there (although the expression sounds more like Trelawny than Byron). Browne, erring perhaps in the opposite direction, records that the 'Cyclopean remains of ancient Samos' (today known as Sami, in Cephalonia) 'from Byron elicited no attention, as he was a more ardent admirer of the present than of the past'.[2]

All the same, they made for the sites on the island that had ancient associations: a rock known locally as the 'castle of Ulysses', a spring and nearby cave on the seashore called the 'fountain' and 'grotto of Arethusa', and the ruins in the north of the island that were reputed to have been the 'school of Homer'. Byron's only recorded reaction to any of these was to seize upon an elderly shepherd near the fountain and drag him back to share the visitors' picnic, on the grounds that the hero of the *Odyssey*, returning in disguise, had been befriended near this spot by the faithful swineherd Eumaeus.[3] As before, it was the unconscious re-enactment of the past by living people against a landscape made significant by story that appealed to Byron.

The sheer, uncomplicated beauty of the places they travelled through undoubtedly affected him as well. Unusually for the time of year, the air was clear enough that from the mountainside above the 'grotto of Arethusa', on the east coast of Ithaca, they could see as far as Santa Maura (today's Lefkada) to the north, Zante to the south, the mountains across the strait, and the Gulf of Patras all the way inland to where it narrows to become the Gulf of Corinth. It was perhaps at the grotto that Byron exclaimed, according to Trelawny: 'You will find nothing in Greece or its islands so pleasant as this. If this isle were mine – "I would break my staff and bury my book." – What fools we all are.'[4]

This time, it sounds more like Byron than Trelawny. Two Shakespeare plays, both of them about magic, are unexpectedly thrown together in this remark. 'Lord, what fools these mortals be', says the child-spirit Puck in *A Midsummer Night's Dream*, in mock-horror at the antics of the human characters. And the quotation that Trelawny's punctuation recognises, though it is not exact, comes from *The Tempest*, where Prospero bids farewell to his magic art – and Shakespeare, it is traditionally supposed, to his career as a dramatist. There is an authentic melancholy about Byron's rare apostrophe, at this time in his life, to the beauty of the Greek landscape. Woven into these feelings, too, is a perhaps half-conscious memory of Shelley: 'This isle and house are mine', Shelley's lightly fictionalised narrator had imagined in 'Epipsychidion', the poem whose fulfilment is set in Greece, and which Byron had read, or reread, not long before taking the decision to come here himself.[5] Much of Byron's time in Ithaca seems to have been spent recalling his own past, and his Prospero-like act of renouncing the 'magic' of his art.

Despite this, some reminders of the present were too pressing to be turned aside. The Resident, Captain Wright Knox, painted a pitiable picture of the plight of several refugee families from Chios and the Morea that had been allowed to settle in the island, and were now living in terrible poverty. It is not clear whether Byron actually met these refugees, but he immediately promised to provide for their relief – and would do so, too, shortly after his return to Argostoli. An ailing widow with three underage daughters, apparently singled out because the family had started out from a position of some wealth in Patras, he decreed should follow him to Cephalonia. There he would maintain them and take a personal interest in their welfare. It was as a consequence of this act of charity that Byron would soon fall in love (perhaps) for the last time in his life, with the widow's adolescent son, Loukas Chalandritsanos.[6]

A chance meeting at the Residency brought the most direct news, yet, of Blaquiere, and the chance to discover, even at second-hand, something of what Blaquiere had learned from his time at Tripolitsa. This was how

Thomas Smith, a former colleague of Browne who happened to be passing through, found himself immediately swept up into Byron's party. Smith had been with Blaquiere, in Corfu, only a few days previously. At once he began to tell Byron what he knew. Back in Cephalonia, this was exactly the kind of information that Byron would have seized upon. Now, as the high spirits of the party swirled through the Residency, he seems not even to have heard Smith out. To the 'increased amazement' of his hearer, he turned the conversation, instead, 'to his works, to Lady Byron, and to his daughter'.[7] While in Ithaca, Byron was determined to dwell more upon the past than any serious plans for the future.

A perhaps surprising topic of conversation during those days was Sir Walter Scott and the 'Waverley' novels. Practically alone among the British literary establishment, Scott had earned Byron's consistent and ungrudging admiration, ever since the two had met at the home of their publisher, John Murray, in 1815. Scott had confessed to Byron his authorship of the *succès fou* of the previous year, the anonymously published novel *Waverley*. Byron had read almost every one of the series of historical novels that followed. A trunkful of them had travelled with him aboard the *Hercules* and would be remarked on by visitors to his house in Cephalonia a little later.[8] Now, on the cusp of his expedition into Greece, Byron kept reverting to the topics of 'Scotland, Walter Scott (or, as his lordship always called him), "Watty," the "Waverley Novels"'.[9] This was one of those occasions in his life when Byron chose to remember that he was 'half a Scot by birth, and bred / A whole one' – or, as he explained to Smith, apropos of some lines by Burns, 'that he too was more than half a Scotchman'.[10] The day before, he had discovered that Mrs Knox, their hostess at the Residency, was a Gordon, distantly related to his mother's Aberdeenshire family. 'The gallant Gordons "bruik nae slight"', he had teased Mrs Knox before the company, and been rewarded with a vigorous avowal that their guest had indeed been unjustly abused by the world.[11]

Perhaps this was more than nostalgia. The kinship between Scott's romantic historical novels and Byron's 'Turkish tales' has been recognised ever since they first began to be published. Scott's retrospect on the failed rebellion of his countrymen against Hanoverian rule in 1745, in *Waverley*, had not been intended as politically radical – quite the reverse. Nonetheless, the success of *Waverley* and its numerous sequels would lay the foundation for much of what has more recently passed for a national consciousness, not just of the Scots, but also of the English. The Scots had failed in 1745, and Byron probably still shared what had always been 'Watty's' view: that the failure of the Scottish cause had been the best thing for Great Britain and (therefore) for humanity. But might there, perhaps, be a role model for himself, in Edward Waverley? Scott's hero is a decent, aristocratic sort, of chivalrous instincts, a 'waverer' between his English loyalties and a desperate, 'romantic' cause – a character more resembling Byron's own, later, Don Juan than any of the 'byronic' heroes.[12] Now that Byron had come to Greece, determined 'to scribble [no] more nonsense',[13] he must have seen the parallels between his own situation and that of the very many leading characters in Scott's historical novels who tread a precarious path similar to Waverley's. It is even possible, during the months that followed, that rereading the Waverley novels really did help him decide which would be the right political path to tread between the modernisers and the warlords on the mainland.

Whatever the case, for at least some of the time in Ithaca, 'Lord Byron's spirits were buoyant and elastic; . . . he overflowed with an inexhaustible fund of anecdote, replete with brilliant wit and humour.'[14] In this frame of mind, his purpose in coming to Greece was all but forgotten. Smith was struck by his 'intention, expressed and implied, more than once, of paying a visit to Sir Walter in the then ensuing spring.'[15] In much the same spirit, while at anchor off Livorno, he had promised to visit Goethe in Weimar. In this mood, which would be noted by other observers, too, after his return to Cephalonia, Byron had clearly no thought that he might be on a one-way mission.[16]

But the violent mood swings, that Browne had noted aboard the *Hercules*, returned. Smith was shocked the morning after his first meeting with Byron:

I never saw and could not conceive the possibility of such a change in the appearance of a human being as had taken place since the previous night. He looked like a man under sentence of death, or returning from the funeral of all that he held dear on earth. His person seemed shrunk, his face was pale, and his eyes languid and fixed on the ground. He was leaning upon a stick.

Almost more shocking to Smith was the suddenness with which Byron recovered himself.[17] But worse was to come.

Saturday, 16 August began with Byron swimming off the quarantine station at Vathy, the island's capital. There followed a ride, in the August heat, across the island, to meet the boat that had been summoned to take them back to Sami, in Cephalonia. While waiting for the boat, Byron swam again. Trelawny challenged him to swim across the strait, a distance of some six miles. Byron refused the challenge, but still 'persisted, in despite of the entreaties of his medical attendant, in remaining a very considerable time in the water, exposed to the ardent rays of a very hot sun'.[18] Once the party had been conveyed across the water, a large meal was provided for them at the British military station at Agia Euphemia. After that, for a night's lodging they had a steep ride to a monastery, high above the village. It was dark before they got there. It was probably Byron who compared the setting to a scene in one of Scott's novels.[19] While the monks gathered inside to welcome their guests, Byron jumped down from his horse, outside the walls, and re-enacted the scene from *Hamlet* in which the hero throws himself into the open grave of Ophelia. From the depths of a stone sarcophagus, he intoned 'unconnected fragments' that Smith recognised as belonging to the episode of the play in which Hamlet muses upon the skull of the jester Yorick. A character not unlike Shakespeare's gravedigger provides the title for another novel by Scott, that Byron knew well, and that must have cropped up often in the conversations of the past days and hours, *Old Mortality*. Byron had come to grips with his old enemy at last.

What happened next has been much described. It had been a long day. Too much sun and too much swimming no doubt contributed, as those who witnessed it thought. Imbibing 'gin swizzle' while being rowed in an open boat in the midday heat, the day before, will not have helped. A severe blow to the head, while riding under a low branch in Ithaca, could perhaps have caused concussion. And there was fatigue – it was dark by the time they reached the monastery. The path was so steep that even Byron had been forced to dismount and cover part of the ascent on his lame foot. It is often said that at the monastery Byron had some kind of fit, a precursor, perhaps, of the 'convulsive' episode he would experience six months later in Missolonghi. But as with the dramatic change in his demeanour that had previously appalled Smith, there is no evidence that on this occasion there was anything physically the matter with him.[20]

Emerging from the sarcophagus and holding forth in a lively manner about productions of *Hamlet* that he had seen, Byron entered the monastery with the travellers. Almost immediately, while the servants were preparing their beds, he retired, not waiting to hear the lengthy speech of welcome that the abbot had begun to deliver over coffee. A few moments later, all hell broke loose. Dr Bruno came running in. His master had been seized by violent spasms, 'his brain was excited to dangerous excess, so that he would not tolerate the presence of any person in his room'. From the *sala*, the rest of the party, which must have included the abbot and the monks, 'could hear him rattling and ejaculating'. Trelawny, Browne, and Smith in turn went in to try to pacify him. Trelawny, years later, would describe a 'paroxysm of rage', accompanied by 'flashing eyes'. Browne adds that 'the paroxysm increased so as almost to divest him of reason'. Smith found him 'standing in a far corner like a hunted animal at bay', and then had a chair hurled at his head for his pains. Eventually, Bruno's 'blessed pills' had their effect and Byron slept, to awake composed and contrite in the morning.[21]

No doubt many factors contributed to Byron's extreme behaviour that night. But a clue to its deeper explanation is provided by Browne: 'like one possessed, he cried out, "my head is burning"'. Byron can have spoken of this to no one, because if he had, they would all have thought of it, and no one did. Neither, apparently, have his biographers, since. But in the boat back from Ithaca, he had been reminiscing about Shelley. And it had been on this day, one year ago, that Byron had swum far out to sea and been 'St Bartholomewed' by the sun, while on the beach Shelley's remains were being consumed by fire.[22]

'A FOOL'S ERRAND'

Next day, the seventeenth, the party was back aboard the *Hercules*, at anchor in the bay of Argostoli. None of the awaited letters from the mainland had arrived while they had been away. Used as he was to letters passing between Italy and England in a fortnight, Byron must have been fuming.

By modern standards, communications within revolutionary Greece were unimaginably slow. There was no postal service. Letters had to be carried on horseback over mountain passes and (in winter) flooded rivers, often for part of the journey also by sea. At every point there was a risk of interception – potentially by the enemy or, in Ionian waters, by the British, but more often by rival factions within Greece itself. Important letters were often copied several times and sent by more than one route. Couriers had to be found who were willing to face the hardships of the journey and could be trusted. For Byron, the return to Cephalonia marked the beginning of a period of intense frustration.

To readers today, and even to many of Byron's contemporaries, including some who were with him, the length of time he spent in Cephalonia has always seemed an inexplicable delay, a sign of wavering, or worse. This was true only during the weeks immediately following the expedition to

Ithaca, and there were very specific reasons for it. Thereafter, the twists and turns of the politics in which Byron would become involved would be dictated, very largely, by the time it took for messengers to cross to and from Cephalonia, and from one part of Greece to another. This part of the story was to be played out with inexorable slowness, interspersed by bursts of sudden activity. At the time, it could easily have seemed, and probably felt, like idleness. Not patient by nature, if he was going to enter the world of Greek politics, of which as yet he knew little, Byron was going to have to learn patience. And the remarkable thing is that he did.

Once letters did begin to arrive, the news they brought was anything but good. Byron's party had been back aboard the *Hercules* for at least a week, before his messenger returned from Missolonghi. With him he brought a courteous reply, dictated by Markos Botsaris from his camp in a small village near Karpenisi and translated into Italian. Almost alone among the warlords, Botsaris enjoyed the trust of Ignatios and Mavrokordatos, and seems to have been consistently loyal in return – no doubt because he was old enough to have known Ignatios during his years as Bishop of Arta, under the rule of Ali Pasha. But along with the letter came the news that three days after writing it Botsaris had been killed during a daring night raid on the enemy camp. This action, on 21 August, would be described by Finlay as 'one of the most brilliant exploits of the war'.[23] But the death of Botsaris deprived Byron, right at the beginning, of the only tenuous contact he yet had with the military forces engaged on the mainland.

It might have been from the same messenger – if not, it was very shortly afterwards – that Byron also heard the first, confused accounts of events at Tripolitsa, while he had been at sea. An early report even had Mavrokordatos killed. Writing just over a month later, by which time he still had received no direct communication from the Morea, Byron would sum up what he had learned at this time: 'that the Greeks are in a state of political dissention amongst themselves – that Mavrocordato was dismissed or had resigned (*L'Un vaut bien l'autre* [the one means much the same as the other]) and that Colocotroni with I know not what or whose party was paramount in the Morea'.[24]

His messenger from Corfu had no better news. Blaquiere had already left for England before the *Hercules* reached Cephalonia. So there had never been any chance of intercepting him. Blaquiere had left no letter to explain his conduct. Of the promised letters from Blaquiere's confidants close to the Greek government, Louriotis and Mavrokordatos, there was no sign either. To cap it all, Byron now discovered that a package addressed to him had arrived at Zante and was being held up there, for a reason that was never made clear. As the dog days of August lengthened, he came as close as he ever did to giving up the entire expedition.

There were other causes of frustration, too. The Ionian bankers to whom he presented his bills of exchange were unable or unwilling to meet his demands. At first, Byron schooled his temper with the supposition that 'Specie [cash] in these islands is nearly as scarce as on the Main.'[25] But he could never bear to think that he was being cheated. The exorbitant rates imposed by the merchant house of Dimitrios Koryalenias (Corgialegno) revived all his old rancour against the Jewish moneylenders in London who had exploited his desperate need for cash in student days. He and Gamba decided, arbitrarily, that 'Coriolanus' was a Jew. A text from St Paul, discovered in the course of religious conversations with Dr Kennedy, became the pretext for a tasteless outburst against all those in the island that Byron thought were determined to exploit him: '"*For there is no difference between a* JEW *and a* GREEK*"* [Romans 10:12]. I intend to preach from this text to Carridi and Corgialegno.' In conversation with Kennedy, concurring with the Apostle, he would add, 'the character of both is equally vile'.[26]

Even with his beloved Souliots the same story was repeated. No longer a colourful accessory with which to disembark in free Greece, the 'Zodiacs', as an intimidated Captain Scott had taken to calling them, had been caught out by Byron in 'various attempts at what I thought extortion'. His indulgence evaporated. By the end of August, with a slackening of the Turkish blockade, Byron determined to ship the Souliots to their homeland. Trelawny, increasingly restless after 'a month [spent] in idleness', thought he had Byron's agreement to go with them and see some action. As Trelawny explained matters to Mary Shelley, writing a week later: 'we seemed both to have taken our separate determination, his to return to Italy and mine to go forward with a tribe of Zuliotes to join a brother of Marco Bozzaris, at Missolonghi'.[27]

Byron's war could have ended then, in lassitude and frustration. But on 1 September the delayed package forwarded from Zante finally arrived. It contained a letter from Hobhouse (now lost) and another from Bowring, written while Byron had been at Livorno, on 22 July. With these were enclosed the minutes of a recent meeting of the London Greek Committee. There were also two letters from Blaquiere.[28]

From Bowring and Hobhouse, Byron learned that the Committee had resolved to use the money so far raised to send a ship to Greece carrying supplies, artillerymen, and 'artificers' with expertise in handling explosives. This was the first mention, although he is not yet named, of William Parry, the 'firemaster' who would become a controversial figure at Missolonghi. Bowring was obliged to acknowledge, as he announced these developments, that this was a retrenchment from the Committee's earlier plans. A few months before, it had been expected that Thomas Gordon of Cairness, the only Committee member who had actually taken part in the Revolution, would be returning to Greece to lead a military force on behalf of the Committee. Now it turned out that Gordon had had second thoughts. In the midst of all this, there was at last a role for Byron himself. In the minutes of the Committee's meeting on 7 July, he read:

Resolved – That Lord Byron be requested to become the agent for the application of the funds or supplies, which the Committee may send to Greece in conjunction with Capt Blaquiere.[29]

He will have groaned to see the name of Blaquiere. Later, in Missolonghi, when he heard Blaquiere called a 'humbug', he would pointedly make no comment.[30] It can only have been deeply galling to Byron to read, now, what Blaquiere had written to him from Ancona at the end of July, evidently hoping to forestall him before he left Genoa for Greece:

I believe I told your Lordship that such arrangements had been made for your reception, as were likely to prevent unpleasantness or delay. I need not say with how much satisfaction the event was looked forward to, but considering <as I now do>, that your presence either here or in England would be infinitely more beneficial to the cause, I must sincerely hope your resolution has been suspended.[31]

What was Byron to do? If another of those Highland Gordons, who 'bruik nae slight', had backed out of coming to fight for Greece, why should he do more? If even Blaquiere now thought Byron could better serve the cause by staying in Italy than he could in Greece, why go forward? Now that he had specific instructions from the Committee, all he was in honour bound to do was wait for their ship to arrive and oversee the handing over of its cargo to the Greeks. That done, he would be free to head back to Italy, and Teresa. It would be a waste of time, and probably demeaning too, to go any further towards a conflict where nobody, apparently, wanted him.

Within hours of receiving these letters, Byron devised a plan whose coherence has ever since been obscured beneath the bland loyalty of Gamba and the conflicted testimony of Trelawny. The *Hercules* was abandoned. The ship would soon be departing for England in any case, as the two months' lease would be up.[32] Having already refused the offer of hospitality from Napier, Byron turned to Delladecima instead. From the Count, he rented a two-storey house in the village of Metaxata, five miles from Argostoli in the south of the island.[33] It afforded peace and quiet, in a beautiful rustic setting, overlooking the approach by sea to Argostoli and with a long view over the straits to Zante.

The forty Souliots were sent on their way. With them, in a gesture as pointed as it was magnanimous, Byron sent medical supplies for the relief of their more deserving compatriots who had been wounded in the battle in which Botsaris had lost his life.[34] Trelawny, who had thought he would be accompanying them, suddenly found himself assigned a quite different role.

While the rest of the party prepared for the move to Metaxata, Trelawny and Browne were hastily briefed for a mission to the Greek Provisional Government, which was still believed to be at Tripolitsa.[35] In their later published accounts, both Trelawny and Browne give the impression that this expedition was *their* initiative, in response to what they saw as Byron's inactivity.[36] But the switch in destination from the mountains of Aitolia, where Kostas Botsaris was fighting, to the seat of government in the Morea, can only have been Byron's doing. Trelawny's letter to Leigh Hunt, written on 2 September, makes clear how quickly the plan had been formed, after the receipt of the letters the day before, and what its purpose was. At that point, Trelawny was expecting to leave for the Peloponnese the very next day 'to commune with the Government[,] and Lord Byron will await here for further instructions from the Committee and the Main[land]. He is resolved to proceed to the Main on the Greeks sending boats, &c., to convey him; in the meantime he makes this his headquarters.'[37]

When Trelawny and Browne left for Pyrgos, in an open boat, under cover of darkness, on the night of 6 September, they went as Byron's agents.[38] They had been given precise instructions. They carried at least one letter, perhaps several. One of Byron's first acts on moving into the house at Metaxata will have been to sit down and compose these letters. It was the first time that he had addressed the government of Greece directly. No such letter now exists. But as Byron informed Hobhouse shortly afterwards, he had 'written to apprize the Gk Government of the possible approach of the vessel indicated by the Committee – and to prepare them to receive it's Continents [*sic*]'.[39]

Also with Trelawny and Browne went an extract from Bowring's letter to Byron, for the benefit of the government, and a hastily scribbled list, in pencil, of eight numbered questions to which they were to seek answers on their travels.[40] Both in their tone and purpose, these questions are revealingly different from the ones that Byron had asked Count Delladecima to forward to the government only a month before. His new exasperation is palpable in question 6, which asks: 'The *actual* and effective power of the executive Government – *so called* at least – and how far it is respected & obliged to the people. – –' Crucially, this time, Byron asks for no advice or instructions for himself. He did, apparently, instruct Trelawny 'to express his intentions of devoting his fortune in their *cause*, &c'.[41] But this he could have done without coming any closer to Greece than he was already. Unlike his earlier declarations, first to Bowring from Genoa, and then made via Delladecima since arriving in Cephalonia, Byron does not place himself at the disposal of the Provisional Government, or commit himself to anything at all.

With Browne and Trelawny on their way, there was once again nothing to do but wait. During the days that followed, he brooded over the letters he had received. If the government in Greece were to respond positively, he was still prepared to follow his emissaries to the Peloponnese, as he had promised Trelawny. But there can have seemed little prospect of this happening. Byron began realistically to take stock.

On 9 September, he wrote to Napier, 'I believed myself on a fool's errand from the outset . . . I will at least linger on here or there till I see whether I *can* be of *any* service in *any* way', though he doubted that he could. This was not, he hastened to add, the same thing as giving up: 'I like the Cause at least and will stick by it while it is not degraded nor dishonoured.' But he could 'stick by it', honourably enough, without setting foot in independent Greece, just as others were doing.

To Teresa, all this time, he had rarely written more than a few lines scribbled on the end of Pierino's letters. Now he wrote more fulsomely and with something like his old warmth: 'I shall fulfil the object of my mission from the committee – and then probably return to Italy – for it does not seem likely that . . . I can be of use to them.' The same day, 11 September, he wrote more tersely to Hobhouse: 'I will endeavour to do my duty by the Committee and the Cause.'[42]

So much, and no more. In between writing these letters, he even started to think about poetry again. This was the moment, rather than later at Missolonghi, when Byron might most aptly have remembered the lines he had put into the mouth of the 'sad trimmer', the onstage bard in the third canto of *Don Juan*:

where art thou,
My country? On thy voiceless shore
The heroic lay is tuneless now —[43]

And it seems that he did, because on 10 September he echoed them at the start of a short fragment of verse, to which he gave the optimistic title, 'Aristomenes. Canto First'.

The Gods of old are silent on their shore
Since the great Pan expired . . . [44]

After this bold beginning the lines peter out in a rather trite lament for the passing of the ancient Hellenic world. It is a weaker version of the nostalgia for an irrecoverable heroic past that Byron had permitted himself in the lines from 1812 that later found their way into *The Siege of Corinth* and in the prologue to *The Giaour*, the following year.[45] The hero of the title does not appear in them. Hardly anyone had heard of Aristomenes of Messenia in 1823, any more than they have today. It seems that Byron's eye had been caught by a phrase in Pausanias' ancient guide to Greece, the book that had been in Hobhouse's hand on their travels together, that he had missed during the Diodati summer of 1816, and that had accompanied him ever since Hobhouse had brought it back to him in Switzerland. Aristomenes was an ancient hero who never made it. According to Pausanias, in the lost work of a forgotten ancient poet, 'Aristomenes is no less celebrated than Achilles in Homer's *Iliad*.' But he hardly deserved it, having lost his war to the superior Spartans. Byron, at this moment of despair on the edge of Greece, saw himself as a latter-day Aristomenes, not a latter-day Achilles. As the poem has it, 'the dream / Was beautiful'. It would have a been a beautiful thing he had dreamed of doing, in Greece. But it was over.

Maybe if the poem had taken wing, the expedition would have gone no further. 'Aristomenes' has had its modern defenders.[46] But it never progressed beyond those eleven lines. There was no going back to poetry. A clue buried in Byron's letter to Napier, written the day before the fragmentary poem, gives a better idea of where he now sensed that he was headed. After the confession that he may have been on a 'fool's errand' all along, he adds: 'and must therefore like Dogberry "spare no wisdom"'. Editors of the letters have recognised the allusion to the comic character in *Much Ado About Nothing*. But the quoted words come not from Shakespeare but from Walter Scott, who misquotes the play in exactly the same way in *Waverley*.[47] The context in the novel is the puzzlement of Scott's hero in his first, baffled attempt to approach and understand the Highland chiefs. Byron, during these September days, was still wavering.

Events would soon show that his first instincts had been right after all. Before his letter to Hobhouse could be despatched, aboard the departing *Hercules*, a 'very pressing' invitation arrived from Missolonghi, signed grandly, in Italian, by the 'Prefect General in Aetolia and Acarnania' – provinces that had not existed by those names since ancient times.[48] Then, on the evening of Thursday, 18 September, Count Delladecima rode out to Metaxata with a package that had just been delivered. Next day, probably at the Delladecima house in Argostoli, Byron met the man sent to do business with him on behalf of Mavrokordatos.[49]

A NATION – OR A FACTION?

Alexandros Mavrokordatos, in the summer and autumn of 1823, was very different from the 'turbaned friend' that the Shelleys had known in Pisa. It was not just that he dressed now in the western manner that had proved such a provocation to Kolokotronis (Plate 7a). Over the past two years, he had expended his considerable personal fortune for the cause. In Tripolitsa, he had been living on his meagre, and probably irregularly paid, salary as Secretary to the Executive. Blaquiere, earlier in the summer, had taken a Boy Scout's delight in sharing the privations of 'Mavrocordato himself stretched on the floor with nothing more than a great coat surrounded by his attendants in the same plight', and hoped that Byron would feel equally inspired.[50] Now, in Hydra, after the debacle with Kolokotronis in July, Mavrokordatos had no official position and no income.

His faithful friend and confidant, Georgios Praidis, painted a pitiful picture, that was clearly intended to touch the heart, as well as the pocket, of their shared mentor, Metropolitan Ignatios in Pisa: 'M is staying in Hydra in the utmost destitution, such as I cannot describe to you. Suffice it to say, that he is staying with Orlandos with a single servant while all the rest of our associates, having long ago sold everything we had, have dispersed hither and thither to make ends meet.'[51] The discomforts were perhaps only relative. Ioannis Orlandos was the brother-in-law of the richest man in Hydra. Orlandos had already been nominated by Mavrokordatos, while he had been in a position to do so, as one of the three deputies to be sent to London to seek a loan for the government. For the time being, that project was dead. But Mavrokordatos was clearly made welcome by the 'primates' of Hydra.

These people were the nearest to a middle class that Greece at the time possessed. They had grown rich from trade, carried on in the ships that, together with those of neighbouring Spetses and Psara across the Aegean, had become the backbone of a fledgling Greek navy since the start of hostilities. Mavrokordatos, with his European ways and modernising ideas, found common ground with these men and worked hard to exploit it.

The first thing he needed was money – not so much for his own comfort as to cut a convincing figure in the eyes of his new hosts. In the peculiar circumstances of the islands at this time, this meant paying the crews of the merchant ships that in time of war would double as a fighting force. Each ship was owned by its captain and crewed by men of the same social class who were bound to him by ties of mutual obligation. Risk was shared, as were the profits from trade or piracy.[52] Byron was by no means the only western volunteer to be shocked by these arrangements. But in Greece at this period there was nothing remotely comparable to the strict, military discipline familiar from western navies. If Byron and others found it incomprehensible that men supposed to be fighting for their country would refuse to put to sea without the guarantee of a cash reward, no more could a Greek seaman comprehend how his British counterpart could submit to the humiliation of being flogged.

So, to gain political credibility in his new surroundings, Mavrokordatos had to have resources. He also had to find a way to follow up the negotiations he had begun in the summer, using Blaquiere as his intermediary, with the British government. The most practical way to do this was to persuade the two government bodies, now precariously united in Salamis, to revive the mission to raise a loan in London. Above all, he needed to regain the political ground he had lost, and soon. From the moment when he had received the letter from Metropolitan Ignatios in Pisa, that had been carried part-way by Vitalis aboard the *Hercules*, announcing that Byron was on his way, it was clear to Mavrokordatos that the means to achieving all these aims now lay with Byron.

Mavrokordatos lost no time. He had been in Hydra for only two weeks himself. The letter from Delladecima, with information about the new arrivals in Cephalonia, and conveying Byron's questions for the government, had not yet reached him.[53] On 27 August, he briefed Praidis for a mission whose first (and, in the event, only) objective was to meet Byron in Cephalonia. Along with Praidis went a bag of diplomatically phrased letters addressed to Byron. Two of these were from Mavrokordatos himself. Another was from the 'Primates of Hydra', in florid language inviting him to their island. Louriotis, whom Byron had met with Blaquiere at Genoa, sent his formal respects. A fifth was from the young Spyridon Trikoupis, whose family was among the most prominent citizens of Missolonghi, and who later would deliver the eulogy over Byron's body. Much later still, Trikoupis would become the first Greek historian of the Revolution.[54]

Mavrokordatos had already written to Byron while he had been at Tripolitsa – evidently as an afterthought in the wake of his letters to more serious political figures in Britain. This letter had been given to Louriotis to deliver on his way to London with Orlandos and Zaimis, the other deputies for the loan. But with that expedition now indefinitely postponed, the letter was still in Hydra. Mavrokordatos now added it to the package, with a brief covering note to introduce Praidis, who could tell Byron more.

Where the earlier letter was effusive but very general in its thanks to the great man for the interest he has begun to take in Greek affairs, the second reflects the urgency of the new circumstances. Mavrokordatos now professed himself convinced, he wrote to Byron, that 'You have an essential contribution to make to the salvation of Greece.' The note concludes with a studied vagueness that Byron interpreted, correctly but with a touch of exasperation, as 'hinting that he should like to meet me there [in Hydra] or elsewhere'.[55] A preserved draft reveals that Mavrokordatos had hesitated whether to reveal his hopes of leaving Hydra with a fleet and coming to meet Byron in western Greece, before deciding not to risk it.[56]

Exactly what form Byron's 'contribution' was supposed to take is hardly spelled out in these letters. Mavrokordatos' longer letter of July gives most space to the financial needs of the Revolution, and Praidis' unwritten instructions seem primarily to have been to use all possible persuasion to raise cash from the distinguished visitor.[57] Neither of Mavrokordatos' first two letters to Byron contains any hint of the subtle geopolitical assessment of the potential for a British alliance that he had set out in his letters to Canning, or in his secret instructions to Louriotis and Orlandos for their mission. At this stage, Mavrokordatos was still looking to Byron as a source of revenue, not as a political ally.

That would change, but not immediately.

Before Praidis reached Argostoli, Byron was already well disposed towards Mavrokordatos. Napier thought highly of his abilities, and Delladecima, a fellow-aristocrat, approved his politics. Byron would not have forgotten, either, what Shelley, and perhaps also Mary, had told him about Mavrokordatos in Pisa. '[H]e is the only civilized person (*on dit* [it is said]) amongst the liberators', Byron wrote to Hobhouse on 11 September, clearly echoing these opinions, before he had yet received any communication from him.[58] Rumours arriving in Cephalonia were still contradictory.

Byron had been dismayed by the evidence that reached him of 'division' within the government and the increasing likelihood that Mavrokordatos had left office. Praidis, when he met Byron just over a week later, on 19 September, should have been pushing at an open door.

But something went badly wrong. Byron in his surviving correspondence and recorded conversations barely mentions Praidis, and seems not even to have troubled to remember his name correctly.[59] Immediately after that first meeting in Argostoli, Praidis reported back to his master a 'long conversation' with Byron. He had had an uphill struggle, he said, to mitigate the unfavourable impression created by the rumours from the Peloponnese. Many of them, he had been obliged to concede, were of course true. Byron listened, 'sullen' and 'moody'. Rousing himself, he declared that his mind was already made up: 'he was not going either to the Peloponnese, or any further than the Peloponnese' (meaning, to Salamis). 'Curtly', he refused to go to Hydra either.[60] This was a very recognisable Byron, to those who knew him. Temperamentally, he was more than capable of shooting the messenger.

For this particular task, the messenger had probably not been well chosen. Praidis was a teacher by education and background. Fiercely loyal to his master, he would remain one of the most indefatigable and biddable of the small band of intellectuals who had gravitated towards Mavrokordatos from the beginning and would serve as his staff officers throughout the Revolution. But Praidis had no aristocratic credentials to his name. He lacked the flair, or warmth, or sheer cheek that could have won Byron over. In a long life devoted to public service, Praidis would go on to fill a series of administrative posts in the Greek state, but never achieved political office, as most did who been active during the Revolution.[61] The meeting ended, from Praidis' point of view, on a slightly brighter note. Byron explained about the emissaries he had already sent to the government in the Peloponnese. He reserved his final answer until he had heard back from them.

Browne and Trelawny, at least at this early stage of their mission, were assiduous in following their master's orders. It had taken them three days on rough mountain roads, that Browne warned Byron would not be suitable for his horses, to reach Tripolitsa. They had found the town still in ruins, after the siege and destruction in 1821, and in the grip of an epidemic of typhus. Mavrokordatos, whom they had been expecting to meet, was of course not there, but they interviewed his 'officers' who remained. The only man of any influence left in Tripolitsa was Kolokotronis. Although they kept this detail from Byron, Kolokotronis effectively had them kidnapped and taken to attend him in his 'palace', where he was laid up with fever. They heard, in detail, the warlord's complaints against Mavrokordatos and his 'intrigues', and were greatly impressed by the force with which he delivered them, ill though he was. 'I trust sincerely', wrote Browne to Byron, 'that a reconciliation may be effected, but from the warmth evinced by Colocotroni, I fear that it will be difficult.' A final nail in Mavrokordatos' coffin, in the eyes of these English radical spirits, was his willingness, not denied by his own supporters, to see a foreign monarch installed eventually on the throne of Greece.

Both interviews were written up at length by Browne, with an even longer letter to Byron, on 13 September. The next day, Trelawny added a blunt message of his own, summing up the situation as both men saw it. One of the Souliots who had accompanied them was despatched at once to deliver the package to Byron in Argostoli. By the same messenger went hasty warnings for Praidis, from Mavrokordatos' men, alerting him to what had happened.[62]

In their summing-up, both Browne and Trelawny concluded that Mavrokordatos had overreached himself and as a result had lost not only office but also 'the confidence of the people of the Morea'. As there was no one in Tripolitsa with the authority to receive Byron's letter on behalf of the government, they had now to press on to Salamis. There, Kolokotronis had assured them, a summit meeting of the Legislative and Executive Bodies would shortly be convened. Arrangements would be made for Byron to attend if he wished. Apparently speaking on behalf of the Government, Kolokotronis further 'recommended the ship with the [London Greek] Committee stores to proceed to Napoli di Romania [Nafplio] – and placed at the disposal of the government'.[63] Byron was not to know that the 'Congress' in Salamis would never amount to more than the fractious and short-lived coexistence of the two governing bodies in the same place, and that Kolokotronis had no more intention than Mavrokordatos of going there himself.

By 21 September, two days after his meeting with Praidis, Byron had received these letters, hard on the heels of the ones from Hydra. His immediate response was to hand over both sets to Napier for an opinion. Napier's advice was categorical, but evidently not what Byron wanted to hear, either. To give his money to the Greeks would be disastrous, Napier warned him. 'Having done so they will pay no attention to a word you say.' The solution that Napier proposed was drastic. Byron should use the available money, instead, to raise a foreign force, seize Nafplio, and 'open the gates to all the people of Greece, but exclude all the warlike chiefs'.

The 'few enlightened men' in the country, such as Mavrokordatos and Trikoupis, would 'stick to you and support you'. 'This scheme', Napier conceded, 'may appear at first a wild one' – not least because he foresaw the likelihood 'of being assassinated by the warlike chiefs the moment they perceived what you were at'. On one point Napier was sound, although it seems he was unable to convince Byron of this immediately: 'it is evident', he added in a postscript, 'that Prince Mavrocordato dares not trust himself in the power of Colocotroni, and not at all that he has become really unpopular'.[64]

But Byron was not convinced. According to Praidis, these letters 'instead of encouraging him, made him more hostile'.[65] Six days later, Byron bundled up the whole package and sent it with a covering note to Hobhouse in London, to pass on to the Committee. His perplexity is palpable. He had been in Cephalonia for a month and a half, and no one on the mainland had taken the slightest interest (except for Botsaris, who had immediately afterwards got himself killed). Now, within the space of a week, he had received one invitation from Metaxas to cross over to Missolonghi, another from the Primates of Hydra, ambiguously backed by Mavrokordatos, and now, according to Browne and Trelawny, the Provisional Government wanted him to go to Salamis. As he summed it up, exasperated, 'No less than three parties . . . a few steps further and a civil war may ensue. – – On all sides they are . . . trying to enlist me as a partizan.'

The legitimacy of his actions had been paramount in Byron's mind from the start. This was what would differentiate his own foray into the world of action from that of so many of his fictional heroes, most recent among them the *Bounty* mutineer, Christian. To Hobhouse he spelt it out, as he would shortly do, regretfully, to Mavrokordatos too: 'I can recognize only the Greek Government – without reference to the *persons* who may compose it . . . [A]s a foreigner I have nothing to do with factions or private preferences of individuals.'[66] This quest for legitimacy must be the reason for one of the most surprising aspects of Byron's behaviour in Greece. Why was Byron, of all people, immune to the charisma of the 'warlike chiefs', to which Trelawny was at that very moment beginning to lose his heart, and whose spell would fall on so many of his close associates over the coming months? Men like Kolokotronis and Trelawny's future brother-in-law Odysseus Andritzou (later known as Androutsos) came straight out of Byron's own 'Turkish tales'. The very character of the 'byronic' hero owed his existence to the warlike traditions of the klefts, out of which these people had emerged in real life. But, having lived imaginatively with them through the years of his fame, Byron knew better than anyone how that kind of enterprise was bound to end. It is yet another indication of how far he had travelled. From the reckless lawlessness of his own fictional rebels Byron was now in full retreat. "[T]is the *cause* makes all', he had written, only six months ago, in *The Island*. How to explain *that* to the warring parties?

Praidis, probably through Delladecima, was pressing him for a reply to Mavrokordatos and the Hydriots. The bewildering 'mass of papers' went to Hobhouse on 27 September. Over the next three days, as he wrestled with the problem of how to respond, Byron tried to make sense of what had happened so far by writing it up in the form of a short-lived diary. It was one of the few moments in his life when he addressed no reader. The 'Journal in Cephalonia' is yet another testimony to Byron's newfound seriousness. It is more than likely that in these pages Byron was trying to explain himself to posterity. And what he wished posterity to know was that he had 'not come here to join a faction but a nation'.[67]

It was the concept of the nation, that essentially new and potent convergence between the collective identity of a people and the self-determination enjoyed by the governments of states, that must confer legitimacy on Byron's enterprise.

This decision now taken, it had to be conveyed to Mavrokordatos and the Primates who had invited him to Hydra. The letter to the Hydriots does not survive.[68] To Mavrokordatos he wrote on 1 October, with the help of Gamba, in courteous diplomatic Italian. He could not, he said, 'conceal his displeasure' at the extent of division among the Greeks, and warned that their hopes of raising a loan in London were bound to be dented by these reports. While things remained as they were, he declared, 'It is very likely that I may decide to remain here watching until a better opportunity is offered to me.' He did, though, hold out the prospect of a meeting, and offered to correspond 'with the frankest sincerity that is known to me and which you so much deserve'. The door was not quite closed.[69]

There matters rested for the next three weeks. Then, once again, everything happened at once. On 21 October, a Tuesday, Byron rode into Argostoli, intending to call on Colonel Duffie. Laconically, two days later, he apologised to the colonel: he had been 'detained by business until too late'.[70] The business will once again have taken place at the house of Count Delladecima. An agent of the Provisional Government had arrived from Salamis. With him came an invitation signed on behalf of the Executive Body and glowing reports of conditions there from Browne and Trelawny.

Anargyros Petrakis had been chosen and briefed for this mission by the Legislature more than a month ago, at the time when Byron's initial queries for the Government had reached Salamis.[71] But it was clear to Praidis, who was present when Byron opened the letters, that all was not well. The letter that Petrakis carried had been signed by the Executive, not the Legislature. In it, Byron was invited to present himself before the Provisional Government of Greece, which might by that time be either at Nafplio (in Kolokotronis' sphere of influence) or Salamis. Byron's generous offer to fund a corps of Souliots for the defence of Western Greece, made during his first week in Cephalonia, was politely refused. The supplies on their way from the London Greek Committee should be disembarked at Nafplio. This had been Kolokotronis' demand to Browne and Trelawny. To Praidis it was self-evident that this meant, 'into the hands of Kolokotronis'.[72]

Praidis drew his own conclusions. He spoke privately to Petrakis and got only 'evasive replies'. He was convinced that Browne and Trelawny had been cosseted and flattered by the Executive in Salamis 'until they described to him [Byron] the joys of the isle of the Blessed'.[73] Praidis' conclusion was shrewd and also substantially correct, as surviving documents and later events would show: 'one can conclude that the two Bodies are still at variance and suspect that the factional spirit [i.e., the opposing faction] is endeavouring to reap the benefit from his Lordship's resources'. Delladecima evidently saw this too. But Byron would not hear a word spoken against 'what he thinks the *Government* has written to him', backed by the reassuring accounts of Browne and Trelawny.[74] None of these letters survives, and neither Browne nor Trelawny would later elaborate on their reception at Salamis. But it was there that Trelawny first met the warlord Odysseus, to whom he would soon transfer his allegiance from Byron. The lost letters will have confirmed, and probably strengthened, the conclusion that both men had already begun to draw while at Tripolitsa, that legitimacy and popular opinion were now firmly on the side of Kolokotronis and the Executive.

Byron's own references to these letters at the time are cautious. 'Brown [*sic*] and Trelawny, having been better treated than others, probably give a much more favourable account than we have yet had, from other quarters', he wrote two days after receiving them. 'The Opposition [i.e., Delladecima and Praidis] say they [i.e., the Executive] want to cajole me – and the party in power say the others want to seduce me – so between the two I have a difficult part to play.'[75] Byron understood the situation better than Praidis supposed. But despite these misgivings, his mind was made up.

Before the day was out, Byron had detailed Constantin Skilitzy (Mavro-kordatos' relative who had been given a passage aboard the *Hercules*) to leave at once for Salamis. Skilitzy was to give notice to the government of Byron's imminent arrival there. Byron himself would make first for Nafplio, as the letter requested. As soon as Skilitzy could oversee the necessary arrangements and return to Pyrgos, the nearest point in the Peloponnese to Cephalonia, Byron would be on his way. He had been waiting only for this. Now, at last, he had instructions from a legitimately constituted body in Greece. The decision was taken on the instant, and no argument would change it.

Praidis was outraged. 'You know how vain the English are', he wrote the same day to Mavrokordatos,

with the result that what honest people could not persuade him to do, with all their efforts . . . he has been moved to do by those people's letters and even more, to cross to the Peloponnese and go to Salamis, something he wouldn't make up his mind to before, when he turned down the invitation to Hydra.[76]

Mavrokordatos' envoy now mobilised all the resources he could think of. To Andreas Zaimis, the primate of Kalavryta and an ally against Kolokotro-nis, he wrote a convoluted letter begging him to have Byron intercepted the moment he landed at Pyrgos. Zaimis himself must explain to him that the Executive that had written to him was in the hands of a fac-tion and did not truly represent the will of the Government. At the same time, Delladecima urged Mavrokordatos to find a way to return to office – for no other reason, it would seem, than to meet Byron's insistence on dealing only with a legitimate authority. At the very least, could not Mavrokordatos contrive to be in Salamis when Byron arrived? These let-ters were carried by the same Skilitzy who also carried Byron's reply to the Executive.[77]

It now looked as though Mavrokordatos' party had lost – not because Byron preferred the warlords, as he might well have done, but because the opponents of a centralised authority had, ironically, been more successful in presenting themselves *as* that authority. Preparations went ahead rapidly for Byron's journey, with Gamba and the rest of his party, to Nafplio and Salamis. By 6 November, it was known that they would be departing for Pyrgos 'within five days at the most'.[78]

Commentators at the time, and biographers since, have been misled by the sometimes languid tone of Byron's letters and conversation while he was in Cephalonia. The evidence from the Greek sources explodes the myth that he settled easily into his old indolent ways and was reluctant to move on. Byron was in reality desperate to move on, and committed himself to do so at the earliest opportunity that was compatible with his principles. The time for wavering was over. He was not an adventurer. He had not come here to strike a pose, for death or glory. He would go only at the behest of a legitimate Greek government. Not for a faction, but a nation.

CHAPTER 9

The new statesman

MAVROKORDATOS FIGHTS BACK

During the very days when Byron was preparing himself to embark for the Peloponnese, on the other side of Greece, on the island of Hydra, three things came together that would decisively alter the balance of political forces on the mainland. One was news of the worsening situation at Missolonghi. Another was the arrival of Byron's emissaries, Browne and Trelawny. Third was Byron's response to Mavrokordatos' first letters, which reached him hard on their heels.

Since the summer, the threat to Missolonghi had greatly increased. The pashas Omer Vryonis of Ioannina and Mustai of Skodra (today's Shkodër) had reached the outskirts of the town at the end of September. A sizeable army of Albanian Muslims, loyal to the Sultan, was now laying siege to the fortified island of Anatoliko nearby, with the support of a renewed naval blockade. If only the islanders of Hydra and Spetses could be persuaded to put to sea, Mavrokordatos would at once secure his own return to western Greece and a chance to repeat his strategic feat of the previous year, in defending Missolonghi.

This made the need for money more acute than ever. The impasse over the deputation to raise a loan from London still dragged on, as the Executive continued to block Mavrokordatos' nominees. The secret negotiations that Mavrokordatos had initiated in the summer, with political figures in Great Britain, depended on the trusted agents he had already briefed, Orlandos and Louriotis. So these, too, were in abeyance. Mavrokordatos has generally been credited with inexhaustible (if sometimes self-defeating) political energy, not least by those observers who thought this a vice. But his behaviour at this crucial point in his career makes one wonder if there was not something of the 'melancholy' temperament of the Romantic poet about this close associate of first the Shelleys and then Byron. Periods of frenetic and highly effective politicking seem to have alternated with intervals of lassitude and inactivity, as happened during those months in Hydra. If true, this guess about his temperament might help to explain why Mavrokordatos was never quite able to consolidate his most significant achievements – either in his association with Byron or later in a long political career.

Browne and Trelawny reached Hydra on 14 October and were put up in the house of Orlandos, where Mavrokordatos was also staying. Trelawny had conceived a strong dislike for the 'prince' before he even met him. Living under the same roof did nothing to change his mind. To Mary Shelley he wrote at length from Hydra, taking a not-disinterested delight in listing the failings of her former admirer from Pisa days. At the same time, the explosive, larger-than-life personality of 'Byron's jackal' seems to have had a tonic effect on his host. It may well have been Trelawny's own idea, as he would claim in the same letter, written before he left Hydra, to put Byron's professed generosity to the test. If money was urgently needed for a fleet to come to the defence of Missolonghi, then why not apply to Byron for a personal loan, repayable out of the much larger one to be raised in London? Trelawny cynically thought this would call his patron's bluff.[1] But Mavrokordatos was not to know that. And, in any case, Trelawny would be proved wrong.

It was at this point that Byron's letter came. Within days of receiving it, Mavrokordatos had swung into action, with a series of interlocking and far-reaching manoeuvres. On the twenty-first, a week after the arrival of Browne and Trelawny at Hydra, he replied to Byron. (This was the same day that Anargyros Petrakis reached Cephalonia, and Byron committed himself to going to the Peloponnese.) The tone of Mavrokordatos' reply is as courteous as before. But this time he matches Byron's offer of a frank exchange between intellectual and social equals. The reason he had resigned from the government, he explains, had nothing to do with any factional interest, as Byron had implied. He had done it precisely so as to avoid greater dissent:

No one is more assured than I, that you have come with the firm intention of aiding Greece: this Greece is already before you, under your eyes, you can see at a glance which is the part of the country endangered, that Missolonghi is blockaded by sea and besieged by land; that the town is short of provisions, and sure to fall to the Turks ... To bring aid to this place, to save it, to save in consequence the whole of Greece, is that to declare oneself for a faction? I do not think so.[2]

Mavrokordatos was not so tactless as to spell out the manner in which he and his new English friends hoped that Byron would 'save' Missolonghi.

It was left to the Legislature in Salamis to mention money, and to name a sum. But the sum *was* named, in a draft in Mavrokordatos' handwriting of a letter to be sent over the signatures of the Primates of Hydra to the Legislative Body in Salamis. That body was requested to make a formal approach to Byron for an advance of 30,000 dollars, the equivalent of 6,000 pounds sterling, repayable out of the loan to be raised in London. This would cover part of the needs of the fleet, the rest to be made up from friendly sources nearer home, for the immediate and urgent defence of Missolonghi.[3] The letter is to be written in Greek, 'which language his Lordship understands perfectly'. The exaggeration can only be due to Browne or Trelawny. But it was a deft diplomatic touch.[4] Not content with that, Mavrokordatos arranged for a similar request on behalf of the Primates to be conveyed to his political rivals, the Executive in Nafplio. That body obliged, one supposes through gritted teeth, since the Executive, too, wanted the money, but not for this purpose. The application by the Executive to Byron for the same sum, 30,000 dollars, signed by its President, Petrobey Mavromichalis, with the names of the other Executive members following, is the only surviving document addressed to Byron that bears the name of Kolokotronis.[5]

At the same time, and again using the Primates as his proxy, Mavrokordatos was finally able to persuade the Legislature to authorise the immediate departure of his chosen deputies for the loan from London. After all, Byron could hardly be expected to offer his own money up front, without at least the prospect of collateral from the much larger sum to be raised in England. In a brilliant piece of strategy, the Legislative was further to charge Orlandos and Louriotis with calling in at Cephalonia on their way to London, to put the request on behalf of the government to Byron in person. In this way the two loans would be inextricably linked, both contractually and in public perception. The smaller loan was to be repaid out of the larger, and the individuals responsible for negotiating both were Mavrokordatos' men.

The keystone of Mavrokordatos' strategy was an official position for himself. On 26 October, the Legislative Body signed the decree instructing Mavrokordatos to proceed to Missolonghi with the fleet. No official title went with this new role, an omission that would lead to trouble later. But, in the eyes of the Legislature, Mavrokordatos was still its President. A second letter addressed to Byron, dated 27 October, spelt this out, and would thereby resolve the issue of legitimacy that had deterred him from cooperating with Mavrokordatos in the first place. But this second letter would travel with Mavrokordatos to Missolonghi and would not reach

Byron until the eve of his departure from Cephalonia, by which time he would no longer need its reassurance.[6]

Louriotis and Orlandos left Hydra on 29 October. The third deputy, Ioannis Zaimis, who had also been nominated by Mavrokordatos, would join them later. With them went the secret orders that Mavrokordatos had drawn up for them in July. As an added insurance for Byron's compliance, they were accompanied by Browne, who had now come over to Mavrokordatos' and the Primates' position.[7] (This was when Trelawny cut loose, and went off to Athens with the warlord Odysseus Andritzou.) Kolokotronis and the Executive had been comprehensively outmanoeuvred. Disgusted, and having no further use for the appearance of legitimacy it gave him, Kolokotronis resigned his position as Vice-President of the Executive, the more freely to embark upon an open campaign against the Legislature.[8] Once again, a political step forward by the modernisers was about to raise the stakes still higher in the simmering civil conflict.

The deputies, with Browne, reached Pyrgos on 6 November. There they learned that Byron was expected to arrive in a matter of days, on his way to Nafplio. There was a local argument in progress about who should receive him and take care of the next stage of his journey. Louriotis and Orlandos knew how much was stake. If Byron were once to disembark at Pyrgos, any money he advanced in response to the appeal by the two government bodies would end up in the hands of the Executive. So, instead of recovering from the rigours of their overland journey as they had planned, and drying out their clothes and possessions that had been soaked by the rains in the mountains, they pressed on at once to Argostoli, to forestall Byron's departure.[9]

Anyone entering the United States of the Ionian Islands from the Ottoman empire was required to spend a statutory period of twenty-one days in quarantine. Byron visited the new-arrivals in the offshore lazaretto on Wednesday, 8 November. During the next few days the number of visitors and the flurry of business they conducted must have alarmed the health authorities, whose vigilance even Napier would have been powerless to overrule. Byron was there every day, talking over their mission with the deputies, showering them with advice about how to proceed with their mission in London. Before they left, he would give them several personal letters of introduction to take with them. He was also, he assured them, anxious to meet Mavrokordatos in person.

At their first meeting, Byron was apparently willing 'to give the full amount of 30 thousand dollars'. But the deputies stayed long enough in the lazaretto, and met Byron enough times, to observe the 'instability and fickleness of his character'. 'His noble lordship', Orlandos concluded, 'is a philhellene' and 'perhaps himself wishes to benefit Greece, but others have influence over his will'.[10] The 'others' in this case can only have been Napier. Although a strong supporter of Mavrokordatos, Napier was as resolute as ever against giving any money into the hands of the Greeks.[11] At their second or third meeting in the lazaretto, Byron haggled the sum down from 30,000 to 20,000 dollars, the equivalent of 4,000 pounds.

The documents were formally witnessed by James Hamilton Browne, Pietro Gamba, and Demetrio Delladecima.[12] Byron had made over a considerable sum from his personal fortune, as requested by the Provisional Government of Greece, 'for the sole purpose of providing prompt assistance for the needs of western Greece'. At a stroke he had proved wrong the cynical speculations of Trelawny, and perhaps others. As cash was scarce in the islands and the Corgialegno brothers with whom he had so far done business courteous but extortionate, Byron determined to send Browne to Malta to raise the money. This meant a delay of about a month, as Browne's quarantine still had a fortnight to run, and the voyage would take a week in each direction.[13] In the meantime, Byron would try to find a quicker way of cashing his bills – as eventually he did. But until the money was in his hands he would have to put off all thought of moving to the Peloponnese. This, too, was a victory for Mavrokordatos and his agents.

SHELLEY'S GHOST

All that he was now learning of the true magnitude of the political crisis in Greece did nothing to improve Byron's estimation of the people he had come here to help. After he had sent off his first letters to Mavrokordatos and the Primates of Hydra, at the beginning of October, and before Petrakis arrived with his invitation from the Government, he still doubted whether there was any good he *could* do. 'I was a fool to come here but being here I must see what is to be done', he wrote to Teresa on 7 October. A few days later, to his half-sister Augusta, who had put him on the spot by asking why he had come 'up amongst the Greeks', he was blandly evasive: 'it was stated to me that my so doing might tend to their advantage in some measure in their present struggle for independence . . . How far this may be realized I cannot pretend to anticipate – but I am willing to do what I can.' Pietro Gamba, answering the same question from *his* sister, Teresa, was more patient: 'the Greek situation has not yet given us any opportunity in which one could believe B's help to be truly efficacious and useful', he explained on 8 October. 'Byron has confirmed his original opinion of these people, but has not therefore changed his intentions.'[14]

Teresa would have been in no doubt as to what that opinion was. She would have heard him say the same things that had shocked Lady Blessington in Genoa. 'The worst of them is – that . . . they are such d—d liars', he expostulated in the privacy of his diary at the end of September; 'there never was such an incapacity for veracity shown since Eve lived in Paradise'. A couple of months later he told the newly arrived Dr Millingen: 'The Greeks are perhaps the most depraved and degraded people under the sun uniting to their original vices both those of their oppressors, and those inherent in slaves.'[15]

Two incidents are revealing of Byron's response to living among Greeks in day-to-day situations. In October, not far from Metaxata, there was a landslip on one of the roads that was being built by Napier's *corvée*. A dozen workers, conscripted from the nearby villages, were buried. Alerted by Napier, who had been summoned from Argostoli, Byron at once rode to the scene. With him went Gamba, Dr Bruno, and Fletcher. There they found a large crowd gathered, including the wives and children of the stricken men. Some had been dug out of the landslip alive. Others might still be trapped, nobody seemed to know. But the men declared it would be too dangerous to dig any further into the unstable earth. According to one eyewitness, Byron at this point 'ordered his valet to get off his horse and thrash them soundly, if they did not immediately commence their work'. Not content with that, 'enraged', he then 'seized a spade himself, and began to work as hard as he could'.[16] The witnesses all dwell on the well-known traits of Byron's character on display in this behaviour: his instinctive philanthropy and propensity towards impulsive action. But more significant is his comment immediately afterwards:

he said that he came out to the Islands prejudiced against Sir T. Maitland's tight government of the Greeks, 'but I have now changed my opinion. They are such barbarians, that if I had the government of them, I would pave these very roads with them.'[17]

Later, towards the end of November, Byron received visitors from the mainland at Metaxata. Notis Botsaris, the uncle of Markos who had been killed in August, and his young son were accompanied by Delladecima, who interpreted for them. Dr Kennedy, who was present, noticed that Byron spoke only two words of Greek during the whole of the afternoon – at the beginning, when he invited the visitors to sit down. The uncle, later a hero in his own right, after the part he would play in leading the Exodus from besieged Missolonghi, two years after Byron's death, cut a fine figure, 'richly dressed' in the traditional kilt and capote of the Souliots. Byron may have looked tenderly on the son, 'a smart-looking boy of fourteen', who on his father's orders was banished to the kitchen and the care of Fletcher. As the visitors prepared to leave, the elder Botsaris drew himself up and delivered a dignified speech of thanks for all that Byron was doing in the 'sacred cause' of Greece. Byron responded more briefly in the same style. But while Delladecima was interpreting his words for Botsaris, and good manners would have dictated that he should continue to give all his attention to the person addressed, Byron turned aside to Kennedy and said: 'These Greeks are excellent flatterers. I do not believe they care one farthing about me personally, though they would be very glad to get my money.'[18]

Reading Byron's letters from Cephalonia, and the narratives of those who were with him, it is hard to escape the conclusion drawn by Iris Origo in a different context: 'when, in 1823, he turned his back on "poeshie", he had come to an end, at the same time, of the stuff of which a large part of poetry is made: human tenderness, passion, attachment'.[19] Origo was referring to the change in his relationship with Teresa after his departure from Genoa. But the insight is equally applicable to Byron's whole life while he was in Cephalonia. The young doctor, Julius Millingen, probably understood best what was going on: 'Divesting himself of every preconceived opinion, he calmly sought to discover, amidst so many contradictory and unfavourable statements, the path that would best lead him to the attainment of his wish, which was the welfare of his newly-adopted country.'[20]

Byron would have remembered, even if he seems never to have quoted them directly, the words spoken by Othello shortly before he murders Desdemona: 'It is the cause, it is the cause, my soul.' His own heart must be no less hardened. As he reiterated for the benefit of Hobhouse on 6 October, underlining the word and insisting on the capital letter he had first given it in Genoa, he was determined 'to serve the *Cause* if the patriots will permit me – but it must be *the Cause* – and not individuals or *parties*'.[21]

The Greeks themselves ('patriots', 'individuals or *parties*') had become just another of the many obstacles standing in the way of the 'Cause'. And what *was* this 'Cause'? Nothing less, as Byron expressed it in conversation with Millingen, than the 'regeneration of a nation'.[22]

Hand in hand with the clear-sighted, even ruthless, forging of this new political Byron, went something darker and more introverted. The poet within him had not entirely been extinguished. In Cephalonia, Byron continued to think of Shelley, who he declared on at least one occasion should have been with him on this expedition, and whose example and early death had spurred him to it. In the earnest young medical officer, James Kennedy, he saw a physical resemblance to his dead friend. It was perhaps for that reason that he submitted good-naturedly, though not uncritically, to being proselytised by this devout adherent of the Church of Scotland, just as he had once responded to the barrage of Shelley's metaphysical atheism. Kennedy knew of Shelley, without of course having read anything he had written, and would hear nothing good about him. It was one of the few categorical disagreements they had.[23] Then, when the thirty-one-year-old George Finlay arrived at Metaxata, fresh from studying law in Germany, during the last week of October, Byron experienced a profound shock.

Finlay had been born and brought up in Glasgow, in the same strict traditions of Scottish Presbyterianism as Byron in his early years. Finlay's rational scepticism, the inheritance of the Scottish Enlightenment, evidently appealed at once to Byron, and shines through the seven volumes of Greek history, from the Roman empire down to his own time, that would become his life's work. He had come to Greece to observe, rather than to fight, as he would explain many years later.[24] After the Revolution, Finlay would make his home in Athens. In the course of a long life, he would keep the secrets of Byron's last months better than anyone else who had shared them. In some respects a parody of the 'canny' Scot, Finlay would later have a bookplate engraved with his personal motto: 'I'll be wary.' The American philhellene Samuel Gridley Howe summed up their acquaintance during the Revolution:

He is a fine fellow and conceals under the air of a man of the world and partly of a misanthrope, a kind heart and delicate feelings. Most people think him cold-blooded, sarcastic and selfish and I once thought so, but he is not. He despises affectation or parade of feelings, but possesses it in reality.[25]

This was the man who arrived, on that late-October morning, at Metaxata to find himself 'fixed' with an 'anxious stare'. Byron, as Finlay later remembered, then 'sat down upon the sofa, still examining me; I felt the reception more poetical than agreeable: but he immediately commenced his fascinating conversation'. It was not until some days later that Finlay learned the cause of this strange reception. 'The next time we met was out riding. Lord Byron told me he had been struck at first by my resemblance to Shelley. "I thought you were Shelley's ghost," were his words.'[26] 'Shelley', Byron went on, evidently warming to this theme, now that the initial shock was beginning to wear off, 'was really a most extraordinary genius', even if he *had* been 'quite mad with his metaphysics'.[27]

A few days later, Kennedy and a fellow-officer called at Metaxata. They were on their way to minister to some of the injured workmen from the road-building accident, and probably hoping to be invited for lunch. Byron was in hospitable mood, so they joined the party, which included Finlay. The conversation, according to Kennedy, was at first 'very general and only desultory'. But soon the earnest young Presbyterian found something to interest him after all. Byron, as Finlay later recalled, 'asked the Doctor [Kennedy] if he believed in ghosts'. Jumping up from the table, he fetched 'his sister's Bible' and from it 'read the account of the appearance of Samuel's spirit' to Saul, conjured up by the Witch of Endor. It was, according to Byron, 'the finest and most finished witch-scene that ever was written or conceived . . . It beats all the ghost-scenes I ever read.' Years before, Byron had made it the subject of one of his 'Hebrew Melodies'.[28]

Now, the Old Testament story that he read to the company had a terrible resonance with his own situation. Saul, the ancient king of Israel, had forfeited the Lord's pleasure and was beyond forgiveness. Saul's situation was exactly what Lady Byron, when many years later she read Kennedy's book, would be prompted to suggest had been her husband's: 'he who thinks his transgressions beyond forgiveness (and such was his own deepest feeling) has righteousness beyond that of the self-satisfied sinner'. Saul's sin had been an act of mercy. This was why, in the course of the same conversation, Byron teased Kennedy by asking him to elucidate a passage in one of the religious tracts he had lent him, 'that in our best actions we sin'. Byron was thinking of himself as Saul, who in the passage he read aloud learns from the ghost that his punishment is upon him: next day, he will die in battle against his people's enemies. It is easy to see how Byron could think of the apparition of Shelley, on the eve of what could well turn out to be his own final battle, in the guise of George Finlay.[29]

The macabre theme continued: 'Lord Byron had some jokes against Dr. Bruno, whom he laughed at for having said that the head of a man will dance on the ground, after it has been separated from the body.'[30] Kennedy would not have recognised this, but Byron was reliving the ghostly conversations of the Villa Diodati, in which the recently publicised theories of galvanism and electricity had been discussed as the key to creating life. Finlay's arrival and chance resemblance to his dead friend had brought all this, too, vividly back. In Diodati days and after, Byron had thought that to revive Greece would be as dangerous, perhaps as deadly, an enterprise as the one undertaken by Victor Frankenstein in Mary's story.

Now, as he prepared to leave Cephalonia in November 1823, he had been reminded of a deeper reason why he had come. The 'regeneration' of a nation was to be the work of a new Prometheus – a project as daring and as transgressive against the established order of things as anything the old Prometheus had done in mythology, or Mary Shelley's 'modern' one in her fable. Prometheus had been punished by Zeus, Saul by the God of the Israelites, Frankenstein by Nature itself – implacable, irresistible forces all. Byron could not say he had not been warned.

Cornered by Kennedy, he would concede, in one of their *Conversations*, 'there is a chain which binds us all, high and low, and our inclination and will must bend to the circumstances of our situation'.[31] Beneath the surface, it must have seemed to Byron that the implacable destiny of the 'byronic' hero was running parallel to his every attempt to confound it, in Greece.

TAKING SIDES

By the time the contract for the loan was signed, Napier was becoming apprehensive that so much philhellenic activity on his watch was starting to attract unwelcome attention from his superiors in Corfu. Two days after the signing, on 15 November, and despite atrocious weather, he hustled the deputies off on the next stage of their journey, to complete their quarantine in Corfu. The Greek boat that had brought them from Pyrgos was sent back. With it went Finlay, a group of newly arrived German volunteers, and the envoy Anargyros Petrakis, who had brought the invitation to Byron.[32]

But still the philhellenes kept arriving. Julius Millingen, newly qualified as a doctor, with his assistant Tindall, landed at Assos in the north of the island and reached Argostoli on the eleventh. Both had travelled under the auspices of the London Greek Committee, and were counting on being paid for their services, as they had no other means of support.[33] Then, on 22 November, came the most high-ranking, after Byron, of all the Committee's members who were prepared to risk their lives in Greece. This was Colonel Leicester Stanhope, who brought with him a cargo of supplies for Greece, including a printing press. The 'typographical colonel', as Byron would later dub him when their relations became strained at Missolonghi, had seen service in India. Sincere and ardent liberal though he was, Stanhope could never see the Greeks as anything other than 'natives', to be treated as recalcitrant children, according to the prejudices then prevailing in the colonial service. Stanhope's liberalism was apt to be doctrinaire, and he had recently fallen under the spell of Jeremy Bentham. At first,

Byron was disposed to humour Stanhope's naivety. Undoubtedly, too, he was encouraged to have at his side 'a member of one of the oldest and most noble families of the British Empire' – as he rather quaintly wrote to introduce his new friend to the warlords of the Peloponnese.[34]

Not even these new arrivals, sent by the London Committee, were encouraged to linger. Napier made an exception only for Byron and his immediate entourage. Millingen stayed just long enough to volunteer to join the Greek fleet when it arrived at Missolonghi. Stanhope would be despatched after a fortnight as Byron's emissary to the Greek government, which was now supposed to be at Nafplio. Napier's policy in this was motivated by more than caution. By this time, the philhellenic fever that swept through the small world of Argostoli and Metaxata that autumn had even the official representative of His Majesty's Government in its grip. Napier himself had just been granted leave to travel to London. His superiors in Corfu were not to know that his purpose there was to offer his services to the Greek Committee as Commander-in-Chief of the Greek revolutionary forces. In this scheme Napier had the enthusiastic backing of Byron.[35]

While all this was going on, Byron's two prime concerns were to follow up the intelligence that Orlandos, Louriotis, and Browne had brought from the mainland and to get his bills of exchange cashed as quickly as possible. On the day the deputies left, 15 November, Gamba wrote on his behalf to ask for information from Count Skilitzy, who had gone ahead to forewarn the government of his intended arrival. In a long reply, Skilitzy more than repaid the debt he owed for his passage aboard the *Hercules*. Writing from Pyrgos on the twenty-second, Skilitzy urged his '*cher ami*' to do all he could to dissuade Byron from coming to the Peloponnese. Conditions there were already very different from what Browne had apparently described (in a letter from Salamis that does not survive). The two government bodies, Gamba was now to tell Byron, had left that island and were attempting to face one another down from the neighbouring fortresses of Nafplio and Argos in the Peloponnese. 'This would not matter if they were separated only by distance', added Skilitzy, 'but in their interests and their opinions they are as much enemies the one to the other as the Turks to the Greeks.'

Harold Nicolson, who published the greater part of this letter, found Skilitzy's analysis 'both involved and unconvincing'. But every detail is fully borne out by the Greek sources. 'I announce to you', wrote Skilitzy, 'that there is a civil war.' Indeed, in the western Peloponnese, the region from which Skilitzy was writing, the first armed skirmishes had already taken place. Byron would have been less than impressed to learn, from a postscript not reproduced by Nicolson, that the President of the Executive, Petrobey Mavromichalis, wanted to borrow 100,000 dollars from him on his own account.[36] This was the equivalent of 20,000 pounds, five times the amount of the loan that had just been concluded to pay for the fleet.

By the end of the month, Byron's information was for the first time as up-to-date as it was possible to be from the distance of Cephalonia. Mixed with the bad was some good. On 7 November, the surrender of the Turkish garrison that had been holding out in the fortress of Acrocorinth had been accepted on behalf of the government by Kolokotronis. News of a naval success in the eastern Aegean back in September had slowly found its way to Cephalonia. All of this Byron reported to Bowring for the London Greek Committee on 29 November.[37]

By this time, Byron had made the acquaintance of a British merchant in Argostoli, Charles Hancock. Hancock's business partner in Zante, Samuel Barff, was offering to make the financial transaction there. This would save time. But until he had the money in his hands Byron could still not think of leaving Cephalonia. This was the moment for Stanhope to set out in his stead, carrying a letter to be delivered, in copies, to the two opposed government bodies. After delivering these to Argos and Nafplio, the Colonel was to take a second letter to Mavrokordatos in Hydra, should he still be there. Informed as he now was about the political situation, and with definite news to impart about the arrival of the funds he was himself contributing to the cause, Byron was ready once again to address the highest authorities in revolutionary Greece.

On the last day of November, he wrote, in Italian, to the 'Governo Greco'. It was a diplomatic pretence that such a thing existed. But, beyond that nicety, Byron did not mince his words. He lambasted the 'rumours of new dissensions in the Greek Government, or rather of the start of a civil war'. As he had done before, in his first letter to Mavrokordatos, he warned sternly that anything of the sort would have disastrous consequences for the fortunes of Greece. Any hopes of raising loans abroad would be cancelled out. For the first time, Byron also showed that he had begun to think in terms that today would be called geopolitical:

the great Powers of Europe, of which none was an enemy of Greece, and which seemed favourably inclined to agree with the establishment of an independent Greek state, will be persuaded that the Greeks are not capable of governing themselves and will arrange some means for putting an end to your disorder which will cut short all your most noble hopes[.][38]

This was rather to exaggerate the benevolence of the Powers of the day, as the author of *The Age of Bronze* perfectly well knew. But Byron had learnt a great deal since writing that intemperate poem, and had really begun to believe that his own country, at least, might come round. To Mavrokordatos he wrote more briefly, two days later. In this letter, the voice rings out, even more clearly, of the statesman that Byron was in the process of becoming. Greece, he wrote, must now choose one of three possible courses: 'either to win her liberty – or to become a dependency of the European sovereigns or a Turkish Province . . . But civil war cannot lead to anything but the last two.' As an example of the second, Byron cited Italy, effectively under Austrian control; of the third, Wallachia and the Crimea. 'But if Greece wishes to become for ever free, truly Independent[,] it is advisable to determine this now or there will be no more time – never again –.'[39]

Evidently Byron had discussed with Delladecima and Praidis what he was going to say in these letters. The latter may have even been employed to copy or translate them. The Count was thoroughly alarmed that the Greeks risked losing their noble benefactor altogether, unless their dissensions ceased immediately.[40] This was undoubtedly the message that Byron wished to convey. But Praidis had caught a different tone:

His Lordship's letter is written in such a way as to make one suppose that it is now his purpose to come to the aid of Greece, not *once he has seen in place* a Government and laws that are respected, but *in order to* secure the position of the Government and respect for its laws, and in that case you can imagine which side he must come down on [emphases added].[41]

The distinction may seem a small one, particularly when couched in Praidis' rather scholastic style. What Praidis was saying was that a viable government and respect for the law were no longer necessary preconditions for Byron to act. Now, he would be prepared to act in order to bring these conditions about.

Byron would never abandon his determination to 'mitigate or extinguish' the internal divisions among the Greeks, as he had expressed it to Bowring on 29 November. But there was more than one way to achieve this. Back in October, his emissaries had reported to him from Tripolitsa the opinion of Mavrokordatos' representatives that they had met there: 'They hope that Lord Byron will act in the differences between the Prince and Colocotroni not as a simple mediator, but in a decisive manner "avec une main de fer" [with a hand of iron] was the expression, as they are convinced the former character would be useless.'[42] Napier thought the same. Orlandos and

Louriotis, in the lazaretto, seem to have been more persuasive advocates than the dogged Praidis. As Byron confessed to Bowring on 7 December, three days after Praidis had reported to Mavrokordatos: 'there is not only dissention in the Morea but *civil war* – by the latest accounts, to what extent we do not yet know . . . Had I *gone sooner they would have forced me into one party or the other* – and I doubt as much now.'⁴³ This was the hardest of all the lessons that he had to learn during his time in Cephalonia: that if he really wanted to benefit what he called the 'Cause', he could not do it by trying to be even-handed or simply to mediate among the factions. Byron's political conception, now that he had one, as Praidis correctly divined, was in all essentials that of Mavrokordatos.⁴⁴

Even as Byron still talked of going to the Peloponnese, the logic of his new position was fast making this impossible. In his letter to the government he confessed frankly, 'I cannot see how my presence in the Morea might be of benefit in the present state of affairs.' With Mavrokordatos and the fleet heading for Missolonghi, where his own money would shortly be needed to pay for it, it could be only a matter of time.

Mavrokordatos went aboard the corvette *Athena* off Hydra on the evening of Sunday, 30 November, the same day that Byron wrote his letter to the Greek government. Two days later, after a rendezvous at sea, eight warships and two fire ships from Hydra, with six more ships from Spetses, under the overall command of Admiral Miaoulis, set out to round the southern tip of Greece and reach Missolonghi.⁴⁵

At exactly the same time, during the first week of December, all the Ottoman land forces were suddenly withdrawn from the vicinity of Misso-longhi and Anatoliko, and the naval squadron based at Patras was cut back to a token presence. It had taken so long for the Greek fleet to put to sea that by the time it did, in the eyes of most observers at the time and ever since, there was no longer any need for it. So thought Byron, for one. As he sardonically observed, on 7 December, while news of the Greek ships' arrival was still awaited in Cephalonia: 'By the special Providence of the Deity the Mussulmans were seized with a Panic and fled – but no thanks to the fleet which ought to have been here months ago[.]'⁴⁶

No more convincing reason has ever been put forward for the coordi-nated tactical retreat by the pashas of Ioannina and Skodra on land and the greater part of the naval force at Patras. Had the Turks and Albanians chosen to confront the Greek fleet in the Gulf and oppose a landing at Mis-solonghi, a significant engagement could have resulted, with consequences for the whole of the rest of the war. That this did not happen may well have been the result of what a later age would have termed effective propaganda.

Rumours of a force on its way, manned by the much-feared seafarers of the islands, and supplied by the incalculable resources of a foreign milord – all no doubt much magnified in the telling – would certainly have had time to cross the water and circulate among the troops. With no reinforcements from Constantinople in prospect, and no sign of a concerted response from the Ottoman high command, the local pashas may well have decided to cut their losses. If this was so, then Byron's loan that launched the ships was his single, but not inconsiderable, contribution to the *military* course of the Revolution.[47]

The withdrawal of enemy forces, though, did lend a sense of anticlimax to the arrival of the fleet. The ships entered the lagoon of Missolonghi on Thursday, 11 December. The day before, an action had been fought off the island of Ithaca that Byron at first thought, when he heard of it, 'will make a very good *puff* – and be of some advantage besides'. He had written too soon. The Greeks, he would discover before long, had infringed the neutrality of the British protectorate, and with horrific violence too. His own diplomatic skills would be called into play to deal with the consequences. And the seizure of a large bounty in cash from the stricken Turkish vessel would prove an even more serious cause of contention.[48]

Still, Mavrokordatos was now a short distance away at Missolonghi, with the fleet that he, Byron, had helped to pay for. On 12 December, the day after the arrival of the ships, he instructed Gamba to add a postscript to a copy of his letter to Mavrokordatos. Praidis would be crossing to Missolonghi any day now and would carry it. In this postscript, Gamba wrote: 'Mr Praidis will communicate to you his [i.e., Byron's] every movement, his every intention – He wishes for nothing better than to join Your Illustrious Highness at the earliest opportunity and to act in accordance with the decree [of the Legislative Body] and for the entire liberation of Greece.'[49]

Writing to Bowring the following day, Byron sounds more hesitant. The financial transaction in Zante was all but complete, but the money to pay the ships' crews had still not arrived. After that would be the time to meet Mavrokordatos. 'I shall probably join him at Sea or on Shore', wrote Byron on the thirteenth. And two days later Praidis, before departing for Missolonghi himself, reported Byron still dithering whether to send the money or bring it to Mavrokordatos in person. From his knowledge of his Lordship so far, Praidis thought the latter more likely – and he would be right.[50]

On 17 December, aided by 'the calm though cool serenity of a beautiful and transparent Moonlight', Byron once again took stock of his situation by resuming his short-lived diary. In it, he wrote: 'I shall probably bon gré mal gré [like it or not] be obliged to join one of the factions – which I have hitherto strenuously avoided in the hope to unite them in one common interest.'[51] The truth was, from the moment when he had signed the loan agreement and named Orlandos as the recipient of the funds, he already had. From now on, Byron was Mavrokordatos' man. And the political fortunes of the modernisers in Greece would depend very largely on what Byron said and did next.

'PASSING "THE RUBICON"'

No sooner had the Greek ships reached Missolonghi than wind and rain made communication with Cephalonia impossible. Praidis was unable to cross over until the seventeenth, taking advantage of the same lull in the weather that encouraged Byron to organise his ideas in his diary.[52] Stanhope, learning that the ships were on their way, had turned aside from his planned course and was already at Missolonghi. There, he had already presented Byron's letters to Mavrokordatos in person. Impatient as Byron now was to embark for the mainland, this was as nothing compared to Mavrokordatos' need to have him there.

With the immediate threat from the enemy gone, Mavrokordatos had found his welcome in the town more muted than he had expected. The governor of the province, he who had written so warmly to invite Byron, back in September, retreated into a huff from which he had not emerged almost forty years later when he published his memoirs. Konstantinos Metaxas thought himself slighted by the appointment of Mavrokordatos over his head, and from this point on did everything he could to make things difficult.[53] The local chiefs and unemployed soldiery that had fallen back upon the town during the previous months' campaign were still there, discontented, without means of support, and with nothing to do. Even more pressing was the problem of the ships and their crews that had come from Hydra.

The Turkish brig that had been driven ashore and looted on the coast of Ithaca had been found to be carrying a huge amount of cash, many months' arrears of pay for the garrison in Patras. Contemporary accounts are at variance as to the actual amount, but Praidis put it at 60,000 dollars, three times the amount that was expected from Byron to pay the crews of these same ships.[54] On arrival at Missolonghi, the Hydriots, who had taken possession of this prize, quarrelled with the smaller contingent from Spetses. Nothing Mavrokordatos could do or say would persuade the ships' captains and crews to remain beyond 25 December. On that day, they would be departing for home, taking their bounty with them. Only the six Spetsiot ships would be left. Their crews, too, were threatening to sail away unless the money promised by Byron arrived soon.[55] No wonder Mavrokordatos was desperate.

He wrote to Byron no fewer than three times during his first week at Missolonghi.[56] But thanks to the weather it was not until 20 or 21 December that Praidis could be despatched back to Cephalonia, to deliver all three letters together, and to prepare Byron to embark on the Spetsiot brig *Leonidas* that would follow a day later. Even this plan went wrong. Praidis, sadly accident-prone, found himself stranded on one of the shoals that guard the lagoon of Missolonghi. It was not until the twenty-sixth that he reached Byron with the letters.[57] By this time the *Leonidas* had been and gone. Now that Napier had departed for London, the port authorities in Argostoli were less likely to be accommodating towards a vessel under Greek colours. The brig had not been allowed to land.[58]

On 23 December, the day the *Leonidas* was sighted, Byron thought he was about to embark for free Greece. Already, in his briefly resumed journal, he had returned to the fantasy he had first begun to entertain when the kilted Souliots laid siege to the *Hercules*. He had even worked out the cost, and decided: 'I could maintain between five hundred and a thousand of these warriors for as long as necessary.' He had been reading the biography of Napoleon, his old hero, that he had acquired while passing through Livorno. The money he had already advanced for the Greek fleet, he noted with satisfaction, was 'double that with which Napoleon the Emperor of Emperors – began his campaign in Italy'.[59]

There is no mistaking the rising tone of excitement in Byron's letters, first when he thought he would be going aboard the *Leonidas*, and then when the package from Missolonghi arrived. (Characteristically, the bearer earns not a single mention.) In the package was the long-delayed letter from the Legislative Body, dated 27 October, requesting him to cooperate with Mavrokordatos as its President for the defence of Missolonghi.[60] In his own letters, Mavrokordatos stressed the urgency of Byron's arrival, but elided its true cause.[61] He would not have been the first or the last politician to represent future prospects as more enticing than they really were. Now, wrote Mavrokordatos, would be the perfect opportunity to clear the last remaining Turkish outposts from the Gulf and to send a land army north as far as Thessaly. In his very first letter to Byron, back in the summer, while he had been outlining the scheme to raise a loan from London, Mavrokordatos had trailed the possibility of gaining possession of the rich agricultural lands of the plain of Thessaly. Then, if there had been an effective central government in the Peloponnese to coordinate efforts in different parts of the country, it might have been conceivable. From the base of Missolonghi in the west, it was no more than a mirage.

This is not to say that Mavrokordatos deliberately deceived Byron. The goal of subduing the remaining Turkish fortresses on the north shore of the Gulf was surely realisable, and also features prominently in Mavrokordatos' letters to the government over the next two months. In a public statement issued at the time he left Hydra, he claimed that these fortresses would be within his grasp, and even set his sights on Preveza, far to the north on the west coast. Others talked in similar terms. Byron's own lieutenant, Colonel Stanhope, enthusiastically added his voice of that of Mavrokordatos, and believed that Patras, at least, with the promised artillery support on its way from England, would 'fall in a fortnight'.[62] If the art of the statesman consists in articulating a vision so that it becomes reality, then Mavrokordatos was at least trying, and Byron would have respected him for it. Words, after all, are things.

Mavrokordatos also went out of his way to flatter Byron, adopting an age-old strategy: 'I do not flatter you, my Lord, if I assure you that I would have hesitated to accept so great a task if I did not found my hopes on your co-operation . . . Be assured, my lord, that on you alone depends the fate of Greece.' That was in the first letter. In the third, he returns to the theme: 'I should never . . . have accepted a task whose magnitude and difficulty I foresaw, had I not counted upon the co-operation of Your Excellency.' There was truth here, as well as flattery. Had it not been for Byron's first letter, for the bark of his 'jackal' Trelawny and the cooperation of his more docile disciple Browne, it is very doubtful whether Mavrokordatos or the fleet would now be at Missolonghi.

Seizing upon a metaphor that was newer and more arresting then than it is today, Mavrokordatos wrote that the Greek forces would be 'electrified' by Byron's presence. Byron joked about this when he wrote to Hobhouse the next day.[63] But he was in a state of high excitement himself. Announcing his imminent departure, he wrote to Hobhouse and Kinnaird in London, and to Barry in Genoa: all the money that can be raised from his own resources, and all that the Committee can attract, must be made available to the cause: 'never mind *me* – so that the Cause goes on – if that is well – all is well'. The property he had inherited in Lancashire, that he had struggled to liquidate all his adult life, had finally been sold: 'if the Rochdale sale has been completed I can keep an army *here*, aye, and perhaps command it . . . Why, man! if we had but 100,000 *l* sterling in hand, we should now be half-way to the city of Constantine.'[64] Even Mavrokordatos would hardly have dared imagine so much.

All thought of turning back had vanished. 'I am passing "the Rubicon"', Byron declared in high excitement to Kinnaird on his last day at Metaxata, 'recollect that for God's sake – and the sake of Greece.' To Barry in Genoa he had already announced: 'I have no intention of an immediate return . . . I must see this Greek business out (or *it me*).' The long-delayed moment had arrived: 'Till now – I could have been of little or no use – but the coming up of Mavrocordato – who has not only talents but integrity, makes a difference.'[65] He was throwing in his lot with a leader he still saw as a '*Washington* or *Kosciusko* kind of man', the nearest Greece had to the founding president of the United States of America or the Polish national hero of the 1790s. Although he expressed it in joking terms ('playing at Nations'), he was about to commit himself, alongside Mavrokordatos, to the joint project of turning Greece into a new, modern nation. To this end, in the euphoria of those last days in Cephalonia, he even contemplated intervening directly in the civil war, exactly as Praidis had understood him to be implying. If the parties would not agree to be united under what Byron had now decided was the legitimate government: 'why we must go over to the Morea with the Western Greeks . . . – and try the effect of a little *physical* advice – should they persist in rejecting *moral* persuasion'.[66]

Byron must have had the option of setting out immediately with Praidis. Even if the Greek boat had been too small to accommodate all of his party, with the horses, printing press, and other equipment, he could have arranged for these to brought on later. Dislike or disdain for the man he called Delladecima's 'friend Raidi' cannot have been sufficient reason. Gamba states, without explanation, that 'Lord Byron declined the offer, and preferred hiring vessels for himself.'[67] He might have thought that the neutral flag of the Ionian Islands would give him better cover en route. If so, he was wrong. He would have enjoyed a much less eventful journey with Praidis.

The real reason was that the money destined for the ships at Missolonghi was still in Zante, awaiting collection. To have sailed into the port of Zante in a Greek warship would have been a flagrant violation of his own country's neutrality – and Byron was throughout punctilious about such matters. So two small vessels were chartered. Byron himself would travel in a *mystiko*, a type of craft whose name means 'secret', no doubt because it was favoured by smugglers and blockade-runners for its speed and small size. A larger craft, a *bombarda*, was hired for the horses and supplies.

All these arrangements took time, and then the weather was against them.' Byron lodged for two nights in Argostoli, at the house of Charles Hancock, the merchant who had helped him cash his bills. There, he seized upon the latest published of Scott's Waverley novels, *Quentin Durward*. The time of wavering was long past. But he could not resist seeing himself once again in the mould of one of Scott's heroes – embroiled in a desperate, 'romantic' cause to which he alone can contribute a decent, honourable, rational humanity. He could not be coaxed out of his room until he had finished *Quentin Durward*.[68]

On the afternoon of Monday, 29 December the boats were ready to depart. The wind was still strong and spray was blowing. Delladecima, who was in Praidis' confidence and knew the urgency, had been doing his best to hustle forward the preparations. But the Ionian count had grown sincerely fond of Byron, too. He reported a pang of conscience when Byron parted from him, that morning, with the words, 'Delladecima, you couldn't wait for me to leave Cephalonia, and now you want me to go aboard in terrible weather – I shall do everything as you wish.'[69]

Friends from the British garrison rowed out with him to the *mystiko*. With Byron in the smaller boat went Dr Bruno, his valet Fletcher, a dog called Lyon, and the young Loukas Chalandritsanos, the son of the distressed family from Patras that he had been supporting since August, whom he had now taken into his service.[70] Byron was full of high spirits, 'animated at finding himself embarked once more on the element he loved'. It must have been from one of those present, if not from his own imagination, that Trelawny captured the vividness of the moment: 'as he sprang aboard the Mistico – and felt the salt spray dash over his face, he rubbed his hands joyously – and said – this is what I like – now hurrah for Greece'.[71]

The short crossing to Zante was quickly made, and the two vessels lay off the port town for twenty-four hours. Byron did not go ashore, but received several visitors, including the Resident, Sir Frederick Stoven, and Samuel Barff, Hancock's business partner from whom he finally took delivery of the 20,000 silver dollars destined for the fleet at Missolonghi, together with some additional 'specie' for contingencies. Sixteen thousand dollars went with Byron aboard the *mystiko*, 8,000 with Gamba on the *bombarda*.[72] It was a lot of money to risk in unsafe waters, the equivalent of almost

5,000 pounds sterling. But there was no other way of getting it into Greece, to where it was needed.

Byron seems to have thought that after leaving Zante he would pick up a Greek escort. Certainly, he blamed Praidis for what happened next. Unknown to anyone aboard the two craft, the greater part of the Greek fleet had abandoned Missolonghi for Hydra, as the crews had threatened, on Christmas Day. Emboldened by their departure, the few Turkish ships remaining in Patras had begun venturing out into the Gulf again. On form so far, an armed Greek brig of war might not have been challenged, so great was the awe in which the islanders were held by the Ottoman navy. But Byron's two boats were an easy prey, despite their Ionian colours and the false papers that had been obligingly provided for them in Zante.[73]

The *bombarda* carrying Gamba, the servants, horses, and stores, was arrested on the high seas and taken into Patras. Byron's own boat had a narrow escape. Challenged in the darkness by a Turkish frigate, and at daybreak discovering the way into the lagoon blocked by another, the skipper ran for the nearest point of land. The *mystiko* found shelter in a creek known as Skrofes ('sows'), on the tip of land where the Acheloos river flows into the sea. Young Loukas and another Greek were despatched, partly for their own safety, by land to carry news of what had happened to Mavrokordatos and Stanhope in Missolonghi. That Byron's feelings for Loukas were more than ordinarily humanitarian can be seen from the sudden vehemence of his language in the letter he wrote to Stanhope for him to carry. Were the boy to fall into the hands of the Turks, 'you know what his fate would be; and I would sooner cut him in pieces and myself too than have him taken out by those barbarians'.[74] Before leaving Cephalonia, Byron had bought two dictionaries for Loukas, who could speak some Italian. Perhaps, in his new life at Missolonghi, he would be able to resume the idyll that had begun with Nicolo Giraud, who at the same age had taught him Italian and some Greek in the Capuchin monastery in Athens, twelve years before.

Even at Skrofes they were not safe. One of the two frigates in sight showed signs of pursuit. To reach the safety of the lagoon of Missolonghi, the *mystiko* would have to tack up-wind, under the guns of the Turkish frigate. There was nothing for it but to head the other way, northwards along the western side of the Acheloos delta. As Byron described it two days later: 'we dashed out again – and showing our stern (our boat sails very well) got in before night to Dragomestre'.[75]

Now called Astakos, this small port is protected by a string of islets and reefs. Here they would be safe from pursuit. The shortest way to Missolonghi from Dragomestre would have been by road. But Mavrokordatos, probably worried as much about the security of the dollars as of Byron's party, was horrified at the idea of a land journey. The long-suffering Praidis was sent with three boats to collect them.[76] Even now Byron's adventures at sea were not over. While they retraced their route through the channel between Skrofes and the island of Oxeia, adverse winds twice blew the *mystiko* on to rocks. As Byron laconically expressed it, 'the dollars had another narrow escape'. So did young Loukas, who had showed sufficient devotion to his master to return with one of the boats, and now had to be saved all over again. This time, Byron told the boy to cling to his back and he would bring him safely to shore – to the dismay of Dr Bruno, who was not much older and could not swim either. In the event, several of the Greek sailors abandoned ship and had to be taken off by one of the other boats. But the *mystiko* remained afloat, the dollars were saved, and no one had to swim for his life.[77]

It was Sunday, 4 January 1824, when Byron entered the lagoon of Missolonghi. Gamba and those aboard the *bombarda*, having been released after a courteous detention by Yusuf Pasha in Patras, had arrived earlier in the day. Byron must have sent word to Mavrokordatos, perhaps by Loukas. He was not going to make himself known, in brine-soaked clothes after a week in an open boat, late in the afternoon on a day of rest. The first thing he did was to take a swim.[78] That night was his last aboard the *mystiko*, that had well lived up to its name and reputation.

At eleven o'clock on Monday morning, 5 January, Byron went ashore. According to the Greek calendar, it was Christmas Eve. The symbolism would not have been lost on him. The whole town had been prepared to receive its saviour. He had dressed for the occasion in a scarlet regimental uniform.[79] If one of the three helmets that he had had made in Genoa was upon his head, nobody present was ever so tactless afterwards as to mention it. He had himself outgrown that gesture. Most probably, the helmets remained in a trunk. Gamba describes the scene: 'Lord Byron's arrival was welcomed with salvos of artillery, firing of muskets, and wild music. Crowds of soldiery, and citizens of every rank, sex, and age, were assembled on the shore to testify their delight. Hope and content were pictured in every countenance.'[80]

Many years later, the painter Theodoros Vryzakis would depict the moment, with a ruined minaret and the silhouette of Varasova, the mountain that dominates this side of the gulf, in the background (frontispiece).

The painter was not quite five years old when Byron landed, and of course not an eyewitness. Despite a fair amount of licence in the composition, Vryzakis would faithfully reproduce the portraits of many of those who had been there. Byron himself is noticeable for his short stature, but has been turned into a civilian. In this iconic representation, it is the poet of *Childe Harold's Pilgrimage* that steps ashore, bringing courage and confidence to the Greeks.

That was not how Byron saw himself. He was here to stand shoulder to shoulder with Mavrokordatos, as a leader – a military leader, should 'chance so happen', but at all events a political leader. As Trelawny, not an eyewitness either, rightly divined, 'The poet had now laid down his pen – and mounted the warrior's plume.'[81] It was the greatest moment of Byron's life. His transformation was complete. The 'new Prometheus' of the Romantic imagination had turned himself into the new statesman.

PART IV

Missolonghi: the hundred days
(January–April 1824)

CHAPTER 10

'Political economy'

A WORKING RELATIONSHIP

The irony would not have escaped Byron, had he been in a position to appreciate it. His whole active life in revolutionary Greece would last only as long as the brief restoration of his hero Napoleon, between escape from Elba and defeat at Waterloo. At the time, though, and in the eyes of all who were there, those first three months of 1824 were meant to be a beginning, not an end. We will do better to think of Byron's hundred days at Missolonghi in terms of the political language of today, as the initial testing time that defines a new leader in office and lays the foundations for what is to follow.

The underlying pattern of those hundred days is as much obscured as illuminated by the many testimonies to the day-to-day tribulations that Byron endured at Missolonghi, the main material on which his biographers have been able to draw up to now. Well-known incidents, reported not long afterwards by Gamba, Millingen, Parry, Stanhope, and others, and reproduced in biographies ever since, either fall into place, or seem less significant, when these accounts are set alongside the primary sources in Greek. The daily accumulation of misery and frustration that emerges from most of these narratives (though not, strikingly, from Byron's own letters) was the result of causes that were often relatively trivial. The very richness of the standard narrative, with its vivid detail on those aspects of lived experience that happened to be recorded, tends to cast Byron in the role of helpless sufferer, observing and enduring, the victim of forces he barely understood and had no chance of controlling.

The truth is that during all but the very last of those hundred days, Byron knew perfectly well what he was doing, and why. He pursued his aims with remarkable consistency of purpose. From start to finish, everything hinged on the new working relationship that he struck up with the man he had come here to support, Alexandros Mavrokordatos.

211

There is no record of their first meeting, that January morning at Missolonghi. For first impressions, we have to rely on inference and the word of others. A British naval officer, who called on Mavrokordatos not long afterwards, described his own reception:

We found the great man surrounded by thirty or forty men, armed after the manner of the country, with richly chased pistols and ataghans, while he, on the contrary, was in a French dress – blue coat, drab waistcoat, wide blue pantaloons, and boots, all much worn and badly brushed. His complexion is swarthy, his face rather broad, an aquiline nose, eyes large, black and expressive; and his countenance displays intelligence and shrewdness; but from wearing his hair turned back, in bushy profusion about his shoulders (he has no neck) and a huge pair of ugly mustachios, he has a singular, and not very prepossessing appearance; his height may be five feet six or seven.

This accords closely with the likeness drawn from life, three years later, by the Bavarian volunteer Karl Krazeisen (Plate 7a). Byron's own stature was estimated by the same observer at just two to three inches more.[1]

Byron was expecting to meet the Washington or Kosciusko of Greece. Mavrokordatos had never forgotten the warning from his mentor back in Pisa, the shrewd Bishop Ignatios: this was a man who could do incalculable harm, as well as good. The two men had similar conceptions of the cause that each was here to serve. Both saw far beyond the small cockpit in which they found themselves, and understood how the struggle to establish an independent Greece could be played out on the wider stage of European geopolitics. It should have been an instant meeting of minds. Some degree of disappointment on both sides was perhaps inevitable.

Byron, probably for the first time in his life, was entering upon a *working* relationship, and one between social equals. It mattered to him, surely, that among the westerners at Missolonghi, Mavrokordatos was still regularly styled 'Prince'. With Murray, his publisher, Byron had been far more intimate than he ever became with Mavrokordatos. But Murray he could bully, and often did, until eventually the relationship had broken down. Something of the kind had been envisaged again, in Ravenna and Pisa, when he and Shelley had planned to work with the Hunts to produce *The Liberal*. But tempers and temperaments had made that a highly fissile project from the start. If Shelley had lived, Byron might have stuck with *The Liberal* a little longer. Now, in Greece, far more was at stake. These two *had* to work together, for the higher good. There was no place at Missolonghi for the kind of posturing and tantrums for which Byron was famous. There was plenty of that already, among the picturesque 'byronic' heroes who strutted and fired off their guns day and night in the streets. The new Byron had to be different.

So it is not necessarily a surprise to discover that Byron was consistently muted in what he said about Mavrokordatos, not only in his letters, but in the conversations that others recorded. After meeting the man himself, Byron never again repeated the comparison with George Washington. Indeed, he would have been in Missolonghi for almost two months, and meeting him almost daily, before he so much as mentions Mavrokordatos in a surviving letter: 'Prince Mavrocordato is an excellent person and does all in his power – but his situation is perplexing in the extreme', he would write to Murray at the end of February.[2] Often, what Byron does *not* say in his letters can be as revealing as what he does.

What Mavrokordatos thought of Byron is no less hard to gauge, from correspondence that is always more or less official. Perhaps the writer feels the need to convince the recipients of his letters of what he finds hard to believe, himself:

He [Byron] desires to be of service in whatever way the Government orders him; 'no danger', he says, 'and no obstacle will prevent me from hastening wherever the Government orders me to go'.

On the subject of his Lordship, this much only I tell you, that the man has the greatest disposition to appear useful in our affairs; he is ready to do anything, so long as he knows it to be of use.[3]

Many years later, George Finlay would sum up what he had seen of Byron and Mavrokordatos at work: their 'intercourse was not intimate. Business and ceremony alone brought them together. Their social and mental characteristics were not of a nature to create reciprocal confidence, and they felt no mutual esteem.'[4] But Finlay did not arrive in Missolonghi until the hundred days were more than half over. Other accounts suggest that from the beginning there *was* an informal, social side to the relationship. Mavrokordatos was in the habit of dropping in on Byron and spending an hour or two with him most evenings, 'like one of his private friends'. Gamba records that they shared an interest in Turkish history.[5] There was perhaps an element of one-upmanship in these conversations, reminiscent of Medwin's account of Mavrokordatos sparring with Shelley over the pronunciation of Greek. But, for most of the hundred days, these occasions seem to have been uniformly amicable and easy-going (no small feat for the Byron of old).

Business there was in plenty. And it is remarkable just how much business these two concluded, right from the very first day. One of their first joint actions was a diplomatic one. The administration of Sir Thomas Maitland, High Commissioner of the Ionian Islands in Corfu, had issued a proclamation denouncing violations of the islands' neutrality during Mavrokordatos' voyage from Hydra. The main issue was the fate of the Turkish brig, whose sailors had been hunted down by the Greeks on shore and whose cargo of silver dollars had been taken while the ship was beached on the coast of Ithaca. Mavrokordatos addressed a personal letter to the High Commissioner, according to Byron 'rather calculated to conciliate – than to irritate'. This was enclosed with another from Byron to his friend Lord Sydney Osborne, who was on Maitland's staff, and whom he asked to intercede. The personal touch would ensure a degree of access that would never have been granted to a leader of the Greeks. Byron's personal assurance would have carried some weight as well, the more so for the offhand informality with which it was given: 'I am doing all I can to convince them [the Greeks] of the necessity of the strictest observance of the regulations of the Islands – and I trust with some effect.' Writing to his government, shortly afterwards, Mavrokordatos would represent this joint diplomatic initiative as having been his own idea.[6] But Byron had been insisting on the need for the Greeks to conciliate the Great Powers, and particularly Britain, since at least the time of his meetings with Orlandos and Louriotis in the lazaretto of Argostoli.[7] He and Mavrokordatos were acting in perfect accord.

THE POWER OF MONEY

Everything else at this time had to do with money. When Byron landed, twenty barrels of silver coin had been carried ashore and distributed among the crews of the ships from Spetses, fulfilling the contract for his personal loan that had been drawn up in November. This was not the only demand upon him. Two days later, as he informed Osborne, he had already 'engaged to maintain a certain number of troops'.[8] It was not that Missolonghi at this time needed defending. Since the hasty lifting of the siege at the beginning of December, no further threat from the north could be expected until late spring, at the earliest. The greatest difficulty facing Mavrokordatos was what to do with the warlike tribesmen of his own side, who had fallen back during the autumn on the town and the neighbouring fortified island of Anatoliko (today's Aitoliko). Missolonghi was crowded with up to 5,000 armed men, about half of them more or less credibly describing themselves as 'Souliots', most with families to maintain and no means of subsistence.[9]

The day before Byron arrived had seen the inauguration of a ten-day assembly of all the military and civilian chiefs of the region, under the chairmanship of Mavrokordatos.[10] Its twin purposes were to secure a formal vote of confidence in his own leadership and to raise money for the upkeep of these soldiers. The first was achieved. The second resulted in a finely worded resolution addressed to the Provisional Government. But everybody knew the Provisional Government had no money to give. All attention therefore turned towards Byron.[11]

There seems to have been some realistic haggling about numbers and back pay (which the Souliots were demanding and Byron refused).[12] This was probably still going on when Byron wrote to Osborne on the seventh. Within a week, terms had been hammered out. Byron would put up the money to pay 500 men in arms, for a year. This was out of his own resources. It was not a loan, as the money for the ships had been. He estimated the total cost for the first year at 20,000 dollars.[13]

Byron's weakness for the Souliots was well known – 'the best and bravest of the present combatants', as he had described them while still in Cephalonia.[14] During his very first week there, he had proposed to the Greek government, via Delladecima, that he might employ a troop of these men. This proposal had been turned down, while the government had been in Salamis and divided. Now, Mavrokordatos was more than happy to accept it on his own authority, here in Western Greece. In return, he offered to put Byron in command and proposed an immediate target for attack – and all this within forty-eight hours of Byron landing.[15]

The target was to be the fortress of Lepanto (Nafpaktos in Greek). Built several centuries before by the Venetians, at the entrance to the Gulf of Corinth, on a cliff with a town and harbour at its base, the castle has ever since commanded the sea and land routes eastwards into central Greece. In 1571, the Battle of Lepanto had been fought in these waters between the combined navies of western Christendom and the Ottoman empire. Victory for 'Don John of Austria', as G. K. Chesterton's poem has it, had checked the westward expansion of Islam into Europe for a century. Now, Lepanto was garrisoned by Albanians who were 'discontented and mutinous . . . because they have not been paid for fourteen months', as Mavrokordatos had written to explain to Byron before his arrival.[16] Conditions in the enemy camp, in other words, were the mirror-image of those in Missolonghi. Before long, Mavrokordatos would ask the government to assign the supreme command of the expedition to Byron.[17] No military skill and very little physical risk would be involved. Everybody knew that the attack Byron was being asked to lead would be a token affair only. The fortress would be surrendered for silver.

At the same time, demands for money kept coming from further afield. In the Peloponnese, tension between the Legislative and Executive bodies had erupted into violence. On 8 December, soldiers under the command of Kolokotronis' son Panos had gone from Nafplio, seat of the Executive, to Argos and broken up the meeting of the Legislature, seizing its archive at the same time. News of the debacle had not long since broken in Missolonghi when Byron arrived. Mavrokordatos reported him 'horrified' and 'shocked'.[18] Since then the Legislative Body had reconstituted itself in the fortified village of Kranidi, in the northeast corner of the Peloponnese – about as close as it was possible to be to the ships and guns of Hydra and Spetses while still being on the mainland. From there, the members of the Executive had been one by one proscribed. While Byron had been in transit and during his first days at Missolonghi, a new Executive was in process of being appointed, and appeared prepared to overrule the rebels by force if necessary.[19] Byron, according to Mavrokordatos, was 'pleased' by these signs of decisiveness on the part of the legislators. His own letters and reported statements studiously avoid any appearance of taking sides. But Gamba's diary for 15 January must reflect his attitude at this time: 'The legislative body were pursuing the same energetic measures as before; and public opinion was daily more pronounced in their favour.'[20]

On the same day, Mavrokordatos received letters from the Legislature, that had been written while the new Executive was still being formed. Enclosed were two more for Byron. Of these, one was an effusion of thanks for all that he had done for the cause so far. The second, more businesslike but equally courteous, explained that, for the protection of the large islands of Euboea and Crete, a further loan of between 20,000 and 30,000 dollars was urgently required, and begged his Lordship to put up the money. As before, it would be repaid out of the larger loan now being negotiated in London.[21] The second of these letters Mavrokordatos was instructed to forward only 'if you think it reasonable and success probable'.[22]

Mavrokordatos could have been forgiven, in the circumstances, for seizing upon the let-out clause and suppressing this second substantial demand on Byron's resources. He had already just agreed to maintain the Souliots. Only ten days had passed since the previous loan, also of 20,000 dollars, had been paid out to the crews of the ships from Spetses. Mavrokordatos knew, although Byron did not, that the Spetsiots had only remained in Missolonghi, after the departure of the larger contingent from Hydra with their captured bounty, to secure this largesse by way of compensation. In a matter of days they too would be gone. Then, there would be no concealing from Byron the truth of how his previous generosity had been abused.

It is surprising enough that Mavrokordatos, knowing all this, handed over the letter. Even more surprising is how Byron responded. Although he was meeting Mavrokordatos daily, he replied to this request in writing the next day:

1. It would take at least two months before the best rates could be raised on the London or Genoa exchange...
2. We shall have had an answer from London, via the deputies, in less time than that, and then the twenty or thirty thousand dollars would be superfluous. If the deputies do not succeed, I shall do everything in my power to satisfy the request of the government of the Morea.
3. The commitment I have made to maintain the Suliot corps, &c. (without seeking any reimbursement) will cost just under twenty thousand dollars...
4. I expect some special letters from England on my private affairs, and then I shall be able to say precisely what I can and cannot do with my own resources during the current year. Meanwhile I shall not go back on the promise I have made already.
5. P. S. Therefore, if the Prince and the Government believe it necessary, we could dispatch an agent to Cephalonia to negotiate in my name and in the name of the Greek Government the amount requested by the Legislative Body.[23]

Mavrokordatos thought this meant 'yes'. Gamba noted, bluntly, 'his means did not allow of such an advance'. Byron himself reported to Hancock, 'I demur for the present', but then added a couple of lines later: 'till I receive letters from England which I have reason to expect'.[24] Byron was fast learning the art of equivocation, in which the undoubted master was Mavrokordatos. But what he might have been expected to say, and did not, was 'no'.

Mavrokordatos, emboldened, pressed home the advantage at once – and with a directness that shows how the relationship had altered since their diplomatic exchanges from a distance. The very next day, he wrote to Byron: 'Mylord, To conclude the matter of the Souliots today, I absolutely need three thousand dollars.' This time Byron agreed without equivocation. But the difficulty of raising extra cash and transporting it from Zante remained. Mavrokordatos would have to wait.[25]

Byron's determination to expend all his disposable income for the good of the cause must have astonished those around him. By 14 January, he had calculated that with the recent sale of his property in Rochdale thrown in, he would have at his 'disposition upwards of an hundred thousand dollars', the equivalent of 25,000 pounds, for use in 1824 alone. The figure he gave to Mavrokordatos at the same time was only slightly lower. Out of an annual income the equivalent of 80,000 dollars, Mavrokordatos reported to the Legislative Body on the eighteenth, his Lordship was prepared to make available everything, bar what was needed for minimal personal wants, 'for the needs of the fatherland'.[26]

On the morning of Monday, 19 January, Byron's party awoke to see 'the Greek fleet making sail, and the Turkish ships standing out of the mouth of the Gulf'. At first Mavrokordatos tried to make out that the ships had only gone to keep watch on the enemy. But nobody can have been fooled for more than a few hours.[27] Gamba reported Byron 'irritated'. It was another of those instances where Byron's silences could be as expressive as words. Two months would pass before he could even bring himself to allude to what he must have seen as a betrayal, when he tersely expressed the hope that in future his money might be put 'to better purpose than paying off arrears of fleets that sail away'.[28] Instead, his immediate fury was curiously displaced.

He took it out on Gamba. In the midst of the military frenzy that had taken hold of Byron's household since their arrival, Pierino had ordered from Zante an expensive set of uniforms, to be tailored in Corfu. Two letters written by Byron on the day of the ships' departure are vituperative with indignation at his lieutenant's extravagance. 'This accursed Cloth merchandizing of Gamba', he called it, and raged on: 'this is what comes of letting boys play the man'. What incensed him about 'Gamba's d—d nonsense' was that 'I have occasion for every dollar I can muster – to keep the Greeks together – and I do not grudge any expence for the Cause.'[29]

At the very moment when he must have been asking himself if his previous generosity had not been wholly wasted, and whether he should now reconsider the commitments he had so recently entered into, instead Byron railed against Gamba for throwing away trivial sums that could have been better used for the 'Cause'. As had often happened in the past, the real target for Byron's anger that day was himself. He needed the anger to conquer his own doubts. In the course of humiliating Pierino and gaining the satisfaction of countermanding these harmless vanities, Byron convinced himself and those around him that the setback of the ships' defection was not going to change his own policy of giving to the Greeks. Suddenly turning the contentious cloth into a metaphor, he all but reveals what had been in his mind, when the ships sailed away: 'as for me – I mean to stick by the Greeks to the last rag of canvas or shirt – and not to go snivelling back like all the rest of them'.[30]

True, by early February he would claim to be exercising a new caution in the promises he was prepared to make: 'I do not like to tell the Greeks *exactly – what –* I *could* or would advance on an emergency – because otherwise they will double and triple their demands.' But this was wisdom learned too late. He had already told Mavrokordatos, with only a 20 per cent write-down of what he believed to be the true position. And, on 9 February, a fortnight after the ships had gone, he would urge Kinnaird to speed up the transfer of the sale money from the Rochdale estate, 'as I shall have occasion for it all – and more – to help on the Greeks'.[31]

Byron's rage was soon over. The next day, 20 January, it had a revealing sequel. He took Pierino out riding, as was his habit, and patiently explained to him the nature of his mission and why it mattered so much. Gamba does not claim to reproduce Byron's words exactly, only 'the substance of what he said'. And of course he omits any mention of the row that had occasioned them. Right at the start, Byron warned that he had 'not much hope of success'. For a moment, this sounds like the disillusioned, despairing Byron of the biographies. But no, it is because the bar he has set for himself is so extraordinarily high: 'those principles which are now in action in Greece will gradually produce their effect, both here and in other countries . . . I am not . . . come here in search of adventures, but to assist in the regeneration of a nation'.[32]

It was the same phrase that he had used to Millingen in Cephalonia – and the fact that it is reported, on different occasions, by both men surely guarantees that it is Byron's. This was why every natural weakness, from Pierino's trifling vanity to his own deepest feelings, and even the 'lava of the imagination' that had once made him a poet, had now to be subordinated to the needs of the 'Cause'.

There was another reason for Byron to be more than usually reflective on that Tuesday afternoon ride outside Missolonghi. In two days' time, on 22 January, it would be his birthday. The year before, in Genoa, he had agonised all winter over the watershed of passing thirty-five. The slowly taken decision to come to Greece had been his response. This time, on the threshold of thirty-six, the results of his annual self-examination came out in the form of his sober admonition to Gamba. By comparison with that far-sighted assessment, the mawkish poem that he produced, half-apologetically, before the assembled company of his friends on the morning of his birthday itself, is a mere footnote. The poem represents a self-pitying glance backward just at the moment when, as its very first line acknowledges, "'Tis time this heart should be unmoved'. What was good for weak-willed, accident-prone Pierino would in future have to be good for Byron too. This was part of the lecture he had delivered on their ride together. The poem's tawdry, worn-out rhetoric about 'Glory and Greece' is beside the point. Only prose, and the rigorous suppression of 'those reviving passions', would do, for the 'regeneration of a nation'.[33]

POLITICS FOR A NEW NATION

It was not just the Greeks who were divided among themselves. Leicester Stanhope had arrived at Missolonghi before Byron, and had already begun making himself useful. A project dear to the Colonel's heart was the establishment of a free press in Greece. The initiative to establish the *Greek Chronicle* in Missolonghi was not necessarily Stanhope's, certainly not his alone. Mavrokordatos had brought a printing press with him from Hydra. The bespectacled young Swiss philhellene from Basle, Johann Jakob Meyer, was already primed to act as editor. A local schoolteacher had been found to translate Meyer's editorials into Greek – and also, as it turned out, to exercise austere control over the language considered acceptable for publication.[34] What Stanhope contributed was energy, determination, and at the start a small injection of cash. Byron was sceptical about the project from the beginning. 'His Lordship . . . thinks the press will not succeed', Stanhope wrote to Bowring on 6 January. 'I think it will.'[35]

By the time of Byron's birthday, on the twenty-second, discord between the two men had reached such a point that, as Stanhope reported to Bowring, 'I am in the habit of putting written questions to Lord Byron for his decision.'[36] It began with the press. For Stanhope, the freedom of the press was an article of his liberal faith. For Byron the poet, the liberty to express himself without fear or restriction had surely mattered no less. He had often enough chafed, fumed, or raged whenever he had found his own freedom of expression threatened. Now, Stanhope's doctrinaire principles and unyielding personality forced Byron to rethink his position not just on this issue, but on several other matters of politics on which the two men clashed, during the last days of January.

It may have been merely his old desire to provoke that prompted Byron to report to Stanhope a conversation he had recently had with Mavrokordatos. If he had been in Mavrokordatos' place, Byron said, he 'would have placed the press under a censor'. Mavrokordatos had demurred, objecting that 'the liberty of the press is guaranteed by the constitution'. This was the Constitution of Epidaurus, of which Mavrokordatos had been the principal architect. Probably, he cited the articles in it that already limited press freedom, explicitly forbidding blasphemy, immorality, and libel.[37] Byron may have been echoing – and doubting – some such reassurance from Mavrokordatos when he shared with Stanhope his fear of 'libels and licentiousness'. This may sound like an astonishing volte-face from the author of *The Vision of Judgment* and *Don Juan*. But Byron, ever since his first visit to Greece, had been a relativist, one of the things that makes him still seem so modern today. The values he had espoused in other times and other places were simply, as he tried to convince Stanhope that night, 'not applicable to this society in its present combustible state'.[38]

A few days later the quarrel burst out again. The occasion this time was a visit from the Royal Navy. Before the Spetsiot warships had sailed for home, they had taken as a 'prize' a caique flying the Ionian flag. The owner of the caique, a Greek, addressed a plaintive note to Byron, begging for the restitution of his livelihood.[39] The British authorities in the Ionian Islands were in no mood to put up with further violations of their neutrality. Whether skipper Louverdos ever got his money back is not recorded. But when Captain Yorke came ashore at Missolonghi from the naval brig *Alacrity* on Monday, 26 January, he brought with him an ultimatum from the Ionian government: he would not depart without at least 200 dollars, which was half the value of the stolen cargo. Byron treated the naval officers to a courteous reception, and some sardonic humour at his own expense.

Mavrokordatos was prepared to accept liability in principle, but tried to defer payment. When this was refused, Byron offered to pay himself. But Captain Yorke was not going to accept reparation for a Greek violation from a fellow-Briton. So Byron had to give the 200 dollars quietly to Praidis, who duly handed them over as though from the Greek government.[40] That evening, Byron told Stanhope what had happened, probably still laughing at the absurdity of the transaction. But Stanhope was not the person to see the funny side of anything. 'I said the affair was conducted in a bullying manner', Stanhope reported indignantly to Bowring two days later, 'and not according to the principles of equity and the law of nations.'[41]

Byron's always-fragile good humour collapsed. He had been touched by the plea of the caique's owner, and horrified that the Greek warships (that he himself had paid for) should have stooped to what he called 'buccaneering' against their own people. Quite apart from humanitarian and legal considerations, on which he declared himself disinterested, he warned that it was the height of political folly for the Greeks to put their future relations with foreign powers at risk in this way. Over the next few days, Byron would say as much in a stern circular addressed to 'the captains of Greek privateers' and to Bowring in London: 'I cannot but condemn the want of discipline and authority which has led to the acts of *piracy* in question (for they are no better).'[42]

That evening, with Stanhope, 'His Lordship started into a passion. He contended, that law, justice, and equity, had nothing to do with politics.' This was Byron's relativism at its most shockingly radical, and Stanhope recoiled from it. Inevitably, the name of the 'immortal Bentham' got dragged in. The quarrel raged fast and furiously. Byron had never read anything by Bentham, but took refuge in casting slurs against the man. Or so Stanhope complained. It was not the first time this had happened. At least, Stanhope raged, 'Bentham had a truly British heart', while Byron, 'after professing liberal principles from his boyhood, had, when called upon to act, proved himself a Turk'. When Byron demanded an instance of this, Stanhope countered with: 'Your conduct in endeavouring to crush the press, by declaiming against it to Mavrocordato, and your general abuse of liberal principles'. 'And yet', retorted Byron, 'without my money, where would your Greek newspaper be?'[43]

Far from being against the press, Byron was actually subsidising it, along with just about everything else that went on at Missolonghi. On the question of Greek actions at sea and the payment of reparations, he could see both sides, was appalled by the behaviour of the Greeks, and had deftly defused diplomatic tension with the representatives of British naval power in the eastern Mediterranean. Immediately after that riposte, he ended the quarrel with Stanhope with a plea for what today would be called pragmatism: 'Judge me by my actions, not by my words.'[44]

Five days later, on 31 January, Stanhope struck back through the columns of the *Greek Chronicle*. The lead article, unsigned, is headed, 'Publicity is the soul of justice. On the freedom of the press.' Whether the words are Stanhope's, or more probably Meyer's, the sentiments could have come straight from the pen of Jeremy Bentham himself: 'Publicity by means of the press . . . gives the most accurate measure of all things; the organs of this most beneficial publicity are newspapers.'[45] But while Stanhope struck back in words, when the occasion warranted Byron would resort to action as he had promised. Almost two months after the initial quarrel, and a month after Stanhope had left Missolonghi, the *Chronicle* had become increasingly outspoken on another issue on which the 'typographical colonel' felt strongly. This was monarchy, both in principle and as a future form of government for Greece. Editorials in March lashed out against the 'tyranny' of the newly restored monarchy in Spain.[46] When Meyer found occasion to express solidarity between the Greeks and the Hungarians and Croats, peoples presented as being subjected to the overweening empire of the Habsburgs, Mavrokordatos intervened to suppress the entire issue of the newspaper.

Byron was eager to enforce this order, confiscating all copies that came into his possession. It was the first of only three occasions in the paper's two-year history when this happened.[47] On the same day, 20 March, the first number of the *Telegrafo Greco* appeared. Written mainly in Italian, the new publication was intended to complement the *Chronicle* by addressing a foreign readership. This time, Byron had taken the precaution of installing his trusted lieutenant, Gamba, as editor – though not without misgivings about Pierino's propensity to get into 'scrapes'. Missolonghi now had two regular newspapers, more than all the rest of Greece. But despite the protestations about freedom of the press in the *Chronicle*, the one was securely controlled by Mavrokordatos, the other by Byron himself.[48]

Could this be the same Byron who had championed the constitutionalist revolution in Spain ever since its beginning exactly four years ago – indeed for longer and more consistently than he had the cause of Greece? The same who from Italy had repeatedly denounced the Austrians as 'barbarians'? Where now was the author of *The Age of Bronze* – a far more intemperate tirade than anything that ever appeared in the schoolmasterly columns of the *Greek Chronicle*?

It is thanks to the long-delayed arrival of the firemaster William Parry that we know the answers to these questions. Parry finally reached Dragomestre on the last day of January, with his artillerymen and a shipload of supplies sent by the London Greek Committee. In another week, he and his stores would have arrived at Missolonghi. Byron, who had been expecting them since September, observed caustically to Bowring, 'I presume from this retardment that he is the same Parry who attempted the *North* pole – and is (it may be supposed) now essaying the *South*.'[49]

Parry would quickly prove a controversial figure, and has remained one ever since. It was hardly his fault that a better-qualified specialist in artillery could not be found, on the terms that the London Greek Committee was able to offer. At least one German aristocratic volunteer refused to serve under Parry and departed. Dr Millingen sneered at the pretension of a man who 'presented himself before the troops with an apron and hammer'. Finlay 'cared little about the apron and hammer but . . . was satisfied that a drunken mountebank was not the person to do anything for [the] good of Greece'.[50] Fond of his drink Parry certainly was. But his real offence came down to class. Parry was not an officer or a gentleman. The Greeks (except for Mavrokordatos) ignored him because they cared nothing for the new-fangled technologies that he was supposed to have brought. The foreigners, liberals to a man and engaged in fighting a war for a new kind of society, would have nothing to do with someone who had never been to the equivalent of an English public school, who could not quote Latin and ancient Greek, and had no military record that he was willing to talk about.

All except Byron. Byron took to Parry at once. Parry had no time for humbug, spoke his mind with a blunt directness that Byron seems sorely to have missed among his new acquaintances in Missolonghi, and at once struck a chord with certain of Byron's own recent antipathies. 'Parry', declared Byron after their first meeting, 'seems a fine rough subject.' Later, he called him 'a sort of hard-working Hercules'.[51] At least until Finlay arrived at Missolonghi at the end of February to displace him, Parry was Byron's chief confidant. During their evenings spent together, Parry listened and took notes. Parry's ghost-written memoir, published the next year, contains the fullest evidence we have for the thinking that lay behind Byron's political choices during his hundred days.

This was how he accounted for his interventions over the press:

He knew it had been said that the Greek insurrection was the offspring of the revolutionary principles to which the sovereigns of Europe were so resolutely opposed. He knew that wherever they suspected the existence of these principles, no appeal to honour, to justice, or even to religion, was of any avail, and that they directed all their energies to stifle in every part of the world every germ of popular independence. He therefore saw in this denunciation [of Austria, in the *Greek Chronicle*], and in most of the political doctrines which were broached in Greece, an invitation to these powers, more particularly to Austria, to take part against the Greeks. It was moreover a justification of their doing so. Lord Byron saw this was hazarding the success of that cause which wholly engrossed his mind, and he was proportionably energetic in his reprobation of what appeared to him both inexpedient in practice, and indefensible in principle.[52]

When it came to his actions over reparations to the Ionian authorities on 26 January, that had also offended Stanhope, Byron explained himself with the exact same logic. Greece was not yet recognised as 'an independent power', by Great Britain or by any other state. 'Whatever may be my opinions as to this part of the conduct of our government,' he explained patiently to Parry, 'these are things I cannot alter; I must take them as I find them.' There was a very simple reason for caving in to the demands of the Royal Navy. The colonial British government that ruled the Ionian

Islands had the power to cut off supplies to Greece or even to intervene in the war on the side of Turkey. 'Knowing this', Byron went on, 'I counselled restitution, not because it was just, for as I say justice has nothing to do with politics, but because it was expedient for us to do so.'[53] Byron had by this time gained a firm grasp of the realities of the political situation he was trying to influence. He was not only a relativist. He was also, at this time in his life, a clear-sighted realist.

On the future form of government that he wished to see in independent Greece, Byron was similarly pragmatic and open-minded. Mavrokordatos was known to favour monarchy as the best solution to the constitutional question that was bound to arise sooner or later if the Greeks succeeded in their aims. Many philhellenes, notably Stanhope and Trelawny, were viscerally hostile to the idea – hence Meyer's editorials in the *Chronicle* and the suppression of its offending issue.[54] The author of *Don Juan*, who had only three years before declared, 'The king-times are fast finishing... the peoples will conquer in the end', might have been expected to be similarly opposed. But not even this principle would Byron allow to stand in the way of the 'regeneration of a nation'.[55] Instead, as he explained it to Parry:

A system of government must and will arise suitable to the knowledge and the wants of the people, and the relations which now exist among the different classes of them... [The Greeks] cannot for ages have that knowledge and that equality amongst them which are found in Europe, and therefore I would not recommend them to follow implicitly any system of government now established in the world, or to square their institutions by the theoretical forms of any constitution... There is no abstract form of government which we can call good... [E]very government derives its efficiency as well as its power from the people.

It was a neat reversal of what Byron had written in his journal ten years before. What had once looked like 'political nihilism' re-emerges as creative openness. As he also expressed it to Parry, 'Time will bring such a system; for a whole nation can profit by no other teacher.' History itself would have to evolve a new system of government that would work in the new circumstances.[56]

Within a few weeks of Parry's arrival, Byron had hammered out a set of principles that built upon the lessons of his rapid apprenticeship in Greek politics while he had been in Cephalonia, and now at Missolonghi. It was typical of his distrust of any sort of abstract theorising that he never set down these ideas in any systematic form. He barely touches on them in letters. It was in conversation, particularly with Parry and with Gamba, that he elaborated his thinking most fully – and, as a result, tantalisingly, we are forced to rely for our knowledge on the notes and later written-up recollections of these two very different witnesses. Essentially, Byron's policies for Greece, while he was at Missolonghi, come down to three fundamental principles. The first was the paramount need for a 'strong national government' with centralised functions.[57] This made Byron unequivocally a 'moderniser', in the terms in which the civil conflict within Greece at the time is understood today. This first principle was a necessary precondition for the other two.

Secondly, Byron recognised, as many others did not, that it was not just money the new state needed, but what today would be called an economic policy. Already he was looking beyond the immediate goal of the arrival of the expected loan from London. There had to be mechanisms for the proper disbursement of the funds, and also to ensure that eventually they would be repaid. On this, Byron was punctilious.[58] He saw that the future viability of the Greek state would depend on its financial probity. (Had he lived longer, he might have been able to mitigate the reputational damage that would begin with the scandals over the two British loans to Greece of 1824 and 1825, and has returned to haunt the country since the economic crisis of 2010.)

Since an economic policy, in the short term, hinged upon the raising of loans abroad, this second principle led seamlessly into the third: the need for a developed and coherent foreign policy. Full independence and prosperity would only ever be possible with the blessing of those Great Powers of Europe that Byron, as poet, had heartily loathed. This meant persuading the hard-headed representatives of those Powers that their own geopolitical interests would be better served by supporting the fledgling Greek nation than by allowing the status quo to remain. To Gamba, a little later, he would spell it out: 'The English government deceived itself at first in thinking it possible to maintain the Turkish empire in its integrity: but it cannot be done; that unwieldy mass is already putrefied, and must dissolve. If any thing like an equilibrium is to be upheld, Greece must be supported.'[59]

Here Byron was invoking what in a few years would come to be called the 'Eastern Question', which would preoccupy the courts and governments of Europe for a century. A new independent Greece, on this way of thinking, would succeed to the mantle of Turkey (not yet dubbed the 'sick man of Europe') as a bulwark against Russia for the powers of the West. It was a bold and far-reaching view of the future of Greece. And it was not only Byron's. It may well be, as some commentators have thought, that he had already foreseen the dissolution of the Ottoman empire at the time when he embarked on the 'Turkish tales'. But all of those principles, and especially the last, had for some time been central to the political thinking of Mavrokordatos too.[60]

Byron and Mavrokordatos, together, were determined to tie the fortunes of the revolution into the economic and geopolitical future of the entire continent. Revolution in Greece was not just a local affair. Every one of the Great Powers must be obliged to take notice of what was happening, must be dragged into involvement – for their own self-interest. Loans of money raised from private speculators in Great Britain were part of that. So was the establishment of good diplomatic relations, so that eventually the powers would *have* to recognise Greece, if only out of the fear that their rivals would do so first. The Greek Revolution must become, as one modern study has it, a 'European event'.[61] Whether Byron himself ever quite believed this or not, he certainly saw the benefits of *presenting* the struggle as being fought 'between barbarism and civilization ... and in behalf of the descendants of those to whom we are indebted for the first principles of science, and the most perfect models of literature and of art'.[62] It was a less grandiose version of what Shelley had written in the preface to *Hellas*.

Finally, there remained the issue of how to resolve the simmering civil conflict within Greece, that stood most immediately in the way of realising those aims. This was about to prove the most intractable of all the political challenges that Byron faced. In the meantime, as January gave way to February, all heads at Missolonghi were turned by the preparations going forward for the assault on the Turkish outpost of Lepanto – with Byron himself as commander-in-chief.

CHAPTER II

Confronting the warlords

LEPANTO: THE FIRST ROUND

By early February, news was reaching Missolonghi that the members of the deposed Executive had regrouped at Tripolitsa. Kolokotronis was on his way there to provide them with military backing. From Tripolitsa, a lengthy proclamation signed by Petrobey Mavromichalis as President of the Executive was put out on 5 February. In it, the deposed president denounced the actions of the rival government at Kranidi and systematically set out to rebut all the accusations that had been used to justify the proscription of himself and his fellow-officers. When it came to laying blame for the breakdown of civil order, the proclamation became strident. All was 'due to the illegal, unjust and absurd presidency of the shamelessly so-called "prince" Mavrokordatos', who was further accused of 'power-lust' and of still harbouring designs to sell out 'this sacred soil' to unspecified foreign interests.[1]

Rumours were being put about the Peloponnese. Mavrokordatos' allies there, the primates-turned-warlords Zaimis and Londos, who were also the main channel through which communications passed between Missolonghi and Kranidi, were becoming edgy. They wrote to him, warning of the rumours that were reaching them from Tripolitsa. According to one of these, Mavrokordatos and some of the merchants from the islands had concluded an alliance with the Catholic Knights of Malta. This was playing on the religious sensitivities of the Peloponnesian population, which was solidly Orthodox. Another story had it that 'your Excellency, either in agreement with us or treacherously over our heads, is going to hand over Greece to the British, and we should wake up to the fact'. How were these rumours to be countered? What was the truth of the matter?[2]

With this letter came a second, dated a day later, and containing a more specific warning. Nikolos Tzavellas at the head of twenty Souliots had just passed through Vostitsa (where Londos had once entertained Byron

228

and Hobhouse). They had previously been at Gastouni, in the northwest Peloponnese, where the local primate, Georgios Sisinis, was under the protection of Kolokotronis. Now they were heading for Missolonghi. While at Gastouni, Tzavellas had been keeping bad company and had 'become considerably imbued with the corrupting aims of the tyrant-lovers' (an allusion to Kolokotronis). Other troublemakers were independently on their way too. But Tzavellas, the writers warned, was determined to 'do as much as damage as he can' at Missolonghi. The damage could be considerable. Zaimis and Londos did not need to remind Mavrokordatos that the Tzavellas clan was one of the most powerful among the Souliots who were even now being drilled by Byron and Gamba in anticipation of the campaign against Lepanto. Kitsos Tzavellas was a key figure in all Mavrokordatos' dealings with the Souliots. Nikolos, the writers of the letter warned, was plotting 'to gather together all those Souliots [at Missolonghi] who will follow him, and others, to bring them over to the Peloponnese to unite with Kolokotronis'.[3] And this just at the time when the deposed Executive was issuing its message of defiance from Tripolitsa. By the time Mavrokordatos read these letters, on Saturday, 14 February, and conveyed their contents to Byron and Gamba, the damage had already been done.

Preparations for the assault on Lepanto had been going on for six weeks. From the beginning, there had been an air of make-believe about them. Byron was fully aware of the deal that had been struck with the defenders. The Albanian garrison would give up the fortress after only token resis-tance, in return for the pay they were owed by their own side. He had even sent to Zante for the money to pay them off.[4] But this did not prevent him from acting out the fantasy to the full. Millingen paints a vivid picture of the walls of Byron's apartment at this time: 'decorated with swords, pistols, Turkish sabres, dirks, rifles, guns, blunderbusses, bayonets, hel-mets, and trumpets, fantastically suspended, so as to form various figures'. According to Stanhope, already on his third day at Missolonghi, Byron had become 'soldier-mad'. A week after that, Stanhope was reporting to Bowring, 'He burns with military ardour and chivalry, and will proceed with the expedition to Lepanto.'[5]

Byron enjoyed drilling and exercising his Souliot troops, whenever the rains let up for long enough. But, revealingly, when it was all over, he would confess to Gamba that 'this enterprise of mine was only a secondary object; my first aim was to know something of those soldiers'. Gamba must have been thirsting to get his own first taste of soldiering, and certainly took those plans seriously. But he understood from the start that, for Byron, Lepanto was never more than a 'secondary interest'. Beyond his lingering fascination with the Souliot warriors, Byron's real and overriding object, as Gamba well knew, was to boost the political and economic strength of the Greek government by every means in his power.[6] A propaganda coup at Lepanto, that would heighten Mavrokordatos' prestige, was one such means. For all the excitement of playing at soldiers, in Byron's mind it was never more than that – a means to a *political* end.

During the first half of February, the preparations gathered momentum. That the expedition was imminent was taken for granted by almost everyone in Missolonghi. Mavrokordatos in his letters repeatedly said so. It was even announced in the *Greek Chronicle*, though, for all his high words about press freedom, Meyer held back from naming the target in print – though of course it was on everyone's lips. From Cephalonia, where the news had already reached, Byron's friends expressed themselves

very anxious you should not expose yourself in the expedition to Lepanto, which we hear you are determined to join. I, for one, do not think your Lordship ought to go a fighting at all, your Lordship's niche in the Temple of Fame is already secured, and fight as you will I . . . think your Lordship's life too great a stake to risk, and would willingly save it over at the expence of Grecian liberty.[7]

On Friday, 13 February, it was announced that the whole regiment of Souliots would parade the next day. The agreement for their terms of service would be read out, and the troops would receive a month's pay in advance. The day after that, Gamba 'was to march with the vanguard of 300 of them, and take up a position under Lepanto'. The expedition would be on its way.[8]

It was on the morning of the day fixed for the parade, Saturday the fourteenth, that Mavrokordatos received the letters that had come from the Peloponnese. A few hours later, he and Gamba met the Souliot chiefs, without Byron. According to Gamba, 'after a tedious discussion, these persons withdrew, and promised to send me their definitive answer in three hours'. The mood of the troops had changed overnight. Tzavellas and his fellow-travellers had arrived. When the answer came, at five in the afternoon, it took the form of a new set of demands. There was no more talk of a parade, or an advance guard setting out for Lepanto. Byron 'burst into a violent passion, and protested that he would have no more to do with these people'.

All next day, the fifteenth, it was left to Gamba and Mavrokordatos to renew negotiations, with the mediation of Kostas Botsaris, the most loyal of the Souliot leaders. Byron refused to attend. Instead, he sent a curt note:

Having tried in vain at every expence – considerable trouble – and some danger to unite the Suliotes for the good of Greece – and their own – I have come to the following resolution. –

I will have nothing more to do with the Suliotes – they may go to the Turks or – the devil but if they cut me into more pieces than they have dissensions among them, they will not change my resolution –⁹

A facing-saving deal was struck: 'a new corps should be raised, no matter from what tribe, composed of six hundred, as before agreed upon'. This was the body that Byron had agreed to pay, at the beginning. Nothing was said about the remainder of the 3,000, that two days before had been ready to set out for Lepanto. With the loyalty of the greater part of the troops uncertain at best, even a token assault was now out of the question. At seven in the evening, Gamba reported this news to Byron.¹⁰

Not long after eight, Byron had the violent seizure that has often been described, and some have thought was an advance warning of his fatal illness two months later. He himself, in its immediate aftermath, described it as 'a strong shock of a Convulsive description', such that several strong men present were unable to hold him.¹¹ Back in August, he had experienced something similar, in Ithaca, though this attack was much more severe and its effects longer-lasting. Then, Byron had been reliving the cremation of Shelley on the same day the year before. All the associated feelings had combined with more immediate contributory causes: exposure to the sun, extreme fatigue, and perhaps recent heavy drinking. This time, Parry's fondness for a vat of cider would at once and ever after be blamed by almost everyone. Byron had certainly been drinking with Parry, Stanhope, and Gamba immediately before it happened. Various manifestations of what today would be called stress have also been invoked, ever since the event itself, and these are plausible enough. The defection of the Souliots and the puncturing of the make-believe surrounding the Lepanto campaign clearly affected Byron greatly. But, just as before, in Cephalonia, there was a specific emotional cause that may better account for the extreme physical reaction that followed.

Gamba was aware of this, but either failed to recognise its significance, or more likely preferred to play it down. In his long account of the events of the previous day, Gamba reports that the Souliots had been urged to defect by a 'messenger sent by Colocotroni . . . What was still more distressing to us was the discovery that this very spy of Colocotroni had been one of those whom Lord Byron had relieved in Cephalonia'.¹² Nikolos Tzavellas, of whom Mavrokordatos had been warned in the letter from Zaimis and

Londos, was none other than the 'Giavella' who along with Fotomaras and Drakos had led the band of forty Souliots to mob Byron when he first arrived aboard the *Hercules* off Argostoli. When the other Souliots had been packed off to Missolonghi at the end of August, Byron had retained Tzavellas and the brothers Georgios and Anastasios Drakos in his service. It was he who had sent all three of them, with the twenty men who had now turned up at Missolonghi, to the northwest Peloponnese at the end of October. At the time when he had been intending to accept the government's invitation and go to Nafplio, these Souliots had been deputed to arrange with Sisinis, the local primate, for his reception when he landed at Pyrgos. Thereafter, presumably, they would have formed his bodyguard on his overland journey.

Possibly Byron had forgotten them, after the arrival of Orlandos and Louriotis in the lazaretto of Argostoli had caused him to change his plans. But they had not forgotten *him*. Now recruited to Kolokotronis' camp and determined to make trouble for Mavrokordatos at Missolonghi, the Drakos brothers went even further, and tried to dun Byron for arrears of wages they claimed were due to themselves and their men for the months when they had gone over to the service of the opposing side in the civil war.[13]

Ever since the time when his beloved Newfoundland dog Boatswain had died and been buried in the grounds of Newstead Abbey sixteen years before, the one thing that Byron hated, despised, and perhaps feared above all others was treachery. Then, in lines literally engraved in stone, he had deplored the faithlessness of his own species, choosing to commemorate his dog as the only faithful friend he had ever known – and this at the age of nineteen.[14] Tzavellas, Drakos, and their men had been the first Greeks to offer Byron a hero's welcome. He had responded with generosity and high hopes for them. Angry and bitter when they tried to take advantage of him in Cephalonia, he had dismissed most of them as soon as he could. But the behaviour of Tzavellas and the Drakos brothers, now, went far further. As well might Boatswain, in Newstead days, have tried to bite off his arm. Among the many other trials and exasperations, the incessant rain and consequent lack of exercise, and Parry's cider, all of which no doubt contributed to Byron's seizure that Sunday evening, the sense of personal betrayal by those 'brave' Souliots was surely the one that struck most deeply.

Parry, who probably knew nothing of the earlier story, and certainly not the epitaph for Boatswain, recorded that the Newfoundland's successor, Lyon, was now Byron's 'dearest and most affectionate friend'. 'Thou art more faithful than men, Lyon', he reported Byron as saying very frequently, before adding, 'I trust thee more.'[15]

During the days that followed, the new disaffection among the Souliots threatened to break out into open insurrection. The first time was a false alarm, caused by two jittery German volunteers who had drunk too much. But the town was put on alert. That was within hours of Byron's seizure. The second was far more serious. A Swedish lieutenant, acting on orders, barred a Souliot from entering the seraglio where the artillery stores were kept. In the fray that resulted, Lieutenant Sass lost his life and the Souliot was severely wounded. For a time it looked as though

the town might be sacked, or that we should at least come to open war. At Lord Byron's quarters, preparations were made as for a siege. The guns were prepared, and pointed towards the gate . . . The main body of the Suliotes assembled round the house, threatening to attack it, and to murder every foreigner.[16]

The foreigners certainly did fear for their safety. Several of Parry's assistants took fright and demanded to be sent home, much to Byron's disgust. Recollecting these events a year later, Stanhope would employ generous licence to evoke the spectacle of Byron confronting the mutinous and dishevelled soldiers from his sickbed: 'the more the Suliots raged, the more his calm courage triumphed. The scene was truly sublime'.[17]

In the midst of the mayhem a series of hastily convened meetings took place. Byron was present on at least one of these occasions, wearing full military uniform, and harangued the Souliot chiefs through an interpreter.[18] By this time, the townspeople were demanding the removal of the Souliots from Missolonghi altogether. A week after Byron's seizure, a new plan of campaign had been cobbled together. The expedition to Lepanto, officially postponed, was abandoned. The paramount need, now, was to remove something like 3,000 armed men as far as possible from Missolonghi. At least, now, there seemed to be no risk of them going over to Kolokotronis. The Souliot leaders, Mavrokordatos had discovered, would not be separated so far from their local power-bases.[19]

Instead, he hit upon the idea of sending them north, into the devastated no-man's-land that had been left behind by the enemy's campaigns of the two previous autumns. Omer Pasha was reported to be having troubles of his own with disaffected Albanians and had been obliged to withdraw as far as Ioannina. The towns of Arta and Preveza were left exposed.[20] Nominally, it was a secret, but most of the leaders knew soon enough that their next target for a token campaign was to be Arta. This way, their men would be able to live off the land – in effect, at the expense of the local Greek peasantry. Even more encouraging, from Mavrokordatos' point of view, was that many of the captains had scores of their own to settle with rival Greek bands in these areas. The Souliots and other armed groups agreed to move to Xiromero, the mountainous region that lies between the main road to the north and the sea. In the event, it would not be until the beginning of March that the troops began to leave Missolonghi: and that not until further threats of disturbances and a desperate plea from the leading citizens had induced Byron to part with yet more money to cover their arrears.[21]

It was the best that could be done in the circumstances. But it was hardly a satisfactory conclusion to the efforts of almost two months. The Albanian garrison at Lepanto sent plaintive messages begging to be 'attacked'. They had still not been paid by their own side and would happily surrender for 'five hundred purses'. But Mavrokordatos' coffers were empty.[22] As for Byron, he was able to conceal his chagrin in part by laying the blame on his illness. He had given up all idea of 'taking the field in person' – at least 'for the present'.[23] The 'Byron Brigade' had been reduced to some 225, in effect little more than a household guard, even if Byron could still boast that it was 'the only *regularly paid* corps in Greece'.[24]

By the first week of March, the emergency had passed. As the troops finally filed out of the town, Mavrokordatos gave vent to his exasperation in a long account of events for the benefit of the government at Kranidi. With weary bravado, he concluded that, at least, 'the plans of the anti-patriots have not succeeded'.[25] But then, neither had his and Byron's. This first skirmish in a civil war, whose main theatre would be far away, had been at best a draw.

DIPLOMACY VERSUS CIVIL WAR

While the excitement had been at its height over Parry's arrival and then the imminent campaign against Lepanto, during the first week of February a development of much greater importance had passed almost unnoticed at Missolonghi. At Kranidi, the newly appointed President of the Executive, Georgios Koundouriotis, was no politician. His principal qualification for office was that his family was the richest in Hydra. Mavrokordatos, during the time of his refuge there, had lived in the house of Koundouriotis' brother-in-law, Orlandos. Mutual respect and shared interest had led to mutual trust. One of Koundouriotis' first acts in office had been to beg and cajole Mavrokordatos to return to the seat of government and help him out. Mavrokordatos' response, while Byron had been actually or apparently 'soldier-mad' about Lepanto, was to insist that, in that case, Byron must be given overall command at Missolonghi, with Londos and someone else of similar standing to support him.[26]

There, for the time being, the matter had rested. Now, on the day the Souliots left town, Mavrokordatos was once again under pressure from Koundouriotis to shift his operations to Kranidi. For Mavrokordatos, this should have been the perfect opportunity – and for Byron too. The two arms of government were now effectively controlled by the islanders of Hydra and Spetses. All of the newly appointed Executive and a working majority of the Legislature were Mavrokordatos' political friends. Officially, he was still the president of the Legislature. He is regularly given this title in letters from the government to Byron, and in the columns of the *Greek Chronicle*. Now, thanks to Koundouriotis' warmly expressed but thinly disguised plea for help in discharging his new duties as President, Mavrokordatos had the perfect opportunity to return to office, virtually unopposed. In effect, he was being offered the chance to take charge of operations that would resolve the civil conflict once and for all. Thereafter he would have been in a position to carry through his own modernising programme unhindered. Mavrokordatos would have become the undisputed political leader of Greece – with Byron at his side.

It was the most important decision of the hundred days. One of history's fascinating counterfactuals is to wonder how Byron might have worked with the government had he gone with Mavrokordatos to Kranidi, and what the political outcome might have been. Another is to imagine what might have been the rest of Byron's life, if he had left Missolonghi for the drier and healthier climate of the northeast Peloponnese in February or March 1824.

Why did it not happen? Back in February, with momentum for the Lepanto campaign seemingly unstoppable, Mavrokordatos could have been excused for temporising, and perhaps saying nothing, either, to Byron. Now, at the beginning of March, without the distraction of a pseudomilitary adventure, with the danger to Missolonghi from friendly as well as hostile forces removed, and while still smarting from their humiliation at the hands of the rebels and their Souliot proxies, both men should have been ready to jump at the chance. Instead, on 2 March, within hours of the departure of the Souliots from Missolonghi, Mavrokordatos laid down conditions. He was willing to go to Kranidi, he replied to Koundouriotis, but only if the Legislative Body were first to accept his resignation, offered three times already, as its President – 'so that by coming there I do not bring on myself new troubles and complications'. He went on, 'I consider it essential for the Government to write also to his Lordship to invite him . . . His presence and his counsel would be of great value there.' But Byron, too, Mavrokordatos seemed to warn, might be lukewarm about the idea. 'Should he fail to come, such a letter from the Government will obligate him.'[27]

It is not hard to work out what the 'troubles and complications' were that Mavrokordatos was determined to avoid at Kranidi. He was well aware of what was being said about him, particularly in the Peloponnese. Many ordinary Greeks believed that his own 'power-lust' was the root cause of the civil war, as the proclamation now circulating there had it. By the beginning of March, he will have known that vital decisions were already being taken at Kranidi without him. If the government was about to go into action against the rebels, then whoever was in charge would have Greek blood on his hands. For Mavrokordatos to have accepted a leading role for himself too soon would have been to give ammunition to his accusers, perhaps even to enflame the conflict further. A more ruthless politician would have risked it. Had he been driven by personal ambition, as his enemies claimed, surely he would not have hesitated. But Mavrokordatos was committed to the long view. And he had Byron to think of, too.

Since coming to Missolonghi, Byron had never repeated his gung-ho threat, made in the high spirits of his final days in Cephalonia, to help resolve the Greeks' internal differences by force.[28] Now, during the first days of March, in letters and conversations he reverted to a topic that had preoccupied him earlier. In his determination to see a 'strong national government' in Greece Byron never wavered. But the way to achieve it, he now insisted, was by 'the healing of these dissensions'. He was himself, he wrote to Barff on 10 March, 'doing all I can to re-unite the Greeks with ye Greeks'.[29] In other words, although he was careful never to say so in so many words, Byron disapproved of the new policy that was emerging at Kranidi, of facing down the warlords by force. As early as 20 February, he had told Gamba, 'I must wait here to see the turn that things take in the Morea, and to receive news from London.' A month later, he would confess to Parry his fear that the government's intransigence towards 'the bravest and most skilful of the military chieftains' would lead to outright civil war.[30]

Mavrokordatos could not possibly risk alienating Byron, over a matter of such importance. He might have tried to talk him round to the government's point of view. But more likely he did not even try. Mavrokordatos could see as well as Byron could that the key to Greece's future lay with the loan that was expected from London. 'Only let the loan be raised, and in the mean time let us try to form a strong national government, ready to apply the pecuniary resources, when they arrive, to the best objects.'[31] So Byron had insisted to Gamba, back in January. Everything else would depend on that. Mavrokordatos' own expedient to remove the Souliots from Missolonghi, as he would later candidly confess, had had the very same aim: to keep the troublemakers at a distance 'until the money should arrive'.[32] After that, everything else would fall into place, without resort to internal violence. A military strike against the rebels, at this juncture, would be at best superfluous, at worst counter-productive. For the government to make war against its own people would only serve to jeopardise the long-term goal. On this, it seems that Mavrokordatos and Byron were in full agreement.

With his second response to the Executive on 2 March, Mavrokordatos bought an interval during which he and Byron could pursue their own independent policy from Missolonghi. It was nothing like a rupture with the government. All the elements of that policy were firmly designed to strengthen the position of the central authority. But in Western Greece, in March, it seemed that there might be more than one way of going about it. While Koundouriotis and the new Executive were preparing to take the field against the rebels in the Peloponnese, Mavrokordatos and Byron, throughout that month, kept up a series of diplomatic exchanges with figures of doubtful loyalty, on whom peaceful leverage might be just as effective.

To one of these, Dimitrios Peroukas (Parucca), in whose house at Argos he had been given hospitality in 1810, Byron went so far as to express himself willing to go as a 'hostage'.[33] To Sisinis, the client of Kolokotronis who had turned his own former Souliot protégés against him, he responded with consummate courtesy, but made no promises. 'I *have heard a good deal* of Sisseni', wrote Byron to Barff, who had been dragged into mediating, 'but not a *deal* of *good*: however, I never judge from report, particularly in a revolution' (Plate 8a).[34] While negotiations continued with both Sisinis and Peroukas, Byron made his own position plain: '*I* am perfectly sincere in desiring the most amicable termination of their internal dissensions – and . . . I believe P[rince] Mavrocordato to be so also – otherwise I would not act with him.' Comparison of Byron's letters with those of Mavrokordatos bears out the truth of this.[35] What is more, when Byron was asked by the government to detach part of his brigade of Souliots, ostensibly to support the siege of Turkish-held Patras but actually for offensive operations against Sisinis at Gastouni, Mavrokordatos intervened to refuse on his behalf.[36]

This policy was effective. Sisinis was indeed playing a double game, as Byron and Mavrokordatos suspected. But he was no fool, and according to his lights was acting conscientiously to protect the inhabitants of his region from the depredations of their better-armed neighbours. To a supporter, Sisinis wrote ruefully, in April, acknowledging how he had been outmanoeuvred:

Our own policy is crumbling from the foundations . . . If it was only a matter of making up to the Milord, that I could take. But then I see Mavrokordatos too, whose intentions are evil and you should know it. And all the time I keep thinking, that the only thing I can do is to abandon my own policy and adopt a new one, and of such a sort, with such fine manners, that maybe that way we can further our old policy [after all]. And this disaster has come upon us because of the loans, because the Milord is going to give it all to the people at Kranidi and that is the basis of their power.[37]

Uncannily, the primate of Gastouni seems to anticipate the worldly wisdom of Don Fabrizio Salina, the fictional hero of the novel *The Leopard* by Giuseppe di Lampedusa, which depicts a comparable situation in Sicily some four decades later.

Byron never knew the extent of his success with Sisinis. But already, on 9 March, an emissary had arrived from Kolokotronis, a certain Lambros. This time (again, no doubt having consulted Mavrokordatos) Byron disdained to reply. But from the message he received he drew the encouraging conclusion that Kolokotronis 'found his influence on the decline'.[38] By 19 March, Byron was optimistic that the 'recent pacific overtures of the contending parties in the Peloponnese' might lead to some 'favourable result'. A week later, he was not so sure. What the 'contending parties' were really trying to do was to drive a wedge between himself and Mavrokordatos, and so gain direct access for themselves to the proceeds of the loan expected from London. Byron had now seen through this ploy. But he had an answer. As he told Parry, probably at about the same time, 'I have advised Mavrocordato to recommend to the government to supply these chiefs with money, but to keep them as short as possible.'[39] That was for after the loan arrived. In the meantime, it was enough to keep the negotiations going, and the warlike energies of the revolution from being dissipated in civil combat.

Of all these diplomatic exchanges, by far the most significant were with the pre-eminent warlord of eastern Greece, Odysseus Andritzou. Odysseus had established his headquarters at Athens. Allied with the young former diplomat in the Ottoman service, Theodoros Negris, Odysseus had for some time been urging on Mavrokordatos a summit meeting of the leaders of western and eastern Greece. The place proposed for this meeting was Salona (pronounced with the stress on the first syllable), today's Amphissa, near Delphi. At the end of February, Finlay had arrived at Missolonghi bearing letters for Mavrokordatos from Odysseus and Negris, and for Byron from Trelawny, who had been won over by Odysseus back in the autumn. When a second batch of letters arrived on 18 March, the newest recruit to Odysseus' camp added his voice to the others. Stanhope had left Missolonghi at the height of the disturbances with the Souliots, to spread the benefits of the press to other parts of free Greece. He had wound up in Athens, and there had become easily convinced that the warlord Odysseus espoused all the utilitarian principles that had been so airily brushed aside by Byron and Mavrokordatos at Missolonghi.[40]

The main object of Odysseus and Negris, as would soon become apparent, was no different from that of the other 'contending parties' who had made overtures. In this, they had been lucky enough to enlist two formidable spokesmen, who might prove more persuasive in their interest than the Ionian intermediaries on whom Peroukas and Sisinis relied. Trelawny and Stanhope had both lost any confidence that they had ever had in the 'prince' and were determined, by this time, to win Byron over to their new friends in Athens.[41] But even if he suspected as much at the time (as surely he did), Mavrokordatos could see the advantage of meeting Odysseus half way. So long as he was not aligned with the rebel chieftains in the Peloponnese, the warlord was potentially a strategic ally whose power and influence might yet be mobilised in the service of the government.[42] A diplomatic success at Salona would do more to enhance the prestige of the modernisers, and therefore also the authority of the legitimate government, than a victory over the Albanian garrison of Lepanto would have done. No Greek lives would be lost. And it was playing to the unique strengths that Mavrokordatos and Byron between them possessed.

The decision seems to have been taken on the spot. Far from being reluctant to go to Salona, as almost all English-language accounts have it, Mavrokordatos wrote at once to Trelawny, Stanhope, and Odysseus promising that he and Byron would both attend – if not at Salona, then at nearby Chrysso (where Byron and Hobhouse had once lodged with the local bishop on their way to Delphi). Byron wrote to Stanhope to the same effect. To Odysseus, Mavrokordatos even gave a date for their departure from Missolonghi – 25 March – and also dangled the allurement of great gains to be made in the north, thanks to the weakness of Omer Pasha of Ioannina.[43]

The decision for Salona had already been taken, and a commitment given, when on 21 or 22 March a new batch of letters arrived from Kranidi. It was now that Byron received this carefully worded note from Mavrokordatos:

> The president of the Executive power . . . writes to me in short that, for the affairs of the highest importance, he believes my presence at Kranidi very necessary; . . . that he would wish to know whether Mylord, were he to be invited to attend the Government would decide to go there; or whether he would accept the general direction of the affairs of mainland Greece . . . that he awaits my response and the frank exercise of my opinion, with impatience.[44]

The new Executive was offering Byron the choice between the two sets of conditions that Mavrokordatos had laid down for going to Kranidi himself, first in February and now in March. But it was left to Mavrokordatos to negotiate with his Lordship. The Greek government seems never actually to have offered these or any other terms to Byron directly.

By this time, Mavrokordatos was in less of a hurry than ever to align himself with a government that was pursuing an increasingly belligerent course against the rebels in the Peloponnese. In the same note to Byron in which he outlined the government's offer, he added news of armed clashes that had taken place in Tripolitsa a month ago. Some of the townspeople there had risen up against the exactions of Kolokotronis' son Gennaios. He also reported that the rebels holding the fortress of Acrocorinth were on the point of surrender.[45] These details seem to have been selectively chosen, and were already out of date. The truth was that Acrocorinth had been forced into submission. The twin fortresses of Nafplio, held by Kolokotronis' son Panos, were under close siege. A government army, 4,000 strong, would shortly be on its way to Tripolitsa, to do battle with Kolokotronis himself. Something of this Mavrokordatos seems to have learned on 23 March, just after he had finished writing his latest report for the government. Diplomatically, in a postscript, he declared himself 'delighted' by these developments. He had little choice.[46] How much Byron ever knew about the details of what was happening in the Peloponnese is impossible to tell. But, by 30 March, he was in a position to report to Bowring, with what degree of acerbic understatement we can only guess: 'the dissensions in the Morea still continue – and hamper them [the Greeks] a good deal'.[47]

All this would be enough to explain Byron's rather listless response to the invitation he had received, via Mavrokordatos, from the government. Given the choice to attend the government at Kranidi or to command at Missolonghi, he wrote to Barff on the twenty-second: 'I am willing to serve them in any capacity they please – either commanding or commanded – it is much the same to me – as long as I can be of any presumed use to them.' The meeting at Salona, where he believed that he and Mavrokordatos could set their own agenda, was more to his taste, and would come first. Gamba reports that Byron 'returned an answer to the government at Cranidi, that "he was first going to Salona, and that afterwards he would be at their commands"'.[48]

There was another reason to hold back from accepting the government's invitation immediately. Hard on the heels of the latest letters from Kranidi had come the first news from London – indirectly, by way of Mavrokordatos' informants in Pisa and Livorno, and Barff in Zante. As yet it was unconfirmed and details were scanty. But on 22 March, Byron learned that a loan had been agreed. Within weeks, the money would be on its way. He and Stanhope were named as commissioners for its disbursement. Neither he nor Mavrokordatos seems ever to have made explicit what must have been uppermost in both their minds. The time for them to arrive at the seat of government would be at the crucial moment, when the funds from London also arrived, to set the seal on the end of civil conflict, confirm the supremacy of the modernisers, and usher in a new phase of the Revolution.

MISSOLONGHI BLUES

During the last ten days of March, it rained so much that the streets of Missolonghi were turned to mud. The town was cut off from the rest of Greece by the impassable Fidari and Acheloos rivers. In these conditions, nobody could have gone to Salona, or anywhere else, as Byron wrote to inform Barff on 3 April.[49] The expedition to meet Odysseus and the leaders of eastern Greece kept being put off. Mavrokordatos will not have been unduly disconcerted by the delay. Every passing day brought the arrival of the loan from London closer. It was a waiting game. Mavrokordatos was good at waiting.

Byron was not. As the rain came down, day after day, and kept him and his companions cooped up indoors, with too little to do and no possibility of exercise, he once again became prey to extreme and abrupt mood swings. Finlay, who got to know him during March and the first ten days of April, observed that 'It seemed as if two different souls occupied his body alternately.' Ever since his convulsive episode in February, at the height of the debacle with the Souliots, as Parry noted: 'Lord Byron's health appeared not thoroughly re-established, and he frequently complained of slight pains in the head, shivering fits, confusion of thoughts, and visionary fears, all of which indicated to me increasing debility.'[50]

Even the normally upbeat Gamba noticed these symptoms. Gamba blamed the rain, which prevented the daily rides that he and Byron were in the habit of taking together. According to Millingen, after his fit, Byron 'fell into a state of melancholy, from which none of our reasonings could relieve him', and began to voice thoughts of death.[51] It was no doubt as part of the same pattern of alternating extremes of mood, and as a response to the boredom of enforced idleness, that he began to resort to pointless, elaborate, and cruel practical jokes. The victims were invariably those most dependent on him: his faithful valet Fletcher, the black American groom Benjamin Lewis, who had previously been in Trelawny's service, Parry the firemaster, and even a Turkish girl prisoner he was intent on saving.[52]

It was an indication of Byron's melancholy, during the doldrums of March, that he once again allowed his thoughts to slide backwards towards the life and the art he had given up to come here. Perhaps what triggered this was a letter from Tom Moore, that reached him at the beginning of the month. 'Your reproach is unfounded', he wrote back indignantly to this voice from his past. 'I have not been "quiet" in an Ionian Island but much occupied with business . . . Neither have I continued "Don Juan" – nor any other poem.'[53] But, during (probably) the last week of March, he thought of it. Grumbling to Parry about what he now called the 'talk and foolery' of the London Greek Committee, he warmed to the idea: 'Well, well, I'll have my revenge: talk of subjects for Don Juan, this Greek business, its disasters and mismanagement, have furnished me with matter for a hundred cantos.' There were to be walk-on parts for Bentham and Stanhope. 'There will be both comedy and tragedy; my good countrymen supply the former, and Greece the latter.' It was a pleasant threat, but not a serious one. He would not start to write again, he told Parry, 'till next winter'.[54]

But it was not quite the whole truth that he had written to Moore. While sheltering from the Turks and the weather at Dragomestre, on his way from Cephalonia, Byron had dashed off a piece of lively doggerel that captured his excitement at being back on the same shore (more or less) from which he and Hobhouse had all those years ago been rescued by Souliot warriors. Rather more accomplished, if hardly great poetry, are the lines, mentioned earlier, that he wrote and read aloud to his entourage on his birthday, 22 January. It was almost certainly during March that he dug out the page on which he had sketched the euphoric verses on the Souliots ('Up to battle! Sons of Suli'), turned it over, and began again.[55]

His theme, this time, was unrequited love. Its object was his 'page', Loukas Chalandritsanos. He had already showed the tenderness of his feelings for the boy during the voyage from Cephalonia. Perhaps it was the association that drew him back to the lines he had written then. The birthday poem, too, had touched on these feelings. But there the emphasis had been on renunciation. The first of the two short poems of March is a love poem, pure and simple. It ends (excruciatingly, to syntactical purists):

> and yet thou lov'st me not,
> And never wilt – Love dwells not in our will –
> Nor can I blame thee – though it be my lot
> To strongly – wrongly – vainly – love thee still.[56]

It was not just that fifteen-year-old Loukas refused to act up to the part, or respond to his advances. In reality, the advances may never have been made. Byron was lavish in his gifts to the young man, but made sure, too, that he knew his place. 'Tea is not a Greek beverage', he instructed his steward, Lega Zambelli, on 2 February, 'therefore Master Lukas may drink Coffee instead – or water – or nothing . . . He will eat with the Suliots – or where he pleases.'[57] This is not the language of the besotted lover. And Byron-the-new-statesman will have been perfectly well aware, from his observations with Hobhouse all those years ago, that the kind of liaison he had once carried on with Nicolo Giraud in Ottoman Athens could never have been publicly accepted in the world in which he was now establishing himself. Far from being the mainspring of his actions in Greece, as some have thought, Byron's feelings for Loukas Chalandritsanos were never more than a nostalgic throwback to his own youth, to his real relationship with Giraud, and still more, perhaps, to its fictional projection in *Lara* – to feelings and experiences that he knew very well could never come again.[58]

What is almost certainly his last surviving poem seems to concede this: 'honours or renown' and 'a new-born people's cry' are more precious to him than any material reward. For these the poet 'could die'. But he is appalled to find himself 'the fool of passion'. The poem's central metaphor is finely ambiguous:

> a frown
> Of thine to me is as an Adder's eye
> To the poor bird whose pinion fluttering down
> Wafts unto death the breast it bore so high –

It seems once again to be a love poem: what brings him down is the loved one's *disdain*. But then come the final lines:

> Such is this maddening fascination grown –
> So strong thy Magic – or so weak am I.

Is it not the fatal attraction itself (the 'Adder's eye') that threatens the proud bird of prey with destruction? This is what the same image had meant, years ago, when Byron had used it in *The Giaour*.[59] Byron at Missolonghi could not afford to be weak, and he knew it.

But these last poems are testimony to the effort it cost him.

By the end of March, Byron had been living among Greeks for eight months, for the last three of those in free Greece. He had still never been close or intimate with a Greek, as he had with friends and lovers of all classes while he had lived in Italy. (Even Nicolo Giraud, his only certain conquest on his earlier travels, though a fluent Greek-speaker and brought up in the country, had French parents.) It was perhaps ironic that Loukas' contempt, indifference, or quite possibly just uncomprehending vanity, had the effect of closing off the only intimate relationship that Byron seems ever to have considered in Greece. But it says something for his attitude, too, that sex with an underage boy was the only form of intimacy he could envisage with the people for whom he was prepared to sacrifice so much.

Even with Andreas Londos, his former host at Vostitsa and now a close political ally of Mavrokordatos, Byron guarded himself against acknowledging ties at the level of personal friendship, beyond obligation. When Londos wrote, through a scribe who translated his words into Italian, to recall 'memories of those happy hours, when in years gone by I had the pleasure of sharing a sweet domesticity with you', and invoking 'feelings of pure friendship', Byron resorted to the high style, praising the struggle and Londos' part in it, but conceded no more than 'the duties of Friendship and the recognition of your Hospitality' in former times. He did end the letter, 'To see you again, and to serve your Fatherland at your side, and under your eyes – will be for me one of the happiest moments of my life.' But the emphasis is on the cause, not the person. A second letter to Londos, written in Greek (by a scribe), is purely businesslike, and avowedly eschews 'compliments'.[60]

The one relationship that really mattered while Byron was at Missolonghi was his working relationship with Mavrokordatos. On the success of that would depend the outcome of his formative hundred days. Politically, and in public, Byron's loyalty never wavered. Privately, he was still happy to 'abuse' many of his old friends, as Finlay would not be the only one to discover at Missolonghi.[61] But he consistently, and quite uncharacteristically, spared Mavrokordatos. The furthest he would go, in answer to a direct question from Parry, was to venture 'that a little more energy and industry in the Prince, with a disposition to make fewer promises would tend much to his advantage'.[62] This had been back in February, soon after Parry's arrival. Byron's restraint is the more striking at a time when almost all the other foreigners who had come to Greece under the auspices of the London Greek Committee were by now openly critical.

It was becoming evident that Trelawny and Stanhope, in Athens, had transferred their allegiance entirely to the warlord Odysseus, who they thought would make a far worthier recipient of the monies from the English loan than Mavrokordatos. Stanhope, Millingen, and Finlay all found a variety of faults in the 'prince', from his lack of true democratic credentials to his devious, 'Asiatic' character and indecisive conduct of affairs. Trelawny, writing at the end of April, would go farther, his antipathy perhaps fuelled by an element of sexual jealousy in a letter addressed to Mary Shelley: 'I hope, ere long, to see his head removed from his worthless and heartless body. He is a mere shuffling soldier, an aristocratic brute – wants Kings and Congresses; a poor, weak, shuffling, intriguing, cowardly fellow.'[63] That, at least, Byron was spared from having to read. But by the end of March he was perfectly well aware of the discontent with Mavrokordatos that surrounded him.

It was Parry who gave him his opportunity, at the end of the month. He and Byron were alone in a punt on the lagoon, surveying the sea fortifications. Out of earshot, a short distance across the water, was Mavrokordatos in another. What the firemaster saw as the lackadaisical attitude of the Greeks to the defence of their town was too much for him to stomach. '"And there,"' he said to Byron, pointing to Mavrokordatos' punt, '"sits the old gentlewoman, Prince Mavrocordato and his troop," to whom I applied an epithet I will not here repeat, "as if they were all perfectly safe".' Parry's reward was to be humiliated as Byron ordered the vessel moved close to the other, then repeated his words to Mavrokordatos in his presence. Parry tells the story against himself. But Byron's purpose on that day, which was most probably 31 March, was surely to give a jolt to the man in whom he had invested so much confidence in public. Parry became his proxy to deliver a withering rebuke that really was Byron's own. Not surprisingly, Mavrokordatos was furious ('very much annoyed', says Parry).[64]

Parry's memoir was ghost-written, and meant to justify his own behaviour and understanding of events against the already-published accounts of Gamba and Stanhope. But here he is, writing to Bowring in his own voice, only a few days before the exchange in the punts:

however the Prince who commands at this place may be competent to direct offices at the Seat of Government, he is by no means actively sufficient at a place like Messalonghi, for although Lord Byron, treats him with the most marked respect and kindness, not only supporting him in every way possible, But actually supplying his private pecuniary wants, and with respect to the Public Service preparatory to the season's Campaign nothing would have been done[.][65]

By the time of the encounter in the lagoon, at the end of March, the working relationship was coming under strain. Mavrokordatos knew that he risked losing Byron's esteem. Ever mindful of Bishop Ignatios' advice, he was bound to be watchful for any sign that their noble benefactor might be 'displeased' and desert them. And Byron could not help being watchful too, now that he knew the efforts being made, in many quarters, to dent his trust in the 'prince'. He did not believe the tales he was told.[66] But the longer the arrival of the loan was delayed, and while the rains still came down, the greater the pressure on the bond that had made Byron and Mavrokordatos such a formidable combination until now.

And then, on the first day of April, the civil war for the second time broke upon Missolonghi. Mavrokordatos' and Byron's alternative policy for confronting the warlords was about to be put to its toughest test yet.

CHAPTER 12

Pyrrhic victory

PRIVATE QUARREL, PUBLIC WOES

Georgios Karaiskakis had no interest either in the civil war or in the affairs of the Peloponnese. It was a chance combination of circumstances that set him on a collision course with the authorities in Missolonghi during the first days of April, and offered up an unlikely scapegoat, just at the moment when Mavrokordatos needed one. The Karaiskakis affair, that rocked Missolonghi for a fortnight, would have the most unlooked-for repercussions. One was to turn an ailing, ranting, foul-mouthed, forty-two-year-old petty chieftain into one of the most revered military heroes of the Greek Revolution (Plate 8b).[1] Another was the effect that the affair would have on Byron.

Karaiskakis during the early months of 1824 had but a single aim: to regain control of the mountainous region of Agrafa, in the foothills of the Pindos some way north of Missolonghi, that he had won for himself in the early stages of the Revolution and held precariously until the campaign by the pashas of Skodra and Ioannina, the previous autumn, had forced him to flee southwards. A victim of tuberculosis, he had sought treatment in Cephalonia. From there, in December, he had written to Mavrokordatos, to beg for his support in regaining control of Agrafa, and to complain of the depredations against his own clients there by his rival Ioannis Rangos, who had moved in and taken over in the meantime.[2] Rangos was one of the chiefs who attended the assembly in Missolonghi at the start of the year and pledged support for Mavrokordatos. Karaiskakis also attended, and seems to have been snubbed or ignored by Mavrokordatos. His name is missing from the list of supporters.[3]

When he left Cephalonia in December, Karaiskakis had travelled part of the way to Missolonghi with Millingen. The doctor had been impressed, and perhaps a little intimidated, by his companion's 'dark scintillating eye . . . deeply sunk in its socket' – the consequence of his illness – and 'fierce glances'. Millingen continued: 'The folds of a yellow ceshmeere, twisted negligently, in the Albanian manner, round his head and the sides of the face, gave to his sallow and emaciated physiognomy a grim – I might almost say, a fiendlike – expression.' Along the way, Karaiskakis regaled the doctor with his grievances and the colourful and violent story of his life. Millingen concluded that his travelling companion 'had not the most distant idea of the meaning of liberty; confounding it with anarchy'. This was not someone on whom a government – any government – could rely. 'He ridiculed the idea of Greeks aiming at the establishment of a regular government; and invariably spoke of it in the most scurrilous terms.'⁴ The lesson that Millingen learned between Cephalonia and Ithaca in the company of Karaiskakis was the same one that Byron and Hobhouse had learned while they travelled south from Preveza to Missolonghi under the protection of Ali Pasha's men in the autumn of 1809. Karaiskakis was one of those fearsome and ungovernable klefts, on whom Byron had based so many of his 'byronic' heroes, and who had more recently proved themselves the most formidable fighters that Greece possessed.

Evidently, Mavrokordatos had confided his suspicions about Karaiskakis' loyalty and motives to Byron as early as January.⁵ When all the armed forces left Missolonghi in early March, supposedly to prepare for the campaign against Arta, some of them did not go very far. Karaiskakis, at the head of 100 men, all that the assembly had allowed him, went no farther than Anatoliko, the fortified island at the western end of the lagoon. There he joined forces with the Tzavellas brothers and their men, who were especially in disgrace with Mavrokordatos after the debacle over Lepanto, and inclined to be fractious anyway, as they were hereditary enemies of the loyal Botsaris clan. Karaiskakis made it loudly known that he was opposed to an assault on Arta, as well as to Mavrokordatos' authority. If there was to be a new concerted campaign to the north, why not head for Agrafa instead?⁶

According to his own values, Karaiskakis was being wholly consistent. All he wanted was to be reinstalled in Agrafa. To this end, and following an age-old convention, he treated with Omer Vryonis, the pasha of Ioannina, as well as with Mavrokordatos at Missolonghi. A bolder stroke was to try to convince Mavrokordatos that Omer actually wanted a deal with *him*. Ever the diplomat, Mavrokordatos took the bait and for a few days (just when he had been looking around for pretexts to put off going to Kranidi) even entertained the idea of a meeting with the pasha in the no-man's-land between Missolonghi and Arta. He was soon disabused. What Karaiskakis had told him about the pasha's intentions was not borne out by other sources. Vryonis would have to make a proper diplomatic approach if he really wanted to discuss terms, Mavrokordatos wrote to inform Karaiskakis on 24 March. Remarkably, and despite all the reasons for caution, he had even sent Karaiskakis a draft of the letter he proposed sending to Vryonis.[7]

Despite this setback, by the end of March, everything seemed to be going Karaiskakis' way. Whether or not Karaiskakis had a hand in this, Omer Pasha had been alerted to the Greeks' designs on Arta and despatched 3,000 troops to reinforce the town.[8] Since the chiefs were traditionally averse to fighting against 'stone walls' or well-defended places, this meant that Agrafa became the obvious next target for a notional campaign, even though it had no strategic importance. On the last day of the month, Mavrokordatos wrote out new orders to be delivered to the chiefs in Xiromero. They would be marching towards Agrafa. This must have been the campaign for which he and Byron drew up plans that were recorded by Parry, though without specifying the target. Now that the loan was on its way, 'Lord Byron's brigade' was to be brought up to strength by redeploying an additional 1,500 men – paid, for the first time, by the Greek government. 'The brigade', the document ends, 'with every material of war, should be ready to march by the 7th day of May for a particular service.'[9]

Karaiskakis had waited for months. He would have waited until the seventh of May. This was exactly what he wanted. He himself was instructed by Mavrokordatos, on 31 March, to rendezvous with the other chiefs at Machalas (today's Fyteies) in a few days' time.[10] All at once, Karaiskakis had less reason to be disaffected than at any time while he had been in the vicinity of Missolonghi.

But the new orders never reached him. Most likely, they were entrusted to his nephew, a young man by the name of Psaroyannopoulos, who was in such excitement to return across the lagoon to Anatoliko without delay that he got into a fight with the local ferrymen. Psaroyannopoulos was roundly thrashed and returned to his uncle in a pitiable state.

Karaiskakis reacted like any kleft, or byronic hero. His prestige had been insulted. The only law he knew was revenge. The next day, 1 April according to the western calendar, a Thursday, Karaiskakis sent 250 of his and Tzavellas' troops into Missolonghi. Unable to find the culprits, they terrorised the town. When they left, the next day, they took with them several leading citizens as hostages. At the same time, a detachment of forty men in flat-bottomed boats rowed across to the fortified island of Vasiladi that guards the entrance to the lagoon and seized control of it.[11]

Karaiskakis' actions caused panic in a town that was already on edge. The day before the spat began, enemy ships had once again appeared off the lagoon. (This was what provided the occasion for Byron, Parry, and Mavrokordatos to be out on punts, inspecting the defences.) On land, a detachment of Turkish cavalry had approached as close as the steep pass overlooking the Gulf of Patras, before turning back. No one, now, talked of Lepanto being ripe for the taking. Yusuf Pasha, in Patras, had re-garrisoned his fortresses with more reliable troops, and was giving notice of the fact.[12] But then, on the morning of Saturday, 3 April, the seven Turkish ships lifted their blockade and sailed away. All the action was now inside the lagoon, where Greek was pitted against Greek. According to the *Greek Chronicle*, 'the Government at dawn took the most drastic measures'. It was a phrase that Mavrokordatos liked to use in his own correspondence. Irregular troops loyal to the chieftains whose power-bases were closest to Missolonghi responded to his appeal and came down from their mountains. Boats were armed and the occupiers of Vasiladi surrounded.[13]

To all appearances, the civil war, that was then coming to a head in the Peloponnese, had spread to Missolonghi – even though, as Gamba correctly noted, in reality 'this was only a private quarrel'.[14] It was a situation that anyone familiar with Byron's 'Turkish tales' should have recognised. But the sense of a more general threat was intensified by the arrival, at the height of the confrontation, of a series of warnings from the government at Kranidi: 'Colonel Stanhope is in Athens, surrounded by the worst troublemakers in Greece . . . What they must be telling the English philhellene, you can imagine for yourself. I fear that they will dupe him. This you must tell to Byron', Mavrokordatos was urgently advised.[15] A captured letter, enclosed as evidence, gave credence to growing suspicions that Odysseus and Negris were actively plotting not only against Mavrokordatos but the government as well. Stanhope, to his credit, would later publish this letter, whose author he would describe as 'one of the most execrable villains that ever existed'. In this way Stanhope would exonerate himself of the charge of complicity, but not of dangerous naivety.[16]

Such was the state of crisis in the town that Mavrokordatos did not bring these letters to Byron himself, but sent Praidis in his stead. This was to become a pattern during the ensuing days, with far-reaching consequences. One face-to-face meeting, at least, there must have been, when these developments were discussed. The new information put quite a different complexion on the proposed conference at Salona. Mavrokordatos had now to consider very carefully whether he should attend. And then there was the problem of what to do about Stanhope's involvement – effectively, now, with the opposing side in the civil war, as Parry noted.[17] Mavrokordatos reported the outcome of this meeting: 'His Lordship had been very much annoyed and wrote ... in appropriate terms, both to Stanhope and the London Committee.' No such letters have been preserved but, again according to Mavrokordatos, Byron

said openly to his friends and to the committee, that Stanhope, being gullible and led astray by those who favoured him with fine addresses on the subject of liberty, without recognising the nature of affairs in Greece and the hidden purposes of those who addressed him, would seriously damage the cause, and that he (His Lordship, that is to say) had no desire to work with him.[18]

Whether or not Byron actually asked Bowring to arrange for Stanhope's recall, as Mavrokordatos believed, he was undoubtedly shocked at the way the colonel's susceptibility was being exploited by the internal enemy – the very same, to all appearances, that was now threatening Missolonghi.

To the immediate crisis Byron responded with his usual cool courage. 'The row has had one good effect – it has put them on the alert', he wrote to Barff on the sixth, perhaps still thinking of Parry's criticisms on the lagoon. According to Millingen, he 'urged Mavrokordato not to fear, but instantly to display all possible energy to defeat the designs of the rebel chief. He offered his own personal assistance, that of the artillery brigade, and of the three hundred Suliots on this service.'[19] Once again, Mavrokordatos was too busy dealing with the emergency to visit Byron. In reply to an anxious message from Gamba, he warned that 'it would be prudent to have our brigade in readiness, and not to suffer them to separate'. It was not long before Byron discovered that his own Suliots would not fire on their cousins of the Tzavellas clan from Anatoliko. The best he could do to save face and not make matters worse was to order them to 'preserve the strictest neutrality'.[20]

The stand-off lasted three days. Mavrokordatos was able to muster a sufficient show of force that Karaiskakis could not have continued the quarrel without serious loss of prestige. Even the law of revenge had its unwritten rules. On Sunday, 4 April, two local chiefs wrote to Karaiskakis, no doubt at Mavrokordatos' instigation, pointing this out in the name of friendship, and urging him to give up the hostages he had taken. In less forgiving tone, Mavrokordatos wrote too. Karaiskakis was to be prosecuted for his actions so far. In the meantime, the hostages must be returned forthwith.[21] The patient application of pressure bore fruit. On Monday, 5 April, Karaiskakis' men surrendered Vasiladi and withdrew from Missolonghi. The hostages returned to their homes. By evening, it was all over.

But not for Mavrokordatos. When, exactly, he perceived his opportunity is impossible to tell. Somebody – surely one of the Europeans, it could even have been Byron himself – while the panic had been at its height, made the connection: the Turks had appeared, after an absence of months, by land and sea. And the very next day a rebel chieftain had threatened to seize control of the town. There must be some sinister link between the two alarms.[22]

Mavrokordatos will have dismissed the idea at once. Temporary truces, deals with their enemy opposite numbers for short-term mutual interest, yes. These were as much a part of the daily life of chieftains, on both sides, as the ferocity with which on other occasions they would massacre the same people, their wives, and their children. It was such an everyday occurrence, there was even a word for it. It was called *kapaki*. But a coordinated act of treachery, involving troops from Lepanto, thirty kilometres the other side of Missolonghi from Anatoliko, and ships from Patras on the other side of the gulf – no, that was just not the way things were done. So Mavrokordatos will have said.

And then he saw the beauty of it. It was the perfect set-up.

Just at the moment when Byron (probably) and the other Europeans (certainly) were accusing him of being irresolute in a crisis, Mavrokordatos had been given the means to win his very own microcosm of the civil war, here in Missolonghi. It was not ethical. But it was deeply political. And it was fiendishly clever. He would show the government, at Kranidi, how a war could be won without recourse to arms and bloodshed. He would make an example of Karaiskakis that no one would ever forget.

There may have been no time. Or it may have seemed too much of a risk. Or, quite likely, by now, he was determined that Byron, too, must be impressed by a *fait accompli*. Whatever the reason, for once Mavrokordatos did not take Byron into his confidence. It was to prove a costly error.

HIGH TREASON

The moment the hostages returned to Missolonghi, on the evening of the fifth, Mavrokordatos went into action. At nine in the evening, Praidis called on Byron, bringing this note from his master:

My Lord,

Constantine Voulpiotti, who is now a guest in the house of your landlord, is strongly suspected of high treason. Not being willing to permit any of the town guard to enter a house inhabited by you, I pray you to order him under charge of your own guards to the outward gate, where the police will be in readiness to receive him.[23]

The original French has been lost, but for the first time the words were there in black and white: *high treason*. The suspect, Konstantinos Voulpiotis, was the father-in-law of Christos Kapsalis, one of the most respected primates in Missolonghi, in whose house Byron had been living for the past three months. His connection to Karaiskakis would prove to be tenuous. But Voulpiotis was necessary to Mavrokordatos' purpose, precisely because in this way Byron could not possibly fail to be impressed, either by the severity of the charge, or by the 'drastic' nature of the measures now being taken.

Byron complied at once. Voulpiotis was arrested and handed over. Late that night, Byron wrote to Barff in Zante. Repeating the terrible words of Mavrokordatos' letter, he confessed his bewilderment: 'What is to become of the father-in-law, I do not know: nor what he has done, exactly.'[24]

Next, Mavrokordatos had to bring in the chieftains who had promised him their support back in January, and secure their complicity in what was about to happen. On Tuesday, 6 April, he wrote to Xiromero, urgently recalling the very troops that he had been at such pains to remove from Missolonghi only a little over a month before. They were to meet him at Anatoliko, the scene of the crime. The message reached them that evening. It was an eight-hour march from Machalas, where most of them were billeted. They arrived late on Wednesday, 7 April. Once again, in the language of the *Greek Chronicle*, the Government was resorting to 'drastic measures'.[25]

But there was a difficulty. Either Mavrokordatos saw this too late, or more likely he was counting on resolving it in the way that had worked so often before. To Byron he wrote, in evident haste, on the sixth: 'The troops of Stornaris, Tzongas, and Botsaris . . . will be at Anatoliko this evening.' They were 1,500 men in arms, and there were no provisions to feed them: 'The treasury is not only empty, but also in debt. All the primates and the captains here are resolved to call upon you and petition you to come to the aid of the fatherland at this critical time, by making another temporary loan.'[26] Once again, Mavrokordatos was too busy to visit Byron himself, and sent Praidis instead. Byron had never got on with Praidis. He had no idea what was happening, and had already become irked at being asked for new personal loans, now that the money from London was supposed to be on its way and he should no longer be having to dig into his own pocket to shore up the government.[27] It was the only time when Byron ever refused Mavrokordatos point-blank. Three days later he wrote again to Barff: 'The Greeks here of the Govt. have been boring me for more money. I have given them a refusal – and as they would not take *that* – *another* refusal in terms of considerable sincerity.'[28]

Rebuffed by Byron, Mavrokordatos took the desperate step of requisitioning flour from Ionian merchants in the town, a serious violation of the islands' neutrality, of which Byron cannot possibly have approved either. 'Mavrocordato', Gamba continues, 'in this unhappy state of affairs, was overwhelmed with calumnies and even insults.'[29] Gamba's loyalty and tact here surely skate over a major row, probably the only one that ever took place between Byron and Mavrokordatos. The insults and calumnies, on this occasion, must have been Byron's. The words of extenuation for Mavrokordatos that Gamba puts into his narrative at this point may reflect his own ineffectual attempt at peacekeeping, at the time.

It is tempting to wonder whether the next evening was not the setting for an episode reported by Millingen, the only one of its kind:

One evening while, as usual, the English gentlemen, then at Mesolonghi, were at Lord Byron's house enjoying the never-failing charm of his society, Mavrocordato entered the room, at a moment, the conversation was most interesting. His lordship received him in a very cool manner; and answered him, with some degree of peevishness; and, notwithstanding Mavrocordato's artful manner of introducing the business, that interested him most, he constantly turned the conversation to another subject. Annoyed to see the prince returning again and again to the charge, Lord Byron got up, and began walking up and down the room. Finding that Mavrocordato persisted in not taking the hint, he could no longer refrain his ill humour; but addressing us, in English, begun by saying: he wished that d—d botherer would regale us with his absence . . . On observing to Lord Byron, that the prince had undoubtedly understood every word he had been uttering, he merely replied; 'I trust he has.'[30]

If this was indeed the occasion, then it was also their last meeting.

That would have been the Wednesday evening, 7 April. The same evening, the troops reached Anatoliko. According to some accounts, Mavrokordatos left Missolonghi the next day, to begin assembling the court martial that would try Karaiskakis. But more likely he had first to deal with provisioning the troops, now that Byron had refused to help. On Sunday, the eleventh, he wrote to Byron from Anatoliko, enclosing a proclamation issued there, that called on witnesses to come forward to the crime of treason. The trial was due to begin at 3 p.m. that day.[31]

There is no official record of the proceedings against Karaiskakis. But an eyewitness was Nikolaos Kasomoulis, the young secretary to one of the chiefs who had been displaced by recent events to wind up in the vicinity of Missolonghi. Kasomoulis' lively *Military Recollections* of his experiences in the Revolution would be written up shortly afterwards but not published until 1939.[32] Kasomoulis frankly confesses that he did not like Karaiskakis. But, in common with most of those present, he watched, spellbound and aghast, as the precursor of so many more famous political show trials went ahead. The hearing was held in the Church of the Virgin Mary. Bishop Porphyrios of Arta, in the full majesty of his robes, presided. The doors were locked. The stalls were filled with armed men. Others sat cross-legged on the ground, all armed to the teeth. It was, according to Kasomoulis, a 'tragic scene'. A pillow was brought for the defendant to sit on, to protect him in his sick condition from the stone floor. And then the proceedings began.

Karaiskakis was accused of plotting with Omer Vryonis to deliver Missolonghi and Anatoliko to the enemy in return for being allowed to return to Agrafa as local chieftain. The father-in-law of Byron's landlord, Voulpiotis, was not accused but called as a witness. Incriminating letters had been found in his possession – but were not produced. Voulpiotis had been granted a passport by Karaiskakis to travel to Ioannina (this much was true, but unremarkable). While there, Voulpiotis had met Vryonis on Karaiskakis' behalf. Karaiskakis blustered and denied everything.[33] He seems to have been too proud even to mention that less than a month ago he had been employed by Mavrokordatos, present in court, to conduct secret negotiations with the same Ottoman pasha, albeit for a somewhat higher purpose.

The judges at this military tribunal were the chieftains and commanders of the irregular forces in western Greece, men much closer in mentality to Karaiskakis than to Mavrokordatos. They had no idea of the kind of legal process that Mavrokordatos was drawing them into. It helped that whatever was going on had the blessing of the Church, to which they all owed the only real allegiance they knew. They were in awe of the responsibilities forced upon them. And enough of them were resentful that Karaiskakis' wilful action had balked them of the plunder of a campaign to turn against him. Karaiskakis himself was uncharacteristically cowed. After a day of inconclusive wrangling among the chiefs, it was decided that the principal witness, who had already been interrogated twice, must be examined again. Voulpiotis was taken to a private house and subjected to a third interrogation, this time by Kostas Botsaris – a man more noted for ferocity on the battlefield than for forensic subtlety, and also the most loyal of the chiefs to Mavrokordatos. Kasomoulis comments drily, 'I was not present at this interrogation. I do not know what they did, or what methods they used on Voulpiotis.' The results were spectacular. This time, contradicting his two earlier testimonies, the witness implicated Karaiskakis on all the charges, even adding for good measure that there had been a plot to kidnap Byron and Mavrokordatos and hold them for ransom.[34]

There was a moment of farce the next day, when Mavrokordatos' secretary gave the wrong version of Voulpiotis' confession to be read out in court. For all their lack of judicial experience, the chieftains then debated hotly whether a man could be convicted on the basis of a changed testimony. But eventually they complied and delivered the verdict that Mavrokordatos had been preparing from the beginning. As these events would be written up a few days later in the *Greek Chronicle*, the more homely (and daily encountered) deviation of 'insubordination' or 'plotting' by a local warlord slid into something much more sinister: 'treason'.[35] Karaiskakis' fit of bad temper had resulted in a conviction as 'a conspirator against the Fatherland and a traitor'. The language and procedures of European jurisprudence had arrived. The warlords – as much those who participated in the trial as the defendant – had been literally confounded.

After such a farrago, there could be no question of invoking the penalty that such a verdict would automatically have carried in Europe at the time. Even Karaiskakis' worst enemies among the chieftains would never have consented to put him to death. But all were, once again, overawed by the severity and the language of the sentence that they soon found themselves pronouncing. The traitor Karaiskakis was 'expelled from the fatherland' and stripped of all rights, honour, and power, all of which, the official text rubbed it in, derived from the Government. Every Greek was exhorted 'to shun his company, and to regard him as an enemy, until such time as he should throw himself upon the mercy of the nation, and beg forgiveness'.[36] As Kasomoulis, in his comment, seems implicitly to have recognised, it was a secular excommunication: 'This proclamation, backed by the Authority of the Nation, divided everyone from Karaiskakis, and no one would dare to take his side or even to go near him, for fear of being polluted.'[37]

The new secular power structures of the 'nation' had appropriated the language of religion, and with it, authority over the minds of the rough chieftains and an impressionable young secretary like Kasomoulis. Mavrokordatos had achieved his object. Even the fractious Tzavellas chiefs repudiated Karaiskakis at once. There could be no question, now, of them responding to the call of the insurgents in Tripolitsa. And all this Mavrokordatos had achieved – as he would soon modestly boast to the Executive in Kranidi, with an implied barb against their own more violent proceedings in the Peloponnese – 'without permitting one drop of blood to be spilt'.[38] It was the perfect vindication of his and Byron's policy.

THE END OF THE HUNDRED DAYS

The verdict against Karaiskakis was delivered at Anatoliko on the morning of Wednesday, 14 April.[39] For most of the previous week, Byron had been left to his own devices. While Mavrokordatos was out of town, overseeing the trial, for the first and only time since he had come to Missolonghi, Byron had nothing to do.

It was now, and not before, that he experienced the intense disillusion that witnesses describe and that most biographers, following Parry's lead, have projected backwards until it becomes the predominant theme of the hundred days. Finlay's authoritative assessment, published many years later, was drawn from what he had observed during March and April – and most of all during the climactic days before he himself took leave of Byron on the evening of the tenth:

> The political information which Lord Byron extracted from Mavrocordatos in their personal interviews, and the proceedings of that statesman in the conduct of the public administration, revealed the thousand obstacles to the establishment of an honest government in Greece. A mist fell from Lord Byron's eyes. He owned that his sagacity was at fault, and he abandoned all hope of being able to guide the Greeks, or to assist them in improving their administration. Not long before his death, he frequently repeated, that with Napier to command and form regular troops, with [Frank Abney] Hastings to arm and command a steamer, and with an able financier, Greece would be sure of victory.[40]

The silent omission of Mavrokordatos' name from the list in the last sentence speaks volumes. Byron never did have much faith in the Greeks. The latest evidence of treason in their ranks was the last straw.

It was during these days, while Mavrokordatos was at Anatoliko, that Byron 'became peevish; and . . . little minded. Losing hope, he lost enthusiasm, and became gloomily sensible to his situation'. According to Millingen's testimony, he had been prepared to cope with almost any depravity, but 'he was not prepared to meet with black-hearted treachery; or to see Greeks themselves conspiring against their own country; courting the chains of their former masters; and bargaining the liberties and very existence of their own brethren'. Compared to this, the treachery of the Souliots he had thought his friends, and who had then subverted the expedition against Lepanto, was as nothing. Then, back in February, Byron had become violently ill. Stanhope, in his account of that episode, had observed, 'The mind of Byron is like a volcano, it is full of fire, wealth, and combustibles; and, when this matter comes to be strongly agitated, the explosion is dreadful.' Now Millingen reported that in the days following the Karaiskakis affair 'The volcanic mind of Lord Byron . . . was thrown by these events into a violent state of commotion.'[41]

No wonder that his health was affected this time too. It was bound to be a vicious circle. The more ill he felt, the more he brooded. The more he brooded, he more ill he became. Parry and Millingen both date the deterioration to the beginning of the month. But, on the fifth, Gamba was reporting to Teresa, 'Mylord finds himself in the best of health.' True to form, Byron's spirits would have rallied during the five days of the emergency. The reaction set in afterwards. This would have been on the sixth or seventh, the days of his confrontation with Mavrokordatos about money for the returning troops, the arrest of Voulpiotis in his house, and the first official confirmation that 'treason' had apparently been at work. Against the date of Friday, 9 April, even the normally upbeat Gamba notes, 'Lord Byron had suffered visibly in his health during the last day or two.'[42]

That morning, a boat arrived from Zante, bringing letters from the islands, from Genoa, and from England. One of these was from Hobhouse, another from his half-sister Augusta, enclosing a silhouette of his daughter Ada.[43] As a rule, Byron would reply at once to letters, particularly from people close to him. But it seems he was in no mood to reply to these. At least, there is no evidence that he ever did. So far as is known, he wrote only business letters that day: two to Barff in Zante and one to Barry in Genoa. The tone of these letters is markedly different from all of Byron's previous ones written from Greece. To both recipients he complained of an unnamed Mavrokordatos 'boring' him for more money. To Barry, who had only just seen the terms of the loan he had made in Cephalonia, and assumed that Byron intended to write off its loss 'with grace', he replied crossly: 'As the Greeks have gotten their loan – they may as well repay mine – which they no longer require – and I request you to forward a copy of the agreement to Mr. Kinnaird and direct him from me to claim the money from the Deputies.'[44]

The letters from London had been almost two months on the way. They had been sent too soon to contain any definite confirmation of the Greek loan. Byron fretted to Barff: 'is it really settled – and how? . . . some say one thing and some another *here*'.[45] To Finlay and to Parry, in conversation, he expressed darker fears. Even if the terms *had* been agreed, as the Greeks had been telling him for three weeks now, the subscribers might still pull out when they learned how bad things really were. News of internal dissension was bound to be damaging enough. Byron had been warning of this from the beginning. But 'high treason' was something else. Perhaps, he even wondered, he had himself unwittingly encouraged his countrymen to invest in a fraudulent enterprise?[46]

The letters written, he went out riding with Gamba. They were caught in heavy rain. Byron's mood was still bitter. 'I should make a pretty soldier, indeed, if I were to care for such a trifle', he snapped, when Pierino suggested they should abandon their usual routine and make straight for shelter. So they dismounted outside the walls, as was their custom, and returned to the Kapsalis house in an open punt. Both men got drenched. That evening, Byron 'was seized with a shuddering', and complained of pain and fever. The next day, Saturday, he was well enough to ride again. This time the rain held off, but apparently his saddle had been still wet from the day before.[47]

On the eleventh, Sunday, Parry spent longer in Byron's company than he had perhaps done for some time. Finlay left for Athens that morning, and the firemaster found himself once again Byron's closest confidant at Missolonghi. This was the day when Mavrokordatos' note from Anato-liko arrived, enclosing the proclamation that had been issued there and announcing the start of Karaiskakis' trial for high treason. This was the occasion when Parry first observed in Byron the signs of what he would later term 'alienation of the mind'. He was 'very unwell', Parry reported, talking 'a great deal, and . . . in rather a wandering manner'.[48] To the fire-master's consternation, Byron seemed to suppose his work in Greece was already completed. He imagined he was about to set sail in a specially built schooner. (The *Bolivar* was in his thoughts, since Barry had told him Lord Blessington was still trying to duck out of paying for it.) Aboard this new schooner, Byron declared that he would shortly be on his way to America, an ambassador seeking recognition for newly independent Greece from the government of the United States. That done, he told Parry, he was looking forward to 'the happiness of domestic life', in a longed-for 'retirement' with his estranged wife and Ada, the daughter that he had not seen since she had been an infant.[49] It was an impossible vision. No wonder Parry was alarmed, when he heard it.

The previous time when Byron had been taken ill, in February, there had been some suggestion that he might return to the Ionian Islands to convalesce. Then, he had courteously but firmly refused.[50] Now, on 11 April, Parry 'earnestly supplicated him to go immediately to Zante', for the sake of his health. This time Byron agreed. Of those who had been present in Missolonghi at the time, only Parry mentioned this fact afterwards. But Parry says that he was himself put in charge of the arrangements, and a year later would be sufficiently sure of his story to reproach Gamba, in print, for having suppressed it. A payment to Parry on the twelfth would have been meant to cover the necessary expenses. And on the same day Sisinis, at Gastouni, who was suspiciously well informed about the latest events in Missolonghi, knew that 'his Lordship is leaving there very soon'.[51]

On Tuesday, 13 April, the second day of the trial at Anatoliko, a 'hurricane' was blowing from the south, with torrential rain. No boat could have put out in such weather. But now, Byron's fever seemed to be receding. Though still 'melancholy and very irritable', he seemed to be over the worst. Next day, the fourteenth, he was sufficiently improved that he could get out of bed. Gamba reports, 'He received many letters, and he told me what answer I was to give to them.'

One of these was from Praidis:

I have just now received a letter from the Prince in which he tells me, as regards the Karaiskakis affair, 'that he was found guilty[,] however to avoid any trouble in the town, he has been ordered to depart, which may happen today'.[52]

The very worst that Byron had feared had been confirmed. The most heinous crime imaginable had been committed against the fledgling state, by one of its own supposed defenders. And now, to cap it all, Mavrokordatos, in whom he himself had invested so much trust, had let the culprit go scot-free – just to avoid the risk of disturbances in the town! That most despicable of all human defects, that Byron had excoriated at the age of nineteen in the epitaph, incised on stone, for a beloved dog, had indeed been rife, right here at the heart of the enterprise to which he had devoted everything.

The price of Mavrokordatos' victory was that Byron, too, had been duped into believing Karaiskakis guilty as charged. In his physically and mentally weakened state, the offence was no doubt magnified still more. He had had nothing to do but brood upon it for the past week. It was the perfect failure of understanding, worthy of any tragedy that Byron himself might have written.

He had been at Missolonghi exactly one hundred days.

'I LEAVE BEHIND SOMETHING PRECIOUS IN THE WORLD'

Five days later, Byron was dead. Mavrokordatos never had the chance to explain his actions. The two men never met again.

Many explanations have been proposed, over the years, for Byron's death, shortly after 6 p.m. on Monday, 19 April, at Missolonghi. The bald facts, recorded at the time by Millingen, were these:

His health had suffered previously very much in consequence of the convulsive fits he fell in in Feby last, but the immediate cause of his death was a rheumatic fever which attacked him from getting wet in a shower. The fever was at its outset very strong, and bleeding was proposed, but he obstinately refused to listen to the urgent remonstrances, and entreaties both of his physician and mine, till the brain was attacked, and the lesions that organ suffered from inflammation became irremediable, his answer to all our arguments was, 'the lancet had killed more than the lance'.

Mavrokordatos, within hours of the event, reported much the same to the Greek government, almost seeming to imply that there had been something wilful about Byron to the last: 'His insistence on not being bled during the first days of the malady, despite the protestations of the doctors, was his undoing.'[53]

To bleed or not to bleed? It was standard medical procedure at the time. Modern opinion tends to blame the doctors, who were certainly very young and inexperienced. In past illnesses, Byron had prided himself on overruling his doctors. This time he was too weak to prevail over them. Blood was taken. And Byron died. The claim of these same doctors, based on a rough-and-ready autopsy, that he would not have lived much longer anyway is as likely to be self-serving.[54] Bruno and Millingen would never live down their part in the death of the most famous Englishman of the age, and did what they could to salvage their reputations.

Once those who were there had had time to reflect, other factors soon came to colour their accounts. Byron had had a superstitious side. The prediction of a fortune-teller, way back in his Scottish childhood, had been much on his mind during his final illness. A fixation with this idea, Millingen believed, 'like an insidious poison, destroyed that moral energy, which is so useful to keep up the patient in dangerous complaints. "Did I not tell you," said he repeatedly to me, "that I should die at thirty-seven?"'[55] (Actually, he was thirty-six.) He had been thinking once more of Shelley, who he believed had 'had an implicit belief in ghosts'. To Millingen, in one of their last conversations before his illness took hold, he recalled how Shelley had foreseen his own death:

You will ridicule, also, a belief in incorporeal beings. Without instancing to you the men of profound genius, who have acknowledged their existence, I could give you the details of my friend Shelley's conversations with his familiar. Did he not apprize me, that he had been informed by that familiar, that he would end his life by drowning; and did I not, a short time after, perform, on the sea beach, his funeral rites?[56]

Parry took a more robust view. The true cause was 'disappointment'. The fever, he insisted, 'was only the symptom of that general disease, which, from the time of my arrival in Greece, had been gradually wasting his frame'.[57] Parry was determined to believe that this had been the case from the beginning. The beginning, for Parry, had been only a week before the defection of the Souliots and Byron's seizure. He had not seen how the hundred days had started. But what he says certainly applies to the week in April when Mavrokordatos was at Anatoliko and afterwards.

One witness to the nature of Byron's last illness, who deserves to be taken more seriously than he has been, is the patient himself. In arguing with Millingen about his treatment, Byron struggled to convince the doctor that his condition belonged to the category 'of nervous disorders, not of inflammatory ones', and added: 'Drawing blood from a nervous patient is like loosening the chords of a musical instrument, the tones of which are already defective for want of sufficient tension.' Bruno gives less detail, but concedes there was a difference of opinion: 'it seemed to him that the doctors did not understand his malady'. Bruno's intransigence is the more surprising in view of his notes written to a fellow practitioner on his patient's seizure back in February, which, he had then concluded, 'depended upon nervous irritability, arising from an excess of *stimulus*'.[58] If his sickness was 'nervous' in origin, as Byron believed – induced or exacerbated by psychological rather than purely physical factors, in the language of today – then both the incapacity of the doctors and the fatal sequel to the bloodletting would be explained.

It is possible that after 14 April, when Karaiskakis' supposed treachery was confirmed, Byron really did give up. He had already consented to leave Greece. Nothing, naturally, can be proved today. But all the signs are there: while he waited for news from Anatoliko to confirm the extreme charges that had been laid against Karaiskakis, Byron was sick in mind, as much as in body. Praidis' note arriving on the fourteenth would have been the *coup de grace*.

In the delirium of his final days, he kept coming back to his daughter Ada – and also to Greece, and all that he had done for the cause. Gamba, loyal as ever, makes out that he was still attending to business, several days after Parry insists that he had lapsed into incoherence.[59] During a lucid interval, he spoke the words that were reported to Gamba, who reproduced them in Italian: *io lascio qualche cosa di caro nel mondo*. What Byron really meant to say has been disputed.[60] But the Italian itself is clear: 'I leave behind something precious in the world.' It is, if nothing else, an affirmation. Despite everything, after those months in Greece, and as his own personal 'war' came to an end, Byron was ready to hand on something that could be precious, not just to himself, but to others after him. In *Don Juan*, during the days after he had seen the body of Shelley consigned to the flames, sent out of the world with the trappings of an ancient Greek hero, he had written:

> And I will war, at least in words (and – should
> My chance so happen – deeds) . . .

Despite the shocks of his last active days, it was the political reality he had helped to create at Missolonghi, and not the poetry to which he owed his fame, that was Byron's last bequest to the world.

Sunday was Easter Day, when the Orthodox population was accustomed to celebrate the Resurrection of Christ. There would have been no church bells in Missolonghi at this time. But, after the morning liturgy, everyone who had a firearm would be expected to let it off loudly and repeatedly (as still happens in some parts of Greece today). Mavrokordatos detailed Parry and Gamba to march the Souliots, who had been under Byron's command, out of the town so that the dying man would not be disturbed by their celebrations. In the streets, patrols urged the citizens to restrain their revelry. That evening Byron sank into a coma, from which he never recovered.[61]

He had arrived in Greece the day before Christmas. He died the day after Easter, at the climax of a week of storms. It was a moment out of one of his own dramatic poems, or a ballad of the Greek klefts. Even while he was alive he had been hailed as a 'saviour', or 'deliverer' – most recently by his old friend and travelling companion Hobhouse, in his last letter that Byron had been able to read.[62] The fortuitous timing of his arrival and death at Missolonghi would ever afterwards give a whole new resonance to these terms of praise.

Epilogue

What had Byron achieved, during his hundred days at Missolonghi? First of all, the complete transformation of himself. As a poet, he had always had a powerful talent for self-invention, a trait that he had projected on to so many fictional creations in his poems and plays. But in the imaginative world of his fictions self-transformation had always ended badly – in futile, if heroic, defiance and the annihilation even of memory. Byron's final transformation of himself into the new statesman was unlike anything he had imagined for a fictional character. Having resisted the call to Greece for so long, once he had heard it and heeded it he overcame all wavering and for the last ten months of his life forged a consistent path. He who had long been fascinated and appalled by the unpredictable forces he recognised within himself, and knew the fickleness of his own mind, suddenly became serious – and stuck to it. As late as 10 March, while he was still recovering from the effects of his seizure, and Barff had offered him the use of his country house in Zante in which to recuperate, he had replied: 'I cannot quit Greece while there is a Chance of my being of any (even *supposed*) utility – there is a Stake worth millions such as I am – – and while I can stand at all – I must stand by the Cause.'[1] No 'byronic hero' ever submitted in this way to anybody or anything higher than himself. That is the nature of the byronic hero, his 'tragic flaw'. And for years Byron had played up to that stereotype in his own life. After the decision for Greece, no longer. In the letters and conversations of his last ten months, the 'Cause' really *was* all.

There is no telling, of course, whether that resolution would have held, if he had lived. Those Greeks who valued his intervention the most – Mavrokordatos, Bishop Ignatios, and their supporters – were acutely aware of the risk that it might not. So was his oldest friend, Hobhouse, back in England. Ironically enough, in the letter that Byron read on 9 April, Hobhouse had expressed himself finally reassured, revealing as he did so his earlier doubts. After everything he had heard from Greece and from the Greek deputies in London, wrote Hobhouse, 'I am in no fear now of your taking a sudden leave of the cause and country.'[2] These jitters had been apparent at Missolonghi, too, while the excitement over the Lepanto campaign had been at its height, and Mavrokordatos had received his first summons to the government at Kranidi. Then, one of his aides had written confidentially to warn Koundouriotis: if Mavrokordatos were to be recalled, all the good work he had been doing with Byron and Stanhope could fall to pieces. Without Mavrokordatos at his side, the writer went on, 'Lord Byron would undoubtedly become displeased very soon, having no instrument through which to put his noble decisions into effect, since the Greeks have no idea how to handle men of his temperament, and at the height of the struggle he could depart and leave us high and dry.'[3]

Byron's reputation had preceded him to Greece. It was this Europe-wide reputation that made his presence there so valuable. But it was a two-edged weapon. Those who knew him best had most cause to fear that he might desert them. That fear became the weak point in the working relationship with Mavrokordatos. Others did their best to exploit it – particularly Odysseus and Negris in Athens, egged on by Trelawny, who knew well this side of Byron's character. But, of all those who tried, it was only Karaiskakis, who had no such intention, who succeeded in driving a wedge between Mavrokordatos and Byron – and, had other factors not combined to cause his death, that would probably have proved only temporary. For all the doubts and suspicions of bad faith, at the time and ever since, the fact is that Byron did *not* desert the cause. He remained true to it at least until his mind began to give way on 11 April, and so far as he was capable, even beyond, until his death eight days later.

How much could any individual have achieved in a hundred days? At an immediate and local level, Byron relieved distresses, particularly for prisoners of war, who would otherwise have been murdered or sold as slaves, and for the destitute.[4] During his first month he lifted morale at Missolonghi and, with the help of his trusted lieutenants, did as much as anyone could have done to mobilise the fissiparous band of foreign volunteers and unruly local armed bands into a fighting force. As he summed it up, good-humouredly, on 7 February: 'between Suliote Chiefs – German Barons – English Volunteers – and adventurers of all Nations – we are likely to form as goodly an allied army – as ever quarrelled beneath the same banner'.[5]

But his real achievement lay elsewhere. Philhellenes, as a rule, brought their prejudices and expectations with them from Europe. It was only natural that they should try to impose these on their new surroundings.

Parry, for one, was alive to the dangers: '*we* introduced plans for codes of laws, and other measures which had for their object to *Anglify* Greece', he would complain presciently in 1825.[6] What makes Byron's contribution unusual, if not unique, is his insistence that the new political realities emerging in Greece should be allowed to forge a new form of governance, never seen before. This was of a piece with his idea of the 'Cause'. It was not any sympathy for the Greeks, as people, that drove him. Instead, he had identified in the Revolution in Greece a turning point in the affairs of Europe. His most important achievement was this, in concert with Mavrokordatos: not just to import European values into Greece (though he certainly did that too), but to try to create, in Greece, political conditions that could then be emulated by the rest of the continent. This was what he had meant, in that homily back in January, when he had assured Gamba that 'those principles which are now in action in Greece will gradually produce their effect, both here and in other countries'. In March, outlining his plans for the foreign-language newspaper that his lieutenant was to edit, he had gone further: 'I cannot . . . calculate to what a height Greece may rise. Hitherto it has been a subject for the hymns and elegies of fanatics and enthusiasts; but now it will draw the attention of the politician.'[7]

Finally, there was his contribution, with Mavrokordatos, to resolving the civil conflict in favour of a centralised authority. If his and Mavrokordatos' joint policy towards the rebels was 'softer' than the government's, it still offered no concessions. (This was exactly what observers like Trelawny and Stanhope objected to.) In all their correspondence with Andritzou and Negris in Athens, with Sisinis and Peroukas in the Peloponnese, Byron and Mavrokordatos were negotiating from a position of strength, and they knew it. The money that was on its way from London had been raised by the legitimate government. The only way to share in the benefits it brought was by recognising that government as the sole authority in Greece. If Byron had lived to go to Salona and meet Odysseus and Negris with Mavrokordatos, the result could have been to bring all the fighting forces north of the Isthmus round to the government side. The shift in the balance of power would have made further resistance in the Peloponnese futile. (It would be in precisely this way, with different personnel, and still not without bloodshed, that the second civil war would be decisively won a few months later.)

So if Byron had lived a little longer, and if his and Mavrokordatos' policy had prevailed, Greece could have been spared the worst effects of two civil wars within a year. Even as it was, the hundred days were not wasted. The disasters at Missolonghi, up to the end of March, were none of them overwhelming. If Byron had been constitutionally stronger, and had recovered from his illness in April, there would have been everything still to play for. In three months, he and Mavrokordatos had laid the foundations, together, for a far-reaching set of policies ready to be implemented once the first tranche of the loan arrived from London. The catastrophic effects of the Karaiskakis affair changed all that. What followed would be much messier. But without Byron and his hundred days, it might not have followed at all.

Even as Byron lay dying, the struggle to create a new kind of political organisation on Greek soil was slowly being won. On 13 April, the day before the verdict on Karaiskakis was reached at Anatoliko, government forces in the Peloponnese were entering the rebel stronghold of Tripolitsa. By this time, there were 4,000 troops besieging the town. When they broke into the outlying suburbs, a series of skirmishes began and the battle quickly spread. Despite the large numbers of heavily armed men involved, it would later be claimed that only one life had been lost, and that accidentally. By the end of the day, Kolokotronis and the remnants of the rebel Executive had agreed to evacuate their capital, though not to give up their arms. They retreated to the stronghold of Karytaina, in Kolokotronis' heartland – much to the annoyance of Koundouriotis, who reprimanded his generals for having allowed it.[8]

News of the government's success in the Peloponnese was not slow to arrive at Missolonghi. On the seventeenth, two days before Byron's death, the *Greek Chronicle* reported, with evident satisfaction: 'The Government has prevailed, and it will not be long before the anti-patriots are punished in a manner commensurate with the acts of which they stand accused.'[9] Mavrokordatos may not have approved of the methods used, but now that the advantage had been gained, he was politician enough to capitalise on it. Everywhere, now, the government party was in the ascendant. Two more months would pass before the first civil war would finally be over – with the surrender of the two fortresses of Nafplio by Kolokotronis' son Panos at the beginning of June. But the power of the rebel Executive had been broken in the Peloponnese, just as Mavrokordatos asserted his authority over the warlords at Anatoliko.

These events, as much as Byron's death, took the wind out of the proposed conference at Salona. Odysseus and Negris brought many of their supporters from eastern Greece, but Mavrokordatos now had incontrovertible reasons for staying away. On the twenty-fourth, he informed Trelawny, who had come hotfoot from Salona to view Byron's body before it could be embarked for England, 'that it is impossible for me to attend or to recognise this conference which has been convened by persons who have no proper authority to do so'.[10] In the event, he sent two middle-ranking representatives in his stead. The rout of the warlords in Tripolitsa and the subtler scapegoating of Karaiskakis at Anatoliko had left the conference without purpose.[11] Odysseus and Negris, perceiving how the distribution of power had shifted, duly made their way to the seat of government – just as they would have been likely to do if the conference had gone as Mavrokordatos and Byron had planned.

At a purely practical level, Byron's death did have one disastrous consequence for Greece. When the brig *Florida* reached Zante on 24 April, carrying the first instalment of the loan from London, Blaquiere, who had travelled with it, was met by the news. The money, 40,000 pounds of it, was taken for safe-keeping into the vaults of Byron's banker, Samuel Barff, while the ship went on to Missolonghi, to convey Byron's remains back to England for burial. With one of the two commissioners dead, Barff decided he could not release the money until the other arrived. When Stanhope reached Zante on 12 May, he was against releasing the funds at all, so long as the country continued in a state of civil war. Stanhope had just learned that he had been summoned back to his regiment in England. He would have to resign his role as commissioner for the loan in any case. There were angry exchanges, by letter, with Mavrokordatos in Missolonghi. After all his doctrinaire rants in Greece against the institution of monarchy and anyone who supported it, Stanhope now rather testily informed Bowring that he was commanded by 'no less a personage than the King of England' and must quit Greece immediately.[12] If Mavrokordatos was right, and Stanhope's recall had somehow been his and Byron's doing, he may have been regretting it now. In the event, the first two instalments of the loan, that had been held up in Zante, would not be released until the end of July.

These delays had devastating consequences for the Greeks. The month of April saw the forces of the Revolution wiped out in Crete (which would not become part of Greece until 1913). In June, the same fate befell the nearby island of Kasos (not incorporated until 1947). In the same month, Psara in the eastern Aegean, one of the three 'naval' islands that had achieved pre-eminence in the war at sea, was totally destroyed by a combined Turkish and Egyptian fleet, with the slaughter of some 8,000 of the inhabitants. To this day, the island has never recovered. All three disasters the Greek government blamed squarely on the untimely demise of Byron, on the behaviour of 'the accursed Stanhope', and the withholding in Zante of the money that would have paid for a fleet to go out from Hydra and Spetses.[13]

Or, as Orlandos, writing from London, would rather gracelessly put it in August: 'How I curse fate for not having left Byron in the land of the living for fifteen days more, until you could have got the money.'[14]

At just the same time, and writing from the picturesque hideout of his patron Odysseus in a cave on Parnassos, Trelawny was making much the same complaint, for an even less noble reason: 'I wish he had lived a little longer, that he might have witnessed how I would have soared above him here, how I would have triumphed over his mean spirit.'[15] Conflicted as ever, and now under the spell of a new master, Trelawny had quickly overcome the awed feelings of his visit to Missolonghi and the forbidden sight of the dead Byron's lame foot (or feet, as he would claim many years later).[16]

Other responses at the time could be equally unsentimental. Jakob Meyer, the editor of the *Chronicle*, boasted privately to Stanhope (surely with some exaggeration): 'Lord Noel Byron died in my arms. How strange that the man who always talked against my newspaper should die in my arms... Thanks be to God, I have won... Byron is dead! Is his death harmful to Greece? No.'[17] Someone else for whom the cause was no less sacred, but who had had his doubts about Byron from the start, was Bishop Ignatios, Mavrokordatos' old mentor in Pisa. Writing to Koundouriotis when the news reached him, the bishop offered words of consolation that surely were more political than spiritual:

We often grieve out of ignorance, when what is presented to us is rather cause for joy than for sorrow. The noble Englishman was good and zealous on our behalf, but as a poet he was frivolous and it is not unlikely that [had he lived] he would have taken umbrage, and left, and written such things against the Greeks as would have done more harm than he ever did good.[18]

Closer to home, Mavrokordatos' personal feelings are impossible to gauge. Three days after the event, his friend and protégé Spyridon Trikoupis read a florid eulogy at a public ceremony with Byron's body present. Out of this tribute was born the enduring legend of the heroic benefactor who had willingly sacrificed his life for a great cause. The orator had met Byron only once, three weeks before his death. It can only have been on the authority of Trikoupis' own imagination, unless perhaps of a bruised and resentful Mavrokordatos, that he could inform his hearers, 'He came... with the determination to die in Greece, and for Greece!'[19]

The formal announcement of Byron's death that appeared in the *Greek Chronicle* on 21 April is unlikely to have been the work of the paper's editor. It will certainly have been sanctioned by Mavrokordatos, and may well have been written by him. Most of what it says is conventional. But the bleak words with which it ends do perhaps convey a personal, as well as a political, realisation of the magnitude of the disaster that is Byron's death: 'The hopes that our nation rested upon this man have failed, and nothing more remains for us but to weep inconsolably for this, to us so cruel, death.'[20] The hopes had been not just the nation's, but very much Mavrokordatos' own.

It was left to an anonymous correspondent from the island of Melos, in the Aegean, to sum up what must have been a hard-nosed but real sense of loss shared by many ordinary Greeks at this time: 'I grieve greatly for the death of lord byron, untimely both for himself and for the fatherland. In such circumstances, even the fact of his presence in Greece was of the greatest benefit.'[21]

It was not only in Greece that the practical effects of Byron's loss were felt. Trelawny was for once not far off the mark when he lamented, on 29 April, that Byron's name had been 'the means chiefly of raising the loan in England. Thousands of people were flocking here...not to the Greeks or interest in the cause, but to the noble poet.'[22] In London, the value of the bonds that been issued in the name of the Greek government, and that had only a few weeks before been oversubscribed, fell over fifteen percentage points on the day that news of Byron's death arrived. Despite some less than respectable insider dealing, the stock value continued to fall, bringing Bowring to the edge of personal ruin, and a complete rupture between the Greek deputies and the London Committee. The arrival in London of Stanhope, bearing the kind of tales from Greece that Byron had always warned would be fatal, completed the mischief.[23] The reputation of the first Greek loan from London, of those who had negotiated it, and of Greek financial probity in foreign markets, would to varying degrees never recover.[24]

Thanks very largely to the loan, the government by the end of 1824 had gained the upper hand in two civil wars – the second rather more violent and widespread than the first. Only when it was all but over, in December, did Mavrokordatos return from Missolonghi to a government that would in the meantime have accepted his often-tendered resignation as President of the Legislature – by which time, as Finlay tartly put it, he had 'allowed all parties to learn that public business could go on perfectly well without him'.[25]

Byron's adherence to Mavrokordatos during the crucial first months of 1824 had ensured that the modernising, internationalist tendency within the Revolution would win out over the locally based power-structures represented by the warlords. But Mavrokordatos' adherence to Byron meant that his own prestige would never recover after Byron's death. The vacancy that Mavrokordatos had failed to fill at Kranidi had already been occupied by Ioannis Kolettis, a qualified doctor from Ioannina who had been co-opted on to the Executive at the same time as Koundouriotis. Like Mavrokordatos, Kolettis enjoyed the benefit of a western education and had gained experience of political service at an Ottoman court – in his case, under Ali Pasha. The 'secretary who spoke German, Latin, French, Italian, Greek, Turkish' and had entertained Byron and Hobhouse to a 'bad dinner' in Ioannina, back in 1809, had been none other than Kolettis.[26] Politically, Kolettis was on the same side. But he had little of Mavrokordatos' idealism. After Byron's death, Kolettis would eclipse Mavrokordatos as the leading moderniser in the crucial final stages of the civil wars, and would outmanoeuvre him decisively again in the course of the two men's long political careers.[27]

Greece entered 1825 with the broad outline of an internal political settlement at last in place. 'The problem of power in the Revolution had found its definitive solution', as one twenty-first-century historian has put it.[28] Emblematic of that shift, and of the effectiveness of the kind of leverage that Byron and Mavrokordatos, together, had promoted, was the transformation of the disgraced Karaiskakis, who in 1827 would die a hero's death at Faliro, outside Athens, in the service of the central government.[29] Karaiskakis is commemorated, today, in the football stadium that bears his name, built near the site. Not all the former warlords would compromise their independence so readily. The fault-line through Greek society that was in evidence at Tripolitsa, when Kolokotronis threatened to drum Mavrokordatos out of the Peloponnese mounted backwards on an ass, and at Anatoliko during the show-trial of Karaiskakis, can be followed through much of the country's history, down to the present day.

Within two years of Byron's death, Greece would face an even greater threat. The long-awaited Ottoman counter-attack came in 1825, with devastating effect. Byron, dead, would be called upon to play a renewed part in mobilising European opinion when the Revolution was all but snuffed out the following year. The posthumous reputation that had been denied to Christian in *The Island*, or the deranged 'giaour', would be assured for Byron's own posterity, when Missolonghi itself was obliterated on Palm Sunday, 1826, two years and three days after he had died there. The enduring 'Byron legend', that began with Trikoupis' funeral oration, would play its part in the extraordinary reversal of fortunes that followed, until, in a few dry words of a diplomatic protocol, signed in London on 3 February 1830, would be born not just the newly minted nation-state of Greece, but the very *idea* of a nation-state on European soil.[30] It was exactly what Byron had foreseen, and had pledged himself to do all he could to bring about while he was alive. In the event, it would not be the United States of America, as he had imagined, but three of the most conservative governments of the Old World (those of Great Britain, France, and Russia) that would give their formal blessing to the sovereign independence of Greece.

In that way, in 1830, the first of the new nation-states of Europe came into existence. Within a few decades, national self-government would have become the norm throughout the continent. In the course of the twentieth century, the self-determination of new nations would sweep away entirely the old monarchical empires against which Byron and so many other Romantics had raised their voices, and sometimes their fists. Belgium, Italy, Germany, the Balkan states after 1878, most of eastern Europe after 1918, down to the break-up of the former Yugoslavia in the 1990s and the recognition of Kosovo in 2008: the list is long and at the time of writing the impetus behind it seems by no means exhausted.

The Greece that Byron fought for – the Greece that still exists, with all the continuing problems inherited from its violent birth – lies at the very foundation of the Europe that we know today. How that came about, in Greece in the years immediately after Byron's death, is another story waiting to be told.

Notes

ABBREVIATIONS USED IN THE NOTES

Abinger	The Bodleian Libraries, University of Oxford: MS Abinger
Apomn.	Ἀπομνημονεύματα ἀγωνιστῶν [*Memoirs of Combatants*], ed. E. G. Protopsaltis, 20 vols. (Athens: Vivliothiki, 1955–7)
Arch. Hydras	Ἀρχεῖον τῆς Κοινότητος Ὕδρας [*Archive of the Community of Hydra*], vol. 9 (Piraeus: Sfaira, 1927); vol. 10 (Piraeus: Zanneios, 1928); vol. 16 (Piraeus: Eleftherios, 1932)
Arch. Kound.	Ἀρχεῖα Λαζάρου καὶ Γεωργίου Κουντουριώτου [*Archives of Lazaros and Georgios Koundouriotis*], vols. I–III, ed. Antonios Lignos (Athens: Sakellarios, 1920); vol. IV (Athens: Sakellarios, 1927); vol. VI, ed. E. G. Protopsaltis (Athens: Library of the General State Archives, 1966)
Arch. Lond.	Ἱστορικὸν Ἀρχεῖον τοῦ Στρατηγοῦ Ἀνδρέου Λόντου (*1789–1847*) [*Historical Archive of General Andreas Londos*], 2 vols. (Athens: Sakellarios, 1914, 1916)
Arch. Pal.	Ἀρχεῖα τῆς Ἑλληνικῆς Παλιγγενεσίας [*Archives of the Greek Regeneration*], 3 vols. (Athens: Library of Parliament, 1971–2) (first published 1857–62)
B	Lord Byron
BCMP	Lord Byron, *The Complete Miscellaneous Prose*, ed. Andrew Nicholson (Oxford: Clarendon Press, 1991)
BCPW	Lord Byron, *The Complete Poetical Works*, ed. Jerome J. McGann, 7 vols. (Oxford: Clarendon Press, 1980–93)
Benaki	Athens: *Historical Archive of the Benaki Museum*
Blessington	Countess of Blessington, *Conversations of Lord Byron*, ed. Ernest J. Lovell (Princeton, NJ: Princeton University Press, 1969) (first published 1834)
BLJ	*Byron's Letters and Journals*, ed. Leslie A. Marchand, 13 vols. (London: John Murray, 1973–94)
Bride	Lord Byron, *The Bride of Abydos*
Bulldog	*Byron's Bulldog: The Letters of John Cam Hobhouse to Lord Byron*, ed. Peter W. Graham (Columbus: Ohio State University Press, 1984)

CCC	*The Clairmont Correspondence*, ed. Marion Kingston Stocking (Baltimore, MD: Johns Hopkins University Press, 1995)
CCJ	*The Journals of Claire Clairmont*, ed. Marion Kingston Stocking (Cambridge, MA: Harvard University Press, 1968)
CHP	Lord Byron, *Childe Harold's Pilgrimage: A Romaunt*
CPWPBS	*The Complete Poetical Works of Percy Bysshe Shelley*, ed. Thomas Hutchinson (London: Oxford University Press, 1943)
Deformed	Lord Byron, *The Deformed Transformed*
Diary	*Hobhouse's Diary*, ed. Peter Cochran, edited from British Library Add. MSS (www.petercochran.wordpress.com/hobhouses-diary)
DJ	Lord Byron, *Don Juan*
EEW	'The Journal of Edward Ellerker Williams', in Maria Gisborne and Edward E. Williams, *Shelley's Friends: Their Journals and Letters*, ed. Frederick L. Jones (Norman: University of Oklahoma Press, 1951)
EJTL	*Letters of Edward John Trelawny*, ed. H. Buxton Forman (London: Oxford University Press, 1910)
Ell. Chron.	Ελληνικά Χρονικά [*Greek Chronicle*] (Missolonghi, 1824–6). Photographic reprint (Athens: Spanos and Nikas, 1958)
Finlay	George Finlay, *History of the Greek Revolution*, 2 vols. (Edinburgh: Blackwood, 1861)
Fotakos	Απομνημονεύματα περί της Ελληνικής Επαναστάσεως υπό Φωτίου Χρυσανθοπούλου ή Φωτάκου [*Memoirs of the Greek Revolution by Fotios Chrysanthopoulos or 'Fotakos'*] (Athens: Greka, 1971) (first published 1858)
Frankenstein	Mary Shelley (with Percy Shelley), *The Original Frankenstein*, ed. Charles E. Robinson (Oxford: Bodleian Library, 2008)
GAK	Athens: Γενικά Αρχεία του Κράτους: Ιστορικόν Αρχείον Αλεξάνδρου Μαυροκορδάτου [*General State Archives: Historical Archive of Alexandros Mavrokordatos*] (1820–4)
Gamba	Pietro Gamba, *A Narrative of Lord Byron's Last Journey to Greece* [translated from Italian by John Cam Hobhouse] (London: John Murray, 1825)
GF	Annotation by George Finlay (British School at Athens Library copy of cited work)
Gordon	Thomas Gordon, *History of the Greek Revolution*, 2 vols. (Edinburgh: Blackwood, 1832)
Hist. Mus.	Athens: National Historical Museum, Archive of Historical Documents
HVSV	*His Very Self and Voice: Collected Conversations of Lord Byron*, ed. Ernest J. Lovell (New York: Macmillan, 1954)

IAM	Μνημεία της Ελληνικής Ιστορίας, τόμ. Ε': Ιστορικόν Αρχείον Αλεξάνδρου Μαυροκορδάτου [*Monuments of Greek History*, vol. 5, *Historical Archive of Alexandros Mavrokordatos*], fascicles I–IV, ed. E. Protopsaltis (Athens: Academy of Athens, 1963–74)
Kasomoulis	Nikolaos Kasomoulis, Ενθυμήματα στρατιωτικά [*Military Recollections*], 3 vols., ed. G. Vlachogiannis (Athens, 1939)
Kennedy	James Kennedy, *Conversations on Religion with Lord Byron and Others* (London: John Murray, 1830)
Medwin	Thomas Medwin, *Conversations of Lord Byron*, ed. Ernest J. Lovell (Princeton, NJ: Princeton University Press, 1966)
Millingen	Julius Millingen, *Memoirs of the Affairs of Greece* (London: J. Rodwell, 1831)
Moore	Thomas Moore, *Letters and Journals of Lord Byron*, 2 vols. (London: John Murray, 1830)
MWSJ	*The Journals of Mary Shelley, 1814–1844*, ed. Paula Feldman and Diana Scott-Kilvert, 2 vols. (Oxford: Clarendon Press, 1987)
MWSL	*Letters of Mary W. Shelley*, ed. Frederick L. Jones, 2 vols. (Norman: University of Oklahoma Press, 1944)
Nat. Lib. Athens	Athens: National Library of Greece, Papers of the London Greek Committee
NLS	Edinburgh: National Library of Scotland. John Murray Archives: George Gordon, Lord Byron, Correspondence and Papers
Parry	William Parry, *The Last Days of Lord Byron* (London: Knight and Lacey, 1825)
PBSL	*The Letters of Percy Bysshe Shelley*, ed. Frederick L. Jones, 2 vols. (Oxford: Clarendon Press, 1964)
PC	Peter Cochran's website (www.petercochran.wordpress.com/). Accessed March–April 2012
Prophecy	Lord Byron, *The Prophecy of Dante*
Prothero	Lord Byron, *Letters and Journals*, ed. R. E. Prothero, 6 vols. (London: John Murray, 1898–1901)
Recollections	E. J. Trelawny, *Recollections of the Last Days of Shelley and Byron* (Boston, MA: Ticknor and Fields, 1858)
Records	E. J. Trelawny, *Records of Shelley, Byron, and the Author*, with an introduction by Anne Barton (New York: New York Review of Books, 2000) (first published 1878)
S&M	*Shelley and Mary: Prepared for the Press by Lady Shelley*, 4 vols. (privately printed, [1882])
Siege	Lord Byron, *The Siege of Corinth*
Stanhope	Leicester Stanhope, *Greece in 1823 and 1824* (London: Sherwood, Gilbert, and Piper, 1825)

TG   Teresa Guiccioli, *Lord Byron's Life in Italy*, translated by
              Michael Rees, ed. Peter Cochran (Newark: University of
              Delaware Press, 2005)
Trikoupis   Spyridon Trikoupis, *Ιστορία της Ελληνικής
              Επαναστάσεως* [*History of the Greek Revolution*],
              4 vols. (London, 1853–7)
West. Rev.   John Bowring, Edward Blaquiere, and William Fletcher,
              'Lord Byron in Greece', *Westminster Review*, 2 (July 1824),
              225–62

PROLOGUE

1. St Clair, *That Greece*; Rosen, *Bentham*; Minta, *Voiceless Shore*; Roessel, *Shadow*; Trayiannoudi, 'Byron in Greece'; Stock, *Shelley–Byron Circle*, 175–97; Cochran, *Romantic Politics*, 209–349.
2. Minta, 'Mavrokordatos'; 'Mesolongi'; 'Consistency'.
3. BLJ III 179: B to Annabella Milbanke, 29 November 1813.
4. Anemon Productions, *1821*; Diamandouros, *Απαρχές* [*Beginnings*]; Gounaris, *Βαλκάνια* [*Balkans*]; Kremmydas, *Τρικούπης* [*Trikoupis*]; Papanikolaou, *Καθημερινή ιστορία* [*Day-to-Day History*]; Papargyriou, *Από το Γένος* [*From Genos*]; Pizanias, *Greek Revolution*; Rotzokos, *Επανάσταση* [*Revolution*]. For the conspiracy theory, see Simopoulos, *Πώς είδαν οι ξένοι* [*How Foreigners Saw*], III 35–201; Kakambouras, *Η βρετανική πολιτική* [*British Policy*].

CHAPTER 1

1. BLJ I 225: B to Hanson, 29 September 1809.
2. Fleming, *Muslim Bonaparte*. For Hobhouse's summing up, see *Journey*, I 109–24; Broughton, *Travels*, I 101–16.
3. Strathcarron, *Joy*, 81–95.
4. In public, Hobhouse put it down to 'accident' (*Journey*, I 1; Broughton, *Travels*, I 1).
5. *Diary*: 23 and 26 September 1809.
6. CHP II 385.
7. The exception was the theatre ('amphitheatre') of Dodona, not recognised as such by Hobhouse, and mentioned only once, in passing, by B (*Diary*: 28 October 1809; cf. *Journey*, I 63–5; Broughton, *Travels*, II 434; BLJ II 134: B to Valpy, 19 November 1811). On not finding any trace of Dodona, see CHP II 469–77 and Minta, *Voiceless Shore*, 81–3.
8. *Diary*: 5 October 1809; cf. *Journey*, I 52; Broughton, *Travels*, I 105.
9. *Diary*: 6 October 1809; cf. 27 October 1809; BLJ I 231 and editor's note.
10. *Diary*: 11 October 1809; cf. BCPW I 275–7: 'Stanzas composed October 11th 1809' and CHP II 424–50; BLJ I 227: B to Mrs Byron, 12 November 1809.

11. BLJ II 9–10: B to Hobhouse, 16 August 1810, from Tripolitsa; BLJ II 16: B to Hobhouse, 2 October 1810; cf. PC (*Byron's Correspondence*): The Marquis of Sligo to the Marchioness of Sligo, 3 August 1810.

12. *Αρχείο Αλή πασά* [*Ali Pasha Archive*], II 153 no. 543.

13. *Diary*: 26–31 October 1809; *Journey*, I 181–4; 548, 574; Broughton, *Travels*, I 152–4. On Psalidas, see Mackridge, *Language*, 145–50.

14. *Diary*: 31 October 1809; BCPW II 266.

15. *Diary*: 8–11 November 1809; cf. BLJ I 229: B to Hanson, 29 September 1809.

16. *Diary*: 13 September 1809 (Forresti told them the story); cf. *Journey*, I 172–5 (not in Broughton, *Travels*).

17. CHP II 595–603.

18. CHP II 613–701 and B's long note on l. 649.

19. *Diary*: 5, 8 November 1809, but on 18 November he refers to 'a tangly dangerous Kleftical pass'. See also *Journey*, I 149–55, 195–7; Broughton, *Travels*, I 138–46, 166–7; cf. CHP II 615.

20. *Diary*: 14 November 1809.

21. For more information and translated examples, see Beaton, *Folk Poetry*, 102–11.

22. Politis, 'Introduction', 51 in *Κλέφτικα* [*Kleftic Songs*].

23. *Diary*: 5 December 1809; B in Finlay II 35 n.; cf. *Journey*, I 225–9; Broughton, *Travels*, I 188–92; cf. Gamba 146–7; Parry 178.

24. *Journey*, I 225–6; Broughton, *Travels*, I 189.

25. BCPW II 204–5, 208, 213; *Diary*: 6 December 1809; cf. *Journey*, I 571, 572; Broughton, *Travels*, I 506, 508; II 485–9; Kitromilides, *Korais*.

26. Hobhouse (*Diary*: 10 December 1809) transcribes the Greek text, which he reproduces with his own translation in *Journey* (I 586–7; Broughton, *Travels*, II 3; cf. on Rigas: *Journey*, I 570; Broughton, *Travels*, I 505). This is the earliest recorded version of the Greek text. For Byron's version, see BCPW I 330–2, 453. On the confusion with Rigas' 'Battle Hymn', see Solomou, *Greek Poetry*, 187–92 and Daskalakis, *Τραγούδια* [*Songs*], 72–103.

27. *Diary*: 9 December 1809; cf. *Journey*, I 225–9; Broughton, *Travels*, I 188–92. For Hobhouse's fuller attempt at rationalisation, see *Journey*, I 584–607; Broughton, *Travels*, II 1–21.

28. *Diary*: 14–15 December 1809. The phrase and the description survive into *Journey*, I 241 and Broughton, *Travels*, I 198.

29. CHP I 612–16.

30. *Diary*: 18–23 December 1809; *Journey*, I 260–84; Broughton, *Travels*, I 215–36; cf. BLJ II 134: B to Valpy, 19 November 1811.

31. *Diary*: 29–31 December 1809; cf. *Journey*, I 286–94, 353–68; Broughton, *Travels*, I 241–51, 307–21.

32. Reproduced as the frontispiece in Spencer, *Fair Greece*.

33. St Clair, *Lord Elgin*; King, *Elgin Marbles*.

34. CHP II 82–126 and B's note on l. 101.

35. CHP II 82–4, 91–2 (quoted), and B's note on l. 84 (BCPW II 284). B was presumably with Hobhouse when he rode by these ruins on the afternoon of 28 December (*Diary*).

36. Moore I 25–6; cf. BLJ II 47: 22 May 1811.
37. BCMP 133 (written 1821); cf. Spencer, *Fair Greece*, 266.
38. Freud, 'A Disturbance'.
39. CHP II 831–2, stanza added in Athens, early 1811.
40. *Diary*: 3 March 1810; BLJ II 46: B to Hobhouse, 15 May 1811.
41. *Diary*: 11 April, 20 March 1810.
42. BLJ I 235: B to Mrs Byron, 19 March 1810.
43. BLJ II 55: B to Hodgson, 29 June 1811; cf. *Diary*: 31 October 1809, 26 February 1810.
44. BLJ II 92: B to Dallas, 7 September 1811.
45. *Diary*: 13–14 March 1810; *Journey*, II 646–52; Broughton, *Travels*, II 55–9.
46. *Journey*, II 647–8; *Diary*: 14 March 1810 and editor's n. 41; CHP IV 1372–7.
47. *Diary*: 13 March 1810.
48. CHP II 797–800.
49. Hobhouse devotes proportionately the largest amount of space in his published accounts to these debates and the details of his investigations on the ground (*Journey*, II 689–798; Broughton, *Travels*, II 117–86).
50. *Diary*: 15 April 1810; BLJ I 236: B to Mrs Byron, 17 April 1810; cf. BLJ I 238: B to Drury, 3 May 1810.
51. *Beppo* 746–7; DJ IV 588–624; cf. *Diary* (PC: editor's n. 114 on entry for 15 April 1810).
52. *Journey*, II 807 (cf. Broughton, *Travels*, II 193–4) significantly amplifies *Diary*: 16 April 1810.
53. *Diary*: 26 April 1810.
54. BLJ I 237: B to Drury, 3 May 1810, and several letters following; *Diary*: 3 May 1810, Byron's addition dated 26 May, and editor's notes 172–4 (PC). Cf. *Journey*, II 808–9; Broughton, *Travels*, II 194–6.
55. *Bride* II 1–54.
56. Cf. BLJ II 245–6: B to Drury, 17 June 1810.
57. 'Written after swimming from Sestos to Abydos, May 9th 1810' (BCPW I 281–2).
58. CHP II 736–7; cf. DJ V and VI.
59. BLJ I 246: B to Drury, 17 June 1810.
60. BLJ I 248: B to Dallas, 23 June 1810.
61. *Diary*: 17 July 1810; BLJ XI 157: B to Scrope Davies, 31 July 1810; BLJ II 3: B to Mrs Byron, 20 July 1810.
62. This is probably the meaning of BLJ II 206–7: B to Charles Skinner Matthews, 22 June 1809, part-elucidated by being recalled at BLJ II 14: B to Hobhouse, 23 August 1810.
63. *Diary*: 6 October 1809; cf. 20 October 1809 and B's note to CHP II 649–92 (BCPW II 198).
64. Minta, who sees Byron as homosexually inexperienced in England, still has him promiscuous when on his own in Greece (*Voiceless Shore*, 77–80, 148–52). See also Crompton, *Greek Love*; Gross, *Erotic Liberal*; MacCarthy, *Byron*, 126–30 and *passim*; Douglass, 'Biographers', 22–3. The evidence from the primary

sources is most fully assembled in Cochran, 'Byron's Boyfriends', 15–36. It is inconclusive.

65. BLJ II 6–7: B to Hobhouse, 29 July 1810; Marchand, *Biography*, I 251–2 and n. 8. The episode is differently understood by MacCarthy (*Byron*, 126–8).

66. See e.g. BLJ II 46: B to Hobhouse, 15 May 1811.

67. PC (*Byron's Correspondence*): Charles Skinner Matthews to B, 30 June 1809 and Cochran, 'Byron's Boyfriends', 35–6.

68. BLJ II 23: B to Hobhouse, 4 October 1810 ('You know the monastery of Mendele [*sic*], it was there I made myself master of the first [pl & opt C]'); BLJ II 25, 29: B to Hanson, 4 and 11 November 1810, B to Hobhouse, 26 November 1810.

69. BLJ II 14–16: B to Hobhouse, 25 September 1810, continued 2 October; BLJ II 89: B to Hodgson, 3 September 1811; cf. BCPW II 193 (CHP II, 'Notes').

70. NLS MS 43427: Nicolo Giraud to B, 1 January 1815. This part of the letter is in Greek. Its opening, in English, is transcribed by Marchand (*Biography*, I 274 n.9).

71. CHP II, 'Notes', section II (BCPW II 202).

72. BLJ II 32, n. 1; Marchand, *Biography*, I 268, both citing CHP II, 'Notes' (BCPW II 206). Hobhouse, who is unlikely to have met Marmarotouris, but whose information will have derived from Byron, adds that he was a 'merchant' and credits him with an original *Life* of Alexander Suvorov, the victor over the Turks at Ismail in 1791, an event that many years later would form the subject-matter of DJ VIII (*Journey*, I 572; Broughton, *Travels*, I 507).

73. NLS MS 43551: Εἴδησις τυπογραφική ['Typographical announcement'], 1 October 1799, Trieste, signed by Ioannis Marmarotouris, Dimitrios Venieris, Spyridon Prevetos. This document refers to a complete translation in twelve volumes. It is not clear what relation, if any, the project bears to the translation of vol. 4 of this work, by Georgios Vendotis and Rigas Velestinlis, that had already been published in Vienna in 1797.

74. Catalogue of the Gennadius Library, Athens: NH 375.61.

75. For an account of the missing material, see BCPW II 295 and PC (*Childe Harold's Pilgrimage*, Cantos I and II), p. 10 and editor's n. 24.

76. BLJ II 22–3: B to Hobhouse, 4 October 1810; Solomou, *Greek Poetry*, 272–92.

77. The phonetic transcriptions of the Albanian songs in CHP II, 'Notes' (BCPW II 196–8), according to B, writing at the time, 'are copied by one who speaks and understands the dialect perfectly, and who is a native of Athens' – the same form of words as he uses elsewhere in the same set of texts to describe Marmarotouris.

78. NLS MS 43550, subfile 1, no. 59.

79. CHP II 693–728 (714, 721 quoted).

80. BCPW II 202: CHP II, 'Notes' II; cf. BCPW II 201.

81. BCPW II 203; cf. 202: 'the real or supposed descendants . . .'.

82. *Diary*: 2 February 1810; cf. *Journey*, I 298; Broughton, *Travels*, I 249; BCPW II 200–1.

83. BLJ II 125: B to Hobhouse, 3 November 1811; cf. BLJ II 114–15: B to Hobhouse, 14 October 1811.
84. BLJ II 25–6: B to Hanson, B to Hobhouse, 11–12 November 1810.
85. BLJ II 40–1: B to Mrs Byron, 28 February 1811; cf. BLJ II 100: B to Dallas, 16 September 1811 and the epigraph of CHP I–II.
86. See e.g. BLJ II 238: B to Drury, 3 May 1810.
87. BLJ II 88, 95: B to Hodgson, 3 and 9 September 1811.
88. BLJ II 68: B to Scrope Davies, 7 August 1811; cf. BLJ II 67–71.
89. BLJ II 110: B to Hodgson, 10 October 1811; cf. B to Dallas, 11 October 1811.
90. CHP II 127–8.
91. CHP II 891–5. The added stanzas are nos. 9, 95, and 96.
92. See e.g. BCPW II 271; cf. Spencer, *Fair Greece*, 287–94.
93. CHP II 88.
94. For differing views on Byron's place within a modern understanding of Romanticism, see e.g. Berlin, *Roots*, 131–4; McGann, *Romanticism*, 236–55; Cochran, *Romanticism*. On Romanticism and war, see Fletcher, *Romantics*, 16.

CHAPTER 2

1. BCMP 20–43. See also Kelsall, *Politics* and 'Politics', 46–8; MacCarthy, *Byron*, 154–7.
2. BLJ III 217–18: 'Journal', 23–4 November 1813; cf. BLJ V 177: B to Moore, 28 February 1817 ('literature . . . is nothing; and it may seem odd enough to say, I do not think it my vocation').
3. BLJ III 242: 'Journal', 16 January 1814, glossed by Kelsall ('Politics', 50) as 'political nihilism'.
4. BLJ XI 179: B to Hodgson, 8 December 1811; BLJ II 163: B to Hodgson, 16 February 1812; BLJ II 181: B to Clarke, 26 June 1812; BLJ II 190: B to Revd Walpole, September 1812; BLJ II 258: B to Lady Melbourne, 21 December 1812; BLJ III 35: B to Lord Holland, 3 April 1813.
5. BLJ IV 172: B to Moore, 15 September 1814; BLJ IV 269: B to Moore, 20 February 1815; BLJ V 48: B to Wilmot, 11 March 1816.
6. Gleckner, *Ruins*; Green, '"Lifeless thing"'; Leask, *Romantic Writers*, 13–67; Manning, *Fictions*; McGann, *Beauty*, 262–4; Rawes, *Experimentation*, 27–49; Watkins, *Social Relations*.
7. Thorslev, *Hero*.
8. *Giaour* 584–674; *Bride* II 350, 380–6, 426–33; *Corsair passim*.
9. See esp. *Corsair* III 521; *Lara* I 127–30.
10. Crompton, *Greek Love*, 210; Leask, *Romantic Writers*, 57–8.
11. *Giaour* 422–38 and BCPW III 418 (B's note and editor's comment).
12. *Bride* II 433–45, 597–620; *Corsair* III 678–96; *Lara* II 598–9.
13. Leask, *Romantic Writers*, 40.
14. *Lara* I 14; 'Il Diavolo Inamorato' 20 (BCPW III 14).
15. *Bride* II 100–1.
16. *Lara* II 259–63.

17. 'The Monk of Athos' (BCPW I 285–7) 12–18, 39; Rawes, *Experimentation*, 39–41; BCPW III 414, 480.

18. *Giaour* 1–6, 103–67; *Siege* 104–5, 345–78 and BCPW III 476–82; cf. Leask, *Romantic Writers*, 33; *Bride* II 350, 380–6.

19. *Lara* II 240–1, 252–3.

20. *Giaour* 6. On the chronology of the versions, see BCPW III 406–13.

21. *Giaour* 755–62.

22. *Giaour*, B's notes to ll. 755 and 781.

23. *Diary*: 28 December 1809.

24. Southey, *Poetical Works*, III 265–6, including a long extract translated from Tournefort, *Relation d'un voyage du Levant* (Paris, 1717).

25. *Diary*: 14 March 1810.

26. *Giaour* 1269–70, 1280, 1301.

27. *Giaour* 1018, 1286–95, 1315–18.

28. *Giaour* 1308.

29. *Giaour* 91–7; B's note to *Giaour* 781.

30. *Giaour* 100–1, 116–17.

31. Gleckner, *Ruins*, 105–6; Leask, *Romantic Writers*, 29.

32. *Giaour* 135, 1301.

33. Holmes, *Shelley*, 172, citing the testimony of Thomas Jefferson Hogg.

34. Polidori, *Diary*, 101.

35. On 1816, see Ellis, *Geneva*. On B and Shelley, see principally Robinson, *Shelley and Byron*, but also Blumberg, *Byron and the Shelleys*; Buxton, *Byron and Shelley*.

36. Häusermann, *Genevese Background*, 6 and plates 1–2.

37. Moore II 23–4 (information from Mary Shelley); cf. Seymour, *Mary Shelley*, 153.

38. PBSL II 34: Shelley to Mary, 23 August 1818; Ellis, *Geneva*, 44.

39. CHP III 860–77 and BCPW II 311: Byron's note to l. 860; cf. BCPW I 275–7; *Frankenstein* 65–6, 100.

40. BCMP 58–63, 329–35.

41. Polidori, *Diary*, 15: Polidori to Henry Colburn, 2 April 1819; Polidori, *Vampyre*, 244.

42. *Frankenstein* 75, 78–9, 80. The phrase 'lifeless thing' comes directly from *The Giaour* (1280).

43. *Frankenstein* 78.

44. *Frankenstein* 101.

45. *Frankenstein* 123, 169.

46. Seymour, *Mary Shelley*, 137–8.

47. BCPW II 201: CHP II, 'Notes'.

48. Pollin, 'Sources', 102. For additional proof that Byron was aware of this version of the myth before 1816, see BCPW III 269 and 459 (supplementary lines to the *Ode to Napoleon*).

49. Pausanias, *Description of Greece*, 10.4.4.

50. CHP III 608–16; BLJ v 76: B to Hobhouse, 16 May 1816. The site of the battle of Chaeronea is mentioned explicitly in B's note to l. 270.
51. BLJ v 74 and 80: B to Hobhouse 1 May and 23 June 1816; *Bulldog* 228: Hobhouse to B, 9 July 1816.
52. Medwin 156; BCPW IV 457; cf. Duffy, *Shelley*, 150–7.
53. 'Prometheus' 45, 47 (BCPW IV 31–3).
54. *Manfred* I 1.153–4.
55. *Manfred* II 4.159; cf. II 2.79–83.
56. BLJ v 268: B to Murray, 12 October 1817; cf. An, 'Manfred'.
57. See e.g. Mellor, *Mary Shelley*, 78–9; Thorslev, *Hero*, 114–15, 215.
58. CHP IV 1459–67.
59. Buxton, *Byron and Shelley*, 18; PBSL I 353–4.
60. For the chronology of the tour, see *Shelley and his Circle*, IV 692–701.
61. PBSL I 480–1, PBS to Peacock 12 July 1816.
62. PBSL I 491: PBS to Peacock, 17 July 1816.
63. Holmes, *Shelley*, citing Horace Smith, who first met Shelley in January 1817.
64. Holmes, *Shelley*, 26 and 431; cf. 182.
65. 'A Discourse on the Manners of the Ancient Greeks Relative to the Subject of Love', in Notopoulos, *Platonism*, 410; 411; cf. Crompton, *Greek Love*, 288–94.
66. DJ I 921–9, IX 601–2; cf. Crompton, *Greek Love*, 96–7; Gross, *Erotic Liberal*, 138–9. See also PBLS II 44 and Holmes, *Shelley*, 448.
67. CHP III 923–76 and BCPW II 298.
68. See especially CHP III 933–4, 941, 952, 959–61 (quoting the *Pervigilium Veneris*), 972 (presumably alluding to the tale of Venus and Psyche in Apuleius' *Metamorphoses*).
69. CHP III 941, 954–8.
70. See e.g. BCPW II 300.
71. BCPW II 298; Marchand, *Biography*, II 633.
72. MWSJ I 122 and n.; Bieri, *Shelley*, 346.
73. BLJ v 107: B to Kinnaird, 29 September 1816.
74. Leigh Hunt in HVSV 336.
75. PBSL I 506–7: Shelley to B, 29 September 1816; cf. Robinson, *Shelley and Byron*, 110.
76. PBSL I 513: Shelley to B, 20 November 1816.
77. CHP III 1059–61, for date of writing, see BCPW II 298.
78. BLJ III 207: 'Journal', 16 November 1813 (cf. III 218); BLJ IV 74; cf. Keach, *Arbitrary Power*, 40–5, 166.
79. 'A Defence of Poetry' [1821] in Shelley, *Prose*, 297; cf. 'A Philosophical View of Reform' [1819–20] (*ibid.* 240).
80. CHP III 1065–6.

CHAPTER 3

1. Most fully recorded by Hobhouse (*Diary*: 11 October 1816–7 January 1817). See also Schmidt, *Rhetoric*; Stabler, '"Awake to Terror"'; Zuccato, 'Fortunes', 80–90.
2. BCPW IV 485.
3. Marchand, *Biography*, II 716, citing the diary of George Ticknor, 20 October 1817.
4. PBSL II 35–8: Shelley to Mary, 23 August 1818.
5. See e.g. Marchand, *Biography*, II 748–9; MacCarthy, *Byron*, 345; Hay, *Young Romantics*, 152–4.
6. PBSL II 41: Shelley to Peacock, 8 October 1818.
7. Robinson, *Shelley and Byron*, 92–4.
8. CHP IV 397–8, 964–5.
9. 'Julian and Maddalo', 182–7; cf. Foot, *Politics*, 231–3.
10. 'Julian and Maddalo', Preface (CPWPBS 189).
11. Duff, *Romance*; Duffy, *Shelley*; Keach, 'Political Poet'; Stock, *Shelley–Byron Circle*, 99–147.
12. PBSL II 44: Shelley to B, 17 October 1818; Holmes, *Shelley*, 448.
13. Boyd, *Don Juan*; Randel, 'Tradition'.
14. DJ II 1551–2. Note that by Canto IV Haidée has become only half-Greek, as she acquires a Moorish mother from Fez (DJ IV 431–56).
15. Origo, *Attachment*, 39–41; Marchand, *Biography*, II 773–8.
16. BLJ VI 168: B to Murray, 29 June 1819.
17. BLJ VI 189: B to Hobhouse, 30 July 1819; cf. DJ IV 825–8.
18. Origo, *Attachment*, 72–3 and 496 n. 18; BCPW IV 499–500. See also the first paragraph of the 'Preface'.
19. BLJ VI 235: B to Murray, 29 October 1819.
20. *Prophecy* II 15–18; cf. *Lara* II 240–1.
21. *Prophecy* IV 91–2.
22. *Prophecy* II 134, 145.
23. Regularly cited is *Purgatorio* VI 76–127 (BCPW IV 503), but see also *Inferno* XXXIII 79–84 (an episode well known to Byron). Even earlier in his career, in *De Vulgari Eloquentia*, Dante 'had seen that the unity of Italy was already a linguistic fact' (Boyde, *Dante*, 100).
24. As long ago as 1926, Byron was said to be 'one of those who did most to make nationalism the religion of the last [i.e., the nineteenth] century' (Brinton, *Political Ideas*, 154), a sentiment echoed by St Clair (*That Greece*, 184), challenged by Rosen (*Bentham*, 301).
25. *Prophecy* IV 11–15.
26. BLJ VI 126: B to Murray, 15 May 1819.
27. *Prophecy* II 1–2.
28. Origo, *Attachment*, 114–20; Marchand, *Biography*, II 815–23.
29. BLJ VI 235: B to Murray, 29 October 1819.

30. DJ III 701–4.
31. Medwin 231, 233 and editor's n. 553; BCPW v 700, note to l. 689.
32. Cochran, *Romantic Politics*, 209–12; *Edinburgh Review* (October 1819), 263–93.
33. DJ III 762–4, 766–7.
34. Brewer, *Flame*, 42–3.
35. Cochran, *Romantic Politics*, 266–72.
36. DJ III 783.
37. BCPW v 700, editor's note to l. 649.
38. DJ III 714, 743–8.
39. DJ III 785–6.
40. DJ III 791.
41. DJ III 792–4.
42. Marchand, *Biography*, II 826–30; BLJ VI 240–6.
43. BLJ VII 125–6: B to Moore, 13 July 1820; Origo, *Attachment*, 186–90.
44. BLJ VII 146: B to Teresa, 29 July 1820; cf. Origo, *Attachment*, 199–200; Mac-Carthy, *Byron*, 382.
45. Origo, *Attachment*, 202.
46. BLJ VII 236: B to Kinnaird, 22 November 1820.
47. BLJ VI 210–11: B to Kinnaird, 19 August 1819; B to Hobhouse, 20 August 1819; BLJ VI 217: B to Kinnaird, 27 August 1819.
48. BLJ VII 44: B to Murray, 21 February 1820; Parry 204–6, 211–13.
49. BLJ VII 80–1: B to Hobhouse, 22 April 1820; cf. CHP III 770–96.
50. Begun on 4 April 1820, completed on 16 July (BCPW IV 521).
51. *Marino Faliero* I 2.316: 'Could I free Venice, and avenge my wrongs...'.
52. *Marino Faliero* II 2.162, 174.
53. *Marino Faliero* III 2.513–15, 517–21; cf. *Lara* I 336.
54. Cf. BLJ VII 186–7: B to Teresa, 29 September 1820.
55. Kelsall, *Politics*, 91.
56. BLJ VII 77: B to Murray, 16 April 1820; cf. BLJ VII 137: B to Murray, 22 July 1820.
57. d'Amico, 'Byron and Italy'.
58. See e.g. BLJ VII 112: B to Moore, 1 June 1820; BLJ VII 184: B to Murray, 28–9 September 1820; Origo, *Attachment*, 227.
59. BCPW VI 611, 613–14.
60. BLJ VIII 43–7: 'Ravenna Journal', 9, 15, 18 February 1821.
61. BLJ VIII 49: 'Ravenna Journal', 24 February 1821; Origo, *Attachment*, 250–1.
62. BLJ VIII 105: B to Moore, 28 April 1821.
63. St Clair, *That Greece*, 23–34, 51–77.
64. BLJ VIII 214: B to Moore, 19 September 1821; cf. Roessel, *Shadow*, 45.
65. BLJ VIII 11, 84, 118, 121, 124 (*Galignani's Messenger*); BLJ VIII 16, 116, 117, 123, 130 (Italian papers).
66. BLJ VIII 122, 135: B to Hobhouse, 20 May, and to Moore, 4 June 1821.
67. The only offence mentioned is having engineered his early return from his previous 'exile' in Crete (*Foscari* II 1.92–101); cf. Manning, *Fictions*, 136–7.

68. *Foscari* I 1.94–125.
69. Explicitly juxtaposed, if ironically, in the words of Loredano (*Foscari* IV 1.265–9).
70. BCPW VI 633 and B's appendix.
71. *Foscari* I 1.128–30.
72. *Foscari* III 1.133–6; cf. 186–90, 273–7.

CHAPTER 4

1. MWSL I 166; Holmes, *Shelley*, 622–3; Seymour, *Mary Shelley*, 261.
2. Millingen 65–6, reproduced in CCJ 473–6.
3. Millingen's testimony is often overlooked or undervalued. Nicolson's wrongheaded caricature (*Journey*, 163–4) has proved influential; see e.g. Woodhouse, *Philhellenes*, 105, 111, 116, 125. Biographical information from NLS MS 43551: J. R. van Millingen, 'Lord Byron and Dr Millingen', unpublished typescript, March 1920.
4. PBSL II 276: Shelley to Peacock, 21 March 1821; Huscher, 'Mavrocordato', 32. For critical reassessment of Mavrokordatos' life and career, see Loukos, 'Οι «τύχες»' ['The "Fortunes"'] and *Μαυροκορδάτος* [*Mavrokordatos*]; Theodoridis, *Μαυροκορδάτος* [*Mavrokordatos*].
5. Panagiotopoulos, 'Κάτι έγινε' ['Something Happened']; Sideri, *Έλληνες φοιτητές* [*Greek Students*]. See also Panagiotopoulos, 'Ιγνάτιος' ['Ignatios'].
6. Mavrocordato, 'Coup d'œil', 3 (quoted), 44–52.
7. Medwin, *Life*, 262–4.
8. PBSL II 292: Shelley to Claire Clairmont, 14[?] May 1821.
9. Eight of the eighteen letters are transcribed, more or less fully, with errors and omissions, in *S&M* III 600–47. All citations in this chapter have been translated from the original MSS (Bodleian Libraries, University of Oxford: MS Abinger c. 45, folios as specified (formerly Dep. c. 516/5)).
10. MS Abinger c. 45, fo. 92: Mavrocordato to Mary Shelley, 31 May [1821].
11. PBSL II 297: Shelley to Claire Clairmont, 8 June 1821.
12. MWSJ I 350: 23 January 1821.
13. MWSL I 223: Mary Shelley to Maria Gisborne, 7 March 1822.
14. 'Epipsychidion' 513 and 'Advertisement' (cf. 422, 430, 507, 542).
15. 'Epipsychidion' 425–8.
16. MWSJ I 359: 1 April 1821.
17. MS Abinger c. 45, fo. 82: Mavrocordato to Mary Shelley, 3 April [1821] (*S&M* III 600–2).
18. Robinson, 'The Shelleys to Leigh Hunt', 53–4.
19. Finlay I 181. For receipt of the news in Pisa, see IAM I 30 no. 15: unsigned letter of 26 March [/7 April] 1821, reporting the arrival of a ship from Patras with first news of the insurrection in the Morea; IAM I 37 no. 21: Praidis to Louriotis, 19 April 1821, confirming the Morea in a state of revolt; MWSJ I 363–4: 24 April 1821.

20. IAM I 32–3 no. 18: Mavrokordatos to [Praidis, Polychroniadis, *et al.*], 2 April 1821.
21. MWSL I 188: Mary Shelley to Maria Gisborne, 5 April 1821.
22. Robinson, who republished the texts, respectively in 'The Shelleys to Leigh Hunt' and 'Shelley to the Editor', interprets the role of the Shelleys differently, and has been followed by subsequent biographers.
23. Robinson, 'Shelley to the Editor', 56.
24. MS Abinger c. 45, fo. 66: Mavrocordato to Mary Shelley, 11 May [1821] (*S&M* III 621–2).
25. Medwin, *Life*, 264.
26. Svolopoulos, 'Η σύσταση' ['The Establishment'].
27. Finlay I 176–7; Philemon, *Φιλική Εταιρία* [*Filiki Etairia*], 363.
28. Philemon, *Ελληνική Επανάστασις* [*Greek Revolution*], IV 513: Mavrokordatos to D. Ypsilantis, 27 October [/8 November] 1821; *Arch. Kound.* I 44: Mavrokordatos to Lazaros and Georgios Koundouriotis, 12 [/24] December 1821.
29. PBSL II 278: Shelley to Claire Clairmont, 2 April 1821.
30. Μάντις εἰμ' ἐσθλῶν ἀγώνων (*Oedipus at Colonus* 1078). Shelley seems never to have translated Sophocles' words, which are rendered at second hand and sometimes quite wrongly in modern editions of his poems. My translation incorporates Shelley's own phrase from the third paragraph of the Preface to *Hellas*, which best conveys the sense of the Greek as Shelley understood it.
31. PBSL II 276–7: Shelley to Peacock, 21 March 1821 and PS by Mary, editor's note.
32. IAM I 32–3 no. 18: Mavrokordatos to [Praidis, Polychroniadis, *et al.*], 2 April 1821; also cited in Huscher, 'Mavrocordato', 30.
33. MS Abinger c. 45, fo. 81: Mavrocordato to Mary Shelley, 3 April [1821] (*S&M* III 600–2).
34. MS Abinger c. 45, fo. 88: Mavrocordato to Mary Shelley, 24 May [1821] ('Please communicate everything to Mr Shelley with my compliments') and fo. 68, undated [1–5 June] ('you may be assured that everything will be communicated to everyone').
35. MS Abinger c. 45, fo. 73: Mavrocordato to Mary Shelley, date inferred from MWSJ I 360: Saturday, 7 April 1821 and editor's note; cf. Finlay I 156.
36. Finlay I 150, 156.
37. MWSJ I 364–5: 24 April 1821.
38. MS Abinger c. 45, fo. 84: Mavrocordato to Mary Shelley, 14 May [1821].
39. MS Abinger c. 45, fo. 65: Mavrocordato to Mary Shelley, 11 May [1821] (*S&M* III 621–2).
40. IAM I 32–3 no. 18: Mavrokordatos to [Praidis, *et al.*], 2 April 1821.
41. MS Abinger c. 45, fo. 87: Mavrocordato to Mary Shelley, 21 May [1821] (*S&M* III 626–8).
42. MS Abinger c. 45, fo. 88: Mavrocordato to Mary Shelley, 24 May [1821]; Gordon I 187.

43. MS Abinger c. 45, fo. 90: Mavrocordato to Mary Shelley, 27 May [1821] (*S&M* III 629–30, part cited in Hay, *Young Romantics*, 202).
44. Sentence omitted in *S&M* III 630, but noted in MWSJ I 368, n. 4.
45. MWSJ I 365: 8 May 1821 and n. 2.
46. MS Abinger c. 45, fo. 95: Mavrocordato to Mary Shelley, 13 June [1821]; MWSJ I 370: 15 June 1821.
47. MS Abinger c. 45, fo. 67: Mavrocordato to Mary Shelley, [22 June 1821], date inferred from MWSJ I 371; Finlay I 162–4; Gordon I 118–21.
48. MWSJ I 371: 24–5 June 1821.
49. MWSL I 202–3: Mary Shelley to Maria Gisborne, 25 June 1821.
50. MS Abinger c. 45, fo. 97: Mavrocordato to Mary Shelley, 25 June 1821 (*S&M* III 647). This is the only letter in the whole sequence to include a full date.
51. MWSJ I 372: 26 June 1821; Protopsaltis, Μαυροκορδάτος [*Mavrokordatos*], 24–6; IAM I 44 no. 27: Louriotis to Praidis, 29 May 1821; Raybaud, *Mémoires*, I 268–70.
52. MS Abinger c. 50, fos. 1–2: Mavrocordato to Mary Shelley, 30 December [1839].
53. Panagiotopoulos, 'Κάτι έγινε' ['Something Happened'], 180–1; Loukos, 'Οι «τύχες»' ['The "Fortunes"'], 106 n. 37.
54. BLJ VIII 104, 163, 171: B to Shelley, 26 April, [30–1 July?], [5? August] 1821.
55. BLJ VIII 154–5: B to Duchess of Devonshire, 15 July 1821; BLJ VIII 157–8: B to Hoppner, 23 July 1821; Marchand, *Biography*, II 913–16.
56. BLJ VIII 158–60: B to Teresa, 26 July 1821; BLJ VIII 174–5: B to Pietro Gamba, 9 August 1821 ('delle vere pazzie'); cf. Origo, *Attachment*, 261–72.
57. PBSL II 336: Shelley to Mary, 15 August 1821.
58. PBSL II 316: Shelley to Mary, 7 August 1821; BLJ VIII 170–1: B to Pietro Gamba, 5 August 1821 ('un parente del [*sic*] Allegra').
59. BCPW VI 643.
60. BLJ VI 82–4, 125–6: B to Murray, 24 November 1818 and 15 May 1819.
61. BCPW VI 646.
62. BLJ VI 82–4: B to Murray, 24 November 1818.
63. BLJ VII 79–80: B to Hoppner, 22 April 1820.
64. BLJ VIII 132: B to Kinnaird, 2 June 1821.
65. BCPW VI 646.
66. BCPW VI 651–2; Medwin, *Life*, 334–5; Robinson, *Shelley and Byron*, 196–8.
67. *Cain* I 1.213–16; cf. Shelley, 'Julian and Maddalo', 182–7.
68. *Literary Gazette*, 19 May 1821 (cited in Robinson, *Shelley and Byron*, 197).
69. BLJ V 160–3: B to Kinnaird, 20 January 1817; cf. Ellis, *Geneva*, 58–9 and 170 n. 19.
70. See MWSJ I 249 and nn. 249–50 and, among many others, Bieri, *Shelley*, 440–6. For 'my Neapolitan charge', see PBSL II 211: Shelley to John and Maria Gisborne, [7? July 1820].
71. MWSL I 205–9: Mary Shelley to Mrs Hoppner, 9 August 1821.
72. BCPW VI 223–3; cf. BCPW VI 668, 670.

73. BCPW VI 223–4; cf. BLJ VIII 239–41: B to Hobhouse, 12 October 1821.
74. BLJ IX 81: B to Moore, [13? December 1821] and PBSL II 368–9: Shelley to B [13 December 1821]; cf. *Records* 65–6.
75. NLS MS 43387: B cited in 'MS Biographical Notes on Byron by Edward John Trelawny' (1832); also cited in Marchand, *Biography*, III 1098 and Origo, *Attachment*, 354; cf. *Records* 43: 'If I am a poet . . . the air of Greece made me one.' The remark itself dates from Byron's time aboard the *Hercules* in 1823.
76. PBSL II 324–5: Shelley to Mary, 8 August 1821.
77. BLJ VII 138; 182; cf. Blessington 51; PBSL II 332: Shelley to Mary, [11 August 1821]: 'a faithful picture they say of modern Greek manners'. 'They' can only refer to Byron.
78. *Hellas*, Preface (CPWPBS 447).
79. BLJ VIII 180, 182: B to Kinnaird, and to Murray, 16 August 1821.
80. BLJ VIII 198: B to Murray, 4 September 1821.
81. BLJ VIII 211: B to Lady Byron, 14 September 1821.
82. BLJ VIII 214: B to Moore, 19 September 1821.
83. For the very few partial exceptions, see BLJ VIII 239: B to Hobhouse, 12 October 1821; BLJ IX 23: 'Detached thoughts' no. 23; BLJ IX 88–9: B to Hobhouse, 18 January 1822 and HVSV 344–5.
84. *Hellas* 696–9.
85. *Hellas* 737–861.
86. *Hellas* 1059.
87. *Hellas* Preface (CPWPBS 447). See further Wallace, 'National Identity'; *Shelley and Greece*, 178–207; Ferris, *Silent Urns*, 108–33; Cox, 'The Dramatist', 74–7; Beaton, 'Re-imagining'.
88. MWSL I 232: Mary Shelley to Medwin, 12 April 1822.

CHAPTER 5

1. PBSL II 433: Shelley to Trelawny, 18 June 1822, and n. 4. For the fullest account, see Cline, *Pisan Circle*; for cultural implications, Schoina, *Romantic 'Anglo-Italians'*.
2. EEW 139: 27 March 1822; BLJ IX 131: B to Sir Walter Scott, [28 March 1822?]; Cline, *Pisan Circle*, 16–25.
3. EEW 125: 14 January 1822; St Clair, *Trelawny*; Crane, *Jackal*.
4. MWSJ I 395–7: 7–9 February 1822; MWSL I 218: Mary Shelley to Maria Gisborne, 9 February 1822.
5. Hay, *Young Romantics*, 3–26.
6. Huscher, 'Mavrocordato', 32; cf. MWSJ I 341, n. 9.
7. EEW 111: 11 November 1821; MWSJ I 383: 11–15 November 1821.
8. Raybaud, *Mémoires*, I 461–85; Gordon I 243–7; Finlay I 267–71. On the fate of the Jewish community, see Fleming, *Greece*, 16–17.
9. MWSL I 212–13: Mary Shelley to Maria Gisborne, 20[?] December 1821.

10. PBSL II 368: Shelley to Claire Clairmont, 11 December 1821; MWSL I 210: Mary Shelley to Maria Gisborne, 30 November 1821.
11. MWSJ I 383–4: 29 November 1821; PBSL II 370–1: Shelley to Claire Clairmont, 31 December 1821.
12. EEW 112.
13. DJ VIII 34–40; cf. 651–2: 'Shade of Leonidas, who fought so hearty, / When my poor Greece was once, as now, surrounded!'
14. DJ VIII 724–824, 1113–20; cf. *The Deformed Transformed* II 3.
15. MWSJ I 426; MWSL I 210: Mary Shelley to Maria Gisborne, 30 November 1821; PBSL II 368: Shelley to Claire Clairmont, 11 December 1821; MWSL I 212–13: Mary Shelley to Maria Gisborne, 20[?] December 1821.
16. EEW 134: 13 March 1822; MWSL I 229: Mary Shelley to Maria Gisborne, 6 April 1822.
17. Gordon I 357–68.
18. Dakin, *Struggle*, 148–50; Brewer, *Flame*, 167.
19. Juan's Turkish adventures begin in Canto IV, written in 1819, but are considerably extended through Cantos VI–VIII, written between January/April and the end of July 1822 (BCPW v 715). See also Cochran, *Romantic Politics*, 293–309.
20. MWSL I 209: Mary Shelley to Maria Gisborne, 30 November 1821; PBSL II 373: Shelley to Peacock, [11? January 1822].
21. PBSL II 379: Shelley to Horace Smith, 25 January 1822; cf. *Records* 49–50.
22. MWSL I 217–18: Mary Shelley to Maria Gisborne, 9 February 1822; EEW 128–30: 7–11 February 1822.
23. MWSL I 221: Mary Shelley to Marianne Hunt, 5 March 1822; MWSL I 223: Mary Shelley to Maria Gisborne, 7 March 1822.
24. PBSL II 393: Shelley to Leigh Hunt, 2 March 1822.
25. PBSL II 399: Mary and Percy Shelley to Claire Clairmont, [20 March 1822]; cf. 398, where Mary writes of 'L.B., whose hypocrisy & cruelty rouse one's soul from its depths'.
26. CCJ 274–7: 10, 17, 21–5 February 1822 and nn.; CCC 169–70: Claire Clairmont to B, 18 February 1822; MWSJ I 398–400: 21–5 February 1822; PBSL II 391–2, nn.
27. Dowden, *Shelley*, II 486–7; Robinson, *Shelley and Byron*, 218, 279.
28. PBSL II 391–2: Shelley to Claire Clairmont, undated, and editor's n. 2 on probable date. For the possibility of a duel, see also MWSL I 226 = PBSL I 398: Mary Shelley to Claire Clairmont, 20 March. That Shelley's fears were unfounded is suggested by Medwin 150, 152, editor's note.
29. CCC 172: Claire Clairmont to Mary Shelley, 9 April 1822.
30. BLJ IX 119: B to Moore, 4 March 1822; MWSL I 223: Mary Shelley to Maria Gisborne, 7 March 1822.
31. EEW indicates numbers of meetings with B: 11 for November, 12 for December, 23 for January, 10 for February (a short month and Shelley and Williams were away for 5 days), 17 for March, 14 in April up to the 22nd.
32. Robinson, *Shelley and Byron*, 177, 203–21 (211 quoted), 273 n. 12.

33. 'Sonnet to Byron' (CPWPBS 658), placed by MWS among 'Poems written in 1821' but MS dated 22 January 1822 (Shelley, *Hellas Notebook*, p. lviv); cf. Holmes, *Shelley*, 673. Compare Schiller ('Ode to Joy', stanza 3): 'Wollust ward dem Wurm gegeben, / Und der Cherub steht vor Gott.'
34. CPWPBS 644–5.
35. Thorslev, *Hero*, 108–11; Lady Byron cited in BCPW VI 683; PBSL II 376: Shelley to John Gisborne, 12 January 1822.
36. MWSJ I 394: 4 February 1822 and n. 2; Medwin 150.
37. BLJ IX 95–100: B to the editor of the *Courier*, 5 February 1822; BLJ IX 101–2: B to Kinnaird, 6 February 1822 and B to Southey, 7 February 1822 and n. 1; cf. EEW 135: 20 March 1822.
38. Cited in Robinson, *Shelley and Byron*, 214; cf. BCPW VI 730–1; Robinson, 'The Devil'.
39. Medwin 153; BCPW VI 517.
40. *Deformed* I 1.266–71, 280–2.
41. BLJ IX 121: B to Moore, 6 March 1822.
42. PBSL I 506–7: Shelley to B, 29 September 1816; cf. Blumberg, *Byron and the Shelleys*, 55–6, 91; Robinson, *Shelley and Byron*, 110.
43. BCPW VI 731, citing Washington Irving; Robinson, 'The Devil', 177–202.
44. Medwin 153–5 (with Trelawny's annotation).
45. MWSL I 289, 299, 311: Mary Shelley to B, undated letters between November 1822 and February 1823.
46. For the fullest account, see Cline, *Pisan Circle*, 91–154.
47. BLJ X 102–3: B to Lady Hardy, 17 February 1823.
48. Cline, *Pisan Circle*, 143.
49. PBSL II 404: Shelley to Claire Clairmont, [10 April 1822]; cf. PBSL II 410: Shelley to John Gisborne, 10 April 1822.
50. Langley Moore, *Accounts*, 318–21.
51. TG 443; MWSJ I 408: 23 April 1822.
52. BLJ IX 147–8: B to Shelley, 23 April 1822.
53. EEW 145; MWSJ I 409: 25–7 April 1822; MWSL I 235–6: Mary Shelley to Maria Gisborne, 2 June 1822.
54. PBSL II 416: Shelley to B, 3 and 9 May 1822.
55. BLJ IX 160–1: B to Shelley, 20 May 1822.
56. PBSL II 423: Shelley to Horace Smith, [c.21 May 1822]; PBSL II 429: Shelley to Claire Clairmont, 30 May 1822.
57. EEW 147: 5 May 1822 and similar, later entries.
58. MWSL I 236: Mary Shelley to Maria Gisborne, 2 June 1822; MWSL I 244: Mary Shelley to Maria Gisborne, 15 August 1822; EEW 155: 24 June 1822.
59. PBSL II 442: Shelley to Horace Smith, 29 June 1822; cf. S&M II 823: Trelawny to Shelley, 22 June 1822.
60. BLJ IX 161, n. 1, correcting Cline, *Pisan Circle*, 164.
61. Cline, *Pisan Circle*, 169–71.

62. BLJ IX 168–9, 174–6, 178: B to Dawkins, 7, 16, 26 June 1822.
63. EEW 155–6: 27 June, 4 July 1822.
64. TG 457–9; Hunt, *Lord Byron*, 9–13; *Autobiography*, III 6–10; Origo, *Attachment*, 317–18.
65. Cline, *Pisan Circle*, 174–6, 244–5.
66. Hunt, *Lord Byron*, 13–14.
67. EEW 156: 2 July 1822; EEW 162–3: Williams to Jane Williams, 6 July 1822; Cline, *Pisan Circle*, 175.
68. EEW 163: Williams to Jane, 6 July 1822.
69. Hunt, *Lord Byron*, 14–15; *Autobiography*, II 133.
70. PBSL II 444: Shelley to Mary, [4] July 1822; BLJ IX 179–80: B to Dawkins, 4 July 1822; Medwin, *Life*, 256.
71. PBSL II 442: Shelley to Horace Smith, 29 June 1822; PBSL II 434–7: Shelley to John Gisborne, 18 June 1822 (p. 435 quoted).
72. BLJ IX 180: B to Dawkins, 6 July 1822; BLJ IX 184–5: B to Dawkins, 15, 16, 19 July 1822.
73. Hunt, *Autobiography*, III 22–5; BCPW V 715; BLJ IX 183: B to Moore, 12 July 1822; Langley Moore, *Accounts*, 336; cf. MWSL I 248: Mary Shelley to Maria Gisborne, 15 August 1822.
74. MWSL I 247: Mary Shelley to Maria Gisborne, 15 August 1822.
75. *Records* 130.
76. TG 477–8; MWSL I 247: Mary Shelley to Maria Gisborne, 15 August 1822; BLJ IX 184: B to Roberts, 14 July 1822.
77. BLJ IX 185: B to Kinnaird, 19 July 1822.
78. In addition to the biographies, see *Records* 128–39; Robinson, *Shelley and Byron*, 220–31; Dane, 'On the Instability'; Roach, *Shelley's Boat*.
79. Marchand, *Biography*, III 1017.
80. For the presence of onlookers on both occasions, especially the second, see *Records* 141, 301 and EJTL 11. Everything in this and the previous paragraph has been drawn from Trelawny's earliest, unedited accounts. For texts, see Marchand, 'Trelawny', 27–8 ('Narrative 1'); EJTL 2–14; and MWSJ I 419–24, on which see also Marchand, 'Trelawny', 11.
81. Marchand, 'Trelawny', 27 ('Narrative 1'); cf. MWSL I 420: the governor 'did not object to our removal of the bodies but to our burning them which was not specified in the order'.
82. EJTL 4; cf., more briefly, Marchand, 'Trelawny', 27 ('Narrative 1'); EJTL 8–9.
83. *Records* 145, where Trelawny also corrects the much-repeated misapprehension 'that bodies washed on shore were obliged to be burnt'; cf. 301: 'so novel a ceremony'.
84. TG 478–81; cf. an unpublished letter from Teresa to B, part-cited in *Shelley and his Circle*, VII 436.
85. Medwin, *Life*, 395.
86. Biagi, *Ultimi giorni*, 53–4, 63–7, citing Dawkins to Prince Corsini, 6 August 1822.
87. Cf. Langley Moore, *Accounts*, 342 and n. 3; Biagi, *Ultimi giorni*, 87–8.

88. MWSL I 251: Mary Shelley to Dawkins, 21 August 1822; cf. Marchand, 'Trelawny', 27 ('Narrative 1'): 'their Familys & friends intreated me to undertake this painful task'.
89. *Records* 145, not in *Recollections*.
90. *Records* 133; *Recollections* 127; MWSJ I 419; Hunt, *Lord Byron*, 195.
91. MWSL I 249: Mary Shelley to Maria Gisborne, 15 August 1822.
92. BLJ II 70–1: B to Drury, 12 August 1811.
93. EJTL 3; cf. 8. See also Hunt, *Lord Byron*, 200; *Autobiography*, III 16; Medwin, *Life*, 397–8; *Records* 140; *Recollections* 129; EJTL 269–70: Trelawny to Rossetti, 18 December [1878].
94. *Sardanapalus* V 1.275–81 and BCPW VI 624–5 (notes on ll. 281, 436–9).
95. *Deformed* I 1.474–80.
96. BLJ IX 197: B to Moore, 27 August 1822.
97. Marchand, 'Trelawny', 11.
98. BLJ IX 191: B to Moore, 8 August 1822; BCPW V 714–15, 736.
99. DJ IX 81–168; Robinson, *Shelley and Byron*, 234–5; Steffan, *Making*, 389–90.
100. DJ IX 94–6.
101. DJ IX 185–7, 193–4, 199–200; cf. Kelsall, 'Politics', 53–5.

CHAPTER 6

1. TG 512–13; 485 and n.
2. Medwin 233, for date, see n. 557; *Records* 180; *Recollections* 152. For once, the context for Trelawny's recollections can be quite securely established: between his return to Pisa from burying Shelley's ashes in Rome and departure with Byron's party on 27 September.
3. Hunt, *Lord Byron*, 58; *Autobiography*, III 53; *Archivio di Stato, Firenze* in Origo, *Attachment*, 324, see also Marchand, *Biography*, III 1036 n.
4. *Diary*: 15–21 September 1822; BLJ IX 211: B to Kinnaird, 21 September 1822; TG 489.
5. Marchand, *Biography*, III 1031–2; Gross, *Erotic Liberal*, 172.
6. *Diary*: 14 September 1816, several entries during October the same year, and editor's note; Marchand, *Biography*, II 651; Forster, 'Karvellas'.
7. *Diary*: 17 September 1822 ('Carvella called this day'). What looks like a separate entry, summarising a conversation with Carvelà the next day, in fact refers to 'yesterday', from which it can be deduced that the Greek lawyer visited Hobhouse only once and Byron not at all.
8. BLJ IX 206–7: B to Murray, 11 September, 1822; BLJ IX 208: B to Kinnaird, 13 September 1822.
9. BLJ IX 207–8: B to Kinnaird, 12 September 1822.
10. DJ XII 42–4, 106–7 (written shortly after 18 October 1822).
11. DJ XII 703–4.
12. *Records* 180; BLJ IX 203: B to Trelawny, 2 September 1822; Medwin 253.
13. EJTL 19–24: Trelawny to Claire Clairmont, 26 September 1822 (passages dated 28 September, 2 October); Hunt, *Lord Byron*, 58–9.

14. EJTL 22; BLJ x 12: B to Murray, 9 October 1822; BLJ x 62: B to Kinnaird, 19 December 1922. See also *Records* 181; TG 490–1; BLJ x 14, 28: B to Augusta Leigh, 12 October and 7 November 1822.

15. Hunt, *Lord Byron*, 59–60; cf. Origo, *Attachment*, 326; Marchand, *Biography*, III 1036; TG 492 (quoted).

16. BLJ x 48: B to Kinnaird, 1 December 1822; Marchand, *Biography*, III 1052, summarising the testimony of Dr James Alexander.

17. BLJ x 56: B to Hobhouse, 14 December 1822; BLJ x 62: B to Kinnaird, 19 December 1822; BLJ x 78: B to Kinnaird, 6 January 1823; BLJ x 82: B to Hoppner, 13 January 1823; BLJ x 112: B to Hoppner, 27 February 1823; BLJ x 137: B to Moore, 2 April 1823.

18. PC (*Byron's Correspondence*): Alexander Scott to Byron, 9 November 1822; cf. DJ I 1697–9.

19. DJ XII 1–3, 9–11; cf. BLJ x 87: B to Kinnaird, 18 January 1823.

20. Seymour, *Mary Shelley*, 314–16.

21. BLJ x 11: B to Mary Shelley, 4 October 1822; cf. Origo, *Attachment*, 319–20.

22. Hunt, *Lord Byron*, 14, 64–8; Origo, *Attachment*, 321–3; TG 483–92.

23. BLJ x 110: B to Kinnaird, 27 February 1823; BLJ x 114: B to Kinnaird, 1 March 1823; BLJ x 120, 123: B to John Hunt, 10 and 17 March 1823 (the latter quoted).

24. BLJ x 36: B to Murray, 18 November 1822.

25. BLJ x 81: B to Leigh Hunt, 10 January 1823.

26. Foot, *Politics*, 343–4; BCPW VII 120. On the political context see Stabler, *Politics*, 179–92; Stock, *Shelley-Byron Circle*, 151–73.

27. *The Age of Bronze* 274–5; cf. *The Island* II 184–5.

28. On Greece, see *Age* 442–3 (cf. 300–1), 298, 717.

29. BLJ IX 215: B to Kinnaird, 24 September 1822; cf. BLJ IX 207–8: B to Kinnaird, 12 September 1822; BLJ x 69: B to Murray, 25 December 1822; BLJ x 86: B to Kinnaird, 16 January 1823; TG 526.

30. BLJ x 86: B to Kinnaird: 16 January 1823; *Age* 568–705 and BCPW VII 120.

31. *Island* I 212–16.

32. *Island* I 35–6. Among commentators, Stabler (*Politics*, 180–97) is notable for emphasising the link between this poem and *The Age of Bronze*.

33. BCPW VII 134.

34. *Island* II 44–6.

35. Shelley, 'Epipsychidion' 422–9.

36. Robinson, *Shelley and Byron*, 237–40.

37. *Island* II 272–97 and B's note to l. 291 (BCPW VII 145).

38. BCPW VII 134; *Island* III 139–41.

39. *Island* IV 261–7.

40. *Island* IV 270.

41. *Island* IV 351–2.

42. *Diary*: 1 March 1823.

43. NLS MS 43530: William Smith to B, 8 March 1823, includes the earliest list. See also Dakin, *Philhellenes*, 42–4; Rosen, *Bentham*, 305–7.

44. Nat. Lib. Athens K1: [Bowring,] draft, 28 February 1823 (initialled, authorship indicated by address, 5 Jeffreys Street).
45. Nat. Lib. Athens K10: Negris to Bowring, 22 April 1822, responding on behalf of the government to his of 18 January; St Clair, *That Greece*, 142. See also Bowring, *Recollections*, 323, for his meeting with Korais (Coray) in Paris in August 1821.
46. Nat. Lib. Athens K10: Ignatios to Bowring, 19 August 1822.
47. Blaquiere, *Report*, 3–4; *Historical Review*.
48. Bowring, *Recollections*, 135–7.
49. Rosen, *Bentham*, 77–9.
50. *Bulldog* 335–6: Hobhouse to B, 8 July 1823, seeming to contradict *Bulldog* 326: Hobhouse to B, 2 March 1823.
51. Nat. Lib. Athens K1: several letters addressed by Blaquiere, March to May 1823.
52. Rosen, *Bentham*, 77–9, 128 and n. 19.
53. Nat. Lib. Athens K1: Bowring to Negris, 28 February 1823; IAM III 158 no. 506: Gordon to Mavrokordatos, 2 March 1823.
54. Nat. Lib. Athens K1: Bowring to J. Reeves, 26 March 1823. See also St Clair, *That Greece*, 150, citing a later letter to the same recipient, which gives yet another version of the purpose of Blaquiere's mission.
55. NLS MS 43530: Bowring to B, 14 March 1823, cited without source by Nicolson (*Journey*, 76).
56. *Bulldog* 326: Hobhouse to B, 2 March 1823, layout transcribed in PC (*Byron's Correspondence*); BLJ x 124–6: B to Hobhouse, 19 March 1823 (p. 126 quoted).
57. Gamba 3–5.
58. BLJ x 114: B to Kinnaird, 1 March 1823; cf. BLJ x 118: B to Kinnaird, 8 March 1823.
59. See e.g. *Bulldog* 333: Hobhouse to B, 11 June 1823.
60. DJ XIV 32, 45–7.
61. DJ XIV 79–80; cf. BLJ x 139: B to Lord Blessington, 5 April 1823.
62. BLJ x 123: B to John Hunt, 17 March 1823; cf. DJ XIV 81–96. See also BLJ x 109, 120, 126, 138, 161.
63. Blessington 35; BLJ x 136–7: B to Moore, 2 April 1823; cf. BLJ x 131–2.
64. MacCarthy, *Byron*, 450–1; cf. TG 529 and n. 7; Peach, 'Portraits', 113–18.
65. NLS MS 43529: Blaquiere to B, Saturday 7 [for 5] April 1823.
66. BLJ x 139: B to Blaquiere, 5 April 1823.
67. BLJ x 142: B to Hobhouse, 7 April 1823; cf. Blaquiere, *Narrative*, II 28 (written May 1824, Zante); Gamba 5; TG 527, 559 (the latter incorrect about the content of Bowring's letter of 14 March).
68. NLS MS 43530: Bowring to B, 14 March 1823, enclosing William Smith to B, 8 March 1823. For the date of receipt of both letters, see BLJ x 179: B to Bowring, 21 May 1823.
69. BLJ x 154: B to Kinnaird, 19 April 1823.
70. BLJ IX 197: B to Moore, 27 August 1822; BLJ VIII 214: B to Moore, 19 September 1821.

71. BLJ x 168–71: B to Bowring, 12 May 1823. On the letter's publication, see PC (*Byron's Correspondence*): John Hunt to B, 6 June 1823; cf. *Bulldog* 332: Hobhouse to B, 11 June 1823; BLJ x 200: B to Hobhouse, 19 June 1823. Bowring wrote to Byron on 2 June, the day of publication, slightly defensively explaining his action (NLS MS 43530).
72. BLJ x 149: B to Hobhouse, 14 April 1823; cf. BLJ x 150: B to Kinnaird, same date.
73. NLS MS 43529: Blaquiere to B, 11 April 1823, from Rome.
74. Marchand, *Biography*, III 1099 n.
75. NLS MS 43427: Lord Blessington to B, 23 May 1823. Marchand transcribes part, only, of this letter.
76. Kennedy 197.
77. HVSV 447; cf. Bieri, *Shelley*, 588. For July as the month of planned departure, see BLJ X142, 178, 193–4, 201.
78. BLJ x 153: B to Kinnaird, 19 April 1824; cf. BLJ x 151: B to Hobhouse, 17 April 1823; Blessington 221.
79. BLJ x 157: B to Lord Blessington, 23 April 1823.
80. BLJ x 152: B to Hobhouse, 17 April 1823; cf. BLJ x 169: B to Bowring, 12 May 1823 ('so as to alleviate in part their distresses').
81. BLJ x 177–8: B to Kinnaird, 21 May 1823; cf. HVSV 373–5.
82. BLJ x 200: B to Hobhouse, 19 June 1823; BLJ x 157: B to Lord Blessington, 23 April 1823; cf. Blessington 220.
83. Blessington 83.
84. Blessington 181–2; HVSV 381 and Marchand, *Biography*, III 1089; MWSL I 384–5: Mary Shelley to Leigh Hunt, 13 September 1823.
85. NLS MS 43529: Blaquiere to B, 28 April 1823, from Zante (part cited in St Clair, *That Greece*, 152), arrival date indicated by postmark; reading collated with a copy in Nat. Lib. Athens K1. The copy has a note in B's handwriting forwarding it to Bowring in London. Marchand (*Biography*, III 1076) recognises the significance of this letter but does not quote from it.
86. BLJ x 195, 197, 199: B to Kinnaird, 8 June; B to Lady Hardy, 10 June; B to Trelawny, 15 June 1823.
87. Nicolson, *Journey*, 82–3; Marchand, *Biography*, III 1078–9.
88. MWSL I 384–5: Mary Shelley to Leigh Hunt, 13 September 1823; cf. Hunt, *Lord Byron*, 70.
89. BLJ x 200–2: B to Hobhouse, and to Barry, 19 June; to Edward Church, 21 June 1823.
90. BLJ x 180: B to Bowring, 21 May 1823.
91. BLJ x 211–12: B to Kinnaird, and to Bowring, 10 and 12 July 1823; Nat. Lib. Athens K6: Memorandum by Col. Stietz, 22 April 1824.
92. NLS MS 43449 and PC (*Byron's Correspondence*): Leigh Hunt to B, 28 June 1823; cf. HVSV 376; Marchand, *Biography*, III 1087 and notes 122–3; Gamba 9.
93. BLJ XI 81: B to Barry, 10 October 1823; cf. BLJ x 152: B to Kinnaird, 19 April 1823 (see also BLJ x 110–11, 113, 118).

94. Marchand, *Biography*, III 1077: Barry to B, 18 June 1823; BLJ x 200: B to Hobhouse, 19 June 1823; *Records* 198–9; additional details in Prell, *Sailing with Byron*.
95. BLJ x 143: B to Hobhouse, 7 April 1823; BLJ x 176–7: B to Hobhouse, 19 May 1823.
96. TG 562, 568; BLJ x 178: B to Kinnaird, 21 May 1823; cf. TG 563.
97. BLJ x 183: B to Lord Blessington, 23 May 1823.
98. TG 553–5, 568–70; BLJ x 190–1: B to Countess d'Ysone, June 1823; BLJ x 197–8: B to Lady Hardy, 10 June 1823.
99. TG 571–4.
100. Origo, *Attachment*, 347: Teresa to Mary Shelley, 10 July 1823; Nicolson, *Journey*, 33–4: Leigh Hunt to B, 13 July 1823.
101. MWSL I 348: Mary Shelley to B, 13 July 1823; Seymour, *Mary Shelley*, 324–5; TG 575.
102. Buxton, *Byron and Shelley*, 14; cf. Lovell, 'Byron and Mary Shelley'.
103. BLJ VII 102: B to Murray, 20 May 1820; Sunstein, *Mary Shelley*, 120.
104. MWSJ II 483: September 1824 (original ellipsis), and editor's note identifying Edward Williams and 'perhaps' B.
105. MWSJ II 478: 15 May 1824.
106. *Records* 200–1; Gamba 9–13; TG 575–8; Moore II 668; Hobhouse, *Diary*: 26 October 1826 (cited in Marchand, *Biography*, III 1089).
107. For the last two, see, respectively, Clubbe, 'By the Emperor Possessed'; *Records* 232.
108. Blessington 83.
109. Blessington 32; cf. Kennedy 295–6; Moore I 213.
110. BLJ VIII 238; cf. VIII 18; Stanhope 511.
111. Mitford, *History*, I 482; Miliori, 'Greek Nation', 21–30.
112. *Records* 212; cf. 201; Stanhope 523; cf. BLJ x 181: B to Bowring, 23 May 1823: 'the Bavarian wonders a little that the Greeks are not quite the same with those of the time of Themistocles – (they were not very tractable then by the bye)'. See also pp. 25–6, above.
113. Blessington 83; HVSV 413.
114. For example, Millingen 6–7, recording a conversation that probably took place in Missolonghi in January 1824: 'Heartily weary of the monotonous life I had led in Italy for several years; sickened with pleasure; more tired of scribbling than the public, perhaps, is of reading my lucubrations; I felt the urgent necessity of giving a completely new direction to the course of my ideas; and the active, dangerous, yet glorious scenes of the military career struck my fancy, and became congenial to my taste.'
115. BLJ x 153: B to Kinnaird, 19 April 1823; Blessington 183.
116. BLJ x 182: B to John Hunt, 21 May 1823.
117. BCPW VII 77 = BLJ XI 29: 'Journal in Cephalonia', 19 June 1823.
118. *Frankenstein* 63; cf. 259 and 27 (editor's introduction).

CHAPTER 7

1. PC (*Byron's Correspondence*): Metropolitan Ignatius of Arta to B, 21 June/3 July 1823. For date of receipt, see PC (*New Byron Letters*): B to Giorgio Vitali, 7 July 1823.
2. NLS MS 43550, subfile 1, nos. 13–18 (all dated 21 June [/3 July] 1823).
3. NLS MS 43530: Bowring to B, 2 June 1823; Stanhope 212.
4. For the earliest indication of this shift, see Μνημεία [*Monuments*], vol. 4, fasc. 11 145–6: Ignatios to the Government of Western Greece, 26 September [/8 October] 1822.
5. IAM 111 355 no. 704: Ignatios to Mavrokordatos, 29 June [/11 July] 1823.
6. IAM 111 420 no. 753: Ignatios to Mavrokordatos, 29 July [/10 August] 1823.
7. PC (*New Byron Letters*): B to Vitali, 7 July 1823; Gamba 287.
8. NLS MS 43519: C. N. Mavrogordato to Barry, 26 June 1823; Gio. L. Mavrogordato to Mr Barker, 28 June 1823; C. N. Mavrogordato to B, 5 July 1823 (partly translated in Nicolson, *Journey*, 88, where the writer is wrongly identifed as a 'brother of Alexander' Mavrokordatos).
9. BLJ x 213–14: B to Bowring, 24 July 1823; cf. Browne in Stanhope 502.
10. NLS MS 43519: George [*sic*] Vitali to B, from Livorno, in French, 28 June 1823. Cf. IAM 111 355 no. 704: Ignatios to Mavrokordatos, 29 June [/11 July] 1823.
11. Browne, 'Voyage', 65–6; S&M IV 950–1: Trelawny to Mary Shelley, 23 July 1823.
12. S&M IV 975: Trelawny to Mary Shelley, 6 September 1823.
13. Browne, 'Voyage', 56–7.
14. Browne, 'Voyage', 66.
15. BLJ x 213: B to Goethe, 22 July 1823.
16. Respectively: Gamba 17; *Records* 209–13 (209 quoted); *Records* 204–5 (not in *Recollections*, see 186); Browne, too, records something similar (in Stanhope 506, not repeated later in 'Voyage'); Browne, 'Voyage', 59.
17. On reasons for calling at Livorno: Gamba 14; *Records* 201. For B's plan to pick up the passengers without stopping, see Browne, 'Voyage', 56; PC (*New Byron Letters*): B to Vitali, 12 July 1823.
18. S&M IV 950–1: Trelawny to Mary Shelley, 23 July 1823; cf. *Records* 201; Gamba 14; BLJ x 214: B to Barry, 24 July 1823; BLJ XI 140: B to Barff, 22 March 1824.
19. Nicolson, *Journey*, 108.
20. Finlay 11 37.
21. Papanikolaou, Καθημερινή ιστορία [*Day-to-Day History*] 229; Anemon Productions, *1821*, DVDs 4 and 5; Kremmydas, Τρικούπης [*Trikoupis*], 72–80; Pizanias, *Greek Revolution*; Rotzokos, Επανάσταση [*Revolution*].
22. Gordon 1 222.
23. Finlay 1 189.
24. Μνημεία [*Monuments*], vol. 4, fasc. 11 151: Kolokotronis to Ignatios, *et al.*, 26 January [/7 February] 1823.
25. *Arch. Lond.* 11 41–2: Proclamation of 24 February [/7 March] 1824; cf. Karapostolis, Διχασμός [*Schism*], 31–55.
26. Rotzokos, Επανάσταση [*Revolution*], 38.

27. Minta, 'Mavrokordatos', 127; Loukos, 'Οι «τύχες»' ['The "Fortunes"'], Μαυ-ροκορδάτος [*Mavrokordatos*], 91–5.
28. Fotakos 473.
29. Papanikolaou, Καθημερινή ιστορία [*Day-to-Day History*], 218–27; Gordon II 7; cf. Blaquiere, *Report*, 8.
30. Nat. Lib. Athens K5: Mavrokordatos to B, from Tripolitsa, addressed to Genoa, 14 July 1823.
31. IAM III 258–62 no. 629: Charles James Napier, Memorandum to the Greek government (in English), '1823 April'; Fotakos 493–4.
32. Millingen 64.
33. Nat. Lib. Athens K5: [Browne,] 'Substance of a conversation held with Colo-cotroni in his palace', enclosed with Browne to Byron, 13 September 1823.
34. Browne, 'Narrative', 404 (omitted from the report cited in the previous note).
35. Dakin, *Struggle*, 109; Rosen, *Bentham*, 78–9; NLS MS 43529: Blaquiere to B, 9 May 1823, from Tripolitsa.
36. See IAM III 354–5 no. 703: Blaquiere to Mavrokordatos, 28 June 1823; IAM III 371–3 no. 712: Blaquiere to Mavrokordatos, 9 July 1823.
37. NLS MS 43529: Blaquiere to B, from Tripolitsa, 9 May 1823 ('my anxiety to learn what your Lordship's plans are, will induce me to prolong my stay').
38. NLS MS 43529: Blaquiere to B, from Tripolitsa, 10 June 1823; cf. Nicolson, *Journey*, 120. There is no basis for Nicolson's assertion that B found this 'paltry note' waiting for him on his arrival in Cephalonia. As it had been addressed to Genoa, it must have been among the forwarded letters that Byron received on 1 September (see pp. 170–1, below).
39. Nat. Lib. Athens K4: Mavrokordatos to Bowring, 5 July 1823.
40. IAM III 347–51 nos. 698–700, all dated 22 June/4 July 1823, and particularly no. 698: Mavrokordatos to Canning, referring explicitly to a previous letter carried by Blaquiere.
41. Dragoumis, Ιστορικαί αμαμνήσεις [*Historical Reminiscences*], 240–4: Mavrokordatos to Orlandos and Louriotis, 22 June [/4 July] 1823 = Loukos, Μαυροκορδάτος [*Mavrokordatos*], 111–14.
42. IAM III 357 no. 705: Mavrokordatos to Louriotis, 30 June/12 July 1823.
43. Trikoupis III 50; Nat. Lib. Athens K5: [Browne,] 'Substance'.
44. Fotakos 495–6; *Arch. Pal.* II 114: Proceedings of the Legislative Body, 10 [/22] July 1823.
45. IAM III 375–8 nos. 716–20: Vice-President of the Legislative Body to the President of the Same [Mavrokordatos], 11 [/23] July 1823.
46. *Arch. Pal.* II 117 = IAM III 378–9 no. 722 (cf. *Arch. Pal.* II 118–25); IAM III 380–1 nos. 723–4: Vice-President of the Executive [Kolokotronis] to Mavrokordatos and reply, 12 [/24] July 1823.
47. Nat. Lib. Athens K5: [Browne,] 'Substance'; cf. Browne, 'Narrative', 404; *West. Rev.* 233; *S&M* IV 981–9: Trelawny to Mary Shelley, 24 October 1823 (cited in Marchand, *Biography*, III 1130); Fotakos 496; Kolokotronis, Απομνημονεύ-ματα [*Memoirs*], 136 ('I'll come and chase you out with lemons, in the same frock-coat you came with').

48. Mavrokordatos' resignation letter is given in IAM III 383–5 no. 727 = *Arch. Pal.* II 123–5.
49. Kolokotronis, Απομνημονεύματα [*Memoirs*], 136.
50. Protopsaltis, Μαυροκορδάτος [*Mavrokordatos*], 92; Gordon II 10.
51. Trikoupis III 50–4, 57.
52. Origo, *Attachment*, 369: Pietro Gamba to Teresa, 26 November 1823.
53. *S&M* IV 964: Trelawny to Leigh Hunt, 11 August 1823; cf. Origo, *Attachment*, 353: Pietro Gamba to Count Ruggero Gamba, 4[?] August 1823.
54. Trikoupis III 42, 46–9; BLJ XI 16. B to Barry, 10 August 1823.
55. *Records* 217; cf. BLJ XI 15, 16, 22, 30, 41,108.
56. BLJ X 213–14: B to Bowring, 24 July 1823.
57. NLS MS 43529: Blaquiere to B, 9 May 1823, from Tripolitsa. Byron had received this letter, in Genoa, on or shortly before 10 July (see BLJ X 211).
58. BLJ XI 30: 'Journal in Cephalonia', 28 September 1823 ('As rather contrary to my expectations I had no advices from Peloponnesus . . . '). Nat. Lib. Athens K5: Mavrokordatos to B, 14 July 1823, from Tripolitsa, addressed to Genoa.
59. Gamba 19.
60. IAM III 259 (see n. 31, above). 'Single': 'simple' in the published text.
61. BLJ XI 25: B to Hobhouse, 14 September 1823; BLJ XI 73: B to Bowring, 10 December 1823.
62. HVSV 410 and 642 n. 15.
63. Moore II 701, 709; Millingen 18.
64. IAM III 421–3 no. 754: D. Dalla Decima [Delladecima] to Mavrokordatos (in Italian), 31 July [/12 August] 1823; cf. *Arch. Pal.* II 138–9: Proceedings of the Legislature, 31 August [/12 September] (the latter cited in Marchand, *Biography*, III 1115 and n.); BLJ XI 54: B to Barry, 25 October 1823.

CHAPTER 8

1. BLJ XI 19: B to Captain Knox, 26 August 1823; BLJ XI 22: B to Hobhouse, 11 September 1823; BLJ XI 30–1: 'Journal in Cephalonia', 28 September 1823; BLJ XI 46: B to Augusta Leigh, 12 October 1823; Gamba 21–8; *Records* 217–21; Browne, 'Narrative', 392–6; Smith, 'Journal' (part reprinted in HVSV 412–25).
2. *Records* 218; Browne, 'Narrative', 392; cf. Gamba 25.
3. Smith, 'Journal' = HVSV 416.
4. *Records* 221.
5. 'Epipsychidion' 513.
6. Gamba 28; Browne, 'Narrative', 393; BLJ XI 19: B to Knox, 26 August 1823 and n. 1; BLJ XI 32: 'Journal in Cephalonia', 28 September 1823; cf. BLJ XI 213–14.
7. Smith, 'Journal' = HVSV 413.
8. Stanhope 511; Gamba 293; Prothero, *Letters and Journals*, VI 428: Hancock to Muir, 1 June 1824; Speer, *Byron and Scott*, 1–19.
9. Smith, 'Journal' = HVSV 418; cf. Browne, 'Narrative', 394.
10. DJ X 135–6; Smith, 'Journal' = HVSV 420.
11. Smith, 'Journal' = HVSV 414; cf. MacCarthy, *Byron*, 472.

12. Speer, *Byron and Scott*, 57–78.
13. *Records* 218; Marchand, *Biography*, III 1110.
14. Browne, 'Narrative', 393.
15. Smith, 'Journal' = HVSV 415.
16. Kennedy 294.
17. Smith, 'Journal', 253–4 and HVSV 415; cf. 'Journal', 268–9, for a similar occurrence during the night of 15–16 August.
18. Browne, 'Narrative', 394; *Records* 58, 219.
19. Browne, 'Narrative', 395: '[the scene] recalled to one's fancy the Mucklestane Moor, depicted in the Black Dwarf'.
20. Cf. BLJ XI 24: B to Hobhouse, 11 September 1823; BLJ XI 31: 'Journal in Cephalonia', 28 September 1823.
21. Smith, 'Journal', 274–5 (written 17 August 1823, and therefore more reliable than the corresponding passages in Browne, 'Narrative' and Trelawny, *Recollections/Records*).
22. Browne, 'Narrative', 395 (on Shelley), perhaps recalled by Trelawny: 'at times I feel my brains boiling, as Shelley's did whilst you were grilling him' (*Records* 218).
23. Origo, *Attachment*, 356: Pietro Gamba to Teresa, 19 August 1823, from Argostoli; Gamba 32: Marco Bozzari to B, 18 August 1823; cf. Nat. Lib. Athens K4: Marco Bozzari ('da Carpenisi piccolo villagio') to Demetrio Corgialegno, 8 [/20] August 1823. See also Gamba 291; Finlay II 10 (quoted).
24. BLJ XI 30: 'Journal in Cephalonia', 28 September 1823; cf. Gamba 29–33.
25. BLJ XI 17: B to Barry, 10 August 1823.
26. BLJ XI 56: B to Barry (PS), 29 October 1823; BLJ XI 58: B to Kinnaird, 29 October 1823; see also BLJ XI 52–3 and Gamba 36–7; Kennedy 248.
27. *S&M* IV 974: Trelawny to Mary Shelley, 6 September 1823, from Cephalonia, part cited in Crane, *Jackal*, 87.
28. *S&M* IV 964: Trelawny to Leigh Hunt, 2 September 1823. Given the infrequent arrival of letters and B's later account of the delayed package (BLJ XI 31), all these letters must have arrived together. On 9 September, B wrote to Napier that he had received two letters from Blaquiere 'dated Ancona' (BLJ XI 20; see BLJ XI 22 for receipt of Hobhouse's and Bowring's).
29. NLS MS 43530: Bowring to B, 22 July 1823, enclosing Minutes of the London Greek Committee, 7 July 1823.
30. BLJ XI 108: B to Charles Hancock, 7 February 1824.
31. NLS MS 43529: Blaquiere to B, 31 July 1823, from the lazaretto, Ancona, with arrival stamp: Genoa, 7 August. The words within angled brackets have been added above the line. It is not clear when B received Blaquiere's two letters written from Corfu on 9 and 16 July, preserved with this one, which had reached Genoa earlier.
32. Marchand, *Biography*, III 1077: Barry to B, 18 June 1823.
33. Lignadis, Δάνειον [*Loan*], 78; Nicolson, *Journey*, 141–2; Origo, *Attachment*, 360–1: Pietro Gamba to Teresa, 8 September 1823.

34. BLJ XI 23: B to Hobhouse, 11 September; BLJ XI 31–2, 'Journal in Cephalonia', 28 September 1823; Gamba 36, 292; Nat. Lib. Athens K4: Konstantinos Metaxas to B, 26 August [/7 September] 1823 (from Missolonghi, thanking him for these supplies).
35. BLJ XI 26: B to Hobhouse, 15 September 1823 ('The Government at Tripolitza').
36. *Records* 222–3; Browne, 'Narrative', 399.
37. *S&M* IV 965: Trelawny to Leigh Hunt, 2 September 1823; cf. IV 974: Trelawny to Mary Shelley, 6 September 1823.
38. Gamba 35; BLJ XI 33: 'Journal in Cephalonia', 30 September 1823; BLJ XI 36, 38: B to Mavrokordatos, 1 October 1823 ('I had sent two Englishmen'); cf. Moore II 681.
39. BLJ XI 23: B to Hobhouse, 11 September 1823; cf. BLJ XI 33: 'Journal in Cephalonia', 30 September 1823.
40. *West. Rev.* 233; BCMP 227, 562.
41. *S&M* IV 982: Trelawny to Mary Shelley, 24 October 1823.
42. BLJ XI 20–1: B to Napier, 9 September 1823; cf. BLJ XI 22, 24: B to Hobhouse, and to Teresa, 11 September 1823.
43. DJ III 713–15; cf. Minta, *Voiceless Shore* (epigraph).
44. BCPW VII 78, 150.
45. *Giaour* 1–6, 103–67; *Siege* 345–78.
46. Solomou, *Greek Poetry*, 300–5; Barton, 'Mythology'.
47. BLJ XI 20 and n. 2; Scott, *Waverley* 155 (chap. 19).
48. Nat. Lib. Athens K4: Konstantinos Metaxas to B, from Missolonghi, 26 August [/7 September] 1823; BLJ XI 25–6: B to Hobhouse, 14 and 15 September 1823.
49. IAM III 501 no. 623: Praidis to the Primates of Hydra, 21 September [/3 October] 1823 (the letters were delivered to Delladecima on 6 [/18] September, Praidis met B the next day).
50. NLS MS 43529: Blaquiere to B, 9 May 1823, from Tripolitsa.
51. IAM III 516 no. 824: Praidis to Ignatios, 26 September [/8 October] 1823.
52. Harlaftis, *History*.
53. IAM III 439–40 nos. 765–6: Mavrokordatos to Praidis, 21 August [/2 September] 1823 (reporting receipt of the letter on 1 September).
54. Nat. Lib. Athens K5: Mavrokordatos to B, 14 July 1823, from Tripolitsa, addressed to Genoa, and Mavrokordatos to B, 27 August 1823, from Hydra, addressed to Cephalonia. Also in the file are letters from the Primates, Louriotis, and Trikoupis of the same date.
55. BLJ XI 33: 'Journal in Cephalonia', 30 September 1823.
56. Benaki 146/1 no. 1269: Mavrokordatos to B, 27 August, from Hydra, autograph draft.
57. IAM III 743 no. 1020: Praidis to Mavrokordatos, 9 [/21] October 1823 ('From what he says, it seems he has no intention of handing over anything until he can come and be informed for himself, on the spot, where the principal necessity lies and moreover to disburse it himself, according to need').
58. BLJ XI 22–3: B to Hobhouse, 11 September 1823; cf. Minta, 'Mavrokordatos', 132.

59. BLJ XI 36, 38, 89 and n.
60. IAM III 501 no. 817: Praidis to the Primates of Hydra, 21 September [/3 October 1823); IAM III 509 no. 824: Praidis to Ignatios, 26 September [/8 October] 1823.
61. IAM II 19–21.
62. Nat. Lib. Athens K5: Browne to B, 13 September 1823 (p. 3ᵛ·) makes these arrangements explicit, as is confirmed by IAM III 460–1, 463 nos. 781, 783: Polyzoidis to Praidis, 1 [/13] September and Lelis to Praidis, 2 [/14] September 1823. Gamba (38) is incorrect when he states, 'we remained a month in that village [Metaxata], without any letters from Messrs. Browne and Trelawny'.
63. Nat. Lib. Athens K5: [Browne,] 'Substance of a conversation held with Colocotroni in his palace'; 'Substance of a conversation which took place with the Officers of Mavrocordato, who remain here', both enclosed with Browne to B, 13 September 1823; Trelawny to B, 14 September 1823. Cf. *Records* 224–5; Browne, 'Narrative', 399–404.
64. Napier, *Life*, I 335–8: Napier to B, 21 September 1823. From this letter, it has been supposed that Kolokotronis had written directly to B ('Colocotroni's [letter] shows . . .'). In reality, Napier refers to Browne's report of the emissaries' meeting with Kolokotronis, enclosed with the letters.
65. IAM III 502 no. 817: Praidis to the Primates of Hydra, 21 September [/2 October] 1823.
66. BLJ XI 27: B to Hobhouse, 27 September 1823; cf. BLJ XI 42: B to Hobhouse, 6 October 1823.
67. BLJ XI 32: 'Journal in Cephalonia', 28–30 September 1823.
68. For its existence, see IAM III 502; BLJ XI 37, 38.
69. BLJ XI 36–9: B to Mavrokordatos, 1 October 1823.
70. BLJ XI 52: B to Duffie, 23 October 1823.
71. *Arch. Pal.* II 138–9: Minutes of Legislative Body, Salamis, 30 August [/12 September] 1823, also cited in Marchand, *Biography*, III 1115; cf. *Arch. Pal.* II 142 and 553.
72. IAM III 516 no. 824: Praidis to Ignatios, 10 [/22] October 1823.
73. IAM III 741–3 nos. 1019–20: Praidis to Andreas Zaimis, and to Mavrokordatos, 9 [/21] October 1823.
74. Respectively: IAM III 741, 516.
75. BLJ XI 52, 54: B to Duffie, and to Barry, 25 October 1823.
76. IAM III 743 no. 1020.
77. IAM III 516 no. 824; IAM III 740–5 nos. 1019–25.
78. IAM III 748 no. 1036: Praidis to Andreas Zaimis, 25 October [/6 November] 1823; cf. *Arch. Kound.* I 199: Orlandos to Lazaros and Georgios Koundouriotis, from Pyrgos, same date; Gamba 51.

CHAPTER 9

1. *S&M* IV 981–9: Trelawny to Mary Shelley, 24 October 1823.
2. Nat. Lib. Athens K5: Mavrokordatos to B, from Hydra, 21 October 1823; part cited in *West. Rev.* 235–6. All Mavrokordatos' letters to B are written in French, all Byron's to him in Italian.

3. *Arch. Lond.* I 151–3, 156.
4. *Arch. Hydras* IX 508–9: Primates of Hydra to Legislative Body, undated draft in Mavrokordatos' hand; *Arch. Hydras* IX 510–11 = *Arch. Pal.* II 607–8: Legislative Body to B, from Salamis, 13 [/25] October 1823.
5. Hist. Mus. 11753 (Spetses Archive): Executive Body to B, 11 [/23] October 1823, from Nafplio; cf. the original covering note in *Arch. Hydras* IX 505: Executive to Primates of Hydra, 11 [/23] October 1823.
6. *Arch. Pal.* II 181, 182: Minutes of Legislative Body, 14 [/26] October 1823; IAM III 552–3 nos. 848–9: Legislative Body to B (original in NLS MS 43550) and Legislative Body to Mavrokordatos, both 15 [/27] October 1823. On the last, and its receipt by B, see p. 201, below.
7. Lignadis, Δάνειον [*Loan*], 115; *Arch.Kound.* I 191, 199.
8. Lignadis, Δάνειον [*Loan*], 103–11.
9. *Arch. Kound.* I 199: Orlandos to Lazaros and Georgios Koundouriotis and IAM III 748 no. 1036: Praidis to Andreas Zaimis, both 25 September [/6 October] 1823; IAM III 569 no. 682: Orlandos to Mavrokordatos, I [/13 November] 1823.
10. IAM III 569 no. 682; cf. *Arch. Kound.* I 202: Orlandos [to the Primates of Hydra], 2 [/14] November 1823; Gamba 51–2.
11. Napier, *Life*, I 335–8: Napier to B, 21 September 1823, an opinion repeated in NLS MS 43530 (two undated letters to B) and unpublished PS to this one, dated 4 November.
12. BLJ XI 60–2; IAM III 566–8 nos. 866–8.
13. BLJ XI 61–2. On the Corgialegno brothers, see Lignadis, Δάνειον [*Loan*], 117–18.
14. BLJ XI 43–4: B to Teresa, and to August Leigh, 7 and 12 October 1823; Origo, *Attachment*, 362–3: Pietro Gamba to Teresa, 8 October 1823.
15. BLJ XI 33: 'Journal in Cephalonia', 28 September 1823; Millingen 6. See also BLJ XI 40: B to Hobhouse, 6 October 1823, alluding to DJ X 679–80.
16. Kennedy 299–300; Gamba 293–4; Bruno in *West. Rev.* 231.
17. Kennedy 300.
18. Kennedy 243–6; Millingen 17–18; IAM III 619 no. 904: Praidis to Mavrokordatos, 22–4 November [4–6 December] 1823.
19. Origo, *Attachment*, 351.
20. Millingen 21.
21. BLJ XI 42: B to Hobhouse, 6 October 1823.
22. Millingen 6; cf. Gamba 122 and pp. 219–20, below.
23. Kennedy 197–200.
24. Finlay, *Journals*, II 886.
25. Howe, *Letters*, I 349.
26. Finlay in Stanhope 511, 512–13.
27. Cited in Sanborn, 'Lord Byron', 346.
28. Kennedy 232–43 (p. 232 quoted); Finlay in Stanhope 517; Kennedy 154–5.
29. Lady Byron in HVSV 450; 1 Samuel 15–28. For the episode of the Witch, see 28:3–25.
30. Kennedy 235.

31. Kennedy 247.
32. IAM III 566 no. 865: Louriotis to Legislative Body, 1/13 November 1823; Finlay, *Journals*, II 887; IAM III 599 no. 888: Orlandos to [Mavrokordatos], 14 [/26] November 1823, from Corfu.
33. Nat. Lib. Athens K4: Millingen to Bowring, 18 November 1823 and BLJ XI 72 n. 2, citing Nat. Lib. Athens K5: Millingen [and B] to Bowring, 7 December 1823 = PC (*Byron's Correspondence*).
34. BLJ XI 66–7, 68: B to the General Government of Greece, 30 November 1823; *Diary*: August 1824 = Marchand, *Biography*, III 1136. On Stanhope's politics, see Rosen, *Bentham*, 44–63.
35. BLJ XI 73: B to Bowring, 10 December 1823; IAM III 680–1 no. 957: Napier to Mavrokordatos, 13 December 1823; cf. IAM III 620 no. 904: Praidis to Mavrokordatos, 22 November/4 December 1823; Napier, *Life*, I 333–4.
36. NLS MS 43530: Skilitzy to Gamba, 22 November 1823, from Pyrgos, in French (translation in Nicolson, *Journey*, 160–2, without PS).
37. Trikoupis III 71–2, 86–8; BLJ XI 64–6: B to Bowring, 29 November 1823.
38. BLJ XI 67–9: B to the General Government of Greece, 30 November 1823 (Greek translation in *Arch. Hydras* IX 559–60).
39. BLJ XI 70–1: B to Mavrokordatos, 2 December 1823, translation adjusted.
40. IAM III 610 no. 894: Delladecima to Georgios Ladopoulos, 18 [/30] November 1823.
41. IAM III 617 no. 904: Praidis to Mavrokordatos, 22 November/4 December 1823.
42. Nat. Lib. Athens K5: [Browne,] 'Substance of a conversation which took place with the Officers of Mavrocordato', 13 October 1823.
43. BLJ XI 72–3: B to Bowring, 7 December 1823.
44. Cf. Gamba 54, 94–6.
45. IAM III 627–30 no. 912: [Mavrokordatos' journal of the voyage,] 18–29 November [/30 November–11 December] 1823; Miaoulis in *Apomn.* VIII 157.
46. Nat. Lib. Athens K5: Millingen [and B] to Bowring, 7 December 1823. Cf. BLJ XI 73: B to Bowring, 10 December 1823; BLJ XI 34: 'Journal in Cephalonia', 17 December 1823 ('The Turks have retired from Messolonghi – nobody knows why'). Cf. Oikonomou in *Apomn.* XIV 307.
47. Support for this view comes from Green, *Sketches*, 166–7 – a witness generally hostile to the Greek cause.
48. BLJ XI 76: B to Bowring, 13 December 1823; BLJ XI 34: 'Journal in Cephalonia', 17 December 1823; IAM III 628–30 no. 912; IAM III 711–14 nos. 982–3; Millingen 39–42; Stanhope 72; Green, *Sketches*, 161: letter dated 23 December 1823, from Zante; Trikoupis III 69–70.
49. Benaki 146/3 no. 1272: copy of B to Mavrokordatos, 2 December 1823, with original PS signed by Pietro Gamba and dated 12 December 1823.
50. IAM III 757 no. 1062: Praidis to Louriotis, 3 [/15] December 1823.
51. BLJ XI : 'Journal in Cephalonia', 17 December 1823.
52. BLJ XI 78–9: B to Teresa, 14 December; NLS MS 43519: Mavrokordatos to B, 5 [/17] December 1823.

53. Konstantinos Metaxas in *Apomn*. VI III–12, published in 1860.
54. IAM III 757 no. 1062.
55. IAM III 673–5 nos. 949, 951: Mavrokordatos to Praidis, 10 [/22] and 12 [/24] December 1823; *Arch. Hydras* IX 506–7: Mavrokordatos to the Primates of Hydra, 12 [/24] December [misdated as 'October'] 1823.
56. NLS MS 43519: Mavrokordatos to B: (1) 1/13 December 1823 (copyist's hand), with autograph PS dated next day; (2) 5/17 December 1823 (autograph); (3) 8/20 December 1823 (autograph). Copies exist in Nat. Lib. Athens K6, Hist. Mus., and GAK. Letters 1 and 3 are published in translation by Nicolson (*Journey*, 173–7), the latter without date. Letter 3 is published in the original French in IAM (III 545–6 no. 655), where the misreading of the date as 'October' seems to go back to a contemporary copy.
57. BLJ XI 82: B to Bowring, 26 December 1823 ('Little need be added to the enclosed Which have arrived this day').
58. This is the most likely reconstruction of the events underlying Gamba 66–7, assuming also that B's letters of 23 and 26 December are immediate responses to the arrival of the two vessels from Missolonghi. NLS MS 43550 (subfile 1, no. 28) includes a note from the captain of the *Leonidas* to B, dated 12 [/24] December, in Greek, placing himself under B's command on the instructions of his admiral. The return of the *Leonidas* without Byron, and Praidis' delayed arrival in Cephalonia, are explained by IAM III 673–5 nos. 949, 951 and III 680 no. 956: Mavrokordatos to Praidis, 10 [/22], 12 [/24], 13 [/25] December 1823. By 28 December, Praidis was back in Missolonghi (IAM III 757).
59. BLJ XI 34–5: 'Journal in Cephalonia', 17 December 1823.
60. IAM III 552 no. 848: Legislative Body to B, 15 [/27] October 1823, from Salamis (translation in Nicolson, *Journey*, 172). The translation leaves the impression that B is being invited to go himself to Missolonghi, but the Greek text does not say so. The evidence that B received this letter now, and not earlier as Nicolson thought, was published by Nicolson himself, as Mavrokordatos refers to this letter specifically in the first of his own three letters brought to Byron by Praidis (*Journey*, 173–5: Mavrokordatos to B, 1/13 December 1823), as was pointed out by Minta ('Mavrokordatos', 136–7).
61. NLS MS 43519: Mavrokordatos to B, 1/13 December 1823.
62. *Arch. Hydras* IX 506–7: Mavrokordatos to the Primates of Hydra, 12 [/24] December 1823; cf. IAM III 688–9 no. 964: Psalidas to Mavrokordatos, 16 [/28] December 1823; IAM III 593 no. 880: Mavrokordatos to Praidis, 9 [/21] December 1823. Similar things are reported by Gamba 114 and in letters from Stanhope to B dated 15 and 20 December (NLS MS 43530, not in Stanhope).
63. BLJ XI 85: B to Hobhouse, 27 December 1823; NLS MS 43519: Mavrokordatos to B, 8/20 December 1823.
64. BLJ XI 85–6: B to Hobhouse, and to Kinnaird, 27 December 1823.
65. BLJ XI 85–6: B to Kinnaird, 27 December 1823; BLJ XI 81–2: B to Barry, 23–4 December 1823.
66. BLJ XI 80: B to Kinnaird, 23 December 1823.

67. BLJ XI 89: B to Muir, 2 January 1824; Gamba 67.
68. Muir, 'Byroniana' = Prothero, *Letters and Journals*, VI 426–31; HVSV 488–9; Kennedy 279–80.
69. Benaki 146/1 no. 1125: Delladecima to Mavrokordatos, 19 [/31] December 1823.
70. Langley Moore, *Accounts*, 395–6.
71. Muir, 'Byroniana' = Prothero, *Letters and Journals*, VI 426–31; NLS MS 43387: 'MS biographical notes on Byron by Edward John Trelawny' (1832).
72. BLJ XI 89–9: B to Muir, and to Hancock, 2 January 1824; Gamba 88–9 (with minor discrepancies); cf. Green, *Sketches*, 164.
73. BLJ XI 89: B to Muir, 2 January 1824; Green, *Sketches*, 166–7: letter dated 4 February 1824.
74. BLJ XI 86: B to Stanhope, 31 December 1823; cf. BLJ XI 88, 90.
75. BLJ XI 88, B to Muir, 2 January 1824.
76. NLS MS 43519: Mavrokordatos to B, 21 December 1823/2 January 1824 (translated, without date, in Nicolson, *Journey*, 186).
77. BLJ XI 90–2: B to Lord Sydney Osborne, 7 January 1824; B to Hancock, 13 January 1824; Howe, *Sketch*, 178.
78. BLJ XI 91–2.
79. Langley Moore, *Accounts*, 367–8, 400 n., correcting Nicolson, *Journey*, 187; cf. MacCarthy, *Byron*, 490–1.
80. Gamba 84; cf. Zambelli in Langley Moore, *Accounts*, 400.
81. NLS MS 43387: 'MS biographical notes'.

CHAPTER 10

1. NLS MS 43551: [James Forrester,] 'Lord Byron in Greece', cutting from the *Examiner* (1824). For description of B by the same observer, see Marchand, *Biography*, III 1167–8; MacCarthy, *Byron*, 492–3.
2. BLJ XI 124: B to Murray, 25 February 1824.
3. *Arch. Kound.* II 41–2: Mavrokordatos to Legislative Body, 6 (/18) January 1824; IAM IV 71 no. 1125: Mavrokordatos to Negris, 16 [/28] January 1824; cf. IAM IV 100 no. 1150: Mavrokordatos to Government, 26 January [/7 February] 1824.
4. Finlay II 24; cf. Minta, 'Mavrokordatos'.
5. Gamba 113, 123, 148–9; Parry 78 (quoted).
6. BLJ XI 90–1: B to Lord Sydney Osborne, 7 January 1824; *Arch. Kound.* II 15: Mavrokordatos to Georgios Koundouriotis, 6 [/18] January 1824.
7. IAM III 565–6 nos. 864, 865: [Orlandos and Louriotis] to Executive Body and Legislative Body (drafts), 1/13 November 1823 ('Lord Byron told us also, that Canning is complaining about the actions of the Greeks at sea . . . and that, if the Greek Government does not take proper care, his excellency [Byron? or Canning?] will be compelled to respond with great displeasure').
8. Konstantinos Metaxas in *Apomn.* VI 111–12; BLJ XI 91: B to Osborne, 7 January 1824.
9. Gamba 89.
10. IAM III 720–3 no. 990; cf. Kasomoulis I 354–6; Millingen 72–9.

11. IAM III 726–8 no. 994: 'Declaration', 26 December 1823 [/7 January 1824]; Trikoupis III 117–18; Millingen 77–9.
12. Gamba 99–101.
13. BLJ XI 93, 94: B to Hancock, 13 and 17 January 1824; *Arch. Kound.* II 41–2: Mavrokordatos to Legislative Body, 6 [/18] January 1824.
14. BLJ XI 35: 'Journal in Cephalonia', 17 December 1823.
15. BLJ XI 91: B to Osborne, 7 January 1824.
16. NLS MS 43519: Mavrokordatos to B, 1/13 December 1823.
17. IAM IV 55 no. 1108: Mavrokordatos to Government, 10 [/22] January 1824; *Arch. Pal.* II 239: Minutes of Legislative Body, 28 January [/9 February] 1824; IAM IV 96–7 no. 1147: Document dated 24 January 1824; cf. Gamba 133–4.
18. IAM IV 71 no. 1125: Mavrokordatos to Negris, 16 [/28] January 1824.
19. Stanhope 68–9, 71: Stanhope to Bowring, 3 January 1824; *Arch. Pal.* II 223; Gordon II 94–5; Trikoupis III 79–80.
20. *Arch. Kound.* II 3: Mavrokordatos to Georgios Koundouriotis, 2 [/14] January 1824 and II 41–2: Mavrokordatos to Legislative Body, 6 [/18] January 1824; Gamba 105; cf. 92, 158–9.
21. Gamba 105; BLJ XI 94: B to Hancock, 17 January 1824. For the letters, see *Arch. Pal.* III 4 = NLS MS 43550, subfile 1, no. 29 and *Arch. Pal.* III 9–10 (and summary in *Arch. Pal.* II 219) = NLS MS 43550, subfile 1, no. 30: Legislative Body to B, signed by Bishop Theodoretos, 21 and 22 December 1823 [/2 and 3 January 1824].
22. *Arch. Pal.* III 3–4: Legislative Body to Mavrokordatos, signed by Theodoretos, 21 December 1823 [/2 January 1824]; cf. *Arch. Pal.* II 217–19: Minutes of Legislative Body, 21 and 23 December 1823 [/2 and 4 January 1824]. For date of receipt, see Gamba 105.
23. GAK 912: B to Mavrokordatos, 16 January 1824 (in Italian), previously published only in IAM IV 68 no. 1122, from a contemporary fair copy adjacent in the file, which is not quite accurate. I am grateful to Peter Cochran for confirming the authenticity of B's autograph from a photocopy. See PC (*Byron and Mavrocordatos*) for transcription and translation (here slightly adjusted).
24. *Arch. Kound.* II 41–2: Mavrokordatos to Legislative Body, 6 [/18] January 1824 ('I see that he is entirely disposed [to give it]'); Gamba 105; BLJ XI 94: B to Hancock, 17 January 1824.
25. *Byron Journal* 1 (1973), 27: Mavrokordatos to B, 5/17 January 1824 (= PC, *Byron's Correspondence*), date corrected by Peter Cochran – personal communication; BLJ XI 96: B to Hancock, 19 January 1824.
26. BLJ XI 93: B to Hancock, 13 January 1824 (PS dated 14th); *Arch. Kound.* II 41–2: Mavrokordatos to Legislative Body, 6 [/18] January 1824.
27. Gamba 118; cf. Stanhope 88, 89: Stanhope to Bowring, 18 and 21 January 1824.
28. Gamba 120; BLJ XI 140: B to Barff, 22 March 1824.
29. BLJ XI 95–7: B to Hancock, and to G. Stevens, 19 January 1824; cf. BLJ XI 93: B to Hancock, 13 January 1824; Stanhope 543–4. The affair would surface again briefly in early March, occasioning Gamba's abject letter of mixed explanation and apology quoted by Nicolson (*Journey*, 239, followed by

Marchand, *Biography*, III 1208) and wrongly dated 24 March (NLS MS 43529: Gamba to B, 4 March 1824; cf. *ibid.*: Hancock to B, 1 March 1824, reverting to the issue).

30. BLJ XI 97: B to G. Stevens, 19 January 1824.
31. BLJ XI 93: B to Hancock, 13 January 1824; BLJ XI 110: B to Kinnaird, 9 February 1824.
32. Gamba 121–3.
33. 'On this day . . . ' 1, 22, 29 (BCPW VII 79–81); Gamba 125–8. For contrasting readings, see McGann, *Don Juan*, 152; Blythe, 'Greek Independence', 185–7; Gurney, 'Publicly Private'.
34. Stanhope 54–5: Stanhope to Bowring, 23 December 1823; Parry 32–4; Koumarianou, Τύπος [*Press*], 34–50.
35. Stanhope 73: Stanhope to Bowring, 6 January 1824.
36. Stanhope 91: Stanhope to Bowring, 24 January 1824.
37. Koumarianou, Τύπος [*Press*], 26.
38. Stanhope 92; cf. Millingen 81–2; Parry 33.
39. IAM IV 54 no. 1107: Maris Louverdos to B, 9 [/21] January 1824.
40. Gamba 135–9; Marchand, *Biography*, III 1167–8; cf. MacCarthy, *Byron*, 492–3.
41. Stanhope 96: Stanhope to Bowring, 28 January 1824.
42. BLJ XI 99: B to Greek captains of privateers, 27 January 1824; BLJ XI 102: B to Bowring, 28 January 1824 (quoted).
43. Stanhope 96–7; Gamba 140.
44. Gamba 103, 140; cf. Stanhope 98: 'Well; you shall see: judge me by my acts.'
45. *Ell. Chron.* no. 6: 19 [/31] January 1824; cf. *Ell. Chron.* no. 9: 30 January [/11 February] 1824 and no. 10: 2 [/14] February 1824.
46. *Ell. Chron.* no. 14: 16 [/28] February 1824; no. 18: 1 [/13] March 1824.
47. *Ell. Chron.* no. 20: 8 [/20] March 1824; nos. 20–1: 12 [/24] March 1824; cf. Millingen 81–2; Koumarianou, Τύπος [*Press*], 27.
48. St Clair, *That Greece*, 187. For Byron's principles in regulating the *Telegrafo Greco*, see Gamba 209–14, 305–7; cf. Millingen 113–14; BLJ XI 134: B to Hancock, 10 March 1824.
49. BLJ XI 103: B to Bowring, 28 January 1824.
50. Gamba 161–3; Millingen 94–7 (p. 95 and GF quoted).
51. BLJ XI 108: B to Hancock, 7 February 1824; BLJ XI 144: B to Kinnaird, 30 March 1824; Parry 12–21; cf. Stanhope 111: Stanhope to Bowring, 11 February 1824 ('Parry is all life and activity'). For contrasting modern assessments, see Nicolson, *Journey*, 210–12; St Clair, *That Greece*, 177–9; Rosen, *Bentham*, 187–94; Crane, *Jackal*, 363.
52. Parry 99; cf. 32–3, 83–4 and Gamba 209–10.
53. Parry 233–4.
54. See e.g. Stanhope 147: Stanhope to Bowring, 21 March 1824; cf. IAM III 753–4 no. 1052: Praidis to Levidis, 12 [/24] November 1823 (on the need to tone down references to a monarchy, in deference to the London Greek Committee – this after Praidis' first meeting with Stanhope in Cephalonia).

55. BLJ VIII 26: 'Ravenna Journal', 13 January 1821.
56. Parry 173–4; cf. 211; BLJ III 242: 'Journal', 16 January 1814, Kelsall, 'Politics', 50, and p. 31, above.
57. Gamba 96, 122, 281; Parry 30, 90–3.
58. Parry 183–4, 233–4.
59. Gamba 213–14; cf. Parry 183.
60. Butler, 'Orientalism'; Leask, *Romantic Writers*, 23–4. For Mavrokordatos' treatise on the subject written in 1820, see pp. 69–70, above. Very similar ideas are expressed in IAM III 348 no. 698: Mavrokordatos to George Canning, 4 July 1823 (in French) and IAM IV 614–15: Mavrokordatos to Government, 8 July 1824.
61. Pizanias, *Greek Revolution*; Gamba 121, 210–13; Parry 83, 170.
62. Gamba 210; cf. Parry 83.

CHAPTER 11

1. IAM IV 73 no. 1128: Zaimis to Mavrokordatos, 17 [/29] January 1824; *Arch. Hydras* X 55–61: President of Executive Body to the Hellenes, 24 January [/5 February] 1824 (p. 56 quoted).
2. IAM IV 103–6 no. 1155: Zaimis and Andreas Londos to Mavrokordatos, 28 January [/9 February] 1824 (p. 105 quoted). Gamba's account of these rumours (167–8) is slightly fanciful. On the Knights of Malta, see St Clair, *That Greece*, 129–31; Lignadis, Δάνειον [*Loan*], 97–100; cf. BLJ XI 104: B to Blaquiere and editor's note; *Bulldog* 342–4: Hobhouse to B, 12 February 1824; *Arch. Hydras* X 44–5: Orlandos and Louriotis to the Primates of Hydra 17 [/29] February 1824.
3. IAM IV 112 no. 1161: Zaimis and Andreas Londos to Mavrokordatos, 29 January [/10 February] 1824, from Vostitsa.
4. Gamba 164.
5. Millingen 90; Stanhope 77, 79: Stanhope to Bowring, 8 and 14 January 1824. Cf. *Arch. Kound.* II 5: Mavrokordatos to Anastasios Londos, 1 [/13] January 1824 ('His Lordship will *perhaps* agree to go to the siege of Lepanto' (emphasis added)).
6. Gamba 192–4 (193 quoted), 96–7.
7. *Ell. Chron.* no. 9: 30 January [/11 February] 1824; NLS MS 43530: Muir to B, 23 January 1824, from Cephalonia.
8. Gamba 165–7 (167 quoted).
9. NLS MS 43354 no. 22 (original version); BLJ XI 111–12: ['Note on Suliotes',] 15 February 1824.
10. Gamba 171–4.
11. BLJ XI 113–14: 'Journal', 15 February 1824 and BLJ XI 121, 123–5; Gamba 174–7; Stanhope 115–16: Stanhope to Bowring, 18 February 1824; Origo, *Attachment*, 377: Pietro Gamba to Teresa, 24 February 1824; Parry 41–6; Millingen 117–20.
12. Gamba 169–70.

13. The evidence for this sequence of events is to be found in five unpublished letters: Hist. Mus. 19441: Nicolla Zavella [Nikolos Tzavellas] to B, 6 November 1823, from Gastouni (where he has arrived, on B's orders, and is waiting to escort him to Sisinis at Pyrgos), in Greek; NLS MS 43550, subfile 1, no. 27: Sisinis to B, 6 [?/18] December 1823, acknowledging a letter from Corgialegno on behalf of B that introduced Tzavellas and heralded B's imminent arrival at Gastouni, in Greek; Hist. Mus. 19444: Athanasios Drakos to B, 18 February 1824, from Missolonghi, in Italian, in a scribal hand; Hist. Mus. 19443: G. Drakos to B, 8/20 February 1824, in Italian, in the same scribal hand; Hist. Mus. 19450: Athanasio Draco to B, 28 March 1824, in French, in a scribal hand (including details of his mission to Sisinis at Gastouni on B's behalf, along with 'le Capitain Nicola Ziavella', and their stay there throughout December and January).
14. BCPW I 224–5.
15. Parry 74–5.
16. Parry 62; cf. Gamba 187.
17. Stanhope 537; cf. Parry 63; BLJ XI 124: B to Murray, 25 February 1824.
18. Parry 63. Probably the same meeting was described by Kasomoulis (I 364, partial English translation in Marchand, *Biography*, III 1190).
19. IAM IV 247 no. 1289: Mavrokordatos to Government, 11 [/23] March 1824.
20. NLS MS 43530: [Mavrokordatos] to B, 'Rapport de l'homme venu d'Arta' (unsigned, undated, but giving the date of Omer's withdrawal as 16 [/28] January); IAM IV 160 no. 1202: Mavrokordatos to Government, 10 [/22] February 1824; IAM IV 183–4 no. 1224: Mavrokordatos to Government, 19 February [/2 March] 1824; Kasomoulis I 367–8; Trikoupis III 119.
21. Gamba 191–2; Langley Moore, *Accounts*, 410; IAM IV 183–4 no. 1224. A formal receipt for one month's wages for the Souliots, in Greek, signed by Mavrokordatos and two officials 'of the Economy', is dated 9 [/21] February 1824 (NLS MS 43550).
22. IAM IV 249 no. 1289: Mavrokordatos to Government, 11 [/23] March 1824; cf. Gamba 180.
23. BLJ XI 117: B to Kinnaird, 22 February 1824; Gamba 192; cf. Marchand, *Biography*, III 1191 ('Byron could not quite admit the extent of his defeat, either to his friends in England or to himself').
24. BLJ XI 142: B to Barff, 26 March 1824; BLJ XI 144–5: B to Kinnaird, 30 March 1824; Parry 71–2; Millingen 94–6.
25. IAM IV 183–4 no. 1224.
26. IAM IV 55–6 no. 1109: Georgios Koundouriotis to Mavrokordatos, 10 [/22] January 1824; *Arch. Kound.* II 58: Mavrokordatos to Georgios Koundouriotis, 26 January [/7 February] 1824.
27. *Arch. Kound.* II 101–2: Mavrokordatos to Georgios Koundouriotis, 19 February [/2 March] 1824.
28. BLJ XI 80: B to Kinnaird, 23 December 1823 and p. 203, above.

29. Gamba 96; cf. 122, 218; BLJ XI 128, 130: B to Barff, 5 and 10 March 1824; cf. Parry 30, 90–3.
30. Gamba 193; Parry 181–2.
31. Gamba 122.
32. *Arch. Kound.* IV 205: Mavrokordatos to Georgios Koundouriotis, 8 [/20 April] 1824.
33. BLJ XI 134–5: B to Demetrius Parucca [Peroukas], 11 March 1824; cf. BLJ XI 130, 138, 141, 143; Gamba 207–8; Parry 91; IAM IV 168–9 no. 1208: P. Rodios to Mavrokordatos, 14 [/26] February 1824 (warning Mavrokordatos that Peroukas is being 'used' by the deposed Executive for its own ends). For B's previous acquaintance with Peroukas, not otherwise attested, see Nat. Lib. Athens K5: Browne to B, 13 September 1823 ('we met . . . [Charalambis] Perruca the Minister of Finance[;] he begs to be remembered to Your Lordship, he mentions your having passed some time in his residence at Argos. I believe that he has written to you'). Byron's correspondent was the brother of this Minister in the deposed Executive.
34. BLJ XI 128: B to Barff, 5 March 1824.
35. BLJ XI 138: B to Barff, 19 March 1824 (quoted). NLS MS 43519: Conte Pier Andrea Mercati to B, 14 March 1824, from Zante, conveys numbered terms on behalf of Sisinis, to which Mavrokordatos gave B a point-by-point response (NLS MS 43530: 'Nouvelles de Corfou', pp. 3–4); cf. BLJ XI 138, 141. See also NLS MS 43550, subfile 1, no. 52: Georgios Sisinis to B (in Greek), 16 [? /28] March 1824 (asking for cannons) and B's reply (*ibid.*, subfile 1, no. 55, also in Greek), 24 March [?/5 April] 1824 (translated extract in MacCarthy, *Byron*, 510 and PC (*Byron's Correspondence: New Letters*)); cf. IAM IV 248 no. 1289 (Mavrokordatos' distrust of Sisinis).
36. NLS MS 43550, subfile 1, no. 42: Executive to B, 20 February [/3 March] 1824 (requesting redeployment for relief of the siege of Patras); IAM IV 247 no. 1289: Mavrokordatos to Government, 11 [/23] March 1824 (refusing redeployment of same troops against Sisinis). The real purpose of the request and the impatience of the new Executive are made clear in IAM IV 227 no. 1264: Kolettis to Mavrokordatos, 2 [/14] March 1824.
37. IAM IV 283–4 no. 1156: Sisinis to Dragonas, 26 March [/7 April] 1824; cf. IAM IV 297–9 no. 1338: Archdeacon Ioakeim to Dragonas, 2 [/14] April 1824; Gamba 242–3.
38. Gamba 206–9, 217–19, 226.
39. BLJ XI 139, 143: B to Barff, 19 and 26 March; Parry 182.
40. Parry 94; IAM IV 174–5 no. 1215: Trelawny to Mavrokordatos, 17 February 1824 (introducing Finlay); Stanhope 124–9: Stanhope to B, 6 and 8 March 1824.
41. Humphreys II 215–17; Parry 84–5, 90–1, 94; Millingen 146–7; *West. Rev.* 252–3; Gordon II 116, 121–2; Nicolson, *Journey*, 234–7; Dakin, *Struggle*, 119; Langley Moore, *Accounts*, 422–4. On Odysseus, see St Clair, *Trelawny*, 101–25; Crane, *Jackal*, 105–58, 169–71, 177–8, 210–12; Anninos, *et al.*, Ανδρούτσος [*Androutsos*].

42. This view is borne out by Gamba's positive account of Odysseus, which must reflect what he and Byron had been told by Mavrokordatos at the end of February (Gamba 198–200), as well as by Mavrokordatos' surviving correspondence with Odysseus and Negris in IAM iv.
43. IAM iv 235–7 nos. 1276–8, all dated 7/19 March 1824; BLJ xi 137, 139: B to Stanhope, and to Bowring, 19 March 1924.
44. NLS MS 43530. The document, in French and possibly incomplete, is headed 'Nouvelles de Corfou'; cf. BLJ xi 140–1, 144: B to Barff, 22 March, and to Kinnaird, 30 March 1824; Gamba 221.
45. NLS MS 43530: 'Nouvelles de Corfou' [Mavrokordatos to B, 21 or 22 March 1824].
46. IAM iv 249–50 no. 1289: Mavrokordatos to Government, PS, 11 [/23] March 1824. For these operations, see *Arch. Lond.* ii 40: Executive to Andreas Londos, 20 February [/3 March] 1824; *Arch. Hydras* x 77: Decree, 7 [/19] March 1824; *Arch. Lond.* ii 44: Executive Body to Londos, 11 [/23] March 1824 (expressing satisfaction that Acrocorinth is now in his possession and confirming that Panos Kolokotronis is besieged in Nafplio); *Arch. Lond.* ii 59–60: Executive to Londos, 20 March [/1 April] 1824 (directing him to lead his forces against Tripolitsa). For summary of events, see Gordon ii 95–7.
47. BLJ xi 147: B to Bowring, 30 March 1824.
48. BLJ xi 141: B to Barff, 22 March 1824 (see also BLJ xi 144–5: B to Kinnaird, 30 March 1824); Gamba 222.
49. BLJ xi 151: B to Barff, 3 April 1824; cf. BLJ xi 142: B to Barff, 26 March 1824; Gamba 227; Origo, *Attachment*, 381: Pietro Gamba to Teresa, 5 April 1824 (date supplied from PC).
50. Finlay ii 22–3; cf. Millingen 16; Parry 86–7; cf. 108.
51. Gamba 203, 219–20, 227, 233; Millingen 118–20.
52. Parry 151–65; Gamba 204–5; cf. Marchand, *Biography*, iii 1189–90, where the connection between the two traits is well made.
53. BLJ xi 125: B to Moore, 4 March 1824; cf. Millingen 10.
54. Parry 192–3 (the date of the conversation is suggested by the last of the incidents listed to be included in the new canto: 'torrents of rain – such a week I never witnessed').
55. BCPW vii 78–83, 150–3.
56. BCPW vii 82, ll. 21–4.
57. Langley Moore, *Accounts*, 403–4.
58. Crompton, *Greek Love*, 328, 334–7. Gross (*Erotic Liberal*, 182–3) proposes that B's feelings for Loukas 'motivated' his behaviour in Greece. See further Langley Moore, *Late Lord Byron*, 175–83. See also *Lara* i 510–90. On the poems, see Gurney, 'Publicly Private'.
59. BCPW vii 83; cf. *Giaour* 842–3.
60. NLS MS 43519: Andreas Londos to B, 'January', received on the 29th (Gamba 145); BLJ xi 103–4: B to Londos, 30 January 1824 (both in Italian; translation of the latter modified); BLJ xi 122–3: B to Londos, 24 February 1824 (in Greek). B's letters are also in *Arch. Lond.* ii 433–5, with photographs of the MSS.

61. Millingen 12 and GF: 'Lord Byron knew the estimation in which I held Moore's Lalla Rhook [and] used to say if I left him too early in the evenings at Missolonghi. Stop a little longer Finlay & I will abuse Tommy Moore.'

62. Parry 37 (12 February); cf. 27.

63. Stanhope 100–1: Stanhope to Bowring, 31 January 1824; Millingen 64–8; Finlay II 33–4; EJTL 82: Trelawny to Mary Shelley and Jane Williams, 30 April 1824.

64. Parry 160–2 (punctuation added).

65. Nat. Lib. Athens K7: Parry to Bowring, 20 March 1824; cf. NLS MS 43529: Gamba to B, 6 March 1824 (Mavrokordatos had been too embarrassed to approach B directly for money for his private needs, and asked Gamba to convey his appeal instead).

66. Parry 84–5, 92–3; Millingen 102–3. The only evidence offered by Millingen is convincingly disposed of by Parry (104–5), whose book had been published earlier.

CHAPTER 12

1. The chief source for what follows is Kasomoulis I 354–90, where justification for these adjectives can be found (I 370–1). See also Ainian, Καραϊσκάκης [*Karaiskakis*]; Paparrigopoulos, Καραϊσκάκης [*Karaiskakis*]; Vlachoyannis, Βιογραφία [*Biography*] (on the early life only). On the trial, see Vlachoyannis, 'Καραϊσκάκης' ['Karaiskakis'], reproduced and amplified in Papasteriopoulos, Δίκη [*Trial*]. See also Papanikolaou, Καθημερινή ιστορία [*Day-to-Day History*], 255–8; Tzakis, 'From Locality'.

2. IAM III 660 no. 936: Karaiskakis to Mavrokordatos, 7 [/19] December 1823.

3. IAM III 726–8 no. 994: 'Declaration', 26 December 1823 [/7 January 1824]; Kasomoulis I 355–6.

4. Millingen 35–7. Millingen's narrative is confused, as he begins by saying that he set out from Argostoli with 'Caraiscachi', as though this was someone to whom the reader had previously been introduced, then later reports how, at Agia Euphemia, 'we were kindly entertained by Mr. T. Caraiscachi'. From the details that follow, it is clear that both episodes refer to Georgios Karaiskakis.

5. Gamba 132–3 (who was mistaken about Karaiskakis' departure for Agrafa).

6. Kasomoulis I 366–8, 371–2.

7. IAM IV 248 no. 1289: Mavrokordatos to Government, 11 [/23] March 1824; IAM III 3–4 no. 376: Mavrokordatos to Omer Vryonis (draft, undated, but clearly part of the same correspondence); IAM IV 253 no. 1292: Mavrokordatos to Karaiskakis, 12 [/24] March 1824.

8. Kasomoulis I 374, 381. According to *Ell. Chron.* (no. 27: 2 [/14] April 1824) the number was 300.

9. Parry 96–7, 328–30. Parry says that this meeting happened on the day when B first told him the news about the loan, which cannot have been long after 22 March. Parry's date, 'April 10', is clearly wrong, and is not borne out by his own day-by-day account on pp. 117–18.

10. IAM IV 263–4 nos. 1305–7: Mavrokordatos to Iskos (twice) and Kitzos Tzavellas, 19 [/31] March 1824 (drafts). See also Kasomoulis I 375–6.
11. *Ell. Chron.* no. 29: 9 [/21] April 1824; Kasomoulis I 374–5; cf. (with some confusions) Gamba 237–41; Millingen 122; Parry 102.
12. For the date of the ships' arrival, see BLJ XI 148: B to Clare, 31 March 1824. On the replacement of the Turkish garrisons, see Green, *Sketches*, 169–70: letter of 6 April 1824, from Zante; Oikonomou in *Apomn.* XIV 308.
13. *Ell. Chron.* no. 29: 9 [/21] April 1824. Marchand (*Biography*, III 1209) follows Millingen 124–5 in giving 5 April as the date of the government's response, which was in fact immediate.
14. Gamba 239. For the possibility that Karaiskakis may previously have attempted to enlist the support of Kolokotronis against Mavrokordatos, see IAM IV 212–13 no. 1252: Karaiskakis to Kolokotronis, 28 February [/11 March] 1824. If the letter was not a forgery (see editor's note), it seems to have had no sequel.
15. IAM IV 232–3 no. 1271 = NLS MS 43550, subfile 1, no. 49: Kolettis to Mavrokordatos, 5 [/17] March 1824; for arrival date, see Gamba 239.
16. IAM IV 206–7 no. 1245: Panagiotis Sofianopoulos to Dimitris Ypsilantis, 25 February [/8 March] 1824; translation published in Stanhope 308–9. On Sofianopoulos, see Stanhope 184 (quoted); Parry 292–7; Millingen 146 (GF: 'a rapacious wretch'). NLS MS 43550 (subfile 1, no. 45) preserves the covering letter that introduced the captured one: Executive to Mavrokordatos, 4 [/16] March 1824 (not in IAM).
17. Parry 84–5, 90–1.
18. IAM IV 320 no. 1362: Mavrokordatos to Government, 7 [/19] April 1824; *Arch. Kound.* II 293–4: Mavrokordatos to Georgios Koundouriotis, 10 [/22] May 1824.
19. BLJ XI 151: B to Barff, 6 April 1824; Millingen 124.
20. Gamba 238 (quoted); BLJ XI 150; Millingen 126.
21. IAM IV 273–5 nos. 1320–1: Dimos Skaltzas and D. Makris to Karaiskakis, 23 and 24 March [/4 and 5 April] and IAM IV 272 no. 1318: Mavrokordatos to Karaiskakis, 23 March [/4 April] 1824; cf. IAM IV 267 nos. 1310–11: Mavrokordatos to Government, 21 March [/2 April] 1824.
22. Gamba 240–1; Millingen 123–5.
23. Gamba 242; *Ell. Chron.* nos. 27 and 29, from which it is clear that Voulpiotis was arrested *after* the hostages had been returned safely.
24. BLJ XI 151: B to Barff, 6 April 1824.
25. Kasomoulis I 376–7; *Ell. Chron.* 29; Gamba 243–4. The phrase is also used in Mavrokordatos' own account (Spiliadis, Απομνημονεύματα [*Memoirs*], II 42–3: Mavrokordatos to Government, 31 March [/12 April] 1824).
26. NLS MS 43519: Mavrokordatos to B, 25 March [/6 April] 1824, partial translation (with mistaken date and context) in Nicolson, *Journey*, 237–8. Number of troops supplied from *Ell. Chron.* no. 26: 29 March [/10 April] 1824.
27. BLJ XI 144: B to Kinnaird, 30 March 1824; BLJ XI 153–4: B to Barry, 9 April 1824 (on the obligation of the Greek government to repay him).

28. BLJ XI 152: B to Barff, 9 April 1824. The date is given in BLJ as 7th, but the MS (Benaki 146/3 no. 1295) fills the bottom half of a sheet begun by Zambelli and dated '8 aprile'. B's numeral could as well be a '9' as a '7'.
29. Gamba 243–4; cf. Parry 103.
30. Millingen 104 and GF: 'I was alone present . . . [N]ot the words I gave Millingen on my return'; cited and discussed in Sanborn, 'Lord Byron', 348 n.; Minta, 'Mavrokordatos', 138, 142.
31. Kasomoulis, who was there, gives 27 March [/8 April] as the date of Mavrokordatos' arrival at Anatolıko (1 377), as does *Ell. Chron.* no. 29. But closer to the event is *Ell. Chron.* 27, which says 'last Saturday' [i.e., 10 April], compatible with Gamba's slightly garbled chronology (Gamba 245–7 and cited proclamation dated '30 March' (i.e., 11 April)).
32. See, in English, Delivoria, 'Notion', 116–17.
33. Kasomoulis 1 380–4.
34. Kasomoulis 1 385.
35. Cf. Spiliadis, Απομνημονεύματα [*Memoirs*], II 44–5, 47.
36. Kasomoulis 1 385–7; *Ell. Chron.* 30: 12 [/24] April 1824: 'Proclamation of the crimes of Karaiskakis', dated 2 [/14] April (quoted).
37. Kasomoulis 1 389.
38. *Arch. Kound.* IV 205: Mavrokordatos to Georgios Koundouriotis, 8 [/20] April 1824; cf. Spiliadis, Απομνημονεύματα [*Memoirs*], II 42–3: Mavrokordatos to Government, 31 March [/12 April] 1824 (the rebels were 'ejected in the most beautiful manner without anybody's nose being bloodied').
39. *Ell. Chron.* 30: 12 [/24] April 1824; Kasomoulis 1 387.
40. Finlay II 25. For date of Finlay's departure, see GF in Moore, *Letters . . . in One Volume*, 490.
41. Parry 107; Stanhope 115–16: Stanhope to Bowring, 18 February 1824; Millingen 126.
42. Parry 106–9 and Millingen 128; Origo, *Attachment*, 381: Pietro Gamba to Teresa, 5 April 1824 (quoted); cf. Marchand, *Biography*, III 1210–11; Gamba 247 (quoted).
43. Gamba 247–8; Parry 109. The letter from Hobhouse can be securely identified as *Bulldog* 342–4: Hobhouse to B, 12 February 1824, as it is so close in date to the letter from Ransom & Co. (10 February) on the bottom of which B wrote to Barff on the 9th, saying that it had been received 'this morning' (BLJ XI 152; Benaki 146/3 no. 1279). For the letter from Augusta and enclosure, see PC (*Byron's Correspondence*): Pietro Gamba to Augusta Leigh, 17 August 1824.
44. BLJ XI 152–4 (on the date of the first of these letters, see n. 28, above) and NLS MS 43407: Barry to B, 25 February 1824, forwarded by Barff on 6 April.
45. BLJ XI 153: B to Barff, 9 April 1824; cf. Gamba 247; Parry 109. The conclusion of the loan was made public on 21 February, by which time this batch of letters will already have been on its way to Missolonghi.
46. Finlay II 25–6; Parry 168.

47. Gamba 247–51 (249 quoted); Parry 109, 115–19; Marchand, *Biography*, III 1211–12 (correcting Gamba on the date of the second ride); Fletcher, in *West. Rev.* 253–4.
48. Parry 116–17, 119.
49. Parry 121–2, 184–5; BLJ XI 153: B to Barry, 9 April 1824 and NLS MS 43407: Barry to B, 28 January 1824 (possibly received at the same time as Barry's final letter on 9 April).
50. Gamba 203–4; BLJ XI 131: B to Barff, 10 March 1824.
51. Parry 116–17; Langley Moore, *Accounts*, 416 (doubting Parry, but providing the evidence that could support his story); IAM IV 288 no. 1334.
52. Parry 118–19; Gamba 251–2; NLS MS 43530: Praidis to B, 13 April 1824 (which must be an error for '14').
53. NLS MS 43531: Millingen to Bowring, 27 April 1824; IAM IV 320 no. 1362: Mavrokordatos to Government, 7 [/19] April 1824.
54. Parry 131. For the doctors' testimonies, see Bruno's diary, cited in Nicolson, *Journey*, 247–62, supplemented by Marchand, *Biography*, III 1212–24; Millingen 128–38; EJTL75–6: Trelawny to Stanhope, 28 April 1824.
55. Millingen 137, 141.
56. Blessington 31; Millingen 130.
57. Parry 129–33.
58. Millingen 131; Bruno, 'Last Moments'; NLS MS 43551: Bruno to Dr George Scott, 2 March 1824 (translated excerpt in letter from the recipient to the editor of *The Times*, 28 January 1825).
59. Gamba 252–8; Parry 124–5.
60. Gamba 264–5; Marchand, *Biography* III, n. to p. 1226, l. 24.
61. Parry 125–8; Gamba 258–9.
62. *Bulldog* 342.

EPILOGUE

1. BLJ XI 131: B to Barff, 10 March 1824.
2. *Bulldog* 342–4.
3. *Arch. Kound.* II 63–4: Georgios Ainian to Georgios Koundouriotis, 28 January [/9 February] 1824.
4. Gamba 109–10; cf. 129–32, 182–3; BLJ XI 97–9: B to Yussuf Pasha, 23 January 1824; cf. BLJ XI 111, 115–16, 118, 120–1 and DJ VIII 724–824, 1113–20. Byron's conduct was held up for praise in the *Greek Chronicle* (*Ell. Chron.* no. 13: 13 [/25] February 1824, p. 4).
5. BLJ XI 108: B to Hancock, 7 February 1824.
6. Parry 134; cf. 282, 308, 314, a view developed further in some twentieth-century Greek historiography; see Simopoulos, Πώς είδαν οι ξένοι [*How Foreigners Saw*], III 35–201; Kakambouras, Η βρετανική πολιτική [*British Policy*].
7. Gamba 121, 210–13 (p. 212 quoted); cf. Parry 83, 170.
8. Trikoupis III 113–14; *Arch. Lond.* II 85–6: Executive to Andreas Londos, 4 [/16] April 1824.

9. *Ell. Chron.* 28: 5 [/17] April 1824.
10. IAM IV 333 no. 1376: Mavrokordatos to Executive Body, 12 [/24] April 1824.
11. Dakin, *Struggle*, 118–19, 124–5; Trikoupis III 128; Gordon II 100.
12. Stanhope 212: Stanhope to Bowring, 16 May 1824, from Zante.
13. *Arch. Kound.* II 411: Georgios to Lazaros Koundouriotis, 5 [/17] June 1824; *Arch. Kound.* III 44: Lazaros Koundouriotis to Orlandos, 17 [/29] July 1824.
14. *Arch. Kound.* III 63: Orlandos to Georgios Koundouriotis, 28 July [/7 August] 1824.
15. EJTL 85–6: Trelawny to Mary Shelley, August 1824.
16. *Records* 231–3; *Recollections* 224–8.
17. Nat. Lib. Athens K8: Meyer to Stanhope, 17 [/29] April 1824 = De Beer and Seton, 'Byroniana', 411.
18. Μνημεία [*Monuments*], vol. 4, fasc. 1 281 = *Arch.Kound.* II 275–6: Ignatios to Georgios Koundouriotis, 19 May 1824.
19. NLS MS 43551: Spyridon Tricoupi, 'Funeral Oration' [printed translation, 1836], p. 6.
20. *Ell. Chron.* 29: 9 [/21] April 1824.
21. *Arch. Kound.* VI 140, undated.
22. EJTL 80: Trelawny to Stanhope, 29 April 1824.
23. *Arch. Kound.* III 36–7: Orlandos to Lazaros Koundouriotis, 11 [/23] July 1824.
24. Gordon II 102–5; Trikoupis III 131–2; St Clair, *That Greece*, 210–15; Brewer, *Flame*, 220–5.
25. Finlay II 33.
26. *Diary*: 19 October 1809 (quoted), named in Broughton, *Travels* I 94; cf. BLJ I 227.
27. Mavrogordatos, Ἧττα' ['Defeat'].
28. Kremmydas, Τρικούπης [*Trikoupis*], 80.
29. Tzakis, 'From Locality'. Against Millingen's negative account of Karaiskakis in 1824, Finlay has written: 'He was a gallant fellow and died like a hero' (Millingen 35: GF).
30. Ministry of Foreign Affairs of Greece, *Foundation*, 30; Beaton, 'Introduction', 1–2.

Bibliography

PRIMARY SOURCES

ARCHIVES – UNPUBLISHED

Athens

Historical Archive of the Benaki Museum. For summary description of holdings, see Tselika, Οδηγός [*Guide*].

National Historical Museum, Archive of Historical Documents.

National Library of Greece, Papers of the London Greek Committee.

Γενικά Αρχεία του Κράτους: Ιστορικόν Αρχείον Αλεξάνδρου Μαυροκορδάτου [General State Archives: Historical Archive of Alexandros Mavrokordatos], 1820–4.

Edinburgh

National Library of Scotland. John Murray Archives: George Gordon, Lord Byron, Correspondence and Papers.

Oxford

The Bodleian Libraries, University of Oxford: MS Abinger.

ARCHIVES – PUBLISHED

Απομνημονεύματα αγωνιστών [*Memoirs of Combatants*], ed. E. G. Protopsaltis, 20 vols. (Athens: Vivliothiki, 1955–7).

Αρχεία της Ελληνικής Παλιγγενεσίας [*Archives of the Greek Regeneration*], 3 vols. (Athens: Library of Parliament, 1971–2) (first published 1857, 1862).

Αρχεία Λαζάρου και Γεωργίου Κουντουριώτου [*Archives of Lazaros and Georgios Koundouriotis*], vols. 1–3, ed. Antonios Lignos (Athens: Sakellarios, 1920); vol. 4 (1927); vol. 6, ed. E. G. Protopsaltis (Athens: Library of the General State Archives, 1966).

Αρχείο Αλή πασά [*Ali Pasha Archive*], 4 vols., ed. Vasilis Panagiotopoulos, *et al.* (Athens: National Research Foundation, Institute for Neohellenic Research, 2007).

Αρχείον της Κοινότητος Ύδρας [*Archive of the Community of Hydra*], vol. 9 (Piraeus: Sfaira, 1927); vol. 10 (Piraeus: Zanneios, 1928); vol. 16 (Piraeus: Eleftherios, 1932).

Ελληνικά Χρονικά [*Greek Chronicle*] (Missolonghi, 1824–6). Photographic reprint (Athens: Spanos and Nikas, 1958).

Ιστορικόν Αρχείον του Στρατηγού Ανδρέου Λόντου (1789–1847) [*Historical Archive of General Andreas Londos*], 2 vols. (Athens: Sakellarios, 1914, 1916).

Μνημεία της Ελληνικής Ιστορίας, τόμ. Δ΄: Ιγνάτιος Μητροπολίτης Ουγγρο-βλαχίας [*Monuments of Greek History*, vol. 4, *Ignatios, Bishop of Hungary and Wallachia*], fascicles I–II, ed. E. Protopsaltis (Athens: Academy of Athens, 1959, 1961).

Μνημεία της Ελληνικής Ιστορίας, τόμ. Ε΄: Ιστορικόν Αρχείον Αλεξάνδρου Μαυροκορδάτου [*Monuments of Greek History*, vol. 5, *Historical Archive of Alexandros Mavrokordatos*], fascicles I–IV, ed. E. Protopsaltis (Athens: Academy of Athens, 1963–74).

MATERIAL PUBLISHED ON THE INTERNET

Peter Cochran's website (www.petercochran.wordpress.com/) (complete works of Byron, edited, including unpublished letters addressed to Byron and *Hobhouse's Diary*).

Lord Byron and His Times, ed. David Hill Radcliffe (www.lordbyron.org/).

BOOKS AND ARTICLES

Ainian, Dimitrios, *Ο Καραϊσκάκης* [Karaiskakis], ed. I. K. Mazarakis-Ainian (Athens: Ermis, 1974) (first published 1834), also reprinted in *Apomn.* 7.

Blaquiere, Edward, *An Historical Review of the Spanish Revolution* (London: Whittaker, 1822).

  Narrative of a Second Visit to Greece, Including Facts Connected with the Last Days of Lord Byron, 2 vols. (London: Whittaker, 1825).

  Report on the Present State of the Greek Confederation (London: Whittaker, 1823).

Blessington, Countess of, *Conversations of Lord Byron*, ed. Ernest J. Lovell (Princeton, NJ: Princeton University Press, 1969) (first published 1834).

Bowring, John, *Autobiographical Recollections* (London: King, 1877).

Bowring, John, Edward Blaquiere, and William Fletcher, 'Lord Byron in Greece', *Westminster Review*, 2 (July 1824), 225–62.

Broughton, Lord [John Cam Hobhouse], *Travels in Albania and Other Provinces of Turkey in 1809 & 1810*, 2 vols. (London: John Murray, 1855).

Browne, James Hamilton, 'Narrative of a Visit, in 1823, to the Seat of War in Greece', *Blackwood's Edinburgh Magazine*, 36.226 (September 1834), 392–407.

'Voyage from Leghorn to Cephalonia with Lord Byron', *Blackwood's Edinburgh Magazine*, 35.217 (January 1834), 56–67.

Bruno, Francesco, 'Last Moments of Lord Byron', *Examiner*, 864 (22 August 1824), 530.

Byron, Lord, *The Complete Miscellaneous Prose*, ed. Andrew Nicholson (Oxford: Clarendon Press, 1991).

The Complete Poetical Works, ed. Jerome J. McGann, 7 vols. (Oxford: Clarendon Press, 1980–93).

His Very Self and Voice: Collected Conversations, ed. Ernest J. Lovell (New York: Macmillan, 1954).

Letters and Journals, ed. Leslie A. Marchand, 13 vols. (London: John Murray, 1973–94).

Letters and Journals, ed. R. E. Prothero, 6 vols. (London: John Murray, 1898–1901).

Chrysanthopoulos, Fotios ('Fotakos'), Απομνημονεύματα περί της Ελληνικής Επαναστάσεως [*Memoirs of the Greek Revolution*] (Athens: Greka, 1971) (first published 1858).

Clairmont, Claire, *The Clairmont Correspondence*, ed. Marion Kingston Stocking (Baltimore, MD: Johns Hopkins University Press, 1995).

The Journals of Claire Clairmont, ed. Marion Kingston Stocking (Cambridge, MA: Harvard University Press, 1968).

Dragoumis, N., Ιστορικαί αμαμνήσεις, Α' [Historical Reminiscences, 1], ed. Alkis Angelou (Athens: Ermis, 1973) (first published 1874).

Finlay, George, *History of the Greek Revolution*, 2 vols. (Edinburgh: Blackwood, 1861).

Journals and Letters, ed. J. M. Hussey, 2 vols. (Camberley: Porphyrogennitus, 1995).

Gamba, Pietro, *A Narrative of Lord Byron's Last Journey to Greece* [translated from Italian by John Cam Hobhouse] (London: John Murray, 1825).

Gordon, Thomas, *History of the Greek Revolution*, 2 vols. (Edinburgh: Blackwood, 1832).

Green, Philip James, *Sketches of the War in Greece*, 2nd edn (London: Hurst, 1828) (first published 1827).

Guiccioli, Teresa, *Lord Byron's Life in Italy*, translated by Michael Rees, ed. Peter Cochran (Newark: University of Delaware Press, 2005).

Hobhouse, John Cam, *Byron's Bulldog: The Letters of John Cam Hobhouse to Lord Byron*, ed. Peter W. Graham (Columbus: Ohio State University Press, 1984).

Hobhouse's Diary, ed. Peter Cochran. www.petercochran.wordpress.com/hobhouses-diary/.

A Journey through Albania (London: Cawthorn, 1813).

Howe, Samuel Gridley, *An Historical Sketch of the Greek Revolution* (New York: White, Gallaher and White, 1828).

Letters and Journals, 2 vols. (Boston, MA: D. Estes, 1906–9).

Humphreys, W. H., 'Journal of a Visit to Greece', in *A Picture of Greece in 1825*, 2 vols. (London: Colburn, 1826), vol. 2, pp. 197–344.

Hunt, Leigh, *Autobiography*, 3 vols. (London: Smith, Elder, 1850).

Lord Byron and Some of his Contemporaries (London: Colburn, 1828).

Kasomoulis, Nikolaos, Ενθυμήματα στρατιωτικά [*Military Recollections*], ed. G. Vlachogiannis, 3 vols. (Athens, 1939).

Kennedy, James, *Conversations on Religion with Lord Byron and Others* (London: John Murray, 1830).

Kolokotronis, Theodoros, Απομνημονεύματα [*Memoirs*], transcribed by G. Tertsetis, ed. T. Vournas (Athens: Drakopoulos, n.d.).

Mavrocordato, Alexandre [Alexandros Mavrokordatos], 'Coup d'œil sur la Turquie' [1820], in A. Prokesch von Osten, *Geschichte des Abfalls der Griechen* (Vienna: Gedold, 1867), vol. 3, pp. 1–54.

Medwin, Thomas, *Conversations of Lord Byron*, ed. Ernest J. Lovell (Princeton, NJ: Princeton University Press, 1966) (first published 1824).

The Life of Percy Bysshe Shelley, ed. H. Buxton Forman (London: Humphrey Milford, 1913) (first published 1847).

Millingen, Julius, *Memoirs of the Affairs of Greece* (London: J. Rodwell, 1831).

Mitford, William, *The History of Greece*, 8 vols. (London: Cadell, 1829) (first published 1784–1818).

Moore, Thomas, *Letters and Journals of Lord Byron*, 2 vols. (London: John Murray, 1830).

Letters and Journals of Lord Byron Complete in One Volume (Paris: Galignani, 1831).

Muir, H. S., 'Byroniana', *Notes and Queries*, 6th series, 9 (1884), 81–2.

Napier, William, *The Life and Opinions of General Sir Charles Napier*, 4 vols. (London, 1857).

Parry, William, *The Last Days of Lord Byron* (London: Knight and Lacey, 1825).

Pausanias, *The Description of Greece*, translated with notes by T. Taylor, 3 vols. (London, 1794).

Philemon, Ioannis, Δοκίμιον ιστορικόν περί της Ελληνικής Επαναστάσεως [*Historical Essay Concerning the Greek Revolution*], 4 vols. (Athens: Karyofyllis, 1859–61).

Philemon, Ioannis, Δοκίμιον ιστορικόν περί της Φιλικής Εταιρίας [*Historical Essay Concerning the Filiki Etairia*] (Nafplion: Kontaxis, 1834).

Polidori, John, *Diary*, ed. William Michael Rossetti (London: Elkin Mathews, 1911).

Polidori, John [*et al.*], *The Vampyre and Other Tales of the Macabre* (World's Classics series) (Oxford University Press, 1997).

Raybaud, Maxime, *Mémoires sur la Grèce*, 2 vols. (Paris: Tournachon-Molin, 1824).

Scott, Walter, *Waverley*, ed. Andrew Hook (Harmondsworth: Penguin Classics, 1985).

Shelley and Mary: Prepared for the Press by Lady Shelley, 4 vols. (privately printed, [1882]).

Shelley, Mary, *Journals, 1814–1844*, ed. Paula Feldman and Diana Scott-Kilvert, 2 vols. (Oxford: Clarendon Press, 1987).

Letters, ed. Frederick L. Jones, 2 vols. (Norman: University of Oklahoma Press, 1944).

Shelley, Mary (with Percy Shelley), *The Original Frankenstein*, ed. Charles E. Robinson (Oxford: Bodleian Library, 2008).
Shelley, Percy Bysshe, *The Complete Poetical Works*, ed. Thomas Hutchinson (London: Oxford University Press, 1943).
The Hellas Notebook: Bodleian MS Shelley adds. e.7, ed. Donald H. Reiman and Michael J. Neth (New York and London: Garland, 1994).
Letters, ed. Frederick L. Jones, 2 vols. (Oxford: Clarendon Press, 1964).
Prose, ed. David Lee Clark (London: Fourth Estate, 1988) (first published 1954).
Smith, Thomas, 'Journal, 12–17 August, 1823', in Charles Mackay, *Medora Leigh* (London: Bentley, 1869), pp. 243–80.
Southey, Robert, *Poetical Works*, vol. 3, ed. Tim Fulford (London: Pickering and Chatto, 2004).
Spiliadis, Nikolaos, Ἀπομνημονεύματα [*Memoirs*], ed. P. Christopoulos, 3 vols. (Athens, 1972) (first published 1851–7).
Stanhope, Leicester, *Greece in 1823 and 1824* (London: Sherwood, Gilbert, and Piper, 1825).
Trelawny, Edward John, *Letters*, ed. H. Buxton Forman (London: Oxford University Press, 1910).
Recollections of the Last Days of Shelley and Byron (Boston, MA: Ticknor and Fields, 1858).
Records of Shelley, Byron, and the Author, with an introduction by Anne Barton (New York: New York Review of Books, 2000) (first published 1878).
Trikoupis, Spyridon, Ἱστορία τῆς Ἑλληνικῆς Ἐπαναστάσεως [*History of the Greek Revolution*], 4 vols. (London, 1853–7).
Williams, Edward Ellerker, 'Journal', in Maria Gisborne and Edward E. Williams, *Shelley's Friends: Their Journals and Letters*, ed. Frederick L. Jones (Norman: University of Oklahoma Press, 1951).

SECONDARY SOURCES

An, Young-ok, 'Manfred's New Promethean Agon', in Matthew Green and Piya Pal-Lapinski (eds.), *Byron and the Politics of Freedom and Terror* (Basingstoke: Palgrave Macmillan, 2011), pp. 102–17.
Anemon Productions, *1821* (8 DVDs) (Athens: Skai TV, 2011).
Anninos, Bambis, *et al.*, Ἅπαντα γιά τόν Ὀδυσσέα Ἀνδροῦτσο [Complete Writings on Odysseus Androutsos] (Athens: Mermingas, 2005).
Barton, Anne, 'Byron and the Mythology of Fact', *Byron Centre for the Study of Literature and Social Change, School of English Studies*, University of Nottingham (Nottingham, 2009) (first published 1968).
Beaton, Roderick, *Folk Poetry of Modern Greece* (Cambridge University Press, 1980; repr. 2004).
'Introduction', in Roderick Beaton and David Ricks (eds.), *The Making of Modern Greece: Nationalism, Romanticism, and the Uses of the Past (1797–1896)* (Farnham: Ashgate, 2009), pp. 1–18.

'Re-imagining Greek Antiquity in 1821: Shelley's *Hellas* in its Literary and Political Context', in D. Tziovas (ed.), *Re-imagining the Past: Antiquity and Modern Greek Culture* (Oxford University Press, forthcoming).

Berlin, Isaiah, *The Roots of Romanticism* (Princeton, NJ: Princeton University Press, 1999).

Biagi, Guido, *Gli ultimi giorni di Percy Bysshe Shelley, con nuovi documenti* (Florence: La Voce, 1922) (first published 1892).

Bieri, James, *Percy Bysshe Shelley: A Biography* (Baltimore, MD: Johns Hopkins University Press, 2008) (first published in 2 vols., 2004–5).

Blumberg, Jane, *Byron and the Shelleys: The Story of a Friendship* (London: Collins and Brown, 1992).

Blythe, Joan, 'Byron and Greek Independence: The Miltonic Vision', in Marios Byron Raizis (ed.), *Byron: A Poet for All Seasons* (Athens: Missolonghi Byron Society, 2000), pp. 178–87.

Boyd, Elizabeth, *Byron's Don Juan: A Critical Study* (New Brunswick, NJ: Rutgers University Press, 1945).

Boyde, Patrick, *Dante Philomythes and Philosopher: Man in the Cosmos* (Cambridge University Press, 1981).

Brewer, David, *The Flame of Freedom: The Greek War of Independence, 1821–1833* (London: John Murray, 2001).

Brinton, Clarence, *The Political Ideas of the English Romanticists* (Ann Arbor: University of Michigan Press, 1966) (first published 1926).

Butler, Marilyn, 'The Orientalism of Byron's *Giaour*', in Bernard Beatty and Vincent Newey (eds.), *Byron and the Limits of Fiction* (Liverpool University Press, 1988), pp. 78–96.

Buxton, John, *Byron and Shelley: The History of a Friendship* (London: Macmillan, 1968).

Cameron, K. N., and D. H. Reiman (eds.), *Shelley and his Circle*, 8 vols. (Cambridge, MA: Harvard University Press, 1961–73).

Cline, C. L., *Byron, Shelley and their Pisan Circle* (London: John Murray, 1952).

Clubbe, John, 'By the Emperor Possessed: Byron and Napoleon in Italy and Greece (1816–1824)', in Marios Byron Raizis (ed.), *Byron and the Mediterranean World, Proceedings of the Twentieth International Byron Conference* (Athens: Hellenic Byron Society, 1995), pp. 105–15.

Cochran, Peter, 'Byron's Boyfriends', in P. Cochran (ed.), *Byron and Women (and Men)* (Newcastle upon Tyne: Cambridge Scholars, 2010), pp. 15–56.

Byron's Romantic Politics (Newcastle upon Tyne: Cambridge Scholars, 2011).

Romanticism – And Byron (Newcastle upon Tyne: Cambridge Scholars, 2009).

Cox, Jeffrey, 'The Dramatist', in Timothy Morton (ed.), *The Cambridge Companion to Shelley* (Cambridge University Press, 2006), pp. 65–84.

Crane, David, *Lord Byron's Jackal: A Life of Edward John Trelawny* (London: HarperCollins, 1998).

Crompton, Louis, *Byron and Greek Love* (London: Faber, 1985).

Dakin, Douglas, *British and American Philhellenes during the War of Greek Independence, 1821–1833* (Thessaloniki: Society for Balkan Studies, 1955).

The Greek Struggle for Independence, 1821–1833 (London: Batsford, 1973).

d'Amico, Jack, 'Byron and Italy', conference paper, *International Byron Society Conference*, Missolonghi, 2009 (forthcoming).

Dane, J. E., 'On the Instability of Vessels and Narratives: A Nautical Perspective on the Sinking of the Don Juan', *Keats–Shelley Journal*, 47 (1998), 63–86.

Daskalakis, A., *Τα εθνεγερτικά τραγούδια του Ρήγα Βελεστινλή* [*The Patriotic Songs of Rigas Velestinlis*] (Athens, 1977).

De Beer, E., and W. Seton, 'Byroniana: The Archives of the London Greek Committee', *Nineteenth Century*, vol. C (September 1926), 396–412.

Delivoria, Yanna, 'The Notion of Nation: The Emergence of a National Ideal in the Narratives of "Inside" and "Outside" Greeks in the Nineteenth Century', in Roderick Beaton and David Ricks (eds.), *The Making of Modern Greece: Nationalism, Romanticism, and the Uses of the Past (1797–1896)* (Farnham: Ashgate, 2009), pp. 109–21.

Diamandouros, Nikiforos, *Οι απαρχές της συγκρότησης σύγχρονου κράτους στην Ελλάδα 1821–1828* [*The Beginnings of the Establishment of a Modern State in Greece*] (Athens: Cultural Foundation of the National Bank (MIET), 2002).

Douglass, Paul, 'Byron's Life and his Biographers', in Drummond Bone (ed.), *The Cambridge Companion to Byron* (Cambridge University Press, 2004), pp. 7–26.

Dowden, Edward, *The Life of Percy Bysshe Shelley*, 2 vols. (London: Kegan Paul, 1886).

Duff, David, *Romance and Revolution: Shelley and the Politics of a Genre* (Cambridge University Press, 1994).

Duffy, Cian, *Shelley and the Revolutionary Sublime* (Cambridge University Press, 2005).

Ellis, David, *Byron in Geneva: That Summer of 1816* (Liverpool University Press, 2011).

Ferris, David, *Silent Urns: Romanticism, Hellenism, Modernity* (Palo Alto, CA: Stanford University Press, 2000).

Fleming, K. E., *Greece: A Jewish History* (Princeton, NJ: Princeton University Press, 2008).

The Muslim Bonaparte: Diplomacy and Orientalism in Ali Pasha's Greece (Princeton, NJ: Princeton University Press, 1999).

Fletcher, George, *Romantics at War: Glory and Guilt in the Age of Terrorism* (Princeton, NJ: Princeton University Press, 2002).

Foot, Michael, *The Politics of Paradise: A Vindication of Byron* (London: Collins, 1988).

Forster, H. B., 'Byron and Nicolas Karvellas', *Keats–Shelley Journal*, 2 (1953), 73–7.

Freud, Sigmund, 'A Disturbance of Memory on the Acropolis', in James Strachey (ed.), *The Standard Edition of the Complete Psychological Works of Sigmund Freud*, vol. 22 (London: Vintage, 2001), pp. 239–48 (first published 1936).

Gleckner, Robert, *Byron and the Ruins of Paradise* (Baltimore, MD: Johns Hopkins University Press, 1967).

Gounaris, Vasilis, *Τα Βαλκάνια των Ελλήνων* [*The Greek Balkans*] (Thessaloniki: Epikentro, 2007).

Green, Matthew, '"That lifeless thing the living fear": Freedom, Community, and the Gothic Body', in Matthew Green and Piya Pal-Lapinski (eds.), *Byron and the Politics of Freedom and Terror* (Basingstoke: Palgrave Macmillan, 2011), pp. 15–32.

Gross, Jonathan, *Byron: The Erotic Liberal* (Lanham, MD: Lexington, 2001).

Gurney, Evan, 'Publicly Private: A Close Reading of Byron's Last Three Poems', in M. Byron Raizis (ed.), *Byron and Greece: Proceedings of the First International Student Byron Conference, 2002* (Athens: Missolonghi Byron Society, 2003), pp. 141–50.

Häusermann, H. W., *The Genevese Background* (London: Routledge and Kegan Paul, 1952).

Harlaftis, Gelina, *History of Greek-Owned Shipping: Making of an International Tramp Fleet* (London: Routledge, 1996).

Hay, Daisy, *Young Romantics: The Shelleys, Byron and Other Tangled Lives* (London: Bloomsbury, 2010).

Holmes, Richard, *Shelley: The Pursuit* (London: Harper Perennial, 2005) (first published 1974).

Huscher, Herbert, 'Alexander Mavrocordato, Friend of the Shelleys', *Keats–Shelley Memorial Bulletin*, 16 (1965), 29–35.

Kakambouras, Dimitris, *Η βρετανική πολιτική, ο Μπάυρον και οι Έλληνες του '21* [*British Policy, Byron and the Greeks of 1821*] (Athens: Istoritis, 1994).

Karapostolis, Vasilis, *Διχασμός και εξιλέωση: περί πολιτικής ηθικής των Ελλήνων* [*Schism and Expiation: On Greek Political Morality*] (Athens: Patakis, 2010).

Keach, William, *Arbitrary Power: Romanticism, Language, Politics* (Princeton, NJ: Princeton University Press, 2004).

'The Political Poet', in Timothy Morton (ed.), *The Cambridge Companion to Shelley* (Cambridge University Press, 2006), pp. 123–42.

Kelsall, Malcolm, *Byron's Politics* (Brighton: Harvester, 1987).

'Byron's Politics', in Drummond Bone (ed.), *The Cambridge Companion to Byron* (Cambridge University Press, 2004), pp. 44–55.

King, Dorothy, *The Elgin Marbles: The Story of the Parthenon and Archaeology's Greatest Controversy* (London: Hutchinson, 2004).

Kitromilides, Paschalis M. (ed.), *Adamantios Korais and the European Enlightenment* (Oxford: Voltaire Foundation, 2010).

Koumarianou, Aikaterini, *Ο Τύπος στον Αγώνα* [*The Press in the War of Independence*], vol. 1 ('Introduction') (Athens: Ermis, 1971).

Kremmydas, Vasilis, *Από το Σπυρίδωνα Τρικούπη στο σήμερα: Το Εικοσιένα στις νέες ιστοριογραφικές προσεγγίσεις* [*From Spyridon Trikoupis to Today: The Greek Revolution in Recent Historiographical Perspectives*] (Athens: Parliament of the Hellenes, 2007).

Langley Moore, Doris, *The Late Lord Byron* (London: John Murray, 1961).

Lord Byron: Accounts Rendered (London: John Murray, 1974).

Leask, Nigel, *British Romantic Writers and the East* (Cambridge University Press, 1992).

Lignadis, A., Το πρώτον δάνειον της ανεξαρτησίας [*The First Independence Loan*] (University of Athens, 1971).

Loukos, Christos, Αλέξανδρος Μαυροκορδάτος [*Alexandros Mavrokordatos*] (Athens: Ta Nea, 2010).

'Οι «τύχες» του Αλέξανδρου Μαυροκορδάτου στη νεοελληνική συνείδηση' ['The "Fortunes" of Alexandros Mavrokordatos in Modern Greek Consciousness'], in *Η Επανάσταση του 1821* [*The Revolution of 1821*] (Athens: Society for the Study of Modern Hellenism, 1994), pp. 93–106.

Lovell, Ernest J., 'Byron and Mary Shelley', *Keats–Shelley Journal*, 2 (1953), 35–49.

MacCarthy, Fiona, *Byron: Life and Legend* (London: Faber, 2003) (first published 2001).

McGann, Jerome, *The Beauty of Inflections* (Oxford: Clarendon Press, 1985).

Byron and Romanticism, ed. James Soderholm (Cambridge University Press, 2002).

Don Juan in Context (London: John Murray, 1976).

Mackridge, Peter, *Language and National Identity in Greece, 1766–1976* (Oxford University Press, 2009).

Manning, Peter, *Byron and his Fictions* (Detroit, MI: Wayne State University Press, 1978).

Marchand, Leslie, *Byron: A Biography*, 3 vols. (London: John Murray, 1957).

'Trelawny on the Death of Shelley', *Keats–Shelley Memorial Bulletin*, 4 (1952), 9–34.

Mavrogordatos, Giorgos, 'Η ήττα του πρώτου εκσυγχρονιστή' ['The Defeat of the First Moderniser'], *Eleftherotypia: Istorika*, 65 (January 2001), 23–7.

Mellor, Anne, *Mary Shelley: Her Life, Her Fiction, Her Monsters* (New York: Routledge, 1989) (first published 1988).

Miliori, Margarita, 'The Greek Nation in British Eyes 1821–1864: Aspects of a British Discourse on Nationality, Politics, History and Europe', unpublished DPhil dissertation, University of Oxford, 1998.

Ministry of Foreign Affairs of Greece, *The Foundation of the Modern Greek State: Major Treaties and Conventions (1830–1947)*, ed. P. Constantopoulou (Athens: Kastaniotis, 1999).

Minta, Stephen, 'Byron and Mesolongi', *Literature Compass*, 4.2 (2007), 1092–108.

'Byron: Consistency, Change, and the Greek War', in Matthew Green and Piya Pal-Lapinski (eds.), *Byron and the Politics of Freedom and Terror* (Basingstoke: Palgrave Macmillan, 2011), pp. 152–66.

'Lord Byron and Mavrokordatos', *Romanticism*, 12.2 (2006), 126–42.

On a Voiceless Shore (New York: Henry Holt, 1998).

Nicolson, Harold, *Byron: The Last Journey*, new edn with a supplementary chapter (London: Constable, 1940) (first published 1924).

Notopoulos, James (ed.), *The Platonism of Shelley* (Durham, NC: Duke University Press, 1949).

Origo, Iris, *The Last Attachment* (London: Cape, 1949).

Panagiotopoulos, Vasilis, 'Ιγνάτιος Ουγγροβλαχίας' ['Ignatios of Hungary and Wallachia'], in Panagiotis Michailaris and Vasilis Panagiotopoulos, *Κληρικοί στον Αγώνα* [*Clerics in the War of Independence*] (Athens: Ta Nea, 2010), pp. 45–80.

'Κάτι έγινε στην Πίζα το 1821' ['Something Happened at Pisa in 1821'], *Ta Istorika*, 3.5 (1986), 177–82.

Papanikolaou, Lysandros, *Η καθημερινή ιστορία του Εικοσιένα* [*The Day-to-Day History of the Greek Revolution*] (Athens: Kastaniotis, 2007).

Papargyriou, Stefanos, *Από το Γένος στο Έθνος: η θεμελίωση του ελληνικού κράτους, 1821–1862* [*From Genos to Ethnos: The Foundation of the Greek State*] (Athens: Papazisis, 2005).

Paparrigopoulos, K., *Γεώργιος Καραϊσκάκης* [*Georgios Karaiskakis*] (Athens, 1867).

Papasteriopoulos, Ilias, *Η δίκη του Καραϊσκάκη* [*The Trial of Karaiskakis*] (Athens, 1961).

Peach, Annette, 'Portraits of Byron', *Walpole Society*, 62 (2000), 100–44.

Pizanias, Petros (ed.), *The Greek Revolution of 1821: A European Event* (Istanbul: Isis Press, 2011) (first published 2009, in Greek).

Politis, Alexis (ed.), *Το δημοτικό τραγούδι: κλέφτικα* [*The Folk Song: Kleftic Songs*] (Athens: Ermis, 1973).

Pollin, Burton, 'Philosophical and Literary Sources of *Frankenstein*', *Comparative Literature*, 17 (1965), 97–108.

Prell, Donald, *Sailing with Byron from Genoa to Cephalonia* (Palm Springs, CA: Strand, 2009).

Protopsaltis, E., *Αλέξανδρος Ν. Μαυροκορδάτος* [*Alexandros N. Mavrokordatos*] (Athens: Society for the Dissemination of Useful Books, 1982).

Randel, Fred, 'Tradition and Critique in the Haidée Cantos of *Don Juan*', in Marios Byron Raizis (ed.), *Byron: A Poet for All Seasons* (Athens: Missolonghi Byron Society, 2000), pp. 129–35.

Rawes, Alan, *Byron's Poetic Experimentation* (Aldershot: Ashgate, 2000).

Roach, Julian, *Shelley's Boat: The Turbulent, Tragic Last Weeks of Percy Bysshe Shelley* (York: Harbour Books, 2005).

Robinson, Charles E., 'The Devil as *Doppelgänger* in *The Deformed Transformed*: The Sources and Meaning of Byron's Unfinished Drama', *Bulletin of the New York Public Library*, 76 (1970), 177–202.

Shelley and Byron: The Snake and Eagle Wreathed in Fight (Baltimore, MD: Johns Hopkins University Press, 1976).

'Shelley to the Editor of the *Morning Chronicle*: A Second New Letter of 5 April 1821', *Keats–Shelley Memorial Bulletin*, 32 (1981), 55–8.

'The Shelleys to Leigh Hunt: A New Letter of 5 April 1821', *Keats–Shelley Memorial Bulletin*, 31 (1980), 52–6.

Roessel, David, *In Byron's Shadow: Modern Greece in the English and American Imagination* (Oxford University Press, 2002).

Rosen, Frederick, *Bentham, Byron and Greece: Constitutionalism, Nationalism, and Early Liberal Political Thought* (Oxford: Clarendon Press, 1992).

Rotzokos, Nikos, *Επανάσταση και εμφύλιος στο Εικοσιένα* [*Revolution and Civil War in the Greek War of Independence*] (Athens: Plethron, 1997).

St Clair, William, *Lord Elgin and the Marbles*, 3rd edn (Oxford University Press, 1998) (first published 1967).

That Greece Might Still be Free: The Philhellenes in the War of Independence (London: Open Book, 2008) (first published 1972).

Trelawny: The Incurable Romancer (London: John Murray, 1977).

Sanborn, F. B., 'Lord Byron in the Greek Revolution', *Scribner's Magazine*, 22 (1897), 346–59.

Schmidt, Arnold, *Byron and the Rhetoric of Italian Nationalism* (Basingstoke: Palgrave Macmillan, 2010).

Schoina, Maria, *Romantic 'Anglo-Italians': Configurations of Identity in Byron, the Shelleys, and the Pisan Circle* (Farnham: Ashgate, 2009).

Seymour, Miranda, *Mary Shelley* (London: Picador, 2001) (first published 2000).

Sideri, Aloi, *Έλληνες φοιτητές στο Πανεπιστήμιο της Πίζας (1806–1861)* [*Greek Students at the University of Pisa*], vol. 1 (Athens: General Secretariat of the Young Generation, 1989).

Simopoulos, Kyriakos, *Πώς είδαν οι ξένοι την Ελλάδα του '21* [*How Foreigners Saw the Greece of the 1821 Revolution*], 5 vols. (Athens, 1979–84).

Solomou, Kiriakoula, *Byron and Greek Poetry* (Athens: National and Capodistrian University of Athens, School of Philosophy, [1976]).

Speer, Roderick S., *Byron and Scott: The Waverley Novels and Historical Engagement* (Newcastle upon Tyne: Cambridge Scholars, 2009).

Spencer, Terence, *Fair Greece Sad Relic: Literary Philhellenism from Shakespeare to Byron* (London: Weidenfeld and Nicolson, 1954).

Stabler, Jane, '"Awake to Terror": The Impact of Italy on Byron's Depiction of Freedom's Battles', in Matthew Green and Piya Pal-Lapinski (eds.), *Byron and the Politics of Freedom and Terror* (Basingstoke: Palgrave Macmillan, 2011), pp. 64–83.

Byron, Politics and History (Cambridge University Press, 2002).

Steffan, T. G., *Byron's Don Juan*, Variorum Edition, vol. 1, *The Making of a Masterpiece* (Austin: University of Texas Press, 1957).

Stock, Paul, *The Shelley–Byron Circle and the Idea of Europe* (Basingstoke: Palgrave Macmillan, 2010).

Strathcarron, Ian, *Joy Unconfined! Lord Byron's Grand Tour Re-Toured* (Oxford: Signal, 2010).

Sunstein, Emily, *Mary Shelley: Romance and Reality* (Boston, MA: Little-Brown, 1989).

Svolopoulos, K., 'Η σύσταση της Φιλικής Εταιρείας: μια επαναπροσέγγιση' ['The Establishment of the *Filiki Etairia*: A Reappraisal'], *Ta Istorika*, 35 (2001), 283–98.

Theodoridis, Georgios, *Ο Αλέξανδρος Μαυροκορδάτος και η δράση του (1791–1821)* [*Alexandros Mavrokordatos and his Activity (1791–1821)*] (Athens: Neohellenic Research Foundation, 2011).

Thorslev, Peter L., *The Byronic Hero: Types and Prototypes* (Minneapolis: University of Minnesota Press, 1962).

Trayiannoudi, Litsa, 'A "Very Life in . . . Despair in the Land of Honourable Death": Byron in Greece', in Richard Cardwell (ed.), *The Reception of Byron in Europe*, 2 vols. (London: Thoemmes Continuum, 2005), II, pp. 419–38.

Tselika, Valentini, *Οδηγός Ιστορικών Αρχείων Μουσείου Μπενάκη* [*Guide to the Benaki Museum Historical Archives*] (Athens: Benaki Museum, 2006).

Tzakis, Dionysis, 'From Locality to Nation State Loyalty: Georgios Karaiskakis during the Greek Revolution', in Petros Pizanias (ed.), *The Greek Revolution of 1821: A European Event* (Istanbul: Isis Press, 2011), pp. 129–49.

Vlachoyannis, Giannis, 'Καραϊσκάκης: η δίκη περί προδοσίας' ['Karaiskakis: The Treason Trial'], *Proia* [newspaper], 8 and 15 January 1933.

Καραϊσκάκης: βιογραφία [*Karaiskakis: Biography*] (Athens: Estia, 1948).

Wallace, Jennifer, 'National Identity and the Greek War of Independence', *Byron Journal*, 23 (1995), 36–49.

Shelley and Greece: Rethinking Romantic Hellenism (Basingstoke: Palgrave, 1997).

Watkins, Daniel, *Social Relations in Byron's 'Eastern Tales'* (London and Toronto: Associated University Presses, 1987).

Woodhouse, C. M., *The Philhellenes* (London: Hodder and Stoughton, 1969).

Zuccato, Edoardo, 'The Fortunes of Byron in Italy (1810–70)', in Richard Cardwell (ed.), *The Reception of Byron in Europe*, 2 vols. (London: Thoemmes Continuum, 2005), I, pp. 80–97.

Index